Transatlantic Antifascisms

Antifascism has received little attention compared to its enemy. No historian or social scientist has previously attempted to define its nature and history – yet antifascism became perhaps the most powerful ideology of the twentieth century. Michael Seidman fills this gap by providing the first comprehensive study of antifascisms in Spain, France, the United Kingdom, and the United States with new interpretations of the Spanish Civil War, French Popular Front, and Second World War. He shows how two types of antifascism – revolutionary and counterrevolutionary – developed from 1936 to 1945. Revolutionary antifascism dominated the Spanish Republic during its civil war and re-emerged in Eastern Europe at the end of World War II. By contrast, counterrevolutionary antifascists were hegemonic in France, Britain, and the United States. In Western Europe, they restored conservative republics or constitutional monarchies based on Enlightenment principles. This innovative examination of antifascism will interest a wide range of scholars and students of twentieth-century history.

MICHAEL SEIDMAN teaches at the University of North Carolina Wilmington, having studied at the University of Amsterdam, University of California, Berkeley and Swarthmore College. His first book, *Workers against Work: Labor in Barcelona and Paris during the Popular Fronts, 1936–38* (1991), has been translated into six languages. Other publications include *Republic of Egos: A Social History of the Spanish Civil War* (2002, Spanish translation, 2003); *The Imaginary Revolution: Parisian Students and Workers in 1968* (2004); and *The Victorious Counterrevolution: The Nationalist Effort in the Spanish Civil War* (2011, Spanish translation, 2012). *Transatlantic Antifascisms* has also been translated into Spanish.

Transatlantic Antifascisms

From the Spanish Civil War to the End of World War II

Michael Seidman

University of North Carolina Wilmington

CAMBRIDGE
UNIVERSITY PRESS

NEW HANOVER COUNTY
PUBLIC LIBRARY
201 CHESTNUT STREET
WILMINGTON, NC 28401

CAMBRIDGE
UNIVERSITY PRESS

University Printing House, Cambridge CB2 8BS, United Kingdom

One Liberty Plaza, 20th Floor, New York, NY 10006, USA

477 Williamstown Road, Port Melbourne, VIC 3207, Australia

314-321, 3rd Floor, Plot 3, Splendor Forum, Jasola District Centre, New Delhi - 110025, India

79 Anson Road, #06-04/06, Singapore 079906

Cambridge University Press is part of the University of Cambridge.

It furthers the University's mission by disseminating knowledge in the pursuit of education, learning, and research at the highest international levels of excellence.

www.cambridge.org
Information on this title: www.cambridge.org/9781108417785
DOI: 10.1017/9781108278386

First published as *Antifascismos, 1936–1945*, Alianza Editorial 2017

First published by Cambridge University Press 2018

Printed in the United Kingdom by TJ International Ltd. Padstow Cornwall

A catalogue record for this publication is available from the British Library

ISBN 978-1-108-41778-5 Hardback
ISBN 978-1-108-40586-7 Paperback

To my family

La lucidité est la blessure la plus proche du soleil.

René Char

Contents

Illustrations

Preface

This study of the two main varieties of antifascism in the major nations of the Atlantic world is, like most books, an individual and collective effort. At the University of North Carolina Wilmington my gratitude includes Paul Townend, Mark Spaulding, Susan McCaffray, Lynn Mollenauer, Aswani Volety, and the Inter-Library Loan staff. A UNCW Research Reassignment, local academic jargon for a sabbatical, allowed valuable time; a Summer Initiative and Cahill Award granted material resources to complete the project. Beyond my home institution, Tom Buchanan, Herrick Chapman, Jean-Pierre Le Goff, William O'Neill, Anthony Oberschall, Josep Parello, Don Reid, Henri Simon, Jens Späth, Nigel Townson, Jean-Paul Vilaine, and especially Hugo García offered encouragement and helpful criticism. Special thanks go to the extraordinarily knowledgeable Stanley Payne. I am indebted to editors Lew Bateman and Michael Watson who shepherded the manuscript through an extremely valuable review process.

Readers should be aware that I have used "Fascist" to designate the Italian brand of fascism, which will remain in lowercase unless it refers to the Mussolinian movement. The use of "Communism" refers to the political parties which were led by the Soviet Union; "communism" in lowercase denotes groups outside of the Third International who demanded collectivization of most, if not all, private property. "Resisters" in uppercase signifies those who fought against the German occupation. "Nazi" is used as shorthand for German National Socialist.

1 Introduction

The historiography of the twentieth century is obsessed with fascism, Communism's competitor for the most brutal and spectacular political movement of the twentieth century. Compared with its enemy, antifascism has received little attention. Publications about fascism outnumber antifascism thirtyfold. A WorldCat keyword search revealed 59,000 titles for fascism and 2,000 for antifascism. Yet in almost all Western countries – except, of course, Italy, Germany, and Spain – fascism was a failure, and antifascism an obvious success, which became perhaps the most powerful Western ideology of the twentieth century. Surprisingly, no historian or social scientist has attempted to define the nature, types, and history of antifascisms in the Atlantic world. This book is an attempt to fill those gaps by analyzing antifascisms in Spain, France, the United Kingdom, and the United States from 1936 to 1945.

Fascism may have been the major political innovation of the twentieth century, but antifascism was even more flexible and dynamic. The more antifascism encompassed a broad range of opinion, the more successful it became. It sought consensus, not synthesis. If fascism was built on its ability to profit from the supposed atomization or anomie of modern populations, antifascism reaped an even greater yield from those characteristics. Although fascists were successful in creating one of the first "catch-all" cross-class movements, antifascists easily trumped them in the Atlantic world. Antifascism's extremely disparate nature has rendered it an appealing but slippery topic.

Fascism's early successes aroused fears in both revolutionaries and counterrevolutionaries and thus provoked a powerful alliance against it. The explanation that "a faltering liberal order" accounted for the success of fascism is qualified by the examination of a victorious antifascism in the Atlantic democracies.[1] Historians and social scientists have ignored the ideological, religious, and racial inclusiveness of antifascism since many have identified antifascism as an ecumenical movement which was primarily, if not exclusively, a movement of the left or, at least, "democratic."[2] The left has identified antifascism with its own progressive orientation and regarded conservative antifascism as an oxymoron. Resistance to fascism was supposedly inseparable from the revolutionary politics which followed World War I.[3] Antifascism is assumed to be the province of major politicians and intellectuals of the left.

My own definition differs and proposes a tripartite minimum. First, antifascism makes working or fighting against fascism the top priority. Thus, antifascists rejected uncompromising anti-Communism and anti-capitalism. They recognized the need to collaborate with Communists and capitalists, even though conservative antifascists completely opposed the Soviet model and revolutionary antifascists the liberal one. Antifascists chose to fight a multi-front war against the Axis, not the Soviet Union or the Western Allies. Both sets of anti-appeasers knew that you could remain particular about your friends, but not about your allies. Second, antifascism refused conspiratorial theories which blamed Jewish and plutocratic plotting for negative social, economic, and political developments, particularly preparations for an antifascist war. Antifascists rejected this form of scapegoating anti-Semitism, even if they shared other varieties. In direct contrast to the German National Socialists, most of them did not regard the Jewish issue as central. Third, antifascists refused pacifism and believed that state power was necessary to stop both domestic fascisms and the Axis war machine. Risking their own empires, they were willing to fight a long and global war to halt the spread of fascism. Antifascism meant concrete sacrifice, not merely hostile attitudes, to defeat fascism.[4]

Like fascism, antifascism adopted distinct forms in different periods. Two basic types of antifascism emerged from 1936 to 1945. The first was the revolutionary antifascism promoted during the Spanish Civil War (1936–1939) and often dominant in countries, like Spain, with a weak bourgeoisie. Revolutionary antifascism identified capitalism and fascism and was uninterested in the considerable differences between Italian and German fascisms or between fascist and authoritarian regimes. The revolutionary antifascism of the Spanish conflict encouraged the end of pacifism among sectors of the left, but because of the Spanish Republic's disrespect for private property and its violent anticlericalism it did not prefigure – as many have argued – the antifascist alliance of World War II. Revolutionary antifascism resurfaced in Eastern Europe with the Hitler-Stalin pact (August 1939–June 1941), when it influenced the behavior of the American, British, and French Communist parties, which condemned the war as "imperialist" and treated all belligerents as real or potential "fascists." Like the appeasers in the 1930s, Communists in this period generally preferred pacifism to antifascism. Revolutionary antifascism also revived at the end of World War II when it became the official ideology of the incipient Soviet bloc and helped to lend it legitimacy against a new adversary – the "fascist" West. As in the Republican zone during the Spanish Civil War, revolutionary antifascism in the new "popular democracies" labeled as "fascist" any opposition – including workers' strikes, revolts, and refusals to work – against Communist-supported governments.

The second type of antifascism was conservative and even counterrevolutionary. The lack of reflection on this sort of antifascism mirrors the general historiographical neglect of counterrevolutions. Another World-Cat keyword search shows *revolution* with 1,350,000 entries and *counterrevolution* with 6,000. The few important exceptions have neglected to study conservative antifascism as a variety of counterrevolution. The classic study described types of counterrevolutions but associated all of them with "monopolistic control of state and government by a *new political elite*," a definition which hardly describes the transatlantic counterrevolutions after World War II.[5] A recent text asserted that in countries where fascism failed to become a mass movement "mainstream conservatives" supposedly rejected "the main tenets of the French Revolution . . . [and] did not feel sufficiently threatened in the 1930s to call on fascism for help."[6] Yet the United States, the United Kingdom, and France all experienced "a sense of overwhelming crisis" which many felt "beyond the reach of traditional solutions," but fascists never came close to taking power in these nations. Furthermore, "mainstream conservatives" actively created and participated in French and British antifascist movements. Instead of desiring "to keep the masses out of politics," counterrevolutionary antifascists – such as Winston Churchill and Charles de Gaulle – wanted to win the masses over to conservative antifascism. Antifascism was not merely defensive and passive but often more dynamic than fascism itself and outlasted its enemy in a war of attrition.

The lack of discussion concerning the character of antifascism stands in sharp contrast to the constant debate over fascism's revolutionary or counterrevolutionary nature. The conflation of the two forms of antifascism has muddled many analyses. A common imprecision – accepted by both fascists and antifascists – is that the Spanish Civil War was the first stage of World War II. Another issue is that the "counterrevolutionary" label is no more popular than "fascist." Both labels are almost always considered insults, and at present no significant political movement calls itself fascist or counterrevolutionary. For example, the Americans labeled their attempt to turn back Communist revolution in Vietnam and elsewhere "counter-insurgency," not counterrevolution. In a similar vein, counterrevolutionary antifascism never claimed to be continuing or restoring the old order but rather instituting a new and more hopeful period of history for which it – like other counterrevolutions – was willing to fight.[7]

Counterrevolution suggests the continuation of the Old Regime under pre-revolutionary social, political, and religious leadership. Successful counterrevolutions can integrate important revolutionary elements but must subordinate them to old-regime dominance. In this study, counterrevolution does not mean a return to the Old Regime – i.e., the period before the French Revolution of 1789 – but rather the continuation or restoration of the prewar old regimes. The antifascist counterrevolution continued or restored the old regimes of the Enlightenment-oriented Atlantic Revolutions of the eighteenth century. These revolutions moved toward political democracy and – unlike communist revolutions – guaranteed individual freedoms and private property rights within a reformist framework. Counterrevolutionary or restorationist antifascism rejected the violations of personal freedoms and the confiscations of property which occurred under both fascism and revolutionary antifascism. Conservative antifascists desired limits on state power and opposed the abolition of the distinction between public and private life, which was a key feature of the Nazi and Soviet revolutions.

Conservative antifascism was hostile to a metaphysical or political search for unity (*Volksgemeinschaft*). It did not collapse state into society. It excluded a *Führerprinzip*, exaltation of youth, militarization of politics, absolute male dominance, and the promotion of a political religion. Conservative antifascism rejected fascist attempts to impose cohesion and preferred traditional pluralism. In the 1930s and 1940s, its greater breadth and inclusiveness allowed it to surpass fascists by constructing coalitions in which working-class parties and trade unions allied with capitalists to achieve and maintain political power.

Counterrevolutionary antifascism defended – although not always by democratic means – the old regimes of liberal democracy. It could be labeled liberal antifascism, but the terms "counterrevolutionary," "conservative," and in the French case "restorationist antifascism" are preferred, because to defeat its domestic and foreign foes this form of antifascism used methods and gathered supporters that were not entirely liberal or democratic. Along with feminists, social democrats, and trade unionists, the proponents of counterrevolutionary antifascism comprised conservatives and traditionalists, who included antidemocratic racists in the American South and elsewhere. Its most consistent advocates were conservatives and imperialists (Churchill and de Gaulle) or social democrats (Franklin Roosevelt), not Communists (Joseph Stalin). After World War II in Europe where the victorious Atlantic powers dominated, counterrevolutionary antifascists either continued or reestablished conservative republics or constitutional monarchies based on the principles of the Enlightenment-influenced eighteenth-century revolutions. This transatlantic attempt to found a rehabilitated European order replaced the Axis alternative and eventually won a complete victory when Communism collapsed in 1989.

Counterrevolutionary antifascism assembled economic, political, and cultural leaders. Capitalists who distrusted statism allied with trade unionists who wanted welfarism; artists, intellectuals, and leftist politicians who feared potential fascist repression joined with religious traditionalists. Conservative antifascism easily appealed to large numbers who rejected fascism's elitism – whether racial or social. Antifascists achieved a perhaps shallower but broader consensus than fascists. The ultimate success of antifascism showed the relative narrowness and instability of the fascist coalition, which excluded large sectors of the left, liberals, and racial minorities. Fascism formed an exclusivist political religion which refused coexistence with other political convictions.[8]

Both counterrevolutionary and revolutionary antifascists came to see that violent expansionism was intrinsic to the fascist project. They ultimately rejected the generalized guilt which attributed the rise of Nazism to an allegedly unjust peace settlement and viewed ferocious fascist dynamism – not the Versailles Treaty – as the principal cause of conflict. Unlike their fascist enemies, they did not promise a quick victory but, as in World War I, an extended struggle against a potent enemy. During World War II, they responded to fascist aggression by developing a cult of heroism which relegated victims to a secondary position.

Antifascists did not always equate Nazi Germany with Fascist Italy until the latter joined Germany as an ally in 1940. Before Benito Mussolini's entry into World War II, conservative antifascists in the Atlantic world were much more anti-Nazi than anti-Fascist. They hoped – correctly until the fall of France – that the conservative forces of the Italian monarchy and military would keep Italy out of the conflict. Although ultimately unsuccessful, antifascists attempted to divide the two fascist powers, and they adopted a range of policies on the Spanish Civil War. Counterrevolutionary antifascists might regard the Spanish dictator, Francisco Franco, as a potential ally or friendly neutral. However, they did not overestimate the weight of Italy and Spain and were willing to battle Germany despite those two countries' alignment with the Axis. Conservative antifascists did not underestimate the strength of the democracies, nor were they resigned to the supposed authoritarian wave of the future. They recognized that Nazism was the most revolutionary, dangerous, and aggressive form of fascism. To crush it would leave the less radical Italian and Spanish fascisms vulnerable. Antifascists did not hold an uncompromising position on "totalitarianism," thereby allowing them to ally with Communists and the Soviet Union.

A study of antifascism should include not only elites but also ordinary people who collaborated with fascism or resisted it in their everyday lives. During the German occupation, French workers engaged in sabotage, strikes, and slowdowns. Spanish, British, and American working-class organizations cooperated in their nations' wartime antifascism, although not all wage earners followed their leaders and, like French workers, resisted work. However, the effectiveness of this resistance to wage labor was limited, and an examination of Spanish, French, American, and British defense workers' strikes and refusals to work demonstrates that resistance to work was unable to defeat either fascist regimes or antifascist ones. In other words, state antifascism from above was essential to crush fascism on both domestic and foreign fronts. A history of antifascism needs to engage with recent social historical approaches, but the victory of antifascism cannot be explained solely by social history. Nonetheless, denials of labor suggest leisurely and irenic practices of a post-fascist civilization.

Counterrevolutionary antifascism grew rapidly in the late 1930s. The Italian invasion of Ethiopia in October 1935 provoked Emperor Haile Selassie's traditionalist antifascism, which anticipated that of European conservatives later in the decade (Figure 1.1). Both the venerable Ethiopian Empire and later the British Empire would defend their domains against an aggressive fascist imperialism. The United Kingdom offered the Christian emperor asylum in 1936 and in 1941 restored him to the throne, thus prefiguring its policies toward European and Asian antifascist monarchs at the end of World War II. Antifascists initiated global and often spontaneous grassroots protests opposing the Italian invasion. Demonstrations against the Ethiopian invasion were generally organized along ethnic and racial lines and included Black nationalists, radicals, and assorted anti-imperialists. Yet antifascism based on a combination of anti-imperialism, race, or religion – as Jewish movements against Nazism would also demonstrate – remained ineffective without the mobilizing capacity of powerful national states, all of whom (including the Soviet Union) permitted the Duce to conquer Abyssinia.[9]

The September 1938 Munich crisis, the subsequent German annexation of the Sudetenland, and the November 1938 *Reichspogromnacht* (Night of the Broken Glass) helped to turn an overwhelming majority of Britons and French against the Nazi regime, the most radical expression of fascism. The German invasion of the conservative republic of Czechoslovakia in March 1939 shattered most appeasers' faith in the

Figure 1.1 Ethiopian Emperor Selassie protests Italian invasion of his country at the League of Nations in 1936. Getty Images.

reasonable intentions of the Nazis and further undermined pacifism. The Spanish Civil War had divided leftist and rightist antifascists, but the leftist republic's collapse in April 1939 encouraged conservatives and Catholics to join counterrevolutionary antifascists who supported private property and respected traditional religion. Hitler's invasion of Poland in September 1939 demonstrated the anti-appeasers' calculation that Nazism was more dangerous than Communism.

In the United States, isolationist sentiment also eroded in the late 1930s but remained powerful in Congress, the Midwest, and among certain economic elites and ethnicities, including African-Americans. Like their appeasing counterparts in Great Britain and France, American isolationists based their arguments on pacifism, anti-Communism, or, to a lesser extent, anti-Semitism. As in Europe, fierce fascist expansionism discredited their reasoning and helped the Roosevelt administration to convince conservative Democrats and Republicans to aid the British, whom American public opinion favored because the United Kingdom was actually fighting fascism. Likewise, American and British opinion provided crucial support for de Gaulle's Free French when both

Roosevelt and Churchill wanted to replace the French leader with some-one more pliable. With the support of the Allied armies and the backing of much of the French bourgeoisie and army – including French gener-als who had fought against the Allies – the restorationist de Gaulle took power in France in 1944.[10]

The defeat of Nazi Germany in 1944–1945 led to the return of the conflict between revolutionary and counterrevolutionary antifas-cism. In Eastern Europe, in countries with weak bourgeoisies, the Sovi-ets imposed many elements of their model. Revolutionary antifascists who had organized volunteers or fought in Spain – including Josip Broz Tito (Yugoslavia), Walter Ulbricht (DDR), and Klement Gottwald (Czechoslovakia) – became national leaders in the new "popular democ-racies." A precedent for these regimes could be found in Republican Spain during its civil war, the subject of the next chapter.

2 Revolutionary Antifascism in the Spanish Civil War, 1936–1939

Neither Japanese aggression against China (1931–1932) nor the Italian conquest of Ethiopia (1935–1936) aroused the same level of international emotion and commitment as the Spanish Civil War and Revolution (1936–1939). Antifascism came dramatically to worldwide attention when the Spanish conflict offered antifascists an opportunity to work and fight against their enemies (Figure 2.1). From its beginning in July 1936, the Spanish Civil War eclipsed all other international events until the Munich crisis of September 1938. Forty thousand persons from all over the globe volunteered to fight for the Spanish Republic in the International Brigades, and tens of thousands more worked in their native lands in a host of pro-Republican and antifascist organizations. The Spanish Civil War allowed antifascists (including first lady Eleanor Roosevelt) to overcome the various varieties of pacifism which World War I had generated.

The Spanish Revolution

The most intense and spontaneous revolution that any European country would ever experience occurred in the Republican zone during the Spanish Civil War. Spain's unique historical development explains the outbreak of the only revolution and civil war in Europe of the 1930s. Spain did not follow the pattern of development of northwestern Europe or North America. The long Reconquest from the eighth to the fifteenth centuries helped to ensure the dominance of a numerically large aristocracy linked to a church which maintained for hundreds of years a crusading mentality characteristic of the Middle Ages. Thus, it was hardly surprising that Spanish monarchs became the police of Rome and its Counter-Reformation. Militant intolerance constituted one of the foundations of modern Spain. The expulsion of the Moors and, perhaps even more importantly, that of the Jews were good lessons (if often ignored) on how to destroy a potential middle class.

The great movements of early modern history – the Reformation and absolutism – were aborted or adopted less vigorous forms than in other

Figure 2.1 Antifascist street parade at Eastbourne (England), 29 April 1938. Getty Images.

Western European nations. The eighteenth century accentuated the differences between Spain and the rest of Western Europe and North America. In the Iberian Peninsula, the Enlightenment was largely unoriginal and derivative. Its Spanish advocates were less influential than in other major Catholic nations of the West, notably France but also Italy. The Enlightenment agenda of rationalism, productivism, and meritocracy proved harder to implement in Iberia. The rejection of the Enlightenment's anti-noble and anticlerical agenda was most evident during the Napoleonic period when large numbers of Spaniards fought a fierce *guerrilla* (significantly, a Spanish coinage) against the French invaders and their revolutionary principles.

Even after the era of the Atlantic Revolutions, traditionalist Spanish landlords, backed by the army and the clergy, maintained their economic and social dominance over large areas of the peninsula. In certain regions, such as Andalusia and Extremadura, landlessness was aggravated by the near monopoly of large landowners and rapid demographic growth. Unlike its northern European neighbors, Spain had a great mass of peasants thirsting for land into the twentieth century. Throughout the nineteenth and twentieth centuries, the church maintained overwhelming ascendancy over many educational and welfare bureaucracies. The separation of church and state on the French or American model was never fully accomplished. During the nineteenth and first half of the twentieth century, tolerant Christian democracy remained a minor current among Catholics. The sale of church lands and the loss of its landed wealth made clerical institutions more dependent on the rich than previously. In response, popular anticlerical attitudes proliferated. Just as separation of church and state proved tenuous, so did the subordination of military to civilian rule. *Pronunciamientos* – direct military intervention in politics – punctured the nineteenth and early twentieth centuries and encouraged confrontations between revolutionary and counterrevolutionary forces.

Except possibly in the Basque country and Catalonia, no class of energetic industrialists ever emerged. The more advanced economic development in these regions encouraged peripheral nationalisms. National unity, which had originally been based on a shared or imposed Catholic faith, was never fully consolidated, and in the most prosperous areas of the peninsula, regionalism grew during the Restoration monarchy (1874–1931). Yet demands that the national government provide economic and physical protection circumscribed both Basque and Catalan nationalisms. Even in these purportedly dynamic areas of the peninsula, until the middle or end of the twentieth century, industrial survival depended on protection against foreign competition as well as defense against radical workers' movements. Iberia's previous history of intolerance and persecution haunted Spanish development. Catholic Spain had a difficult time opening its elites to the talented, such as Protestants and Jews, who were often in the avant-garde of economic and cultural development in other European nations.

The Second Republic (1931–1939) modeled itself on the ideals of the French Revolution and the French Third Republic. Simultaneously, it intended to go beyond liberty and fraternity and introduce more social equality. Yet it faced special problems in trying to achieve its project in backward Spain. Given its literacy rates and economic development, 1930s Spain was at the level of England in the 1850s and 1860s or France in the 1870s and 1880s.[1] The French Third Republic (1870–1940) had begun after significant spurts of industrialization and modernization during the Orleanist Monarchy (1830–1848) and the Second Empire (1852–1870). It had also proved capable of maintaining bourgeois order by crushing ruthlessly the last major working-class revolt, the Paris Commune of 1871. Furthermore, the Third Republic took decades to secure itself politically. Only in 1905 was the church separated from the state and the military subordinated to civilian control.

The Spanish Second Republic inherited even graver social and political problems and tried to solve them more quickly than its French counterpart. At the same time, Spain had a much stronger and better-organized working-class movement which, unlike the embryonic French Third Republic, it could not or would not smash militarily. Further troubling its existence, the democratic Spanish Republic was swimming during the 1930s against the authoritarian and fascist currents that had overwhelmed countries at similar levels of economic and social development in eastern and southern Europe. A coalition of the enlightened urban middle classes, who were grouped in various Republican parties, with the working classes of the Socialist party and its trade unions dominated the first years of the Republic. This alliance attempted to imitate the progressive Western model of non-revolutionary change. However, its program of reduction of military spending, gradualist land reform, and anticlericalism alienated the still-powerful forces of military officers, landowners, and the church. In fact, anticlerical sentiments in the governing coalition were so influential that authorities initially refused to intervene when mobs began burning churches in Madrid at the Republic's founding.

As the Republic failed to resolve the profound problems that it had inherited, the right gathered strength. In 1931 the dominance of anti-Republican components of the clerical right was uncertain, and some Catholics were willing to give the new regime a chance. However, the strength of reactionary Catholicism grew as the Republic offered religious freedom to non-Catholics and instituted other measures – such as divorce, civil marriage, dissolution of the Society of Jesus, and secular education – which ended the confessional state. These fairly conventional steps separating church from state were needlessly complemented by gratuitous attacks on religious practices that alienated Catholics who were potential supporters of the Republic. The elimination of parochial education was particularly galling to the faithful. New legislation that secularized Catholic cemeteries and banned Holy Week processions offended many believers.[2]

The attempt to reduce the power of the military was nearly as infelicitous as the efforts to decrease the influence of the church. Manuel Azaña, prime minister of the Republican-Socialist government, was highly influenced by the French model of civilian control of the military and tried to adapt it to Spanish conditions. Yet it was much more difficult to impose civilian superiority in a nation whose elites had frequently depended on direct military control of the state to ensure order and protection of property. Azaña's reforms (1931–1932) removed what he considered the anachronistic judicial functions of the army and drastically reduced the size of the bloated armed services. Despite the needed downsizing and the generosity of retirement benefits, the reforms estranged a large number of officers.

In retrospect, it is evident that the reforms of the first two years of the Republic alienated as many as they pleased. The progressive legislation aroused as much distrust and disaffection among property owners, military officers, and Catholics as devotion and gratitude among wage earners and enlightened bourgeois. In other words, if the Republic's reforms created a social base of support which would be committed to its defense, it also provoked a counterforce which became dedicated to its destruction. The Republic's labor legislation distressed some small farmers by raising wages of their workers and restricting labor mobility. Small holders who leased land to sharecroppers or rented it in tiny parcels found that their tenants delayed payments.[3] Angry small farmers, fearful large landowners, and devout Catholics formed the electorate of the clerical and well-financed CEDA (Confederación Española de Derechas Autónomas) formed in 1933.

During the elections of November 1933, the divisions among the left prevented the Socialists from forming an alliance with the left Republicans. On the radical left, the anarchosyndicalists of the CNT (Confederación Nacional del Trabajo), probably the most influential anarchist movement in the world, gave no respite to the new regime and provoked periodic revolts. The CNT enthusiastically propagated its anti-political ideology and advocated electoral abstention.[4] The right, principally the CEDA, profited from middle-class and Catholic fears concerning the collectivist and anticlerical direction of the new Republic. So did the misnamed Radicals – actually a centrist grouping – which emerged from the voting with 104 deputies; the CEDA with 115; and the Socialists only 62. The Radical party formed the government in December 1933, but by October 1934, the Radicals concluded that they could govern only with the support of the CEDA. After Hitler had come into power in a rightist coalition in January 1933 and a conservative-fascist alliance had violently repressed the Austrian Socialists in February 1934, many on the left worried that the right-wing Catholic party would acquiesce in a "fascist" coup d'état in Spain. Even the moderate and Catholic president of the Republic, Niceto Alcalá Zamora, doubted that the CEDA leader, José María Gil Robles, would be loyal to the Republic and was reluctant to call him to form a government.

Nevertheless, on 4 October 1934 Alcalá Zamora permitted the creation of a cabinet that included three ministers from the CEDA.

The following day in Asturias, militant coal miners, who had been progressively politicized by what they viewed as the failure of the "social" Republic and radicalized by deteriorating working conditions, began the famous Asturias insurrection, the prelude to the civil war and revolution that was to erupt two years later. Twenty to thirty thousand Asturian miners rebelled against what they perceived to be the "fascist" orientation of the new right-wing government in Madrid. In several weeks of intense action, General Francisco Franco and his African troops brutally suppressed them. One of the lessons that many leftist militants drew from the Asturias repression was a wish to eliminate "fascists" – the officer corps and their civilian and clerical supporters – before they could exterminate antifascists.

In Catalonia, at the same time as the Asturias revolt, Catalan nationalists declared the "Catalan state within the Federal Spanish Republic." This attempt at Catalan independence failed miserably, and it clearly demonstrated the limits of Catalan nationalism, whose social base was too narrow to form an independent nation. The unsuccessful insurrections in Catalonia and Asturias allowed the rightist government to repress the left. Various estimates placed the number of political prisoners in Spanish jails at between 20,000 and 30,000 individuals. Throughout 1935 the left correctly feared a continued government crackdown. In southern rural areas, numerous workers were fired, wages lowered, and working conditions changed arbitrarily.[5] The government's intention was to create – as the French had done after the Paris Commune of 1871 – a republic of order that could protect private property and the church. The effort was, as will be seen, ultimately unsuccessful. Furthermore, corruption scandals that discredited the Radical party weakened the ruling coalition.

The left drew together to end the right's repression or what they often termed "fascism." In January 1936 the Socialists, Republicans, POUM (Partido Obrero de Unificación Marxista), UGT (Unión General de Trabajadores), Catalan nationalists, and PCE (Partido Comunista de España) formed the electoral coalition known as the Popular Front. The PCE obeyed the Third International's (Comintern) new initiative for a broad antifascism, which was particularly appealing in Spain and France. Seeking allies among socialists and progressive bourgeois, the Comintern narrowly defined fascism in 1935 as "the open terrorist dictatorship of the most reactionary, chauvinistic and most imperialist elements of finance capital."[6] The new ecumenical policy attempted to defend the Soviet state against growing Nazi power but left open the possibility of future revolution. It also responded to global grassroots antifascist and anti-Nazi sentiments among Communists as well as the entire left. With Hitler's consolidation of power during and after 1933, Moscow viewed fascism as the dangerous last gasp of capitalism and much worse than the liberal democracy from which it had sprung.

The Spanish electoral campaign of 1936 polarized voters. The right was divided, and its more moderate components, including a few Christian democrats, enfeebled. In February the Popular Front won an important victory. Nationwide, it captured 47 to 51.9 percent of the votes, compared to 43 to 45.6 percent for the right. The fascist Falange won merely 46,466 votes or 0.7 percent, conceivably the lowest voting percentage of a fascist party in all of Europe. The Popular Front narrowly gained a national majority but enlarged it by fabricating results in Cuenca and Granada.[7] The left's victory and electoral manipulation heightened rightist suspicions that the Popular Front would violently secure the separation of church from state, further reduce the power of the military, encourage regional nationalisms, and promote sweeping land reform. In addition, the weight of the radical left in the Socialist party (PSOE, Partido Socialista Obrero Español) and the influence of the CNT raised the specter that it would not be the moderate republicans, such as Manuel Azaña who would secure features of the unfinished bourgeois-liberal revolution but rather, as in Russia in 1917, working-class revolutionaries who wished to abolish private property. Local authorities illegally dismissed rightist municipal councilors and protected neither the possessions nor the lives of their political and social adversaries.

Reports of the victory of the Popular Front in the elections of February 1936 led to another wave of church burnings, riots, and even prison revolts. The Republic became symbolic of unrest and disorder to many Spaniards. By mid-March 1936, Prime Minister Azaña privately worried about the arsons of convents and rightist headquarters, in addition to unprovoked attacks on military officers. Azaña admitted that he had lost count of the more than 200 casualties and assassinations since the formation of his Popular Front government on 19 February. By early April, the government had removed 9 of 46 recently appointed provincial civil governors for their failures to prevent or control strikes, illegal land occupations, political violence, and arson. Others were transferred at the request of Socialists who objected to the governors' attempts to impose Republican legality at the expense of their own militants and armed militias. Many communities prohibited Catholic schools; several municipalities banned Catholic tombstones; and others tolerated the looting of gravesites.[8]

The left downplayed these acts or justified them in the name of "antifascism." The governments of the Popular Front were more likely to persecute rightists who were responsible for violence than leftists who committed similar acts. Azaña was hesitant to use the army to jail or shoot protesters and rioters, many of whom supported his coalition. On the other hand, he was also reluctant to disarm the military because it might be needed to stop insurrections organized by the extreme left. The poorest sectors of the population, who probably suffered the most from the Great Depression, exerted powerful pressures for change. Tenant farmers knew that the Popular Front government would be disinclined to move against them. Consequentially, tens of thousands of small holders and farm workers throughout Spain, but mainly in the center and the south, illegally occupied land. In late March in the province of Badajoz, more than 60,000 peasants, under the direction of the Socialist FNTT (Federación Nacional de los Trabajadores de la Tierra), seized more than 3,000 farms. Shouting "Viva la República," they began tilling their new land. Nearly 100,000 peasants appropriated more than 400,000 hectares by the end of April 1936 and perhaps 1,000,000 hectares on the eve of the civil war. In contrast, during 1931–1933 land reform had settled only 6,000 peasants on 45,000 hectares. In many cases, in early 1936 rural wages doubled.[9]

Conservatives along with some small and medium landowners concluded that revolution had already begun. They and their Catholic workers provided the growing social base for the Falange. As many strikes occurred between April and July 1936 as during the entire year 1931. In Barcelona, "endemic" work stoppages erupted for less work and more pay. Domestic and foreign businessmen reacted negatively. The Catalan capitalist elite repeated its hoary, but partly credible, warning that "the reigning anarchy" might destroy its firms. In early July 1936, the director of General Motors in Spain advised the Workers' Metallurgical Union that it was considering shutting down its Barcelona assembly factory, in large part because of increased labor costs. "Workers' non-stop demands for salary raises" made the company ponder laying off its 400 employees. To make matters worse, "workers are not laboring with the same efficiency as previously."[10]

In May 1936, a number of Madrid workers dined in hotels, restaurants, and cafés and then walked out without paying. Their wives, accompanied by armed militants, went "proletarian shopping" in grocery stores and disregarded the bill. A similar wave of "social crimes" occurred in Tenerife. In Melilla (Spanish Morocco), Communists and Socialists insulted military officers in public and traded clandestinely with the French zone to acquire weapons. In provincial cities, such as Granada, attacks on shops, factories, and even the tennis club frightened both big and small bourgeois who rushed to join the Falange. A good number of Andalusian workers pilfered from shops and neglected to pay rent. As certain historians have indicated, the right-wing media doubtlessly attempted to manipulate fears of property owners, but the latter were inclined to believe the harmfulness of "disorder" and "unrest" because of their own confrontations with the multifaceted class struggle. In other words, contrary to some recent histories, public order was not merely the pretext for the military rising but rather its context.[11]

In addition to threats to property, the right feared persecution by the increasingly politicized police forces of the Republic, whose actions would culminate in the assassination on 13 July 1936 of an extreme-right leader, José Calvo Sotelo. For the first time in the history of parliamentary regimes, a detachment of state police murdered a chief of the parliamentary opposition.[12] The assassins were close to the "moderate" Socialist leader, Indalecio Prieto, who protected them from any investigation. Another prominent Socialist, Margarita Nelken, hid the killers, one of whom later became a powerful Republican security chief during the civil war. The magnicide helped to convince a wavering General Franco to join the rebellion against the Republic. Political and social violence in Spain reflected the underdeveloped and polarized nature of Spanish society and the inability of its weak state to control either supporters or opponents. The absence of what important sectors of the right considered to be a neutral and efficient state encouraged them to rebel.

The disorders and demands following the victory of the Popular Front promoted plotting against the Republic by a broad coalition of anti-Republican forces. Among them were fascist Falangists; ultraconservative monarchists known as Carlists; and more traditionally "liberal" advocates of Alfonso XIII, the Alphonsines. They were joined by members of the armed forces determined to smash the Popular Front, which they associated with the "anti-Spain" of Marxism, Freemasonry, Catalan and Basque separatisms, and Judaism. Their anti-Republican coalition would call itself Nationalist. Antifascists did not refer to their enemies as "Nationalists" but, as they had during the Asturias revolt in 1934, as "fascists." The latter included the entire right before and during the civil war.[13]

When another *pronunciamiento* occurred on 18 July 1936, Spanish Communist, Socialist, and anarchist militia prevented its successful execution (Figure 2.2). Unlike the previous coups, the rebellious officers and their civilian supporters had to confront the armed activists of the parties and unions of the left which claimed to represent the Spanish people or, more specifically, the working class. Without these male and female fighters of the PSOE, UGT, PCE, POUM, CNT, and FAI (Federación Anarquista Ibérica), the military rebellion would have easily succeeded. Leftist militias' guerrilla warfare defeated it in Madrid,

Figure 2.2 Male and female militia fighters on the march at the beginning of the Spanish Civil War, July 1936. Keystone/Getty Images.

Barcelona, and in the developed north, thus keeping the most urbanized and advanced parts of the peninsula in loyal hands. In addition to the commitment of leftist organizations, the loyalty of police and Civil Guards was also a decisive factor. In the major urban centers, professional Republican forces of order often joined amateur militia.

Militants on both sides felt that their enemy had to be quickly eliminated. A mixture of social, political, and religious hatreds spurred killers of all persuasions to begin the bloody birthing of a new society cleansed of its enemies. As in the postwar civil wars in Finland and Hungary, when revolutionaries confronted counterrevolutionaries, the right proved more murderous than the left. During the Spanish conflict, the Nationalists would assassinate 130,000 leftists; the Republicans 50,000 rightists. Revolutionary leftists developed their own technique of the poor man's coup d'état. They came together in small groups to murder in cold blood rebellious or even potentially rebellious military officers, rightists, bourgeois, and priests. A squad knocked at the door, politely requested the victim to accompany it, and, when out of sight, shot him. These *paseos*, as they were known, seemed to have developed as a spontaneous practice among activists in the areas controlled by the Republic. Although later in the war some officials did make efforts to

stop *paseos*, during the first months of the conflict Republican governments tolerated or at least did not halt them. For example, about half
of the clergymen killed were executed in the first six weeks of the war.[14]
Potential victims tried to hide their identity by going underground or
disguised themselves by wearing "proletarian" clothes.

Throughout Republican Spain, iconoclastic fervor persecuted the
property and people of the church. Church burnings destroyed the symbols and rituals of the old order as revolutionary firing squads "executed" holy statues. Priests suffered their greatest massacre since the
French Revolution. Nearly 7,000 members of the Catholic clergy were
killed, including 13 bishops, 4,172 diocesan priests and seminarists,
2,364 monks and friars, and 283 nuns. Local revolutionaries might spare
the lives of the rich and right-wingers, but they were usually implacable
with priests. Clerics possessed the unfortunate qualities of being both
hated and easily identified. Furthermore, "fascist" clergymen gained a
highly embellished reputation for firing on revolutionaries from church
towers. As in other major European civil wars – English, French, or Russian – religion both created and revealed the gap between revolutionaries
and counterrevolutionaries. The revolutionaries' massacres and numerous acts of iconoclasm showed their desire to replace the old religion
with their new secular faith. Nationalist sympathizers reported brutal
ceremonies that recalled the rough justice of the French Revolution.
On 5 September 1936, in Murcia a Republican firing squad executed
a priest, the Falange provincial leader, and an unidentified man. Their
bodies were handed over to a crowd of 5,000 whose members hacked
off ears and notably testicles from the corpses. The priest's remains
were hung at the door of his church. In many towns in the Republican
zone, long-buried bodies of priests and nuns were exhumed and publicly
ridiculed.[15]

Militants of the Popular Front who prevented the military rebellion
from triumphing in half of Spain intensified the revolution that the rebellious officers were trying to halt. The activists – Socialists, Communists, and libertarians – collectivized numerous farms and most factories in the Republican zone. The anarchists demonstrated their desire
to defend the newborn revolution by abandoning their anti-statism and
joining governments for the first time in history. Their participation
in the Generalitat (Catalan government) in September 1936 and the
national government in November reinforced the Republic's radical reputation. Anarchist armed squads imposed "class justice" in Barcelona
by eliminating the local bourgeoisie and confiscating their property
(Figure 2.3). Urban anarchists also requisitioned supplies from the
peasantry, exacerbating urban-rural tensions. Although Communists
attempted to downplay the revolutionary nature of the Republic in the

Figure 2.3 CNT-UGT collectivized food store in Barcelona during Spanish Revolution. Getty Images.

civil war, their attitude toward the Spanish Revolution was more complex than is often stated. Even if they usually insisted that Spain must remain at the stage of bourgeois democracy and eventually attempted to suppress both revolutionary "Trotskyites" of the POUM and anarchists of the CNT, Communists immediately supported revolutionary terror against both their "bourgeois" and "proletarian" opponents. In fact, they contributed more to the killings than perhaps any other revolutionary organization.[16]

Spanish antifascism and its even more brutal rightist enemy became intolerable to many of Spain's most accomplished liberals. Both camps repulsed the philosopher, novelist, and academic Miguel de Unamuno: "The critiques of the intellectuals will disturb both sides. If the fascists do not shoot them, the Marxists will."[17] After welcoming the attack on the Republic in the summer of 1936, Unamuno quickly became disillusioned with the Nationalists. Their war on critical thinking, militaristic sloganeering ("Long Live Death!"), and resentment against Catalans and Basques led to his famous public outburst at the University of Salamanca on 12 October 1936 during a ceremony marking Columbus Day. In front of cocked weapons and fascist war cries ("Death to Intellectuals"), he made the most courageous defense of academic freedom in the twentieth century by telling the outraged Nationalists that their words and actions profaned the temple of the intellect. His liberal defiance led to his house arrest and his death a few months later.

Like his friend Unamuno, Salvador de Madariaga – an author, diplomat, and internationalist – remained neutral during the civil war because he believed that both sides – Marxism and fascism – were equally destructive of freedom. Madariaga, who received threats from the left and abandoned the Republican zone, explained his position: "I could not speak for the Rebels, for they stood against all that I hold true; I could not speak for the Revolutionists, not only because I did not believe in their methods (nor, in the case of some of them, in their aims) but because they did not stand for what they said they stood for. They filled their mouths with democracy and liberty but allowed neither to live."[18] After the war, Madariaga remained in exile and, as president of the Liberal International, became a key leader of the movement to replace the enduring Franco dictatorship with a non-Communist, democratic regime linked to Western Europe and the United States.

Like Madariaga and Unamuno, the philosopher José Ortega y Gasset had originally supported the Republic, but he too became alienated by its failure to control the "masses," the subject of his most famous work. Furthermore, at the eruption of the revolution in Madrid, some of the Republic's supporters pressured him to sign a statement in favor of the government and against the *pronunciamiento*. Feeling threatened, the philosopher chose exile in France from where he criticized the ignorance of Western intellectuals, specifically Albert Einstein, who imagined the Republic as a bastion of liberty. The journalist, Manuel Chaves Nogales, also condemned both camps. Chaves had been an enthusiastic supporter of the Republic, but its violence led him to take increasing critical and geographical distance from it. In early 1937, he wrote from his French refuge: "Today's prize is the fatherland. The truth is that between the choice of a pale Ethiopia, to which General Franco condemns us, and a western Kyrgyzstan that the Bolshevik agents desire, it is better to roam the world and find a part that is still habitable."[19]

These four liberals knew that the Republic had gone far beyond the "bourgeois democratic" stage of the French Revolution of 1789. They recognized that the Republican zone was hardly democratic in any usual sense because the entire right had been eliminated – sometimes physically – and the parliament played little or no role during the war. Furthermore, the Spanish Revolution endangered many more types of private property than seigneurial dues and church and émigré possessions confiscated during the French Revolution. Communist, Socialist, and anarchist goals sharply contrasted with those of French revolutionaries of 1789 who had declared private property a "sacred right of man" and who planned to promote a free-market economy. Despite calming rhetoric meant to reassure both the domestic and foreign middle classes, Communist attitudes toward private property were hardly bourgeois. Instead, they were inspired by Lenin's New Economic Policy (NEP, 1921–1928) to protect small property to win over the petty bourgeoisie. Communists also advocated nationalization of large employers and participated with both Socialists and anarchists in the management of collectivized farms and factories. The PCE planned a prototype of "popular democracy" in which large-scale capitalism and "fascism" – i.e., all conservative groups, whether democratic or not – would cease to exist. Their exclusively leftist republic guaranteed private property only temporarily, as Communist and even Republican leaders admitted when speaking candidly.[20]

By February 1937, the PCE conceded that the situation had gone beyond the defense of a "democratic, parliamentary republic" since the basis of capitalism in agriculture, industry, and finance had disappeared and the domination of the church had ceased. In June, 1937, Dolores Ibárruri – the celebrated Pasionaria who became the female icon of the Republic – labeled Spain a "parliamentary and democratic Republic of a new type . . . as communists we do not renounce our desire to bring about in time the victory of socialism, and not only in Spain, but all over the world. We are Marxists-Leninists-Stalinists, and therefore we adapt our theory to the revolutionary possibilities of the given moment, without renouncing our ultimate aims"[21] (Figure 2.4). Following the Comintern line during the Popular Front, Communists thought that they must defend democracy because fascism totally eliminated the possibility of working-class betterment, let alone revolution. Nevertheless, Communists in the 1930s were never fully committed to parliamentary democracy and always kept the goal of establishing some variation – mostly along the lines of the NEP – of the Soviet model in Spain. Communists would often claim that they were merely defending democracy in Spain, but their vision of democracy was quite different from that of conservative antifascists because Communists believed that the defeat of fascism would lead to the victory of socialism.

In this most profound workers' revolution in European history, Communists, Socialists, anarchists, and their allied trade unionists assumed that wage earners would labor devotedly in their newly collectivized farms, factories, and workshops. The militants were soon disappointed, because workers resisted work under the revolutionary political and trade-union leaderships that had instituted various forms of democratic workers' control. Many wage earners continued to demand more pay

Figure 2.4 Dolores Ibárurri (Pasionaria), Spanish Communist leader, salutes members of the International Brigades. Getty Images.

and persisted in their attempts to avoid the constraints of factory space and time. The anarchosyndicalists of the CNT and the Socialists and Communists of UGT who ran the collectives in Barcelona, Spain's most important industrial area, opposed many of the workers' desires that they had supported before the revolution and civil war. Instead, the activists called for more work and sacrifice. Rank-and-file workers frequently ignored these appeals and acted as though the union militants were the new ruling elite. Refusals to work became major points of conflict between rank-and-file workers and militants, just as they had been when the bourgeoisie controlled the productive forces. These new industrial managers were continually beseeching the rank and file not to request wage hikes during the difficult times of war and revolution, but their pleas for more work and sacrifice were frequently ignored in various industrial sectors.

The constant demands of the workers, which began very early in the revolution, frustrated the union leaders. The unions were forced to confront major problems of absenteeism and lateness, phenomena that have existed in varying degrees throughout the history of labor. The anarchosyndicalist and Communist press frequently criticized the workers' adamant maintenance of these traditions. Skipping work indicated the rank-and-file's determined dislike of the factory, however democratic. Sickness multiplied the number of workdays missed. Tobacco breaks and alcohol abuse, subjects of reprobation in wartime Spanish socialist realist propaganda, contributed to the loss of worktime. Sabotage and theft – which implied a great detachment from the libertarian or communist principles of cooperation in production – continued during the Spanish Revolution. Faced with these varied forms of working-class resistance to work and workspace, the unions and the collectives cooperated to establish strict rules and regulations that equaled or surpassed the controls imposed by capitalist enterprises. Wage earners' direct and indirect refusals to work conflicted with the militants' urgent need to combat the Nationalists through greater production of clothing and weapons. To make workers work and to reduce resistances, the urban revolutionary elite implemented piecework, elimination of holidays, medical inspections, and dismissals.

Resistance to work in agrarian collectives was similar. For example, in the Colectividad Campesina Adelante of Lérida, members initially performed their jobs satisfactorily, but quickly problems appeared.[22] The most important difficulty concerned how much collectivists should work. Some argued for infinite sacrifice; others wanted to define precise working hours. When the latter were established in January 1937, disinterested wage earners ignored them and "came late and left early." The divide between "those who work a lot and others who hardly do anything" became the major impediment in this and other agrarian collectives. Throughout 1937, workers departed early and abandoned their tools by the roadside. Proposals for elimination of the work-shy proliferated. The general assembly of the collective decided to award itself the right to discharge "anyone who works poorly" and "those who get drunk."

A veteran militant, who was one of the most active and respected of the Lérida collectivists, proposed that "we expel the gypsies. They are very young and have many children." Gypsies, of course, never adopted the productivist lifestyle propagated by activists of multiple modern "isms." As George Orwell noted, during the apex of the revolution they continued to beg on the streets of Barcelona.[23] The family wage scale made large families financially burdensome for the collective, and conflicts erupted between big families who took advantage of the collective's social and medical services and those with fewer or no offspring. A similar problem concerned the exertions of the elderly and their contribution to the community.

Gender strife also persisted. Women were almost always paid less and sometimes treated as second-class members. In many collectives, they could not vote and were rarely elected as officials. The sexist male leaders of the Lérida collective concluded that "the problem of women is similar in all the collectives. It is a result of egotism and lack of spirit of sacrifice. Unfortunately, there are few that are conscientious collectivists. Female comrades must do certain jobs, such as cleaning and washing." Gender discrimination was tied to an often unspoken but pervasive bias against all those – women, elderly, and gypsies – who were not considered full-fledged producers. One of the most important UGT leaders who was also a prominent Communist concluded that it was the conduct of the workers that most endangered the collectives. In a confidential conversation with CNT members of the Optical Collective, the economist Estanislao Ruiz i Ponseti said that although few would state it publicly, the workers were merely "masses," whose cooperation was unfortunately necessary for the success of the enterprises.[24]

The Communists regarded worker resistance to work and refusals to follow their activist leaders as potentially "fascist." The Spanish Civil War, above all the controversial May Days, pioneered the identification of workers' revolts with "fascism." In early May 1937 in Barcelona, armed members of the CNT and the POUM took to the streets to protest the increasing control of the revolution and war effort by the centralizing Republican government, which Socialists and Communists fully supported. As in East Germany in 1953, Hungary in 1956, and Poland in 1970 and 1981, governing elites labeled as "fascist" workers' resistance to Communist or Socialist policies. This implausible accusation of "fascism" was rooted not only in the short-term vicissitudes of Communist antifascism during the 1930s but also in the longer-term faith in the "workers' state" or "popular democracy" which could identify all its enemies – whether worker or bourgeois – as both "capitalist" and "fascist." Thus, all parties and groups outside the Communist-backed organizations harbored the germs of fascism.

Foreigners and the Spanish Revolution

In the first crucial months of the war, the Nationalists received the highly effective aid of the Germans and Italians, who initiated the Axis in Spain in response to Spanish revolutionary antifascism. Hitler's and Mussolini's claim to be fighting "communist revolution" in Spain seemed plausible to many on the right and even the center. In July 1936 Franco originated the first major airlift in history, and by August 1936, the airlift had transported more than 10,000 soldiers from Morocco to the peninsula with the help of the fascist powers. Several months later, the number had risen to 14,000 along with hundreds of tons of equipment and arms. Moroccan mercenaries were among the elite of Franco's forces and were instrumental in conquering large swaths of southern and central Spain. The North Africans, whose numbers would reach 80,000, were joined by 72,000 Italian ground troops over the course of the Spanish conflict. Following the airlift, Nazi aid to the Nationalists was largely devoted to supporting the Condor Legion, whose destruction of the Basque town of Guernica won international notoriety. This 5,000- to 6,000-man aircraft group, which was assembled in Spain in November 1936, was one of Hitler's most important contributions to the Nationalist victory.

German and Italian assistance to Franco was timelier, more persistent, and more regular than Soviet aid to the Republic, which arrived in substantial amounts only in the autumn of 1936. The Republic tried to narrow the foreign assistance gap by employing approximately 40,000 International Brigaders. The Internationals, whom Communist networks largely recruited, proved more interested in ideology and less in booty than Franco's African mercenaries. The Internationals often developed into excellent and committed soldiers whose gung-ho initiatives contrasted with ordinary Spanish soldiers' desires to maintain the live-and-let-live nonviolence on quiet fronts. The Internationals frequently felt themselves superior to their more passive Spanish Republican comrades.

Antifascist volunteers from France, the United Kingdom, the United States, and many other nations emphasized that their fight in Spain was in defense of democracy and Spanish independence against German and Italian "invaders" (Figure 2.5). The antifascist struggle morphed into a patriotic one. The conflation of patriotism and antifascism – which was initiated during the Popular Fronts – permitted easier recruitment in the democracies where volunteers and aid for the Republic vastly outnumbered those for the Nationalists. For example, the American trade-union leader David Dubinsky, of the International Ladies' Garment Workers' Union, became treasurer of Labor's Red Cross for Spain – soon to become Trade Union Relief for Spain – and dispersed more than $100,000 for the Republic. Although Dubinsky was an avowed anti-Communist, he asserted in 1937: "There is no civil war in Spain. It is an invasion of a democratic country by hostile forces of fascism and Nazism

Figure 2.5 Spanish Civil War, British volunteers in the International Brigades, 1937. Getty Images.

as part of a plan to subdue workers in every land. American labor cannot ignore this threat to itself." Dubinsky's antifascism during the Spanish Civil War anticipated the attitude of the major trade-union federations after the US entry into World War II when American labor organizations emphasized that the struggle was against "fascism" whose imposition of "monopoly capitalism" had transformed its population into "slaves." The main French and British trade unions often shared this view and were firmly pro-Republican. At the same time, UK trade-union leaders feared that the Spanish war would spread beyond its borders and that Communists might impose their dictatorship in Spain.[25]

Aware of the need to appeal to democratic public opinion, many International Brigaders, including the nearly 3,000 Americans mostly grouped in what became known as the Abraham Lincoln Brigade, tried to mask their revolutionary commitment. When the Lincolns sang "The Internationale," they claimed for public consumption that it was "The Star-Spangled Banner."[26] The name of their unit, officially the Abraham Lincoln Battalion, conjured images of a fight for democracy, not socialism. As Communists, most Lincolns accepted a rapprochement with the capitalist West in the form of the Popular Front only as a temporary expedient. They regarded themselves as part of a "proletarian army," even if – like leftist militants in Spain – they had a very orthodox and unrealistic view of Spanish workers. Their Manichean vision of the conflict made it impossible to completely understand the "Spanish people" that they were supposedly defending. The Lincolns' antifascism nonetheless contained militant anti-racism in the form of the US Communist Party's pioneering affirmative action policies that promoted African-Americans and thus contrasted clearly with the widespread discrimination in the US armed forces and society. The introduction of affirmative action *avant la lettre* is undoubtedly one of the reasons the Lincolns' political reputation survived their military defeat.

Like the Lincolns, other International Brigaders never lost their close links to the Communist Party. Following Pasionaria's line, many British volunteers defined the Republic that they served as a "democratic and parliamentary republic of a new type." An Eastern European Jewish-Communist commissar, who had volunteered to fight in Spain, constantly referred to his "revolutionary" commitment and his colleagues' desires to "fight for the proletarian cause." Most of the famous (or infamous) figures who led the post-1945 Communist regimes were involved in the Spanish conflict, including the German Ulbricht and the Czech Gottwald. Josip Broz, the future Marshal Tito who became the head of the Federal People's Republic of Yugoslavia, organized International Brigade volunteers from the Balkans and central Europe. At the end of World War II in their "people's democracies," these men put into practice the Communist theory that the world wars had initiated an era of socialist revolutions.[27]

The assassinations of clergy, military, and bourgeois accompanied by massive property confiscations in Spain convinced a broad range of public opinion across the Atlantic and beyond that the Spanish Republic had become a revolutionary state unable to impose order and discipline on its supporters. With good reason, many non-Communists refused to believe that members of the Comintern had ceased to be dedicated revolutionaries. Some Soviet officials – for example, the foreign minister, Maxim Litvinov – saw the contradiction of their own policy which aimed for broad antifascist alliances with democratic moderates and yet supported a revolutionary republic. Despite the wishes of the Comintern, Litvinov opposed Russian involvement in Spain because he realized that the Spanish Revolution would hinder Soviet attempts to align with the democratic West.[28] Although Stalin decided to intervene in Spain, he ultimately downplayed popular antifascism and favored traditional diplomacy and alliances among states.

Spanish Republicans' commitment to revolutionary anti-capitalism alienated powerful businessmen and diplomats. US Secretary of State Cordell Hull denounced the Barcelona workers' seizure of American corporate property, specifically the General Motors plant in that city. Thus, as one of the most prominent Lincoln Brigade veterans admitted, Communists were unable to alter US public opinion and convince in sufficient numbers "other democratic forces" to aid the Spanish Republic.[29] The same political ineffectiveness and inability to persuade democratic governments to assist the Republic repeated itself in the United Kingdom and France. The revolutionary antifascism of Communists, Socialists, anarchists, and the POUM scared moderates, conservatives, and Catholics throughout the world. Western policies of nonintervention in the Spanish Civil War may not have stopped fascism – as critics claimed a Western intervention would have – but nonintervention prevented a deep division within and among the Atlantic democracies. Nonintervention distanced counterrevolutionary antifascism from revolution and communism and would help to make it respectable among moderate, conservative, and Catholic opinion.

The United Kingdom, France, and the United States deplored German and Italian intervention in Spain on the side of Spanish counterrevolutionaries and fascists. In August 1936 the French Prime Minister – the Socialist Léon Blum – proposed an official policy of nonintervention. Blum's proposal was designed to help the Republic by restraining the flow of German and Italian aid while preventing a wider European war, and Azaña and the Soviets initially supported it. Britain and France would have appreciated a quick Republican or even a Nationalist victory that preserved the European status quo. In retrospect, nonintervention did not serve the Republic's cause, and nearly all the European powers ignored it at some point. Nevertheless, it localized the Spanish war, preventing Madrid from becoming a new Sarajevo. Nonintervention delayed the formation of the two blocs – fascist and antifascist – which would eventually go to war in late 1939. In addition, nonintervention served Blum's domestic agenda because his own Socialist party (Section Française de l'Internationale Ouvrière, SFIO) had an intransigently pacifist wing which refused French military intervention for any reason.[30]

Although nonintervention angered French communists who were part of Blum's own Popular Front coalition, it won the support of Blum's other major coalition partner – the Radical party. Despite its name, the latter was the French Third Republic's swing party and represented its center. Aiding revolutionary Spain would have alienated the Radicals and ruptured the tripartite coalition of the French Popular Front. This Popular Front was a non-revolutionary, center-left coalition, superficially similar but – as we shall see – profoundly different from the Spanish Popular Front. The Radical support of nonintervention reflected the fact that the majority of the French press was favorable to the Spanish Nationalists. Influential French Radicals suspected that Communists were attempting to enlarge the Spanish conflict into a general war in defense of Soviet interests. In general, the French right, including leading Radicals, altered the Popular Front's electoral slogan, "fascism means war," and instead insisted that "communism equals war." The right and even much of the center vowed complete neutrality because they held that Moscow controlled the Spanish Popular Front. The prominent right-wing deputy and journalist Henri de Kérillis, who would become a leading anti-Nazi by the end of 1936, strongly supported the Nationalists throughout the conflict. Kérillis detested Spanish "revolutionary convulsions ... anarchy and murder" and feared that conservative Britain would abandon its French ally if the latter entered an antifascist bloc with Republican Spain and the Soviet Union. Kérillis, the editor of L'Écho de Paris, attempted to sabotage any French aid to the Republic by publishing sensationalist articles on secret arms traffic between France and Spain.[31]

Nonintervention reflected the distaste of the Atlantic establishment (including Roosevelt's State Department) for the Spanish Revolution. The French ambassador to Spain, Jean Herbette, who had been the first French envoy to the Soviet Union, judged that the radical left dominated a Spanish Republic that was acting unconstitutionally and advised Paris to follow the British policy of complete nonintervention. The majority of ambassadors – including the British and French – left Madrid for the tranquil territory of southern France. In vain, the Republican government sharply protested this nearly unprecedented exit. Foreign diplomats also estranged the Spanish Republic by attempting to aid approximately 7,000 persons who had been labeled, rightly or wrongly, as fascists and were threatened by revolutionary violence. The envoys of many nations engaged in what was one of the most massive asylum and rescue efforts in the history of international diplomacy. As late as January 1938, the Republic violated the Turkish delegation's diplomatic immunity by entering its legation and arresting its Spanish asylees. Ambassador Herbette's successor, Eirik Pierre Labonne, who was initially more sympathetic to the Republic, became convinced in February 1938 that it continued to be dominated by atheist and anticlerical "extremists" who had little in common with France or Great Britain. Many of his colleagues shared the consensus that the Republic was not democratic. Although attaining office at approximately the same time as its Spanish counterpart, the French Popular Front refused official assistance to a sister Republic under attack from anti-Republicans and fascists.[32]

Nevertheless, Blum experimented with a policy of limited covert aid to Spain in the summer of 1936 and again in late March 1938. This policy, termed *non-intervention relâchée* (relaxed nonintervention), disregarded British objections and opened France's southern border for arms deliveries until 13 June 1938. The French Popular Front government also permitted the passage over the Pyrenees of volunteers – mainly International Brigaders. However, French military assistance was insufficient to allow the Spanish Republic to defeat the Nationalists. Like the French rearmament effort initiated during its Popular Front, which is discussed later, aid to the Spanish Republic demonstrated no deep commitment to stemming fascism in Spain or elsewhere. Instead, acquiescence for weapons' flow to its southern neighbor served as a warning to Spanish Nationalists and Italian Fascists not to ignore French interests in the Mediterranean. After a number of important Nationalist battlefield successes, normalization of the relations between France and Nationalist Spain began in May 1938, as Franco pledged neutrality in the event of a European war. The normalization process culminated on 24 February 1939 when the French parliament, from which had emerged the Popular Front government of 1936, recognized the victorious Franco regime by 323 votes to 261.[33]

The regularization of French diplomatic relations with Franco's Spain did not lessen Italian aggressiveness toward French interests. Mussolini encouraged his media to endorse what the entire French political spectrum considered unacceptable Italian claims on Nice, Corsica, and Tunis. A few French antifascist rightists saw Franco's alliance with Germany and Italy as dangerous for their own nation and its empire. Lieutenant-Colonel Henri Morel, the French military attaché in Madrid and a member of the anti-Semitic and monarchist Action Française, urged Blum to block Axis pretensions in the Mediterranean. On 20 March 1938 Morel told the prime minister that "a French king would make war" to stop France's encirclement by the fascist powers and the potential disruption of communications with its North African empire, where half of its army was stationed. Although Morel's nationalism originated on the extreme right, it transformed him into an "ardent antifascist." It is impossible to know whether Morel's advice would have led to a better outcome for France and Spain, but he shared fewer illusions than his military superiors who hoped to detach Italy from a German alliance. At the end of 1938 the French government was still hoping for support from Nazi Germany to check Italian ambitions in the Mediterranean, but the Nazi regime unsurprisingly reaffirmed Axis solidarity. As the Spanish war ended in February–March 1939, the influx of Spanish Republican refugees compelled the French government to divert troops to its Spanish border and thus hindered a potential mobilization against Fascist Italy. Franco's triumph undermined the French position in the Mediterranean and offered the Italians and Germans a friendly Iberian power which could help them isolate France from North Africa, the heart of the French Empire.[34]

Great Britain was central in the decisions concerning nonintervention since it was France's principal ally in the 1930s. Britain warned its continental partner to be cautious about aiding the Spanish Republic. At the end of July 1936 Prime Minister Stanley Baldwin told French President Albert Lebrun that the United Kingdom would remain neutral if the Spanish conflict led to war between France and the Axis. British pressure on Blum to stop arms shipments to Spain increased in early August. In the United Kingdom, even more than in France, official opinion viewed the Spanish Republic as unable to control extremists and protect property. This combination made the Republic unlikely to support British interests in the Mediterranean. Many high-ranking British foreign service officers, including permanent under-secretary Robert Vansittart and his deputy Alexander Cadogan, feared that the "Bolshevik" contagion that started in Spain in the summer of 1936 would soon infect Popular Front France. The conservative papers and the liberal *Manchester Guardian* criticized the Republic in July 1936 for failing to control its "extremists." In September 1936, the Labour Party and the trade unions overwhelmingly seconded nonintervention. British conservatives were either indifferent to the conflict or regarded the Republican coalition as encouraging revolutionary terror against their Spanish conservative counterparts. The killings of Spanish naval officers by Republican sailors provoked wide sympathy for the Nationalists in the Royal Navy. As in France, a number of rightists who were pro-Franco were not necessarily pro-Hitler. Some – such as the prolific and bestselling author Major Geoffrey McNeill-Moss – praised the Nationalists but wanted to stop the Nazis. The poet Roy Campbell propagandized for Franco but would denounce Nazi Germany and enlist in the British army.[35]

Like the French right, the British right's attitudes toward Communism and the Soviet Union hardened during the Spanish conflict. Hitler and Mussolini found a sympathetic audience in the democracies and elsewhere when they invoked anti-communism to justify

their pro-Nationalist activities. Germany and Italy successfully encouraged an anti-Soviet stance throughout Europe. Poles, Romanians, and
Yugoslavs – allies of the French and friendly to Britain – were nonetheless positive toward the anti-communist interventions of the fascist powers, and their attitude weakened France's attempt to tighten its Eastern
European alliances.[36] As Litvinov had seen, Soviet aid to the Republic
made conservatives uneasy about supporting it and discredited analysts
who had regarded the Soviet Union as too preoccupied with its internal
problems to promote revolution abroad.

The Spanish conflict divided the politically aware British public as
had no other foreign question since the French Revolution, and this discord encouraged official policy to maintain a certain balance between the
two sides. At the beginning of the war, the government restricted pro-
Republican speakers from entering the country but provided facilities to
Republican vessels in Gibraltar while limiting exports and communications from Nationalist Spain. Despite increasing pressure from *franquis-
tas*, the government remained reluctant to grant belligerent rights to the
Nationalists since this would allow them to blockade Republican ports.
At the start of the conflict, the British left – including Labour and the
Communist Party of Great Britain (CPGB) – supported nonintervention
because it believed – like Blum – that the balance of forces favored the
Republic. The reaction of Franco's agent in London, the Duke of Alba,
to this rather even-handed British policy revealed the fascistic mindset
of the Nationalists. Alba imagined that foreign minister Anthony Eden
and Vansittart led a Judeo-Masonic conspiracy against Spain. Faced with
the intervention of the Axis powers in Spain, these two British diplomats
increasingly preferred a Republican victory after 1936 when their worries
of a communist contagion spreading to France lessened.[37]

Winston Churchill personified the divisions produced by the Spanish
Civil War among conservative antifascists. Like a good number of his colleagues on the right, Churchill believed that neither side was admirable
and that both endangered democracy. In July 1937, he accused the
Republic of being a "mere mask" for Communist revolution. His dislike
of the Republic alienated the pro-Republican left in Britain and elsewhere. To limit Axis gains in Iberia, he became dissatisfied with nonintervention and wanted to end the conflict quickly. As an antifascist, he
had no wish to see a Spanish regime allied with either Italy or, still less,
Germany. However, as a conservative, he detested the Spanish Revolution and was erroneously inclined to blame the Soviet Union for it. He
proposed international mediation which would impose a centrist government that would halt the war and revolution. Churchill distrusted

both Spanish sides, an attitude that Roosevelt and other antifascist political leaders in the Atlantic world shared. Churchill became more sympathetic to the Republic during 1938, but he never advocated aid to it. On 23 February 1939, five weeks before the end of the conflict, he wrote, "as long as the issue of the war hung in the balance, it would have been wrong for Britain to throw her weight on either side of the scale." After the war, he explained: "In this [Spanish] quarrel I was neutral. Naturally I was not in favour of the Communists. How could I be, when if I had been a Spaniard they would have murdered me and my family and friends? I was sure, however, that with all the rest they had on their hands the British government were right to keep out of Spain."[38] Churchill regarded any one-sided British intervention as disastrously divisive both domestically and internationally.

The Spanish conflict led many pacifists in the democracies, especially in Great Britain, to modify their position and accept the necessity of war against fascism. The British left rallied to the defense of the Republic and began to curtail its peace promotion in favor of antifascism. The young British poet and International Brigader John Cornford wrote, in a poem composed shortly before his death in Spain: "O understand before too late/Freedom was never held without a Fight." Another youthful bard, Julian Bell – who also perished in Spain ("the poets exploding like bombs," as W. H. Auden put it) – wrote to novelist E. M. Forster that to be antiwar meant submitting to fascism. In late 1938 the pacifist polymath J. D. Bernal became convinced that the dictators had to be combated and embarked upon mobilizing science as fully as possible to prepare for the coming conflict. Labour MP Ellen Wilkinson's commitment to the Spanish Republic led to her abandonment of pacifism. The Spanish war helped to convince a divided Labour Party to adopt a more positive attitude toward national defense. Despite the passionate anti-Republican sentiments of its Catholic members, pressures from the left forced Labour to end its support for the policy of nonintervention in late 1937 when it called for the right of the Republic to buy arms. Even so, major trade-union leaders continued to assert privately that nonintervention prevented a larger European war.[39]

In Britain, public support for the Republic rose from 57 percent in March 1938 to 71 percent in January 1939, compared with only 10 percent supporting Franco. Even a small current of Tory opinion was pro-Republican by the end of the conflict. The Duchess of Atholl, a Conservative MP from Scotland, did not share Churchill's views on Spain and was a firm supporter of the Republic. Against his advice and because she was very isolated in the Conservative Party, she resigned her parliamentary seat as a Tory in 1938, ran as an independent, and lost. She authored a Penguin Special, *Searchlight on Spain*, which defined the struggle as one between Republican democracy and fascist dictatorship. It sold 100,000 copies in a week during June 1938, demonstrating the continuing ardent interest in the conflict in Great Britain.[40]

Humanitarian sentiments in Britain overwhelmingly favored the Republic, which received much greater shipments of non-governmental aid than the Nationalists, despite the latter's solid support from the Catholic Church. Pro-Republicans opened "Spain Shops" throughout the country which sold Spanish Republican goods and collected donations for the victims of the conflict. As in the United States, the trade unions accumulated contributions which totaled hundreds of thousands of British pounds. The Aid Spain committees – Republican Spain, of course – was the largest movement of international solidarity in UK history. Aid Spain promoted a de facto left-wing unity and was a pale British equivalent of the Popular Front since – unlike the Fronts in Spain and France – Labour refused to ally with the CPGB. British trade-union leaders suspected that Communists were attempting to maneuver France into a war with Germany over Spain. In contrast to the French Socialists after 1934, British Labour officially attempted to block antifascist cooperation with Communists. Labour's analysis of fascism differed distinctly from more radical left interpretations. It attributed the fascist upsurge not to capitalism but rather to the growth of Communism, and it believed that democratic and nonviolent means were the best way to combat the extreme right. Labour feared that cooperation with Communists would result in violent street protests which would create more, not fewer, fascists. As in France, in Britain the Spanish Civil War divided the left as much as it united it.[41]

A War of Religion

The Spanish conflict was the greatest European war of religion in the twentieth century. The inability of the Second Spanish Republic to integrate a large body of Catholics greatly harmed it domestically as well as internationally. As a result, Catholicism became the most cohesive cultural force in the Nationalist zone and the most important source of *franquista* support in Britain, France, and the United States. In contrast to its counterparts in Germany and Italy, the Spanish fascist party, the Falange, became ultra-Catholic. The Spanish war divided clericals from nonbelievers and split the Christian community. Violent anticlericalism in Spain renewed the objections that the Russian and Hungarian revolutions had triggered immediately after World War I, when many learned that leftist revolution meant the destruction of religion as well as private property. Republican anticlerical outrages rendered the conflict in Spain particularly problematic for Christians. Almost immediately after the outbreak of the Spanish conflict, the Catholic Church organized meetings in support of the Nationalists where speakers recounted stories of leftist atrocities against the faithful. The church easily tapped into a neo-traditionalist current of opinion in Great Britain among a few nostalgic intellectuals who romanticized the Middle Ages and many more persons who respected religion. Pro-Republican Anglicans, who seemed unconcerned with the church burnings and priest killings, infuriated their anti-Republican Catholic compatriots. Auden, whom the Republic had employed as a propagandist, returned to his ancestral Anglican faith after the war when he wrote that the closing of churches that he had witnessed in Barcelona "shocked and disturbed" him and perhaps motivated his later rejection of politics.[42]

Even if not pro-Franco, British Catholics' opposition to their hierarchy's defense of the Spanish Church was extremely limited. Working-class Catholics remained consistently hostile to the Republic. Walter Citrine, an influential trade-union leader and a committed antifascist, regretted Republican atrocities and fretted that Catholic workers might abandon unions that adopted a pro-Republican position. Union leaders may have feared feeding the development in Britain of a confessional union movement resembling those on the continent. Furthermore, Citrine and other labor leaders did not regard the civil war as a struggle between fascism and democracy but rather as a conflict within an undemocratic and feudal society that distracted attention from a resurgent Germany, which constituted the real danger to both British interests and the labor movement. Labour leaders were also reluctant to ally with the Soviet Union in Spain or Communist-front organizations in the United Kingdom. The revolutionary assault on the church also offended Protestant traditionalists. Conservative Protestants – such as the devout Methodist and tourist industry pioneer Henry Lunn – defended persecuted Catholics and refused any reconciliation with pro-Republican opinion in Great Britain. The mainstream Archbishop of Canterbury, Cosmo Lang, backed the government's nonintervention policy, which was supported by the majority of the Christian press and the Anglican Church Assembly.[43]

The war also divided Protestants in America. Leading conservative newspapers – *Chicago Tribune, Washington Times, Dallas News* – excoriated a Republic which expropriated private property and repressed religion. William Randolph Hearst's press empire, including the *New York Journal* and 13 percent of all American dailies, emphasized the

Republic's similarities with the Russian Revolution. Hearst's *Cosmopolitan* reported that a "Red government" had been established in Madrid. It justified the military rebellion as a "protest" against the destruction of authority, religion, and "Spain's most beautiful historical monuments." The magazines of another American press magnate, Henry Luce, were more nuanced. On the first anniversary of the war, *Life* offered a critique of the Spanish elite that could have emanated from a Marxist: "The ruling classes of Spain were probably the world's worst bosses – irresponsible, arrogant, vain, ignorant, shiftless, and incompetent... The reason for the civil war was simply that the people... had fired their bosses for flagrant incompetence and the bosses refused to be fired." In 1937, Luce's *Fortune* castigated the "feudal" Spanish Church, army, and landlords. *Time* noted in 1939 that Madrid had become a symbol of "Spanish resistance to fascism." Many in the Protestant middle classes opposed what the venerable and respected *Christian Century* called "fascist-clerical insurgents."[44]

As in Britain, American Catholics looked to the Vatican for leadership and disproportionally favored Franco, isolationism, and appeasement policies even after the German occupation of Prague in March 1939. Their opinions were politically significant because Catholics were approximately 20 percent of the population in the United States in the 1930s. Although labor unions with a predominantly Protestant or Jewish membership were pro-Republican, those with a majority Catholic membership – United Mine Workers and Congress of Industrial Organizations – vetoed support for the Republic. University students' advocacy of the Republic also followed religious belief. The radio priest and philo-Nazi Father Charles E. Coughlin, whose program reached millions of listeners, organized the effective lobbying group Keep the Spanish Embargo Committee. Supported by the Catholic hierarchy and media, it played an important role in resisting US pro-Republican intervention in the conflict. In April 1937, George Shuster, an editor of the relatively liberal Catholic *Commonweal*, published comments critical of Franco. His magazine's circulation immediately fell 25 percent, and he was compelled to resign. *Commonweal* remained ambivalent toward the Nationalists but generally favored them over the Republicans. In fact, it admonished the French Catholic author Georges Bernanos for his unrelenting criticism of the Spanish clergy who supported Franco's forces and connived at their numerous unjustified assassinations of leftists.[45]

The Paulist publication *Catholic World* was still more pro-Nationalist and thus more representative of Catholic opinion. It reproduced articles by the Franco enthusiast Douglas Jerrold, even as it criticized the Caudillo's apologetic attitude toward Fascism and Nazism.[46] *Catholic*

World defined supporters of the Republic or the "Loyalists" as "any Anarchist, Syndicalist, Socialist, Nihilist, Marxist, Bolshevik, or Communist who believes in the destruction of all loyalty to law, government, or property; who executes nuns, priests, monks and all solvent citizens." It lauded Franco as the soul who "drives from Spain the enemy of Spanish ideals, of Spanish faith, of the Spanish character." Franco was a humanitarian, "a lover of men and a defender of the Church." It quoted with approval the statement of the English Hispanist E. Allison Peers, who described the war as "the crusade of a Christian people against the attempt to subject them to godless rule." Like another Catholic dictator, the Portuguese António de Oliveira Salazar, Franco was establishing "Christian liberty" and "social democracy" against the wishes of "Masonic purveyors." The Paulists certified that the Caudillo was not fascist nor another Hitler or Mussolini.[47]

Following grossly exaggerated numbers circulated by the Vatican, which were common throughout the Catholic press, *Catholic World* inflated the number of priests killed to 16,000 and nuns to 15,000. The Paulist monthly generally ignored or denied Nationalist repression and praised "the élan and courage of the New Spain," in which – it falsely asserted – there was "complete religious freedom." *Catholic World* was skeptical of Bernanos' eyewitness account of Nationalist atrocities and dismissed reports of the destruction of Guernica by Nationalist air power as inaccurate or as Loyalist propaganda. Like other Catholic publications, it accepted Nationalist misinformation at face value and asserted that "the fleeing reds" destroyed the "holy city of the Basques." Paulist publications falsely claimed that "the first aggressors in Spain were France and Russia." Franco supposedly accepted foreign aid only after 35,000 foreign volunteers had assisted the Republic. *Catholic World* implied or stated that Republicans were pawns of Moscow. The magazine reproduced an article from the English Catholic *Blackfriars* which rejoiced that "the victory of General Franco . . . will bring the end to a painful conflict of conscience to millions of Catholics throughout the world."[48]

Despite firm Catholic support for the Nationalists, by mid-1938 Franco's prospective victory aroused the concerns of certain American diplomats, Ambassador William Dodd in Berlin and former (Republican) Secretary of State Henry Stimson. They petitioned for a weakening of the Neutrality Act and the end of the arms embargo on the Republic. Influential congressmen, including the usually isolationist Senator Gerald Nye, joined the initiative, which surprisingly gained the support of Secretary of State Hull. However, their plan was blocked by newly appointed American Ambassador to the United Kingdom Joseph

Kennedy, a Catholic who supported Neville Chamberlain's appeasement policies. Kennedy's stance was backed by many US Catholics (including the progressive Dorothy Day) and conservative Protestants who protested passionately against assistance to "Bolsheviks and atheists," leading Roosevelt to abandon the campaign to end the embargo.[49]

At the beginning of the Spanish Civil War, the overwhelming majority of French Catholics – even including liberal ones, such as novelist François Mauriac – favored the ostensibly pious Nationalists over the unmistakably anticlerical Republicans. In July 1936, Mauriac warned Prime Minister Blum in the right-wing *Le Figaro* that Catholics "would never pardon" French intervention on the side of the Republic, which was an integral part of "the International of Hate." For traditionalist Catholics throughout the conflict, Franco remained the defender of "Christian civilization against Marxist barbarism." *La Croix*, perhaps the most widely circulated and most influential French Catholic daily, echoed the Vatican line and came to wish for a Nationalist victory. Robert Schuman, who would become a chief architect of postwar European unity, reflected the views of the French hierarchy. In early 1939 he resigned from a small French Christian democratic group – the Parti Démocrate Populaire – because it was not sufficiently pro-Franco.[50]

Although the Catholic Church hierarchy and most of its faithful were pro-Franco, antifascism nevertheless had a Christian component. The Basque Nationalists were the most significant Iberian advocates of Christian democracy, but their short-lived regional government demonstrated the weaknesses of conservative antifascism in Spain. More than in any other area of the Republic, the Basque country rejected both communism and fascism and attempted to protect property rights and freedom of religion. However, the Basque government, which was dominated by Catholics, endured only nine months before Franco's forces crushed it in June 1937. Basque collaboration with the Republic legitimized the latter in the eyes of Christian democrats who, like the exiled Luigi Sturzo, refused both leftist revolution and Francoism. Sturzo, a priest and a founder of the Italian Partito Populari, proclaimed the fundamental incompatibility of fascism and Catholicism.[51]

A cohort of the most distinguished group of French Christian democrats – Mauriac and Catholic philosophers Jacques Maritain and Emmanuel Mounier – joined Sturzo to sign the manifesto, "For the Basque People." Composed in reaction to the Condor Legion's bombing of Guernica, the signers maintained "the Basque people are Catholic, and Catholic worship has never been interrupted in the Basque country." Thus, Catholics had the duty to protest the inexcusable destruction of Guernica and to halt the atrocious massacre of civilians.[52] To justify his signature on a document that might "supply steam, or rather blood, to the Communist engine," Mauriac asserted that the Basques were neither the "accomplices of Moscow" nor mass murderers who had dishonored the Republican cause. Indeed, Basque priests' popular Catholic trade unions effectively fought revolutionary communists and anarchists. Mauriac, the future Nobel prize winner in literature (1952), thought it "dreadful" (*épouvantable*) that millions of Spaniards equated fascism and Christianity and therefore hated both. He might have added that it was equally mistaken that many Catholics in Spain and throughout the world confused antifascism and communism during the Spanish war.

The failure of the Vatican to condemn the bombing of Guernica and, more generally, the pro-Franco mood among Catholics and conservatives distressed Christian democrats. The martyrdom of the "profoundly Catholic" Basques estranged Mauriac from the Nationalists.[53] Maritain objected to the Nationalist belief in the crusading militaristic ideology of Christ the King. Jesus "is not a warlord but a king of grace and charity, who died for all men and whose kingdom is not of this earth." Bernanos, who had been a member of Action Française, seconded Maritain. The Nationalist violence accompanied by Church complicity, which Bernanos had witnessed firsthand on the island of Mallorca, repulsed him. While Christian democratic antifascism remained a minority current among European Catholics during the Spanish Civil War (even Bernanos remained skeptical of it), it inspired support for the Basque nationalists and anticipated Catholic backing for the Western Allies during World War II.

Much more than Catholics, Protestants in the Atlantic world were willing to express support for the Spanish Republic. Their critique of the Roman Catholic Church, which had originated in the Reformation, commonly made them more anti-authoritarian and antifascist than Catholics. Some Protestants even viewed the Roman Church to be a precursor of twentieth-century fascist or communist "totalitarianisms." In one poll 39 percent of American Catholics supported the Nationalists, compared with only 9 percent of Protestants and 2 percent of Jews. In another 1938 sample, 83 percent of Protestants favored the Republicans but 58 percent of Catholics favored the Nationalists. Protestants generally saw the Republic as attempting to establish a liberal democracy. Methodists and Baptists – notably those in the US South – solidly supported the Republic and viewed the Nationalists as perpetuators of the Inquisition. So did Episcopalians, Presbyterians, Mormons, and Christian Scientists, who appreciated the Republic's "complete religious freedom," at least for Protestants.[54]

Attuned to public attitudes, President Roosevelt initially sympathized with the Loyalists, although he was unsure of their dedication to democracy. He avoided a commitment to the anti-Catholic Republic which would have divided his ecumenical Democratic coalition, where Catholics played important roles both as voters and important office-holders, often for the first time in American history. In December 1936, his administration introduced a Joint Resolution that prevented American intervention in the Spanish war, and it passed both houses of Congress with only one negative vote. However, by 1938 the increasingly evident and unabashed expansionism of the fascist powers convinced Roosevelt to encourage Spanish Republican resistance against a possible, if not probable, German ally in southern Europe. In March 1938 Secretary of State Hull, aware of Nationalist atrocities and critical of Italian intervention in Spain, forcefully condemned their massive bombing of Barcelona.

Significantly, suspicions of Spanish Nationalists also grew among isolationists. North Dakota Senator Gerald Nye – an early member of the antiwar and isolationist America First but, like many American politicians, a Mason – believed the US embargo on war material to Spain disproportionally helped the obsessively anti-Masonic Franco and wanted to lift it in 1938. While public opinion continued to favor the Republic, it nevertheless desired to maintain the embargo on arms shipments. To aid the Republic, Roosevelt allowed his antifascist secretary of the treasury, Henry Morgenthau, to purchase $14 million of Spanish silver, despite objections from Franco's American lawyer and President Dwight Eisenhower's future secretary of state (1953–1959), John Foster Dulles. The dollar amount of the silver purchase was sevenfold more than the relatively substantial Loyalist fundraising efforts in the United States. As in Britain, where Spanish Republicans amassed tenfold more than Nationalists, in America too Loyalist fundraising produced perhaps ninefold more revenue than similar efforts by *franquistas*. In 1938 Roosevelt took another measure to encourage the Republican war effort by personally naming a Committee for Impartial Civilian Relief in Spain. It provided a modest amount of food aid for starving Republicans until Catholic opposition blocked it. As in France and Britain, US religious and political divisions stymied substantial assistance to the revolutionary Republic. In January 1939 the president admitted that by failing to aid the Republic, his administration had committed a serious error. At that time, his goal was not to rescue the collapsing Republic but rather to convince Congress and the American public to help Britain, France, and China in any future war against Germany, Italy, and Japan.[55]

Culture Wars

The Spanish Civil War stimulated some of the greatest cultural achievements of the twentieth century. Although revolutionary antifascism during the Spanish conflict had little in common politically, economically, and militarily with counterrevolutionary antifascism during World War II, both shared much artistically. Their shared aesthetics in Spain are one reason why many have conflated both types of antifascism. An antifascist culture that pluralistically portrayed its heroes and victims found its promised land in the Spanish Republic. Spain became a symbol of hope and tragedy for a wide variety of antifascists and provoked unprecedented participation by artists and writers. The involvement of future Nobel prize winners in literature was striking. Mauriac, Albert Camus, Pablo Neruda, Octavio Paz, Claude Simon, and Ernest Hemingway were all fervently pro-Republican. The Spaniard Camilo José Cela was the sole pro-Nationalist.

The death of the polyvalent artist Federico García Lorca convinced sympathizers of the Republic that it fought for a tolerant civilization against fascism's barbarism. Murdered by Falangists at the beginning of the conflict, Lorca became antifascism's most famous martyr. The news of his assassination spread rapidly around the world, and no Spanish writer since Cervantes aroused as much interest outside of Spain. His life and death have continued to spark numerous books and films. His passing, like those of Lord Byron and Percy Shelley, was the loss of the young poet/martyr, and it elevated him above his work. "He was innocence against barbarism, the angel against the beast, the truth against the lie." More than 100 American poets protested his murder, including William Carlos Williams, who asserted that Lorca conveyed the authentic Spanish popular voice. In September 1936 at Buenos Aires, the International PEN Clubs took up his case with the goal of defending freedom of expression. The American author Theodore Dreiser pursued this line of protest and in November 1938 visited Barcelona to laud the fighting spirit of Spanish Republicans.[56]

Artists who supported the Spanish Republic formed a creative Popular Front, which, similar to its political counterpart, attempted to unite different currents of antifascism. The artistic front accepted various styles which flourished during the 1930s while exploring new expressions of modernity. It generally permitted much greater freedom than its fascist rivals. In 1936 the leftist American Artists' Congress pursued an ecumenism which embraced aesthetic diversity and welcomed bourgeois, proletarian, realist, and modernist artists.[57] This tolerance successfully attracted practitioners who felt uncomfortable within the narrow confines of Soviet-inspired art. These American artists would view the Spanish Civil War as a struggle to defend democracy against a fascist assault.

The best artistic example of the development of counterrevolutionary antifascism was Hemingway's novel *For Whom the Bell Tolls*, his most popular book and the biggest seller in American fiction since *Gone with the Wind*. Hemingway had personal experience of the civil war as a journalist and patron of the Lincoln Battalion. The hero of his novel, Robert Jordan, was an American Hispanist who was devoted to the Republic. Rather incredibly, though, Jordan had little interest in politics. He was certainly not a revolutionary Communist, Trotskyite, or anarchist but simply a decent American and generic antifascist who volunteered to fight the fascist foe. Published in October 1940, after the Hitler-Stalin pact, the novel reflected a reignited US anti-Communism. The author derided the PCE leaders, Pasionaria and Enrique Líster, whom he had previously praised as heroine and hero in the socialist realist documentary film *The Spanish Earth* (1937). In his novel, Hemingway portrayed Pasionaria as a mendacious propagandist and Líster – a high-ranking Republican officer – as a phoney working-class leader. The Hollywood version of *For Whom the Bell Tolls* (1943) highlighted counterrevolutionary antifascism even more than the novel. Robert Jordan, who was played by Gary Cooper, stated, "This [the Spanish Civil War] is a war between the Communists and the Fascists, with the poor Spanish people somewhere in the middle."[58]

The equation of the two ideologies meshed with the conception of "totalitarianism" advanced by conservative antifascists. In the era of fascism and communism, counterrevolutionary antifascists defended bourgeois society and struggled against its two frightening and unprecedented foes. If communists were often successful in using "fascism" for their own purposes, counterrevolutionary antifascists employed "totalitarianism" equally effectively. The concept appealed to centrists, religious traditionalists, and social democrats, who opposed both communism and fascism. In the interwar period anxiety about new forms of revolution – whether of the left or right – promoted the "totalitarian" notion. Those who desired to avoid the counterrevolutionary label and who insisted on accepting the legacy of the eighteenth-century democratic revolutions wielded "totalitarianism" as a weapon against their enemies. Communist duplicity in Spain – their claim to defend democratic freedoms but their violent opposition to all criticisms of the Bolshevik "workers' state" – distanced George Orwell, Arthur Koestler, and Franz Borkenau from the Soviet orbit. In Spain, all three either spent time in jail or were compelled to dodge police. They would be among the chief advocates of the concept of "totalitarianism" to classify Communist activities and equate them with Nazi practices.[59]

Unlike the "totalitarian" states of the Soviet Union and Nazi Germany, the politically semi-pluralist Republic encouraged aesthetic diversity. This convinced many – appropriately in the artistic domain – that the Republic offered a higher level of liberty than the Nationalists. The Spanish Republic possessed the relative aesthetic openness of Fascist Italy and promoted a popular art which produced the most creative and attractive socialist realist posters of any revolutionary movement. The Communist Josep Renau may have been one of the most accomplished practitioners of the visual socialist style, but the poet Miguel Hernández displayed a similar "realism" in his portraits of collective bravery: "Thirty peasants, as one, discharged their rifles." The poet concluded with fulsome praise of the fighting ability of Republican soldiers: "In the heart of the fronts of Extremadura, there is an unbeatably combative human material. We must use all its heroism for it to yield fully its fruit." Hernández also mirrored the xenophobic patriotism of both sides in the war: "That they leave our land / they stain our soil / those dirty foreign claws."[60]

Despite the dominance of socialist realism in the Republican homeland, *Guernica* marvelously demonstrated that the Republic did not restrict artists' sovereignty. Picasso's brand of antifascist art made its rivals seem atavistic (Figure 2.6). The painter and sculptor Ramón Gaya attacked Josep Renau – who was a fellow member of the Alliance of Antifascist Intellectuals and the General Director of Fine Arts, as a "Communist of the most orthodox strain," who produced socialist realist propaganda (Figure 2.7). For Gaya, Renau's posters were advertising, not art: "For an artist to be with the people and work for the popular cause, it is not essential that the people understand or enjoy his work. And today, Picasso ... shows that I am right. Pablo Ruiz Picasso, the most difficult of painters, is with the common people."[61]

The alleged *bon mot* of Picasso during the Nazi occupation of Paris demonstrated the clout of his brand of artistic antifascism. Upon seeing a photo of *Guernica* in Picasso's apartment, a German officer purportedly asked him, "Did you do that?" Picasso responded, "No, you did." Both artist and officer were correct. *Guernica* did not attain universal value because of its evident antifascism. Indeed, some Marxist critics – including the British art historian and Soviet spy Anthony Blunt – felt that its political message was too esoteric for ordinary folk.[62] It became the most renowned picture of the twentieth century because of its generic but transcendent antiwar message. *Guernica* attempted to overcome the

Figure 2.6 Pablo Picasso, *Guernica* (1937), arriving at Madrid, 1981. Getty Images.

divisions between revolutionary and counterrevolutionary antifascism and to unify them in horror against a common enemy who used massive and modern firepower to kill unarmed men, women, infants, and animals in the symbolic capital of the Catholic and democratic Basques. The Popular Fronts' slogan equated fascism and war, and the painting illustrated the plight of war's victims. *Guernica* achieved antifascist unity by invoking victimhood, not militancy. Picasso had considered including a clenched fist, the symbol of the Popular Fronts, but ultimately decided to eliminate this literally heavy-handed gesture. The canvas condemned the fascist perpetrators only in absentia, an aesthetic strategy which rescued it from being considered propaganda.

The artist created the picture for the Spanish Republican pavilion in Paris at the World's Fair of 1937, the showcase cultural project of the French Popular Front. Picasso's depiction of the bombardment intensified transatlantic sympathy for the Republic. The painting's message especially resonated in Great Britain, where British newsreels depicted Guernica as "the most terrible air raid our modern history can yet boast." After the experience of World War I, when German aircraft repeatedly attacked London, British opinion was particularly sensitive to the nation's vulnerability to aerial assault. Guernica's destruction convinced William Temple, [Anglican] Archbishop of York and future

Figure 2.7 Josep Renau, "Peasant, defend with weapons the government which gave you land," 1936. Getty Images.

Archbishop of Canterbury, who had been neutral, to switch to the pro-Republican side. In London in October 1938 leading personalities – the writers E. M. Forster and Virginia Woolf; the publisher of the Left Book Club, Victor Gollancz; the surrealist artist Roland Penrose; and the maverick Tory the Duchess of Atholl – sponsored an exhibit of the monumental canvas. Sketches of the painting toured Britain during November and December, and a second London exhibit attracted 15,000 visitors, each offering a pair of boots for Republican soldiers as the price of admission. The reception of *Guernica* in May 1939 in New York City celebrated the painting's message and its modernist style. The bombing had inspired protests against the Spanish Nationalists even among prominent American conservatives, such as the recently defeated Republican presidential nominee Alf Landon and the isolationist senator William Borah. The American exhibition – supported, among others, by authors Hemingway, Dreiser, Edna St. Vincent Millay; physicist Einstein; and Roosevelt's Secretary of the Interior Harold Ickes – raised funds for the Spanish Refugee Relief Campaign to assist the hundreds of thousands of Republican exiles who had escaped to France as the Republic was collapsing.[63]

Hollywood celebrities – Shirley Temple, James Cagney, Edward G. Robinson, Orson Welles, and Paul Muni – also supported Republican fund-raisers. Actor Frederic March hosted a showing in his home of the documentary *The Spanish Earth* (1937). Some of America's most renowned artists – authors Hemingway, John dos Passos, Lillian Hellman, and Archibald MacLeish; and musicians Marc Blitzstein and Virgil Thomson – had collaborated on the film. The audience at March's home included Errol Flynn, Dashiel Hammett, Dorothy Parker, King Vidor, Fritz Lang, and lesser luminaries. Jazz musician Benny Goodman and blues artist Leadbelly (Huddie William Ledbetter) performed at benefits for Spain.[64]

The End of the Spanish War and Revolution

Despite much sympathy from progressive public opinion in the Atlantic world, revolutionary antifascism in Spain proved unable to defeat its counterrevolutionary enemy. The Spanish Revolution deprived the Republic of support from Catholics and conservatives in the democracies. Just as importantly, the revolution disrupted the Republican economy. Many urban workers interpreted the revolution as a welcome opportunity to liberate themselves from working, rent, and taxes. Given the massive inflation of the Republican currency, peasants and rural laborers refused to trade their hard-earned harvests for valueless government paper. They frequently retreated into autarchy and withdrew food from urban areas and the Republican army. Frustrated by peasant hoarding and perceived profiteering, undisciplined soldiers violated property rights and looted. The Republican economy sustained a vicious cycle in which the collapse of the currency discouraged food producers, who withdrew into self-sufficiency and thus infuriated consumers – whether workers or soldiers – who responded by bartering or pillaging.

The Nationalist victory was a victory of fascism, and it bolstered the prestige and confidence of Germany and Italy. Yet paradoxically, the fascist triumph provided positive opportunities for antifascism. Conservative antifascists could henceforth focus on the central German threat, not the Spanish diversion. Antifascists no longer needed to disperse their energies among a number of fronts – Ethiopia in 1935–1936, Austria in 1938, and Spain from 1936 to 1939 – and could concentrate their political and cultural energies against Nazism. Most importantly, the end of the Spanish conflict freed antifascism from its association with revolution, communism, and anarchy. The war's closure permitted antifascists to construct a broader alliance with Catholics and conservatives in the face of persistent German and Italian expansion against non-revolutionary states. The conflict's termination mended the rift between Britain and France over Italian aggression in the Iberian Peninsula, where the French were much more hostile to the empire building of their Mediterranean rival. The end of the Spanish war facilitated a coalition which would eventually defeat the Axis in World War II. The outcome of the Spanish conflict was not only – as many historians have argued – an example of appeasement of fascism by the Western democracies, but unexpectedly a critical step toward the formation of an altered antifascist unity. In fact, in 1937 Hitler expressed the desire for the Spanish war to continue as long as possible – even to the end of 1940 – in order to divide his potential enemies. In other words, Franco may have won the war too quickly from the Nazi perspective, rather than too slowly as many of his critics and some supporters have argued. Perhaps the revolutionary Republic had to be defeated before a more inclusive antifascist coalition could occur.[65]

The leaderships of both major British political parties were relieved that they could now concentrate on containing Germany and Italy.[66] The opposition between anti-appeasement Conservatives who distrusted the Spanish Republic and Labourites who wanted to assist the latter disappeared. Similar divisions between right and left over Spain also vanished in France and the United States. The right lost the opportunity to flaunt the obvious contradiction of the Spanish Republic that the left defended

Figure 2.8 Spanish Republican refugees in France, 1939. Getty
Images.

as a bastion of liberty but which permitted assassinations of conservatives
and priests. After the Spanish war, a new coalition of antifascists who
respected religious tolerance and pluralist politics surfaced in the major
Atlantic nations. The German invasion of a non-revolutionary republic,
Czechoslovakia, in March 1939 converted opinion in the democracies to
resolute antifascism. The British and French would go to war because of
the German destruction of the conservative republics of Czechoslovakia
and Poland but would not risk conflict for their Spanish revolutionary
counterpart.

Franco's victory compelled nearly 500,000 Spaniards into French
exile in February–March 1939 (Figure 2.8). France received these Spanish Republican refugees ambivalently. In the 1930s, France sheltered the
largest number of immigrants in the world. Even so, the Spanish Republican exiles constituted the greatest single wave of refugees that it had
ever hosted, even if the majority returned to Spain within a year. Neither
French nor Spanish officials had expected such a sudden and substantial
influx, likely the greatest number that any democratic country had ever
accepted at one time. No other nation was willing to host hundreds of
thousands of defeated "Reds" in the middle of the Great Depression,
which had multiplied xenophobia and social/political tensions throughout Europe and North America. The French right generally protested
their influx, whereas the left defended them. Their acceptance by a

post–Popular Front center-right government saved many from potential massacre or long imprisonment. As a result, the Interior minister, the Radical Albert Sarraut – despite his anti-Communism – earned the hatred of the right, and by the spring of 1939 his vigorous defense of most exiled Spaniards had made him their hero.[67]

Initially the French government treated these exiles shamefully. They were confined to "concentration camps" or what, after the Nazi experience of death camps, many contemporary historians prefer to call "internment camps" or, more poetically, "camps of contempt" where conditions ranged from the uncomfortable to the horrible. One of the most infamous, Argelès-sur-Mer, humiliated and sickened the veterans of the Republican army by failing to provide sufficient clothing, housing, sanitation, and clean water. Dishonor and dysentery were the results. Other camps for civilian refugees were less awful. Leftist and Christian democratic groups in French society pressured the center-right government to improve the refugees' reception, and in many cases their humanitarian efforts were successful.

The need for soldiers and workers on the eve of World War II rapidly released many Spaniards from internment camps. Despite some Communist opposition following the signing of the Hitler-Stalin pact in August 1939, thousands of Spanish antifascists enrolled in the French military and its auxiliary forces to combat the Germans in 1940. They distinguished themselves in warfare in the spring of that year both in Norway and in France. During the Battle of France, 1,000 Spaniards lost their lives in defense of their adopted country. At least 5,000 were captured and became the first deportees from France to perish at the Mauthausen concentration camp. Immediately following the French defeat at the end of July 1940, de Gaulle's nascent Free French movement had only 7,000 men at its disposal; several hundred of them were Spaniards. Many other Spanish refugees, including a large block of Communists, would later join the Resistance.[68]

Even if the goal of most Spanish exiles was to avoid working for the Germans, at the end of 1940 25,000 were laboring – under varying degrees of compulsion – in the Organization Todt, which was building the Atlantic Wall, fortifications designed to prevent Allied invasion. In addition, significant numbers of Spanish workers in France enrolled in the French Foreign Legion, where they became the most numerous foreign group.[69] During the North African campaign of 1942–1943, French Legionnaires of Spanish origin quickly transferred their loyalties to the Allies. Their bravery throughout the war – when approximately 6,000 died fighting the Axis – impressed Free French General Philippe Leclerc, a devout Catholic and imperialist, who awarded them places of honor in the first ranks of troops who liberated Paris in August 1944. During World War II, the conservative French Third Republic and then the Gaullist Resistance restrained the revolutionary currents of Spanish antifascism. Thus, Spanish exiles would contribute to the victory of the broader antifascist alliance of World War II in contrast to the defeat of their own more radical and less inclusive coalition during the Spanish Civil War. The differences between the two antifascisms refute the common belief that the Spanish conflict was the first battle of World War II.

At the end of that war, the Western Allies became reluctant to overthrow Franco because they suspected that the alternative would not be a conservative republic or constitutional monarchy but rather another Spanish revolutionary regime. The Anglo-Americans' nonintervention policy maintained their position adopted in the civil war, which held that communism or anarchy was more dangerous than fascism. During the German occupation of France, the Communist-led Unión Nacional Española (UNE) had attempted to build a broad coalition of monarchists, traditionalists, and members of the CEDA, but non-Communist Republicans remained wary of PCE hegemony. On 3 October 1944, the UNE launched the Val d'Aran invasion across the Pyrenees, and 5,000 Spanish Republicans entered their homeland from France to spark a popular uprising against the Franco regime. The rapid failure of the invasion showed the lack of support within Spain itself for the Communist-dominated guerrilla movement. Once again, the Spanish antifascist coalition that undertook the incursion remained too narrow to attract the kind of conservatives and traditionalists – such as de Gaulle, Leclerc, or Churchill – who had entered, if not created, the antifascist resistance in the democracies. The collapse of the invasion led to the de facto recognition of the Franco regime by de Gaulle's Provisional Government on 16 October 1944. After Franco's death in 1975, when a significant part of the *franquista* conservative base agreed to a democratic constitutional monarchy, a broad coalition terminated the regime. Only when the prospect of revolution had disappeared would the former Western Allies unreservedly support the Spanish transition to democracy. The conservative constitutional monarchy of the Transition finally fulfilled the wishes of counterrevolutionary antifascists of the 1930s and 1940s.

3   The Antifascist Deficit during the French Popular Front

In contrast to Spain, France had steadily and consistently industrialized from the middle of the nineteenth century onward, and its development of the productive forces had, as in other advanced Western nations, severely restricted the revolutionary possibilities of working-class organizations. The French had created a thriving national market and slowly forged national unity. In the first third of the twentieth century, regionalist movements did not pose a threat to the indivisibility of the nation. Again, in direct contrast to Spain, there were no attempts at coups d'état in the 1920s, and the conspiracies of the 1930s against the Third Republic failed miserably. The French, too, had separated church from state and military from civilian government. After the Dreyfus affair anticlericalism was no longer the burning issue that it continued to be in Spain. Although French anticlericalism did not disappear in the interwar era, it progressively dwindled and declined.

Furthermore, in France and particularly in Paris, careers were open to the talented, regardless of religion. The French bourgeoisie became progressively de-Catholicized and widened its ranks to include considerable numbers of Protestants and Jews, some of whom played essential roles in the most modern industries – electricity, automobiles, and aviation – that in Spain were either backward or nonexistent. The assumed aristocratic values of venality, idleness, and titles gradually waned, as that of *réussite* (success) took their place. The most modern and active part of the bourgeoisie defended the virtues of work and talent. As the Socialist leader Jean Jaurès stated, "the bourgeoisie is a class that works." Periodic economic crises forced this class to renew itself, and it enlarged its numbers and broadened its base. In the 1930s, the French standard of living was probably the highest in continental Europe.

Domestic Antifascism

Throughout late modern European history, France often initiated new political ideas – revolution, rights of man, Bonapartism, and, finally,

52

antifascism. Since "fascism" became a pejorative term almost immediately, the neologism "antifascism" came to denote the opposition of the left to the new Italian regime. From 1922 to 1924, Communists identified fascism and capitalism and thus argued that they were the only antifascists. By 1926, French Communists became somewhat more ecumenical and attempted to constitute a "single antifascist front" in which Communists would lead a coalition of socialists, trade unionists, and even democrats. Fearing PCF (Parti communiste français) manipulation, non-Communists remained unenthusiastic about joining PCF militants in a common cause. At the end of the 1920s until the mid-1930s, the PCF used the term "fascism" to stigmatize all other political movements. The Comintern labeled non-Communist forces "as varying forms of hyphenate fascism, the number one enemy being the 'social fascism' of social democratic parties."[1]

Historians have attributed the success of fascism in Italy and Germany to the division of working-class organizations – principally the split between the Socialist and Communist parties. Although a major factor in the victories of fascisms, the inability to unite was merely one of the many failures of early antifascism. Perhaps more important was that those who considered themselves antifascists had an erroneous analysis of the phenomenon. For most of the French left, fascism became synonymous with the eternal counterrevolutionary who had combated the French Revolution and resurfaced during the Dreyfus affair. In other words, fascism was merely another way to designate moneyed and clerical reactionaries. Overlooking the mass radicalization which formed the base of fascism, many progressives interpreted it as the new face of finance capital. Marxists equated Bonapartism and fascism and believed that the latter announced the final crisis of capitalism. The dominant leftist analysis argued that fascism was a reactionary movement and assimilated it to the traditionalist or capitalist right.[2]

Whether Trotskyite, dissident communist, anarchist, or Socialist, revolutionary leftists often shared with more moderate comrades the same analysis of fascism as a purely reactionary phenomenon. Unlike the moderates, who desired a broader antifascist alliance, radical leftists posited that antifascism had to be revolutionary, not merely a defense of the bourgeois republic. Revolutionary antifascists reminded Communists of their pre–Popular Front position which had equated fascism and capitalism. In the SFIO, the revolutionary wing of Marceau Pivert adopted the position of Largo Caballero and insisted that workers seize control of the means of production. Likewise, Trotsky reminded his followers of the need to make revolution and argued that antifascism was merely a cover for counterrevolutionary manipulation.

Whether communists or social democrats, Marxists underestimated the radical nature of their reinvigorated enemy. Léon Blum equated fascism with the monarchist nationalism of the fin-de-siècle. Hitler represented "a reactionary fascist," a new Déroulède, whose hyper-nationalism had challenged the Third Republic at the end of the nineteenth century. The left comprehended neither fascism's dynamic militarism nor Nazism's racial revolution. The French left supposed that their own domestic fascisms – which lacked the unity, vigor, and popularity of their German and Italian counterparts – were more dangerous than their foreign equivalents. French antifascists were more willing to fight the extreme-right leader Colonel de la Rocque than Adolf Hitler: "In a word, the [right-wing riots] of 6 February 1934 hid [Hitler's chancellorship] of 30 January 1933." This national navel-gazing was common not only in France but also in the United Kingdom and the United States, where alarm about domestic weapons makers and capitalist warmongers outweighed uneasiness about foreign aggressors.[3]

The French Popular Front originated from the struggle against what was perceived as internal fascism – the alleged *coup de force* by the right-wing leagues of 6 February 1934. Using physical and verbal violence, the *ligueurs* attempted to assault the Palais Bourbon, the locus of parliamentary power in France. Various corruption scandals involving major political figures had partially discredited the Third Republic in the mid-1930s and encouraged the extreme right to attempt to overthrow it. However, the police proved loyal to the regime and prevented the demonstrators from reaching the National Assembly. During the confrontations, 15 died, 14 of whom were members of the right-wing leagues, and nearly 1,500 were injured. Street pressure led to the formation of a new government of "national union" which included right-wing parliamentarians and, for the first time, Marshal Philippe Pétain, a World War I hero. The left believed that the extreme right had attempted to imitate Mussolini's March on Rome, and it equated the right – including the conservative government of "national union" – with what Blum called "the fascist reaction."[4] Socialists used the "fascist" label almost as indiscriminately as Communists.

The exaggerated fear of domestic fascism inspired the leftist unity of the Popular Front. The left coalition became committed to the defense of the democratic parliamentary republic, even if capitalist. French leftist activists began to invigorate a movement "against fascism and war" one year after Hitler had taken power. Six days after the rightist riots, on 12 February 1934, the CGT (Confédération générale du travail) called for a general strike to defend the republic. As in other democracies, French trade unionists had good reasons to oppose fascism, which they viewed as a lethal form of union busting. When the unions' antifascism was connected to work stoppages, the results were impressive: 45 percent of workers in Paris and the provinces followed the general strike, and the Parisian demonstration assembled 300,000 persons. Antifascism easily outmatched at least sixfold the numbers of its enemy in the streets.[5]

Antifascism in France was largely non-revolutionary. Communist party activists mobilized and temporarily defended the French republic, a position which allowed them, perhaps for the first time, to become integrated into the nation. Their new orientation reflected the progressive, although uneven, "nationalization" of the PCF, which had become the most important non-Russian European Communist party after the collapse of the German branch in 1933. Negotiations between the major labor federations, the Communist CGTU (Confédération générale du travail unitaire) and the non-Communist CGT, began in 1934 and eventually culminated in the reunification of the CGT in March 1936. Thus, Communist trade unionists joined their more moderate colleagues who wanted to combat fascism by bolstering democratic and parliamentary traditions.

The enlightened middle classes, who wished to protect republican liberties and who included many war veterans, buttressed the antifascist coalition. As mentioned, the Radicals were the swing party of the Third Republic, and they represented a large portion of the French middle classes who were devoted to democracy and the protection of small private property. Even though many of their constituents were skeptical of the Popular Front's economic program – particularly its proposal to limit the workweek to forty hours – the Radicals joined the coalition. In numerous districts Radical deputies often depended on the votes of Communists and Socialists to win elections (Figure 3.1). Freemasons, whose members included prominent Radicals, were particularly active and founded numerous Popular Front committees throughout France.[6]

The Popular Front won the May 1936 general elections, and in June Blum became the first Socialist and first Jew to become prime minister of France. In contrast to Spain, where a pre-revolution and then a full-scale revolution erupted in the Republican zone after the victory of its Popular Front, the stability of the French state and society precluded large-scale political and anticlerical violence and spontaneous collectivization of private property. Nevertheless, when Blum took office in June, wage earners profited from the Socialist leader's stated reluctance to use force against them to launch a great strike wave, which extended to the French Empire. Workers occupied factories, thereby surpassing the program of the Popular Front, which called for a shorter working week, higher wages, paid vacations, and nationalization of defense

Figure 3.1 Socialist leader Léon Blum and Communist leader Maurice Thorez at Popular Front rally, 10 June 1936. Getty Images.

industries. The work stoppages of June were followed by many months of resistance to work – absenteeism, lateness, fake illnesses, low productivity, slowdowns, indiscipline, indifference, and even sabotage. As in Barcelona, these actions and attitudes generally harmed output and decreased productivity. Indiscipline that challenged industrial hierarchy was hardly compatible with the greater commodity consumption that the Popular Front promised. More than any other aspect of the Popular Front, the work stoppages and the subsequent refusals of work in large factories alienated conservative and centrist members of the Radical party who believed that nefarious Communist maneuvers encouraged workplace indiscipline which was damaging the French economy.[7] Despite the untiring efforts of an extreme left of militant Marxists and anarchists, the work stoppages did not become revolutionary. French workers wanted higher pay and less work, not an anarchist, councilist, or Soviet revolution.

The Popular Front prefigured the Vichy regime of World War II by fighting more against the internal than the external enemy. When it began to govern in June 1936, it banned the right-wing leagues that had participated in the riot of 6 February – La Rocque's Croix-de-Feu, Jeunesses patriotes, Solidarité française, and Francisme. This prohibition obtained broad support from centrist French politicians, such as Laurent Bonnevay, deputy from the Rhône since 1902. Bonnevay considered himself a "moderate Republican" but not "moderately Republican." In other words, he was fully committed to the conservative Third Republic and supported the disarmament of the extreme-right Leagues.

Also like the future Vichy regime, the Popular Front sought to reconcile the workers and the middle classes. Yet the forty-hour week divided the two. Wage earners certainly considered it an antifascist reform, and they fittingly identified fascism with a long and tiring work routine at low wages. However, many peasants, small business owners, and the elderly considered the strict application of the short workweek as legislated laziness, above all when workers in other major European nations were laboring many more hours. The goal of the forty-hour week was to stimulate the economy by forcing employers to hire more wage earners, but the limited number of skilled workers in France created a production bottleneck. Higher wages produced an inflationary situation where more money was available to purchase the same or a diminishing number of commodities. In France in 1937, when the forty-hour week was in effect in many industrial branches, production was 25 percent inferior to that of 1929, whereas Britain and Germany had significantly exceeded their 1929 levels. Moreover, the British believed that the forty-hour week sent the wrong message to Hitler about Allied preparedness.[8] The Germans could make their limited numbers of skilled workers work many more hours than the French. In addition, fascism reduced trade-union barriers to dilution and deskilling in weapons production.

The briefer workweek showed the ambivalent nature of Socialist and even Communist antifascism since the PCF and its followers in the CGT fought hard to preserve a workweek which hindered French arms production. In metallurgical factories, the forty-hour week obligated employers to hire relatively unskilled workers who were less productive than their more experienced counterparts. The inability of the limited numbers of skilled workers to work more than forty hours, when prior to the Popular-Front legislation they had labored 52 to 60 hours, resulted in a significant loss of output and increased costs, which were particularly dramatic in naval shipbuilding. In this context it should be noted that even though the wage earners of the indispensable British ally were laboring 48 hours per week, the United Kingdom still suffered from a severe skilled labor shortage in 1938. In addition, the French trade unions increased their authority on the shop floor and encouraged an atmosphere of refusal of wage labor. After the long workweeks and harsh discipline of the early thirties, the proliferation of permissiveness may have pleased workers, but worker gains alienated employers and their supervisory personnel. A good number of both became more sympathetic to fascism, which they identified with tighter workplace discipline and higher output.[9]

From the second half of 1936 to the end of 1938, the Socialists, Communists, and CGT fought to maintain the forty-hour week despite the opposition of the entire right and center and increasing evidence that the shortened workweek delayed arms production. Disregarding growing international tensions between France and both Italy and Germany in 1938, the French left and the workers themselves demanded the preservation of the shortened workweek and substantial bonuses for overtime. For example, an overwhelming majority of workers of two aviation firms – the nationalized SNCASE in Argenteuil and the privately owned Gnôme et Rhône on Boulevard Kellermann – objected when in April 1938 government arbitration terminated the forty-hour week in aviation.[10] Thus, the forty-hour week was not merely a "symbol" for workers but rather their most important gain from Popular Front legislation. Increased free time regenerated a French leisure industry that began to cater to workers' weekend and vacation needs.

Foreign Policy in the Popular Front Era

Like leftists, rightists also had great trouble understanding the new Nazi phenomenon, which they often viewed as a continuation of the policies of Wilhelmine Germany. Not only militarily but just as importantly intellectually, both left and right were fighting the last war. Both assumed the established German business and military leaders would circumscribe the power of the Nazi party. During the 1930s and even in the early years of World War II, the French – including Jacques Maritain – underestimated what Maritain called "the capacity of the Nazi revolution for violence and destructiveness." French analysts also continued to underrate popular backing for Nazism and maintained their understanding of the regime as a mask behind which the old elites pulled the strings.[11]

The conservative French ambassador in Berlin, André François-Poncet, persuaded himself in 1932 that the German Nationalist Party would not permit Hitler to take over the government, and throughout the 1930s he continually misjudged the Nazi menace to France. Prominent French politicians, such as the rightist André Tardieu, assumed the early fall of the Führer. Tardieu, the former prime minister and member of the post–6 February conservative government of "national union," asserted in mid-1934 that a French agreement with Hitler was

unnecessary since the Crown Prince would shortly replace him. Many –
but not all – politically interested British and French citizens also mistakenly assumed that the Nazi regime would collapse because of its supposedly irrational economic policies.[12]

L'Économie nouvelle, a prominent French business publication, was
somewhat sympathetic to the Nazi experiment. The monthly declared
that it was "absolutely certain" that during the Weimar Republic Jews
had monopolized money and power without popular support. The magazine lamented the assassination of the prominent Weimar politician
Walther Rathenau, but stated that Rathenau – a Jew himself – understood that it was dangerous for any minority "without deep roots in
a country to manage it." Accepting German right-wing claims at face
value, it affirmed that since 1918 France had failed to negotiate with
"the true Germany." The journal expected Hitler to retain power and
enter a "constructive" period of dictatorship. Nevertheless, the Nazis'
violent desire for conquest worried these representatives of French business. The National Socialists had no morality, no desire for cooperation
with other peoples, no wish for intellectual freedom, but only a vicious
need to dominate. Like the Soviets, they adopted autarchic policies and
dumped German goods.[13]

Another business publication, *La Journée industrielle*, shared the
ambivalence of *L'Économie nouvelle*. Its editor, Claude-Joseph Gignoux –
the head of the most important French employers' organization during
the Popular Front – opposed Nazism, even if Gignoux would eventually
become a member of Vichy's Conseil National. Although he admired
Hitler's and Mussolini's restoration of an apparently bourgeois order and
their intensification of work, his periodical was hostile to the Nazis' violence and aggressive foreign policy which, it asserted, endangered peace
and the French position in Europe. In addition, the Nazi state's domination of the economy, protectionism, and autarchic policies alienated Gignoux' liberalism. In September 1938, *La Journée industrielle* would refuse
collaboration with what it considered a warmongering Nazi regime.[14]

The left continued to be equally, if not more, undiscerning. In
1933, Blum stated, "one does not fight warmongering by developing
warmongering" and "nationalist pride...contributes...to the creation
of an environment for the growth and success of fascism." As late
as 1934, Blum held that Mussolini was more dangerous than Hitler.
Blum disagreed with the Communists and his Socialist colleagues, such
as Jean Zyromski, who posited that a Franco-Russian alliance could
block German aggression. Blum expressed skepticism during 1934 that
French rearmament and the proposed Franco-Soviet treaty would bolster French security and opposed the treaty on pacifist grounds. Like

the British Conservative leader Neville Chamberlain during the same decade, Blum was reluctant to ally with the Soviet Union because he feared that an agreement with it would accelerate the arms race and provoke conflict with Germany.[15]

After the signing of a toothless Franco-Soviet pact in 1935, the Socialists – unlike the PCF – refused to vote credits for national defense and had expelled those who had voted for them in 1933. Following the official announcement of German rearmament and compulsory military service in March 1935, the SFIO did approve increases in military spending. Yet the Socialist-led Popular Front appealed to many pacifists by opposing "war preparations." Blum's fear of inciting war led him to reject until 1939 military intervention to stop fascist aggression. Like his Socialist and pacifist colleague Paul Faure, Blum consistently opposed preventive war against Nazism and assumed that the capitalist arms race – not fascism – caused armed conflict. Likewise, in Great Britain, Clement Attlee kept his similarly divided Labour Party together by supporting collective security and opposing rearmament until 1937–1938 and conscription until 1939.[16]

French Socialists and their partners insisted on the nationalization of defense industries, more as an antiwar than an anti-capitalist measure. According to the Popular Front, nationalization would prevent private owners from lobbying for war. In August 1936 the Popular Front government nationalized a dozen factories, mainly in aviation, but – unlike the Spanish Republic – it compensated their owners and left them in management positions, thereby setting a precedent for postwar French (and British) nationalizations. These nationalizations also anticipated the postwar antitrust measures of the Allied occupiers of Germany and Japan. Not the workers themselves but the French parliament initiated and approved these reforms, which it justified by citing expected improvements in labor relations and economic efficiency.[17]

During the formative phase of the Popular Front in 1935 and when Blum took office in June 1936, he argued for eventual general disarmament. The Socialist leader persisted in believing that the supposed injustices of Versailles were the cause of the fascist dictatorships' aggression. Guilt over Versailles was one of the foundations of Socialist pacifism, championed by Blum and even more consistently by Faure. Blum and his party had been hostile to the Versailles Treaty and believed that reparations imposed on Germany were too severe. Throughout the 1930s Faure's pacifists – who composed perhaps 40 percent of the party – attributed German aggression to justified resentment over Versailles. Syndicalists had argued in 1931 that France would be responsible for the collapse of the Weimar Republic if the postwar treaties were not revised.

Anti-Communist trade unionists would fault Versailles for causing European war. Versailles culpability would become a key ingredient of French syndicalist and pacifist support for collaboration with the Nazis. The left often concluded that vengeful right-wing French nationalists were responsible for German fascism. Before the Popular Front, the Communists too had blamed French "imperialism" for provoking German chauvinism. Not fascism but the supposed injustices inflicted on Germany generated threats to peace.[18]

On 15 June 1938 the popular antiwar humor magazine *Le Canard enchaîné* maintained that the Versailles Treaty had reduced "a great people to slavery" and had led them to support a dictator posing as a prophet. *Le Canard* posited that the French nationalist right – Charles Maurras, Pierre-Étienne Flandin, Léon Bailby, and others – were responsible for the *Anschluss*, Germany's annexation of Austria in March 1938. Oddly enough, the French nationalist right had its own form of Versailles guilt and blamed the treaties on Masons, namely the presidents and prime ministers of the United States, United Kingdom, and Czechoslovakia – Woodrow Wilson, David Lloyd George, and Edvard Benes. Sectors of the right held the French architect of Versailles, Georges Clemenceau, accountable for making France the policeman of Europe and stimulating German *revanche*.[19]

Versailles' war guilt clause did more damage to antifascism in France, Britain, and elsewhere than to German nationalism. Blaming the Great War solely and simplistically on the Germans allowed for the reversal of war culpability and helped to legitimize the Nazis. Versailles culpability assumed French and British injustice and German victimization. Versailles remorse was necessarily Gallo- and Anglo-centric and thus obscured the dynamics of Nazi militarism. Versailles guilt induced large sectors of the left and the right to excuse German aggression. British Conservatives, Liberals, and Labourites agreed that Versailles' attempt to maintain Germany as a second-class power was unworkable and that the treaty be revised in Germany's favor. By 1933 all major British newspapers – which possessed perhaps the most avid readership in the world – had accepted the critical view of Versailles and, more importantly, could not adjust their feelings of culpability to the unfamiliar situation of the Nazis in power. They blamed Versailles and the French for the rise of Nazism. Before 1933, G. E. R. Gedye, one of the most famous British interwar correspondents, attributed the elevation of "an obscure fanatic like Adolf Hitler" to French imperialism. In December 1936 the semi-official *Times* reproached the French foreign minister Louis Barthou and the Franco-Soviet pact for stimulating Germany's "unlimited rearmament." Anti-Versailles and Francophobic sentiments were also common in the Dominions, especially South Africa, whose prime minister, J. B. M. Hertzog, sympathized with German aspirations in the mid-1930s. South Africans, Canadians, and Australians feared Japanese militarism more than German. Many Americans also considered the French as the chief threat to peace in the early 1930s. Guilty conscience made the so-called status quo powers – France and Britain – nearly as revisionist as Italy and Germany.[20]

The peace movement helped to obstruct any firm action against fascist aggression. French "integral" pacifists saw the Versailles system as the origin of Europe's interwar troubles. They predicted that if Hitler proved himself a warmonger, then the German people would revolt against his regime. Feminist pacifists, such as the English activist Vera Brittain, wrote that Versailles "sowed the seeds of Hitlerism." The British section of the Women's International League for Peace and Freedom argued in March 1933 that "conditions in Germany are largely the result of unjust treatment since the war by this [United Kingdom] and other nations." While condemning Nazi cruelty, the British section continued to oppose the war effort well after September 1939. Only feminists who were willing to abandon their pacifism were actively antifascist.[21]

From the Rhineland to Austria

In March 1936, three months before the French Popular Front came to power, Nazi Germany remilitarized the Rhineland. The Communists and the Socialists (including Blum) accepted with resignation or pacifist pride the change of the status quo. The feebleness of the French economy and its dependency on Germany discouraged a vigorous response to the entry of German troops on France's border. Furthermore, the French general staff overestimated German military strength and refused to take unilateral action against the Reich. French military leadership preferred to avoid an immediate conflict and instead planned to fight a future war far from France in Eastern Europe. At the same time, like other Western elites, the French general staff disdained the Red Army and distrusted the Soviet alliance, which, it felt, would provoke German aggression.[22]

A small minority of prescient counterrevolutionary antifascists were ignored. The deputy political director of the Foreign Ministry, René Massigli, argued that the absence of any riposte to Hitler's aggression would open the path to German domination of Europe. Massigli demanded a firm response to the German remilitarization of the Rhineland, which he predicted would damage France's eastern alliances with the Little Entente (Czechoslovakia, Yugoslavia, and Romania),

Poland, and the Soviet Union. The German success unquestionably intimidated the Reich's neighbors in Western as well as Eastern Europe. The remilitarization of the Rhineland encouraged Belgium to abandon its alliance with France and return to neutrality. As Churchill pointed out well after the event, the lack of a forceful response to the Rhineland coup prefigured the Munich appeasement. The fear of upsetting financial markets – always sensitive to war scares – encouraged concessions to Nazi Germany. In the 1930s the British and French subordinated their antifascism to the demands of investors; in contrast, the Germans made markets subservient to rearmament and militarization. The occupation of the Rhineland provided a more favorable opportunity to stop German expansionism than the Spanish Civil War because the latter involved a revolutionary-counterrevolutionary confrontation that the former did not. Camille Chautemps, a Radical who would become prime minister of a Popular Front government from June 1937 to March 1938, warned Blum against intervention shortly after the outbreak of the Spanish conflict. He told Blum that no one would understand why France would risk war for the revolutionary Spanish Republic when it had not for the Rhineland. A military response to Hitler's move on the French border would have been the clearest possible act of conservative antifascism and might have discouraged the fascist powers from further expansion in Spain and elsewhere. Some have speculated that the German military could have overthrown its ex-corporal if his Rhineland gamble had failed.[23]

An overwhelmingly pacifist left helped to block an antifascist response to the Rhineland's remilitarization. The headline of the *Le Canard enchaîné* read "Germany invades . . . Germany." Faure judged the threats of the French government to respond by force to the military occupation to be more dangerous to peace than Hitler's violation of the Versailles Treaty. The official Socialist position, endorsed by Blum, was to negotiate a solution at the League of Nations. The Rhineland remilitarization showed that the French Popular Front was much more comfortable rallying the left against domestic fascism than combating its more lethal foreign strain. In May 1936, *Manchester Guardian* correspondent Alexander Werth confirmed the self-absorption of the Popular Front, which had "an almost unbelievable indifference to international affairs."[24]

By failing to take countermeasures to protect its own borders, France handed the Nazi regime a great victory and encouraged future aggression. As Massigli had predicted, the German occupation of the Rhineland rattled France's eastern allies, who lost confidence in the reliability of their major partner who had remained passive in the face of its most dangerous enemy.[25] The inability of France to take unilateral action

against Germany increasingly tied it to Great Britain, which was determined to appease the Nazi regime and to discourage a Franco-Soviet
alliance. British Francophiles, such as Churchill, who were receptive to
an anti-Nazi alliance with the Soviet Union remained a very small minority in the United Kingdom.

In 1935 the rightist Flandin government had negotiated the Franco-
Soviet pact, and on 27 February 1936 the French Chamber ratified the
treaty of mutual assistance, despite the opposition of 164 conservative
deputies. Hitler used this pact to argue that Germany remilitarized the
Rhineland in March 1936 because of its "encirclement" by France and
Russia. This pretext found a friendly hearing in France but even more so
in Britain. Germany successfully played the victim not only of Versailles
but also of Communist Russia to a British audience which feared the
Soviet Union. Despite the fact that French anti-Bolshevism prevented
any concrete military understanding and rendered the pact ineffectual,
Nazi diplomacy successfully employed the Soviet threat to divide the
United Kingdom from France. As powerful currents of anti-French feeling circulated in rightist public opinion and in the majority Conservative
Party, Britain strongly opposed forceful action to counter the Rhineland
coup. The Tory Prime Minister Stanley Baldwin believed Versailles to be
"iniquitous" and feared that the French would unleash "another great
war in Europe. They might succeed in smashing Germany, with the aid
of Russia, but it would probably only result in Germany going Bolshevik." The expectation of war leading to Communism was an article of
faith among numerous Conservatives. Neville Chamberlain and many
others felt that the Germans had good cause for their grievances. British
opposition made it difficult for France to bolster its alliance with the
Soviet Union. After the Rhineland invasion, W. P. Crozier, editor of the
liberal *Manchester Guardian*, cast doubt on an Anglo-French alliance that
might lead his country into an unwanted war with Germany. The United
Kingdom's first prime minister from the Labour Party, Ramsay Mac-
Donald (1924, 1929–1935), celebrated the remilitarization that finished
off "that blot on the peace of the world, the Treaty of Versailles."[26]

No war could be fought over the defense of Versailles, whether for the
Rhineland – whose demilitarization had been accepted by the Germans
in the Locarno treaties of 1925 – or later for Czechoslovakia, a democratic republic and the key Eastern European ally of France. The *Manchester Guardian*, which was generally quite critical of the domestic policies
of the Nazi regime, asserted six months after the Rhineland's remilitarization that Germany had behaved as any other great nation would.
Despite its coverage of mounting German atrocities, it opposed military
measures against the Reich until 1939. To mainstream Anglicans, the

"criminal injustices of Versailles" excused most German actions. Even as late as the summer of 1939, the Christian press could not criticize the peace rallies of the British Union of Fascists (BUF) because both were offering the same pacifist arguments against war. Like many others, these Christians viewed Germans as victims, not dangerous enemies, and ignored the distinction between pre- and post-1933 Germany. They failed to see that the rise of Nazism was a revolutionary change that altered the context of Versailles revisionism.[27]

In Eastern Europe, Britain acted less as an ally of France than as an arbitrator. Pacifist and Germanophile sympathies affected a wide range of political and intellectual leaders. Former Liberal Prime Minister David Lloyd George – resentful of his party's poor showing in the 1935 elections and Britain's rejection of "great men" like himself – called Hitler "the greatest German of the age." He also wrote in September 1936, "the establishment of a German hegemony in Europe which was the aim and dream of the old-pre-war militarism, is not even on the horizon of Nazism." He believed that Hitler was determined never to quarrel with Britain again. The well-known historian Arnold Toynbee shared Lloyd George's analysis, sympathized with German remilitarization, and convinced himself that Hitler desired peace. In this atmosphere, in March 1936 the leader of the BUF, Oswald Mosley, began his somewhat successful pro-German and anti-Semitic peace campaign.[28]

When Blum became prime minister in June 1936, he thought he could negotiate with the Nazi regime over disarmament and – in line with French public opinion until the end of 1938 – was willing to make colonial and economic concessions to the new Reich. Like his British counterpart, Neville Chamberlain, Blum had confidence that compromises with fascist powers would lead to peace. As prime minister, he stated, "we do not intend to doubt the word of a former soldier [Hitler] who for four years knew the misery of the trenches." Blum believed that a few concessions within the broader context of an alliance of the democracies could reintegrate Germany and Italy into a European concert. On 24 January 1937, he made friendly gestures to Germany by promising that France was ready to forget the Rhineland invasion and offered to open economic discussions. French and British appeasement also shared an influential economic component that tended to view the rise of fascism as a result of the Great Depression and imagined that economic compromises, such as the lowering of tariffs, could incorporate fascist dictators into a peaceful, capitalist Europe. The British and French leaders supposed that they were still dealing with Weimar politicians who negotiated in good faith over reparations and other economic issues.[29]

As has been seen, Blum's Popular Front government refused overt aid to the Spanish Republic to avoid deep divisions within both the nation generally and the Socialist party specifically. The French Popular Front's dread of wider European conflicts trumped its antifascism. Pacifism, national unity, and Socialist party cohesion took precedence over fighting foreign fascism. The social democratic Blum would not risk civil and world war to take decisive steps to aid revolutionary Spain. The latter aroused an anti-Communist reaction and encouraged the French and British right to view Stalin, not Hitler, as their main enemy (Figure 3.2). To rightists, fascism in Spain – the alliance of Spanish Nationalists, Fascists, and Nazis – seemed to be an effective way to block Communist influence.

Soviet support for the Spanish Republic, its own revolutionary record, and the corresponding rise of a fellow (but non-revolutionary) Popular Front in France bolstered profascist sentiment in Great Britain. Throughout 1936–1937, Germany continued to stir sympathy among conservative sectors of British opinion. The anti-Bolshevism of British conservatives, who were often hostile to France, diluted their desire to check Germany in the east. The persistent expansionism of Nazism would force them to choose between Germany and the Soviet Union, but until the German occupation of Prague in March 1939, most conservatives chose to oppose the Soviet Union. A combination of anti-Communism and anti-militarism reinforced by Versailles guilt rendered France and Britain impotent against the new Reich.[30]

Nevertheless, obstacles to good relations between Germany and the United Kingdom persisted, specifically in 1937 when Germany's renewed desire for colonies alienated prominent Tories – Leo Amery, Duncan Sandys, and Henry Page Croft. Anti-Nazism moved others to warn about the fate of the native populations under German imperial control, given Nazi cruelty to the Jews. In June 1936, the Francophile anti-appeaser Duff Cooper, who was Secretary of State for War, had affirmed British friendship with France. Both countries' "interests were identical and . . . were threatened by the same danger."[31] The new king – the philo-German, anti-Communist, and pacifist Edward VIII – strongly disapproved of Cooper's speech. Edward's sympathies for Nazism, which his father had condemned, and the new sovereign's disregard for his position as constitutional monarch contributed to his reputation as "irresponsible." Increasing Conservative government pressure led him to abdicate at the end of 1936. In 1937, Churchill and a few other Tory MPs proposed containment of Germany and opposed the revision of Versailles.

These counterrevolutionary antifascists were not yet influential. In November 1937, in discussions with British Prime Minister

Figure 3.2 "Communism Means War," poster produced during French Popular Front. Getty Images.

Chamberlain and his foreign minister Anthony Eden, French Prime Minister Chautemps and foreign minister Yvon Delbos had already concluded that France should not guarantee the existing territorial and political settlement in Czechoslovakia. At that time Chamberlain thought that the Nazi leaders had no desire or intention of making war. In January 1938, he rejected Roosevelt's proposal for an international conference of democratic powers to impede the fascist dictators' expansionism in favor of British efforts to pacify them. Churchill termed this missed opportunity Chamberlain's "rejection of the last frail chance to save the world from tyranny otherwise than by war." Churchill's assessment may have been hyperbolic, but Chamberlain spurned a possible transatlantic alliance, the basis of Churchill's hopes and future policy as prime minister during World War II. In February 1938 Chamberlain's desire to reach an agreement with Italy and his refusal of Roosevelt's initiative helped to trigger the resignation of Eden, the most popular figure in the government and a strong supporter of collective security through the League of Nations. Chamberlain and Lord Halifax – Eden's replacement at Foreign Affairs – distrusted the American president's foreign and domestic innovations and considered him an unreliable ally.[32]

Eden's resignation allowed Chamberlain to move to a more pro-Franco and pro-Fascist position. His government passively accepted the German annexation of Austria (*Anschluss*) in March 1938 and registered only a purely formal protest against the violation of Austrian sovereignty. The French submissively seconded British unwillingness or inability to protect Austria from German domination. Although Mussolini renounced his previous opposition and recognized the *Anschluss*, Chamberlain's government still believed that it could woo the Duce away from a German alliance. Much of the French right, the military, and even the Popular Front government held the same misplaced hopes. As prime minister, Chamberlain was willing to negotiate seriously with both Italy and Germany but not with the Soviet Union.

In France, Blum once again became prime minister a day after Hitler's annexation of Austria, and he attempted to erect a very broad coalition which would include Communists and anti-Nazi conservatives, such as Louis Marin and Paul Reynaud. Blum's proposed "national union" approximated the domestic and international alliance of the World War II Allies. The French Communists agreed to Blum's proposal, but nearly the entire right, including its democratic and republican parties, objected to Communist participation and to the left's commitment to the forty-hour week. The right's antifascism was deficient because it still considered the Communists – both foreign and domestic – as the chief enemy. Thus, conservatives insisted on the ostracism of the PCF from any governmental participation throughout 1938.[33] Although the French

Popular Front was initially able to incorporate the center – i.e., the Radicals – into its antifascist coalition, its economic policies remained too leftist to prefigure the alliance of revolutionary and counterrevolutionary antifascism. Only when transatlantic antifascism could integrate traditionalists and nationalists of the center and the right would it be successful.

Rearmament

As early as 1936 the Baldwin government embarked on a rearmament program, supported by Conservatives, which began to help prepare Britain for the coming war. Yet Chamberlain, Chancellor of the Exchequer in Baldwin's cabinet and his successor as prime minister, implacably opposed "unlimited" rearmament and did not make it Britain's top priority even after the *Anschluss*. He reasoned that massive weapons production would unbalance the economy, destabilize the country, and, by dividing Europe into two armed camps, undermine his own foreign policy to achieve agreement with the fascist powers. Chamberlain mixed modest rearmament with appeasement and never abandoned his quest to find "decency in [fascist] dictatorship." Although it was a necessary step toward antifascism, rearmament in itself did not guarantee firmness toward Hitler. Instead, it could act to ensure British isolation from continental affairs. Appeasement and anti-Bolshevism did not preclude increased military spending. In contrast with Chamberlain's relative moderation, Churchill demanded massive British rearmament – especially improving its air force – as early as March 1933 when Hitler was quickly consolidating his power. In the context of his advocacy of firm alliances with both France and the Soviet Union, Churchill reiterated his warnings about German air power throughout the 1930s. Although his estimates of German air strength were sometimes inaccurate, his lack of complacency made him more lucid about the military capabilities and popular support for the Nazi regime than any other major politician of the Western democracies. He never expected the Nazis to stop their expansionism without an uncompromising stance by the great powers.[34]

Like Chamberlain, in 1936 during the Spanish conflict Blum initiated the first serious interwar rearmament program of 14 billion francs; however, as in Britain, a major military expenditures program that was essential for national survival had to wait until 1939. Before that year, the results of French rearmament efforts were negligible. In 1936 France spent 26.5 percent of state revenues on defense while German military expenditure was 62.4 percent of state income. According to historian (and Resister) Jean-Louis Crémieux Brilhac, "Daladier and Blum took the initiative to rearm France in 1936, but it remained embedded in a pacifist religion which some pushed towards angelism." French rearmament took the form of selective doses of limited spending on the air force (1934–1935), army (1936–1937), and again air force (1938–1940). The autumn 1936 program devoted 14 billion to rearmament, to which was added 12 billion in spring 1938; in contrast, the spring 1939 program was 65 billion. Military expenditures increased in France from 6 percent of national income in 1936 to 8 percent in 1938, but the great change came in 1939 when they reached 28 percent of national income. The French attempted to keep military spending in check in order to balance the budget and maintain the value of the franc. France's slow recovery – compared to Germany or the United Kingdom – retarded its rearmament. In 1933 France produced one kilo of steel for each German kilo, but by 1938 Germany produced three kilos for every French kilo.[35]

British military expenditures jumped from 7 percent of national income in 1938 to 22 percent in 1939. The Royal Air Force was the recipient of a growing portion of the military budget in the 1930s and became the principal priority. By 1939 it received more funding than any other service branch, which laid the groundwork for its victory in the Battle of Britain. The priority and prestige of the air force allowed it to attract volunteers for more than half of its positions. These eventually included a number of wealthy American anglophiles who were determined to defeat the Nazi regime. While the British spent just over 7 percent of their national income on defense as late as 1938, the Germans disbursed more than double that amount. German rearmament already consumed 13 percent of GNP in 1936, 17 percent in 1938, and soared to 23 percent in 1939. Only the Soviet Union devoted a greater share of its national budget. Although the French and British efforts were formidable when added together, Nazi Germany far outclassed them before 1939. In other words, the level of rearmament that the Allies pursued was ineffective in preventing fascist aggression and ultimately deterring conflict. In the 12 months before the war, the French and British caught up with and surpassed the Germans but failed to coordinate and execute their strategies effectively. The British effort, however, was more rapid and efficient than the French. The initial German lead was partially responsible for the quick fall of France in 1940. Although the Socialist Blum and the Conservative Chamberlain obviously had clear ideological differences, their governments made roughly similar efforts to prepare for the coming conflict that, as in World War I, they envisaged as a war of attrition in which the democracies with their superior resources and resolute political will would eventually triumph. The democracies' concerns about budget balancing and currency stability prevented them from matching the military efforts of the Reich or the Soviet Union. Only when Churchill became prime minister in 1940 did the British, like the Germans years before them, completely abandon orthodox budgetary caution.[36]

Until the invasion of Prague, both the French and British used their rearmaments as bargaining chips to deter the fascist powers rather than to mobilize their nations for the coming war. In the spring of 1937, the British pressured Paris to retard its naval building program so that Germany would not renounce the 1935 agreement which limited the tonnage of the Kriegsmarine to 35 percent of that of the Royal Navy. British opinion remained ambivalent about a military pact with France since it would have meant an admission of failure to reconcile with Germany and Italy as well as involvement in France's eastern alliances. The reticent rearmament of both Britain and France became not an alternative to appeasement but rather a different aspect of it. Arms were not principally for fighting but for negotiating a European détente, based on a renunciation of Versailles and the reestablishment of the conventional balance of power among the great nations.[37]

Munich

Deferred British and French rearmament contributed to the signing of the Munich Agreement of 30 September 1938. This accord granted Germany control over the area of Czechoslovakia known as the Sudetenland, inhabited by approximately 3 million ethnic Germans. Czechoslovakia was a product of the postwar settlement and had enemies on the right who regretted the collapse of the Catholic Hapsburg Empire and on the left who condemned Czech borders as too punitive toward Germany. The Munich Agreement marked the culmination of the political and diplomatic failures of the Western powers. In the name of the democratic principle of self-determination, Britain and France allowed Nazi Germany to annex the wealthiest and most fortified regions of Czechoslovakia. Not only did the agreement decisively weaken the Czechoslovak state, but it also alienated the Soviet Union, an ally of Western-oriented Czechoslovakia. After the French concessions in the Rhineland, the Soviets had little faith in their 1935 pact with France. Yet the Russians were prepared to support Czechoslovakia in September 1938 if France backed its own eastern ally. The French and, of course, the British resisted signing any military convention with the Russians. After Munich, the Soviet Union – the standard-bearer of revolutionary antifascism – began to explore the possibility of an alliance with Nazi Germany, which resulted in the Hitler-Stalin pact less than one year later. Munich would deepen the division between revolutionary and counterrevolutionary antifascisms initiated in the Spanish Civil War.

Chamberlain was the proud architect of Munich. Unlike his predecessor, Stanley Baldwin, who had declined to meet Hitler, Chamberlain flew to visit the Führer three times and Mussolini once, but he never attempted to deal directly with Stalin. The British prime minister privately expressed the opinion that "Jewish-Communist propaganda" fooled those who doubted the peaceful motives of Hitler and Mussolini and who opposed his policies. The charge that Jews and Communists were warmongers was common among fascists of various sorts as well as in Chamberlain's circle. Thus, he and his cabinet endorsed the identification of Jews with revolutionary antifascism and maintained little interest in an agreement with the Soviet Union. Chamberlain stated that he had "the most profound distrust of Russia. I have no belief whatever in her ability to maintain an effective alliance, even if she wanted to." Like the German chancellor, the British prime minister underestimated the Soviet Union. Chamberlain believed that the only alternative to his appeasement policies was war. His refusal of antifascism had as its corollary the rejection of the need and the usefulness of even a temporary alliance with the Soviet Union. Until September 1939, Chamberlain was too anti-Communist to be antifascist.[38]

Fear of Czechoslovakia's Soviet ally and of war itself deterred many British rightists from defending France's closest partner in Eastern Europe. Foreign Secretary Halifax told a German audience that only Bolshevism would benefit from a European war. Even when Churchill's conversations with the Soviet Ambassador revealed that the Soviet Union was prepared to respond with force if Germany attacked Czechoslovakia, the British government did not wish to align itself with the Soviets. Influential newspapers – such as *The Times, Daily Telegraph*, and *Manchester Guardian* – followed the analysis of the British military and underrated the value of the Red Army and the Soviet Union as an ally against Germany. Thus, it is not surprising that the Munich Agreement provoked comparatively little dissent – only 20 Tory back-benchers abstained (of a working majority of approximately 400), compared to 80 who resisted the Conservative government's reformist India Bill of 1935.[39]

In 1936 and 1937 Blum had also proved reluctant to reinforce cooperation with the Soviet Union. At the end of 1937 the Popular Front foreign minister Delbos visited France's Eastern allies – Poland, Romania, Yugoslavia, and Czechoslovakia – but he pointedly omitted a trip to the Soviet Union and pressed the Czechs to make concessions to their German minority. Unlike his Socialist colleague, Faure, Blum may not have been an advocate of "unconditional pacifism," but he was enough of

an anti-militarist politician to concede German domination of the Sudetenland. Furthermore, French military officers, diplomats, and politicians – with the exception of the Communists – also underestimated
the Red Army and feared that the Soviet Union wanted to provoke a
war which would weaken, if not destroy, the conservative French republic. French and British leaders accepted the impressions of the anti-
Communist American aviator Charles Lindbergh, who disdained Soviet
and admired German military power. "The Lone Eagle" – who had
become an international hero by flying solo across the Atlantic in 1927 –
propagated the myth of the invincibility of German arms, especially its
Luftwaffe, even though the Soviet air force equaled the German in the
autumn of 1938. His belief in Nordic racial superiority influenced his
Germanophile assessment. In addition, he viewed the situation through
his anti-Communist and anti-Versailles lenses, which faulted the British,
French, and the Americans – not the Germans – for the European pow-
der keg. France neglected to encourage Czech-Soviet air force cooperation, which might have been very effective in preventing Germany from
gaining the air superiority on which its short-war strategy depended.[40]

The French general staff consistently overestimated the capabilities of
the German armed forces and calculated that a Franco-Soviet *entente* to
defend Czechoslovakia would cause war and revolution that would benefit only the Communists. French policy makers of the left and right
showed little willingness to defend Czechoslovakia despite Czech Francophilism. The Czechs had modeled their constitution on the Third
Republic and had close political and economic ties with their Western ally. Since 1925 both countries committed themselves to mutual
assistance in case of aggression. Nevertheless, until December 1938,
Blum "pushed his friends very far to conciliate Hitler." Blum's brief
second government of March–April 1938 did little to revive a Russian alliance, which he had deliberately neglected during his first term
in office. He reaffirmed the treaty with Czechoslovakia when he again
became prime minister after the *Anschluss*, but Britain made clear that if
France defended Czechoslovakia, it could not count on British help.[41]

Blum came to believe that the Sudetenland could be separated from
Czechoslovakia if the latter received guarantees that it would be preserved. In the Socialist newspaper *Le Populaire*, he had written that he
was prepared to shake the bloodiest hand for peace and wholeheartedly approved the meeting between Chamberlain and Hitler at Berchtes-
gaden on 15 September. As a longtime opponent of the Versailles Treaty,
Blum welcomed the Munich Agreement as an opportunity to "return
to work and get some sleep. We can enjoy the beauty of the autumn
sun." His attitude toward Chamberlain's concessions to Hitler was more

ambivalent: "War has probably been avoided, but under such conditions that even though I have always fought for peace, I cannot be joyful and am torn between cowardly relief and shame." Nevertheless, he supported Chamberlain and French Prime Minister Édouard Daladier, for whom he expressed "gratitude." He found the Munich Agreement "honorable and equitable" and rejoiced that it had preserved peace. Like the overwhelming majority of British and French politicians, he was unable to see that it would have been more advantageous to fight with approximately 40 Czechoslovak divisions in 1938 rather than without them in 1939. Furthermore, as a Socialist and a disciple of Jean Jaurès, he opposed the offensive and mobile strategy proposed by Colonel Charles de Gaulle and supported the defensive and static one adopted by the French military establishment. After the war, Blum admitted that he had failed to break over Munich with powerful pacifist currents in his party. He also regretted not responding militarily to Hitler's accession to power and the remilitarization of the Rhineland.[42]

Blum was aware that fighting German aggression in the Sudetenland would have entailed a split in his SFIO, whose pacifist wing was powerful. Thus, unlike his British counterpart – the anti-Munich Labour Party leader Clement Attlee – Blum preferred pacifism to antifascism in 1938 and, in any case, chose party unity. To prevent fascists from taking state power and destroying the SFIO was one of the major reasons behind his support for the Popular Front. Although the contexts were quite different, Blum resembled the Spanish Socialist Indalecio Prieto, who had also refused to divide his party. In 1936 Prieto knew that revolutionaries in the PSOE were provoking a violent reaction from the right, but he tolerated them for the sake of party unity. In 1938 (and even in July 1940 after the fall of France), Blum recognized that unconditional pacifists were mistaken but cooperated with them to keep the party intact. French Socialists' support for Munich reflected fears that Czechoslovakia would become – as Serbia had been – the trigger of world war. Thus, Munich was hardly a refutation of the "values of the Popular Front," and Blum's coalition proved incapable of "Defending Democracy." The French Popular Front was less antifascist than historians have indicated.[43]

Mussolini's assessment of the negotiations over the Sudetenland was more accurate than either Blum's or Chamberlain's. Like the Führer, the Duce trusted in the necessity of war for national survival and was willing to gamble for victory with the highest stakes: "As soon as Hitler sees that old man [Chamberlain], he will know that he has won the battle. Chamberlain is not aware that to present himself to Hitler in the uniform of a bourgeois pacifist and British parliamentarian is the equivalent of giving a wild beast a taste of blood." Extraordinarily enough, Mussolini's analysis was shared in Britain by a number of refugee antifascist intellectuals – Franz Borkenau, Aurel Kolnai, and Sebastian Haffner – who presciently argued that military force would be needed to stop Nazism. In contrast, Blum continued to believe that a *deus ex machina* in the form of Roosevelt's intervention could resolve the Sudetenland issue. The Roosevelt administration, however, reaffirmed its neutrality in case of war. The president himself initially approved the Munich Agreement and telegraphed Chamberlain, "Good man."[44]

With the exception of the Communists, French leftist opinion generally backed the agreement. The left-leaning, Christian democratic *L'Esprit*, which had opposed the Ethiopian War and fought nonintervention in Spain, had nonetheless legitimized the *Anschluss* as an inevitable result of the hated Treaty of Versailles. *L'Esprit* criticized appeasement but rejected armed opposition to fascism until 1939. Even after Munich, it recommended disarmament as the solution to the European crisis. The Christian democrat and future Resistance leader Georges Bidault seconded *Esprit*'s position. Like other sectors of the left, many Christian democrats deluded themselves that the Nazi regime would succumb to its own internal contradictions.[45]

The pacifism of Paul Faure's Socialist faction shared the right's international anti-Communism. The *paulfauristes* maintained that Stalin was trying to provoke a war between the Western democracies and Germany; moreover, they sometimes hinted that Jews were involved in this endeavor. Faure's anti-Communism did not prevent him, like many Marxists, from identifying fascism and capitalism. Thus, he saw no point in siding with Anglo-American (or even less Soviet) imperialism over its German competitor. His anti-militarism made him complicit with aggression and willing to ally with the right to stop war. Both pacifists and anti-Communists – the two were usually difficult to separate – believed that the Soviet defense of Czechoslovakia aimed to provoke a conflict which might eventually spread Communism. The example of the Spanish Republican zone where war had promoted the collectivization of private property and the elimination of its owners was fresh in their minds.[46]

Peacemongers were so powerful at the end of 1938 that they forced the antifascists of the PCF, the only party to support a firm anti-Munich position, into the political ghetto that it had inhabited before the Popular Front. Well-known authors – Jean Giono, Alain (Émile-August Chartier), Victor Margueritte, and Surrealist leader André Breton – refused to sign Communist Louis Aragon's post-*Anschluss* petition to "offer the nation an example of fraternity" in the face of the Nazi challenge. Writers, such as Giono, proclaimed the uselessness of heroism and the need for peasants to sabotage all preparations for war. Jean Renoir's *La grande illusion* (1937) and Jean-Paul Sartre's *La nausée* (1938) displayed a pacifist desire to refute the "myth of German barbarism."[47]

More radical leftists, including members of the Trotsky's Fourth International, shared the pre-Popular Front Communist analysis and posited that the confrontations between fascist and democratic powers were a result of equally condemnable "imperialisms." After the *Anschluss*, the revolutionary Pivert believed that Daladier's government, which had replaced Blum's in April 1938, marked the first step toward a French "fascist dictatorship," even though the entire Popular Front initially supported the government of the Radical prime minister. Pivert rejected fighting for the Czechs because, in his view, the French Socialist party had permitted the suppression of the Spanish Revolution. His extreme-left faction was expelled from the SFIO in April 1938.[48]

For other revolutionaries, Czechoslovakia's original sin was its bastard creation by Versailles.[49] The philosopher Simone Weil – full of Versailles and other varieties of guilt – posited that Czechoslovakia was an unviable state that oppressed the Sudeten Germans, an analysis shared by many across the political spectrum. In 1938 Weil – who had gone to Spain in 1936 to fight for its workers' revolution – had little if any objection to German domination of Czechoslovakia. In May 1938 she claimed that the hegemony of the Reich "might not be, in the end, a misfortune for Europe."[50] Other revolutionaries – Maurice Chambelland and Pierre Monatte of the *Révolution prolétarienne* – chose pacifism over antifascism, whether revolutionary or not. Like the Socialist reformists around the journal *Syndicats*, these radicals backed the Munich Agreement.

Munich obtained broad support in France. A poll taken in October 1938 revealed that 57 percent approved the agreement and 37 percent rejected it. A mélange of peace promotion and anti-Communism, often tinged with xenophobia and anti-Semitism, rendered the pact popular, demonstrating a rare occasion when uncritical pacifism could be as shortsighted as unrestrained militarism. The French right and extreme-right press supported Chamberlain and considered that the British alliance made a Soviet alliance unnecessary. Indeed, many deemed the Munich Agreement positive because it ignored the Soviets. Most of the French right and non-Communist French left continued to undervalue the Soviet Union, which had failed in Spain and had been debilitated by purges. Both rightists and leftists worried that a weakened USSR was trying to maneuver France into a war with Germany.

Moderates endorsed Munich. The left-center *Oeuvre*, representative of the Radical party, assumed – as did so many others – the rationality of the Führer during the Munich crisis and postulated that concessions would restrain his militancy. In the second half of 1938, another Radical paper, *La République*, divided the French into conflicting parties of war and peace. The Communists supported the former, and intelligent Frenchmen the latter. *La République* believed in the good sense and reasonableness of Nazi Germany, in contrast to the alleged warmongering of Communists and other *bellicistes*. Only when Hitler repeated his demands for German colonies in November 1938 did *La République* reluctantly agree to try to check German expansionism. The centerleft *Depêche de Toulouse*, which had national influence, reluctantly supported the Munich accord only to take a harder line toward Germany at the beginning of 1939. In whatever order, Communism and war – not Nazism – were the main enemies. Thus, those who accepted the need for war – Communists, anti-appeasers, and Jews – were the real foes.

The moderate rightist papers – *Le Temps*, *Le Figaro*, and *La Croix* – used the Czechoslovak crisis to attack French and foreign Communists, not Nazis. In late May 1938 as the Czech crisis grew, *Le Temps*, the authoritative center-right daily, declared that that Hitler had expressed sincerely his "desire for peace." Even after the Rhineland and *Anschluss*, *Le Temps* – which often reflected the opinions of elite government and business circles – had "no reason to doubt his [Hitler's] sincerity" for peace. Like the other dailies, the prestigious *Temps*, which continually congratulated itself for its "realism," proved unable to understand Nazism, which it viewed as a reactionary movement caused by the failures of democracy and the provocations of the extreme left. The rightwing *Figaro* accepted Nazi propaganda uncritically and concluded that Munich meant the beginning of European cooperation. Its foreign editor, Waldimir d'Ormesson, judged Germany's eastward expansionism "rather desirable." Disregarding the hatred of France found in *Mein Kampf*, the French press and even high-level officials often took the German chancellor's professions of Francophilism at face value. The sensationalist mass circulation daily *Paris-Soir* praised the "understanding" of Hitler during the Munich discussions and became the advocate of "the most demoralizing pacifism."

French veterans – nearly half of the entire male population and one quarter of the electorate – were undoubtedly sincere in their desire for peace, and they assumed that the much more militaristic German veterans were too. Contacts between German and French veterans as early as 1934 were part of the "Nazi charm offensive" during which Hitler emphasized his pacifist solidarity with French veterans. In 1935–1936 major leaders of French veterans' organizations, who demanded neutrality in the Spanish Civil War, took the Führer's word that he had only irenic intentions. Marshal Pétain, an admirer of the dictatorship of General Franco, expressed a desire to resolve crises by speaking directly to Hitler "soldier to soldier." Pétain had consistently preferred that veterans' organizations, instead of political parties, orient the nation. In February 1938, Paul Baudouin, director of the Banque de l'Indochine, promoted a French-German agreement backed by war veterans and based on the defense of a "threatened West." At the same time, peasant leader Henry Dorgères recommended an *entente* between peasants and veterans on both sides of the Rhine. The rural right unanimously approved of the Munich Agreement, and pacifism proved particularly influential in the countryside where almost half of the French still dwelled. In September 1938, André Delmas, secretary-general of the leftist and pacifist Syndicat national des instituteurs, suggested that war veterans Daladier and Hitler would understand each other quite well. At the end of September 1938, the authoritarian Catholic nationalist Colonel de La Rocque, head of the Croix-de-Feu and then in 1936 of the Parti social français, called on the veterans of the Great War – Daladier, Hitler, and Mussolini – to avoid a conflict which could benefit only "bloody and barbarous Bolshevism." Shortly following Munich, on 9 December 1938, Prime Minister Daladier claimed that all French veterans wanted peace with Germany.[51]

Louis Marin, the leader of the conservative Fédération républicaine, was torn between his anti-Germanism and anti-Communism, although ultimately the latter dominated in the 1930s. His federation's Catholic activists, Xavier Vallat and Philippe Henriot, were more than willing to sacrifice a "Hussite" and "Masonic" Czechoslovakia to assuage an anti-Communist Germany which threatened Bolshevik Russia. The conservative Catholic press, while critical of the Hitler regime, gave priority to the fight against Communism. Like the Vatican, its anti-Communism outweighed its antifascism. French newspaper baron Léon Bailby, owner of *Le Jour* and *L'Écho de Paris*, promoted a conservative Catholicism that viewed Moscow as more dangerous than Berlin and thus supported the Munich Agreement.[52]

The extreme right in the form of the venerable Action Française (AF), the reactionary monarchist group which arose from the Dreyfus affair, demanded a joint dictatorship by its founder, Charles Maurras, and Marshal Pétain. The latter became the most popular of all possible candidates for the position of a *chef* who was purportedly above parties and special interests. The anti-Communism and anti-Semitism of AF found much common ground with the Nazi regime. Oblivious of the danger of Nazi Germany to France, the AF celebrated Munich as a victory over "Israel and Moscow." The novelist Louis-Ferdinand Céline, for whom anti-Semitism provided an all-explanatory worldview, charged that warmongering Jews in Moscow, London, and Washington were conspiring to prevent a fruitful French-German alliance. The extreme right rejoiced that France had disregarded its alliance with Czechoslovakia and that both Western democracies had ignored Soviet interests at Munich. The "new man" on display at the Nuremburg spectacles convinced author Robert Brasillach of the virile Nazi superiority over the feminized Western democracies. Fellow writer Pierre Drieu la Rochelle shared Brasillach's conviction and believed that to survive France must reject democracy and become fascist. Brasillach's weekly, *Je suis partout*, reveled in Munich's implicit rejection of Roosevelt's hostility toward the fascist powers. The French extreme right disdained a broad alliance of France, the United Kingdom, and the United States by claiming the latter was "puritanical, Jewish, and materialist." Like the Nazis, they scorned democracies as a veil for Jewish domination. The fascistic right accepted the judgment that the Western powers were as decadent as the Jews and could not match the youthful and vigorous Axis.[53]

Jacques Doriot, leader of the *fascisant* Parti populaire français (PPF), saw the Munich Agreement as the triumph of his own anti-Soviet policies, which had condemned the Franco-Soviet pact of 1935. In September 1938 the right-wing journalist Bertrand de Jouvenel, who had been a member of the PPF, called it a "pact with the devil." According to the Catholic traditionalist, Henriot, the Franco-Soviet pact permitted the Comintern to undermine France domestically. In 1936, Marshal Pétain also voiced his opposition to the pact and fancied Britain as "France's most implacable enemy." The French right generally preferred to ally with Fascist Italy, not Communist Russia. It refused to adopt an antifascist perspective that viewed the major problem as Nazi expansionism. Instead, it blamed the Czech crisis on the presumed Czech oppression of the Sudeten Germans and the faulty diplomacy of the Popular Front. The right wanted to use the Munich crisis to appease the Germans and build closer relations with Francoist Spain.[54]

Despite the fanatical condemnation of Masonry by the extreme right and the fascist powers, who constantly derided "Masonic" Czechoslovakia, the Masons themselves were divided over armed resistance to the Nazi regime. Many of them were pacifists and shared the leftist analysis that fascism was just another form of capitalism. A few lodges even joined the growing anti-Semitic current, which European Masonry had nearly always rejected in the past. Nonetheless, Catholic reactionaries accused Masons of being responsible for war.[55]

A sense of national debility encouraged French and British appeasement policies. Major figures of the Third Republic – Flandin and Joseph Caillaux – argued that peace with Nazism was preferable to war which

Communists encouraged. Conservative British politicians held that the United Kingdom should concentrate on the defense of its empire and Western Europe and abandon Eastern Europe to German dominance. Flandin, several times French prime minister and the leader of the center-right Alliance démocratique, defended a similar position. He emphasized the weakness of France, its desire to avoid conflict with a stronger Germany, and Communist-Jewish warmongering. In 1937 Flandin opposed rearmament and preventive war against Germany. His real enemy was not Nazism, but rather the French Popular Front. He recommended that France affirm its alliance with the British Empire in "the interest of the white race," allow the United Kingdom to improve its relations with Germany, and award Germany *Lebensraum* in Central and Eastern Europe. Flandin's position proved popular among "realists" of both left and right. Defense of empire – inevitably paired with anti-Communism and sometimes with anti-Americanism – took priority over antifascism. Indeed, on the eve of the Munich Agreement, Flandin demanded the arrest of the French Communist leadership.[56]

Caillaux – a former Radical prime minister and president of the Senate's finance committee – and his closest collaborator, Émile Roche – the editor of *La République* – distrusted the "Franco-Russians" who wanted to defend Czechoslovakia. Roche accused the *anti-munichois* of wanting revenge against Hitler who was "guilty only of putting German Jews in concentration camps because the motor of this campaign [to stop Hitler's expansionism in the east] is not only Russian but also Jewish." Caillaux opposed any mobilization of French forces to block German aggression, and on 16 September he publicly proclaimed his desire for the neutralization of Czechoslovakia. In the case of war, he feared not only bombardments but "another [Paris] Commune." Like Flandin, Caillaux advocated turning away from the European continent to focus on the empire. He supported the appeasement efforts of French foreign minister Georges Bonnet, as did other right-leaning Radicals.[57]

Prime Minister Daladier bent to pacifist opinion in France and supported Bonnet, who had no desire to defend Czechoslovakia or to offend Hitler. Like Chamberlain, Bonnet feared that rearmament would destabilize the budget and opposed "warmongers" throughout 1938. France preferred that the British take the lead in negotiations with Germany over the Czech issue since this would tighten the Western alliance and deflect opposition to concessions from France to Britain. Daladier and Bonnet eagerly took shelter "under Chamberlain's umbrella" and engaged in secret diplomacy to abandon their ally. They demoted opponents of appeasement, such as the high-ranking foreign-service officer Massigli. Daladier wanted to be sure that Germany did not invade Czechoslovakia so that France would not be forced to meet its obligations. Thus,

Chamberlain's settlement at the cost of Czech sovereignty pleased the French prime minister. Prior to the Munich meeting of Daladier, Chamberlain, Hitler, and Mussolini, the British and French had essentially agreed to give the Führer what he demanded. To mask their abandonment of Czechoslovakia, they tried to associate the United States with the sellout.[58]

With the important exception of the PCF and isolated individuals throughout the political spectrum, who are discussed in the next chapter, French politicians and their political and media organizations were convinced *munichois* who nursed tendentious illusions about the Nazi regime.

The End of the French Popular Front

Faced with growing international tensions, by the spring of 1938 Daladier was determined to re-impose domestic "order" and increase production. From April to August 1938, he accomplished what Blum could not and formed a government with support from the right and a more skeptical left. Daladier's determination to break strikes and, most importantly, to end the forty-hour week meant an eventual rupture with his Socialist partners. On 25 August 1938, Blum wrote, "the divine-right and reactionary bosses have been attacking the forty-hour week legislation for a year. During the last few weeks, the attack has been more violent and determined than ever. The struggle is political and social, not economic. This is proven because the great majority of industrial firms are working less than forty hours." Like many in and out of the government, Blum was misinformed since in the autumn of 1938 at least 80 percent were laboring forty hours. Blum repeated his hostility to the end of the short workweek in November when he called Finance Minister Paul Reynaud's plan to end five days of eight hours a "vehement declaration of war" against the weekend and, more generally, against the social reforms of the Popular Front.[59]

Blum's position was backed by a united Socialist party which opposed without dissension Reynaud's imposition of a six-day week, piecework, and overtime. Even the so-called antifascist faction of the SFIO, which remained close to the PCF line, labeled Reynaud's productivist measures the domestic equivalent to the Munich Agreement. According to Zyromski's philo-Soviet *La Bataille Socialiste*, "Munich was the capitulation of democracy to external fascism. Reynaud's decree-laws [i.e., executive orders bypassing parliament] are the capitulation of democracy to the domestic fascism of banks and trusts."[60] Faure's pacifist faction also opposed the end of the forty-hour week, the anchor of the Popular Front reforms.

The supposed antifascist defense of the forty-hour week ignored fascist aggression and the large, if not decisive, German head start in weapons production. The pacifist left believed – somewhat magically – that a demographically inferior France with its work-free weekends could compete with Nazi Germany, where wage earners were laboring 50 to 60 hours per week and sometimes more. Nevertheless, Blum argued that "patriotic duty" could be accomplished only by maintaining the existing social gains of the Popular Front.[61] The abolition of the forty-hour week was also rejected by supporters of the Spanish Republic – including the CGT leader Léon Jouhaux, who nonetheless wanted a firm stance against German expansionism, which he considered responsible for the risk of war.

Like the entire left, the PCF defended the workweek "of two Sundays," which it realized was the most popular proletarian achievement of the Popular Front. As their Spanish comrades, many rank-and-file French workers knew that "fascism" meant extended labor under strict discipline. "Antifascism" therefore signified less work and more personal freedom in the workplace. The workers' priorities obviously conflicted with national defense, but the left generally refused to face the dilemma.[62] This evasion was also true for revolutionary antifascists, who often shared with more moderate leftists the same analysis of fascism as a purely reactionary and bourgeois phenomenon. Revolutionary antifascists – anarchists, Trotskyites, dissident Communists, and a few socialists (Pivert and Daniel Guerin) – held that antifascism must be revolutionary, not merely a defense of the bourgeois Third Republic.

Although the forty-hour week contributed to the weakness of French rearmament, notably in aviation, and therefore encouraged concessions at Munich, even after Munich in October 1938, the Socialists rejected granting full powers to the Daladier government unless the prime minister promised not to alter the abbreviated week. Socialists, Communists, and their trade-union supporters refused to recognize what their counterparts in Spain and elsewhere had learned – that effective preparation for war and war itself demanded a long and intense workweek. Daladier's and Reynaud's decision to end the forty-hour week meant a rupture with the left, the end of the Popular Front, and intensified military preparations.

The right was as appeasement-oriented as the left, or more so; but the right united in opposing the forty-hour week, which it termed an obstacle for French production and national defense. The theme of putting France back to work dominated the right and the center throughout 1938. Therefore, it was not "the problem of foreign policy" that destroyed the Popular Front in 1938, but rather the forty-hour week, which involved both foreign and domestic concerns.[63] Counterrevolutionary antifascists – such as Reynaud and a post-Munich Daladier – tied increased production to resistance against Nazism. Although he was a member of Flandin's sometimes pro-Franco Alliance démocratique, after a visit to the Reich at the end of 1937 Reynaud became alarmed by German war preparations. He wrote in major French press organs of the necessity to prepare for conflict by boosting defense production and reaffirming the Soviet alliance. Along with Georges Mandel, Reynaud was one of the leaders of the minority anti-Munich faction in Daladier's cabinet. Reynaud proved instrumental in busting strikes at the end of November 1938 and ending the forty-hour week.[64] His measures restored investor confidence, which financed more intensive rearmament that allowed France to pursue a policy of firmness toward the fascist powers in 1939. The Reynaud-Daladier government proved to be more antifascist than the Popular Front itself. Like most of the right, even after Munich, it refused to give Germany total *carte blanche* in the East.

The French Popular Front fostered a hesitant counterrevolutionary antifascism. Neither fascism nor the extreme right took power during the Popular Front period beginning in June 1936 after its electoral victory and ending in November 1938 when the forty-hour week was terminated. Although the leftist coalition was successful in battling the domestic extreme right, the Popular Front was unable and unwilling to stop fascist expansionism abroad, whether in Spain, Austria, or Czechoslovakia. Therefore, its antifascism was only partial. It was symptomatic that the largest demonstration involving foreign affairs during the period of French Popular Front governments did not concern the *Anschluss* or the Munich Agreement but instead protested the violent intervention of Italian Fascism into France itself. In response to the assassination of the Italian Socialists Carlo and Nello Rosselli by Mussolini's agents on 9 June 1937 at Bagnoles-de-l'Orne, 200,000 persons accompanied the corpses to the Père-Lachaise cemetery.[65] The left coalition could not extend the working week beyond forty hours to compete with Italian or German workers. Given that a large part of Popular Front supporters were pacifists and anti-Communists, it remained unprepared to confront militarily the Nazi regime. The [Communist] weekly *Regards*, "the illustrated magazine for workers," concluded that Munich had given the Popular Front the "final blow. At Munich when the Popular Front caved in to fascism – so completely that no one can deny it – it no longer existed. It died because it did not know how bring to life its fundamental doctrine: resistance to fascism."[66]

4   British and French Counterrevolutionary Antifascism

The United Kingdom experienced a sensation of decline during the Great Depression. Even so, liberalism and social democracy remained vigorous. The British economy recovered more quickly in the 1930s than either the German or French. The rise in real wages and living standards for those with jobs reinforced relative economic and political stability. The British slump was never severe enough to cause a mass of voters to abandon the established parliamentary parties, which were – in order of importance – Conservative, Labour, and Liberal. Still, during the 1920s and 1930s fascism aroused sympathy among some Conservatives. Until late 1934, the BUF maintained an aura of respectability because its right-ist supporters were perceived as traditionalists and its leftist opponents as antidemocratic and violent. Disgruntled Tory businessmen in declining sectors, such as cotton industrialists who bankrolled right-wing orga-nizations, tinkered on the edges of the extreme right. Yet in general, British executives were reluctant to support fascist organizations, which had to rely largely on foreigners for financial backing. Another factor that diminished the fascist appeal was the diminutive nature in Britain of the Communist Party, which had often provoked fascist reaction among the middle and upper classes on the continent.[1]

The dominant Conservative Party exerted much greater efforts to attract Liberals and Non-Conformists than fascists. The party retained roots in nearly all sectors of society, even drawing a large number of unorganized workers, and it regularly gained approximately 30 percent of the working-class vote. Thus, Conservatives were reluctant to engage in an all-out attack on the labor unions and the incipient welfare state. The Tory success in creating an inclusive mass party ultimately made it hostile to British fascist movements, which seemed unnecessarily vio-lent and divisive. Indeed, it has been argued that Baldwin insisted on the abdication of Edward VIII because of the King's lack of respect for con-stitutional procedures and his pro-German meddling in foreign affairs.[2]

Mosley's desire to imitate foreign dictators estranged potential sup-porters on the right. Lord Rothermore, whose newspaper empire had supported the BUF Blackshirts, had second thoughts after the Night of the Long Knives in June 1934, when Hitler and his military conspirators murdered a potential opposition movement within the Nazi party. All major newspapers – including the Tory press – unyieldingly opposed any form of British fascism. Mosley unwisely linked his own political fate to that of the Führer, whom the British public regarded as the most dangerous ruler in Europe. Public opinion usually blamed street violence on the fascists, not their enemies. Faced with the hostility of both elites and masses, domestic fascists never posed a serious threat to the British political system. Some Tories might view foreign fascism as a barrier against Communism, but almost all thought it inappropriate for their own country.[3]

Even if the BUF's endorsement of appeasement profited from the anti-war sentiment of the 1930s, the party aroused great opposition among the left. In a manner similar to the ecumenism of the French Popular Front, British antifascism assembled representatives of Labour, trade unions, women's organizations, League of Nations Union, progressive churchmen, Independent Labour Party, and CPGB. Personalities as varied as the Communist Willie Gallacher; the Labourites Arthur Greenwood and Aneurin Bevan; the historian A. J. P. Taylor; and the Bishop of Manchester rallied against fascism in Platt Fields in Manchester in 1934. Working-class organizations exposed fascism's deserved reputation for eliminating the right to strike and imposing a long and intense workweek at low pay. Responding to Sir Oswald Mosley's ambitious plan to protect the beleaguered cotton industry in Lancashire, a letter of December 1934 to the *Cotton Factory Times* concluded acerbically, "Sir Oswald is going to protect the Empire. He has promised to put you [the workers] on the same footing as your Italian and German counterparts. What more can you ask him for? Hail Mosley – the man with a mission."[4]

In the second half of the 1930s British intelligence and security services saw the danger of indigenous fascism not in its own potential for domestic growth but instead in its incitement of an antifascism which the revolutionary left could manipulate. In both Manchester and London, the CPGB was willing to confront the Blackshirts physically. Mosley's opponents usually vastly outnumbered his supporters. The British fascists, approximately half of whom were Catholic (fivefold their percentage in the general population), faced a hostile and sometimes violent public reaction. On 7 June 1934 Mosley's proposed rally at London's Olympia exhibition center provoked a counter-demonstration by much of the left, including many Labour Party members. In the United Kingdom, as in France and the United States, antifascist and fascist disorder reinforced the state's claim to a monopoly of violence. The police, judiciary, and security services adopted measures to restrict the civil liberties and media access of fascists. The BBC banned Mosley for over three decades. In 1934 the Air Ministry refused BUF members permission to fly in aviation clubs subsidized by taxes. In September 1936 Arnold Leese, founder of the Imperial Fascist League (1929) and an enthusiastic devotee of the Third Reich, who had charged Jews with ritual murder of Christians, was sentenced to six months' imprisonment for "conspiring to create a public nuisance."[5]

Antifascists prevented or disrupted 57 percent of the BUF's public meetings in 1936. The most famous of all confrontations, Cable Street on 4 October 1936, spurred intensified state antifascism. The Battle of Cable Street pitted a few thousand BUF Blackshirts, who attempted to invade the East End, against hundreds of thousands of antifascists. The East End sheltered a large Jewish population, including many Jews who were extraordinarily active fighting fascism in and outside the CPGB. Police protected the Blackshirts against the much larger number of their enemies who were determined that the fascists "shall not pass." Considerable violence erupted when the authorities attempted to clear the road to allow the BUF march to proceed, and antifascists responded by battling the forces of order. Approximately 80 protesters were arrested and 73 police injured.[6]

The most significant official reaction to the violence was the passing of the Public Order Acts of 1936–1937 which outlawed political uniforms and gave the state unprecedented power to ban political demonstrations and extreme anti-Semitic expression. By supporting nearly without dissent the antifascist Public Order Acts, Conservatives decisively disassociated themselves from the BUF. All major parties promoted state antifascism and cooperated to prevent British fascists from imitating the successes of their Italian and German counterparts. The British political system effectively employed the state to constrain, if not eliminate, the BUF and other extreme-right movements. Following the declaration of war in 1939, authorities banned fifth-column activities and outlawed British fascism, just as they limited the right to strike and resistance to work. In May 1940, Mosley's persistent peace campaign during wartime led to the Churchill government's decision to crush the BUF and intern 750 of its most active members, including the aspirant Führer along with other prominent extreme rightists. By November 1943, when the United Kingdom seemed likely to win the war, authorities released Mosley from prison, sparking protests from trade unions and even the putatively libertarian National Council for Civil Liberties.[7]

Tory participation demonstrated the pluralism of British antifascism. Fascism in Italy, Germany, and Spain may have synthesized conservative and revolutionary-right interests, but antifascism in the major Atlantic powers successfully juggled interests that were much more diverse. Fascism was generally exclusivist, but non-revolutionary antifascism was inclusive, reflecting the pluralist virtues which it defended. If fascism was a "religion," as the Italian philosopher Benedetto Croce claimed, antifascism was not. In fact, antifascism welcomed the support of both secularists and believers. The presence of religious believers and clergymen in British antifascist movements signified their largely conservative nature. The support of religious traditionalists has consistently marked the European counterrevolutions against the French Revolution of 1789, Revolutions of 1848, Paris Commune of 1871, and Spanish Civil War. Perceived Nazi and Fascist godlessness bolstered the synthesis between religion and country in antifascist nations.

In the mid-1930s, antifascism in the United Kingdom and France domesticated the revolutionism of Communists, anarchists, and Trotskyists and thus resurrected a new *union sacrée*. Despite fears that antifascism would lead to communist domination, as had occurred in large part in Spain, the danger of fascism disciplined the left in the democracies and reduced its revolutionary and anti-parliamentary wings. The extreme left (anarchists and Trotskyists) protested the counterrevolutionary nature of antifascism, but the overwhelming majority of antifascists agreed that they could succeed only if revolutions were contained or delayed.

British Reactions to Foreign Fascism

Initially, only a perceptive few viewed Hitler's seizure of power of 1933 as a civilizational rupture. Like many progressive Europeans and Americans, the *Manchester Guardian* journalist F. A. Voigt had been critical of the harshness of the Versailles Treaty, but, as early as 1932, he realized that even the driest account of the rise of Nazism in Germany would appear sensationalistic to readers. He uncommonly grasped that the Nazi revolution – like those in France (1789) and Russia (1917) – was not "a purely domestic affair, but a matter of universal concern. All Europe, indeed the world, and not least the British Commonwealth, will pay heavily for failure to see that this is so."[8] Voigt asserted with considerable foresight that Nazi anti-Communism was a mask for German imperialism, which would inevitably continue as long as the Nazi regime was in control. Versailles revisionism would embolden the new Reich to use its power to achieve European hegemony. Voigt held Nazism to be more dangerous to the West than Communism because the former sought to subvert Christianity from within. His critique echoed many of the themes of the most thoughtful continental antifascist intellectuals.

The Third Reich in power quickly repulsed one-time sympathizers, such as *The Times* reporter G. E. R. Gedye. An expert on the German-speaking world, Gedye had accused interwar France of perpetuating European instability, but the Nazi regime's violence and torture horrified him. In June 1933 he explained that supposed French excesses did not excuse the viciousness of the Hitler regime: "Condemnation of those who tease and torture an animal until it loses normal control and flies at the nearest victim in a passion to be free does not involve approval of the maddened animal." His newspaper was pro-appeasement but hostile to the new Reich's savage domestic conduct. Although certain British intellectual luminaries – the novelists Henry Williamson and Wyndham Lewis, and the historian Arnold Toynbee – seemed initially well disposed to Nazism, most intellectuals eventually concluded that it represented a return to barbarism and a regression to paganism. By the late 1930s Toynbee, Williamson, and Lewis had all thoroughly rejected Hitler and his regime.[9]

Admiration for the Nazis remained very limited, even if a number of conservatives welcomed their abolition of unemployment. Arnold Wilson, the philo-fascist Tory MP, held that the ceremony of the Labor Service (*Arbeitdienst*) "would have satisfied the early saints, who held that *Laborare est orare*."[10] Yet devotion to the work ethic could not prevent the Hitler movement from being "culturally constructed" as the enemy of civilization. Nazi lawlessness disgusted Conservative opinion. Conventional wisdom held – wrongly – that the Hitler regime had deliberately burned down the Reichstag in 1933. Much of the British public found the Nazis' crude political anti-Semitism distasteful, and the major parties in Britain avoided it and sometimes sanctioned members who toyed with it. Mainstream politicians considered Nazi anti-Semitism a barrier to Anglo-German understanding. The British rejection of extremist Judeophobia also meant a refusal of the Nazi worldview in which Jews were the all-purpose perpetrators of Communism, capitalism, and ultimately antifascism.

The public book burnings and the expulsion of world-famous intellectuals reinforced the regime's barbaric reputation. Whereas the French accepted several hundred thousand Jewish refugees, the British admitted a smaller but more select number of tens of thousands, including prominent German-Jewish scholars and scientists. In 1933 the Academic Assistance Council formed to help accommodate emigrant intellectuals. In October, in collaboration with other refugee organizations, a fundraiser for the council was organized at the Royal Albert Hall, where Albert Einstein lectured for the first time to a general audience. He was joined on the podium by Cambridge physicist Lord Rutherford, Conservative politician Austen Chamberlain, editor of *The Times* Geoffrey Dawson, the Bishop of Exeter, and the director of the London School of Economics, William Beveridge, who was particularly active in recruiting and retaining European Jewish scientists.[11] No prominent leftists spoke.

A still broader coalition backed manifestos on "Liberty and Democratic Leadership," published in February and May 1934, which defended democratic rule, freedom of expression, and – somewhat inconsistently – international reconciliation. The manifestos were signed by 144 prominent individuals, including trade unionist Ernest Bevin, antiwar activist Vera Brittain, art historian Kenneth Clark, Conservative Harold Macmillan, socialists Hugh Dalton and George Lansbury, writer Aldous Huxley, eugenicist Julian Huxley, authors Virginia and Leonard Woolf, and historians John and Barbara Hammond. These intellectuals, artists, and politicians demanded protection of free inquiry. No Communist initialed these declarations in this pre–Popular Front period. The signers represented millions of Britons of various political persuasions who were dedicated to the customary defense of their democratic liberties and rights.[12]

In response to the rise of French antifascism, in 1935 Labour MP Philip Noel-Baker and novelist E. M. Forster agreed to organize intellectual celebrities into a British section of the Paris-based Comité de Vigilance des Intellectuels Antifascistes. The initiative developed into an association entitled For Intellectual Liberty, whose president was Aldous Huxley. The scientist J. D. Bernal, sculptor Henry Moore, author Leonard Woolf, and historian R. H. Tawney joined Huxley on the executive committee. The society pledged to defend democratic and individual liberties independently of all party interests. The French Popular Front found another positive echo in Great Britain when in the spring of 1936 the young Tory MP Harold Macmillan – whose election in his constituency depended on attracting Labour and Liberal votes and whose book was tellingly named *The Middle Way* (1938) – toyed with the idea of forming a cross-party forum of antifascists to create democratic unity.[13] The leadership of both the Labour and Conservative parties rejected his proposed British Popular (or People's) Front and refused to collaborate publicly with revolutionaries and Communists.

If politicians failed to imitate French political antifascism, British publishers nonetheless promoted a cultural Popular Front. Allen Lane's inexpensive Penguin Specials, which were devoted to current events, became the great publishing success of the late 1930s. They outsold competitors, such as the philo-Communist Left Book Club, by hundreds of thousands of copies. The first Penguin print was Edgar Mowrer, *Germany Puts the Clock Back* (first published in 1933, reissued in 1937). Its title indicated the dominant antifascist analysis, which French and American analysts shared after 1933, of Nazism as a reactionary movement. Almost all the seventeen titles of the Penguin series covered events from a center-left position and won praise for their "non-partisan" defense of democracy.[14] The series reflected the cultural dominance of conservative antifascism in the late 1930s. On the BBC, E. M. Forster championed established British liberties, which he called the basis of civilization. His broadcasts mirrored a pervasive antifascist, especially anti-Nazi, commitment among the British public.

More quickly than any other major politician, Churchill grasped the political and diplomatic potential of transatlantic antifascism. His early anti-Nazism allowed him to overcome Conservative sectarianism and made him acceptable to trade-union and Labour leaders whose organizations had been equally dogmatic in rejecting formal talks with Tory rebels.[15] In many ways, Churchill created a much more inclusive coalition than the either the French or Spanish Popular Fronts. Unlike the latter, which had only leaders from the left, Churchill would guide the antifascist alliance from the right. As early as 1934, despite his pioneering and unquestioned anti-Communism, he saw that an international antifascist alliance must include the Soviet Union to block potential German expansion. At the same time, his own conservative antifascism refuted the Marxist argument, both before and after the Popular Front, that only the working class could be antifascist. Similarly, the counterrevolutionary transatlantic antifascism that Churchill initiated undermined the extreme-right analysis that fascism was the only means to prevent communist revolution. In fact, the capitalist and "plutocratic" Churchill (as both German Nazis and American isolationists labeled him) and his eventual social democratic partner, Roosevelt, would become the chief antifascist counterrevolutionaries. The success of their future alliance refuted predictions advanced by both communists and anti-communists that a new world war would lead to the collapse of capitalism.

As early as July 1934, Churchill robustly endorsed collective security through the League of Nations. He became an even more fervent champion of the latter, which included the Soviet Union, in response to the German seizure of the Rhineland in March 1936. This position brought him a close contact with the Labour opposition, led by Clement Attlee, also a staunch supporter of the League. However, as has been seen, the overwhelming majority of Churchill's own Conservative party feared that British retaliation against German moves in the Rhineland would redound to the benefit of the Soviet Union and foster the spread of communism. Churchill's fellow Tories refused to connect aggressive Nazi foreign policy with its brutal and persecutory domestic behavior. Instead, they accepted German expansion and trumpeted their dislike of Bolshevik Russia.

In 1936 Churchill became the center of an elite and discreet antifascist alliance, the Focus in Defence of Freedom and Peace, which included prominent trade unionists, churchmen, businessmen, Labour, Liberals, and Conservatives. In contrast, Churchill's Tory rival, Neville Chamberlain, was relatively uninterested in building a coalition with Liberals and Labour, whom his Conservative predecessor, Stanley Baldwin, had successfully wooed on a number of occasions. Like the French Popular Front, the Focus group began in 1935 to mobilize public opinion against the dangers of German National Socialism and, above all, to encourage rearmament. It was particularly devoted to a modernized air force that could confront the growing Luftwaffe. Wickham Steed, a former editor of *The Times*, played a particularly active role in Focus. Overcoming his deserved reputation as a zealous anti-Semite, Steed warned the British and North American publics of the dangers of Hitlerism, whose aggressions would disturb the balance of power on the continent. Others in the Focus group emphasized Nazi paganism, its challenge to traditional religions, and violations of property rights. No French equivalent to the ecumenical Focus group existed. Instead, on the eve of war in August 1939, more than a dozen Socialist and rightist pacifist deputies – including Flandin, Radical dissident Gaston Bergery, and neo-Socialist Marcel Déat – created might be termed a de facto and short-lived anti-Focus, the Anti-war Coordinating Committee, which wanted to avoid conflict with Germany at any cost. In the French Senate, former Prime Minister Pierre Laval sought the same goal. In the British parliament, a similar peace lobby materialized, but its members lacked the stature of their French counterparts.[16]

The Communist presence in the French Popular Front ensured the Focus group's hostility to that alliance. Nor did Focus press for British intervention on the side of the Spanish Republic. The absence of a powerful Communist party in the United Kingdom allowed Churchill and his followers to initiate a broader coalition than in France, where – as had been seen in 1938 – anti-Communism prevented inclusive antifascist alliances of right and left. Focus anticipated the British establishment's ultimately resolute resistance to fascism that sparked World War II. In Britain, the internal threat of Communism could not be used effectively to scare the middle and upper classes into the fascist camp. The CPGB never had more than 20,000 members at its peak in 1939, compared to a Labour Party with 400,000 members.[17] Focus ignored British

Communism and promoted a counterrevolutionary antifascism which rallied elites from almost the entire political spectrum to what the group termed the cause of "ordered freedom" or what Marxists called bourgeois democracy. Ultimately, the defense of this vision of freedom – i.e., representative democracy, extensive liberty of expression, religious tolerance, predominance of private property, and trade-union rights – would take precedence over peace.

Fascist union busting deeply disturbed labor leaders, such as Bevin and Citrine, a Focus participant and the general secretary of the Trades Union Congress (TUC) who had opposed Churchill's determined strikebreaking measures during the 1926 general strike. Unlike the German trade unions and Socialist Party (SPD), whose origins in the authoritarian Wilhelmine period preceded the Weimar Republic, both Labour and the TUC were products of liberal democracy and were determined to defend it. As early as 1933, the Labour Party published a pamphlet, *Democracy versus Dictatorship*, which depicted Nazi violence against trade unionists and condemned both left and right tyrannies. Also in 1933, the TUC issued its report on fascism, *Dictatorship and the Trade Union Movement*, which equated communism and fascism and advocated representative democracy, which it believed could achieve Labour's goals. Fascism's reputation for the hyper-exploitation of wage earners continually damaged it among both organized and non-organized workers in the Atlantic world.[18]

Yet Labour and trade-union leaders' antifascism had limits. They remained reluctant to conclude an antifascist alliance with the CPGB since they believed that Communism and fascism grew concurrently, and violent opposition to one triggered the growth of the other. Furthermore, Bevin and other union officials held that Communists would destroy the union movement. In their estimation, the German Communist Party had divided workers' organizations and thus opened the door to the Nazi seizure of power. By equating Communism and Nazism, British Labour's version of totalitarianism shared the perspective of intellectuals who denounced both movements. Thus, the Labour leadership rejected a coalition with British Communists to stop domestic fascism, even if it would later accept an alliance with the Soviet Union to fight against the international variety.[19]

In contrast to the future Axis, the inability or unwillingness of the Soviet Union to conquer territory outside its European borders from the early 1920s until the Hitler-Stalin pact of 1939 ensured that it would not arouse the same fears among the public as Nazi Germany. Although generally hostile to both Nazi Germany and the Soviet Union, during the Great Depression British opinion tended to favor the Soviet Union as a better alternative. In April 1939, 87 percent expressed a preference for a military alliance with the Soviets, a figure which varied little over the summer. Even if more murderous than German National Socialism until World War II, Soviet Marxism appeared more rational than the Nazis' Nordic racism. Many British intellectuals – among others the classic theorist of imperialism, J. A. Hobson – defined fascism as the product of a bankrupt capitalist system and excluded the possibility of an antifascism friendly to capitalism. Furthermore, before the Hitler-Stalin pact, support for the Soviet Union tapped into a current of revolutionary antifascism which desired to imitate aspects of the Soviet model. British Marxists and fellow travelers – including the historian Maurice Dobb; the Fabian Socialists Beatrice and Sidney Webb; composer Ralph Vaughan Williams; and authors H. G. Wells, Virginia Woolf, and Bertrand Russell – frequently championed the Soviet experiment, arguing that it had inspired community, sacrifice, and social progress. John Strachey, a Labour MP, and G. D. H. Cole, an architect of Guild Socialism, sympathized with the Soviet Union, which they saw as successfully planning a post-capitalist future. John Maynard Keynes took a more critical, if not disdainful, position toward Communism and a planned economy in general, but he reflected the growing consensus among economists that the state should play in larger role in stimulating production and especially consumption. If the Conservative government had accepted Keynes' willingness to borrow and risk inflation, it might have embarked upon a more ambitious armaments program.[20]

By the late 1930s Communist influence had grown within British antifascist organizations. Victor Gollancz's Left Book Club fashioned a publishing Popular Front that attracted a broad spectrum of the left. Gollancz named Stalin the man of the year in 1937 for his guidance of a society which was purportedly abolishing exploitation. In his own volume for the club, poet Stephen Spender argued that liberalism was morphing into fascism and therefore advocated communism. Beatrice Webb applauded "a new [Soviet] civilization with a new metaphysic and a new rule of conduct." She and her husband published the laudatory *Soviet Communism: A New Civilisation?* (1935), which answered its title's question in the affirmative. Indeed, in the second edition, which was issued in 1937 during the Great Purge trials, the Webbs dropped the question mark. Bernard Shaw endorsed the book as a masterpiece, and it was still regarded as the last word after 1941 when the Soviet Union returned to the antifascist fold.[21] Shaw and the Webbs were correct that the Soviet Union introduced a new civilization; however, it was one based on a revolutionary one-party dictatorship that engaged in massive repression of its political opponents. Its economic policies destroyed Russian agriculture, and its industrialization, although successful militarily during World War II, failed in peacetime. Nevertheless, until the Hitler-Stalin pact, transatlantic pro-Soviet attitudes seemed to expand and intensify as fascism became more aggressive.

The *Anschluss* of March 1938 further undermined pro-German sentiment in Great Britain, where sympathizers had asserted that the "unfair" constraints of Versailles made Hitler's demands for national self-determination reasonable even if his methods were deplorable. Gedye's reporting on the vicious pogrom in Vienna in March 1938 was particularly hard-hitting. The cruel and unprecedented violence against Viennese Jews that accompanied the *Anschluss* distinguished it from the Rhineland coup and compelled the public to become more conscious of the links between Nazi domestic and foreign aggression. Right-wing British Conservatives attacked the "absolute . . . abandonment of morality and religion in the satrapy of Herr Hitler." Tories had hoped that Italian Fascism would take a course different from German Nazism. The *Anschluss* disappointed them because it demonstrated both Nazi aggression and Fascist complicity in the German conquest.[22]

Catholic philo-Fascists attacked Hitler's regime as "barbaric" but remained favorable to Mussolini. In the 1930s, imperialist Britons admired the Duce for restoring Italian self-respect and pride in the imperial past. Churchill and others acted on the hope that Mussolini could become a British friend or ally, a faith which prevailed among many Conservatives even after the *Anschluss*. Britain and France had attempted sporadically and ineffectually to discourage Italian expansionism in Africa during 1935. When the pugnacious Duce ignored them, the European democracies accepted the Italian *fait accompli*. Much of the British right came to regard the Italian invasion of Ethiopia in 1935–1936 sympathetically. Although Labour favored sanctions against Italy, many Conservatives – including anti-Nazis, such as Churchill and Austen Chamberlain – thought that Italian rule would impose some order and progress on Ethiopian Emperor Selassie's primitive and slave-owning country. Fascinated by dictatorship and convinced of Western superiority, they condoned Mussolini's African adventure. Tory reluctance to impose sanctions and the pursuit of appeasement undercut the League of Nations that only a minority of Conservatives believed essential for collective security. Seeing the confluence of German and Italian interests, Hitler cleverly used both the Ethiopian conflict and the Spanish Civil War as diversions which allowed German rearmament and expansionism. The Führer took advantage of the divisions between and within the democracies and occupied the Rhineland during the Abyssinian war. In 1936, the fascist powers proved more successful in splitting London and Paris than the democracies in dividing Italy and Germany. The military historian, Basil Liddell Hart, concluded that Britain and France missed in Ethiopia their best chance of checking Fascist aggression.[23]

The Ethiopian war repeated patterns of colonial conquest and anticipated future developments. The Italian Fascists gathered 500,000 men – the largest expeditionary force ever engaged in a colonial campaign. Like the British, French, and Spaniards in their colonial wars in the 1920s, the Italians resorted to poison gas to defeat enemy tribesmen. The Fascists embraced blatant racism in the name of a "superior civilization" and employed unsurpassed colonial violence – the most intense bombing campaigns ever and indiscriminate attacks against civilians. The silence of Pope Pius XI concerning Italian atrocities mirrored his passivity regarding Nazism. Ironically, despite the right's acquiescence to Fascist invasion, Selassie's traditionalist antifascism anticipated that of European conservatives later in the decade. The Ethiopians and then the British used imperial troops to defend themselves against aggressive fascist colonialism and eventually succeeded in forming powerful coalitions with other national states that would largely restore the status quo ante.[24]

British Catholics and Protestants regularly employed a discourse that placed Christianity as an alternative to both fascism and communism, even if fear of the latter often surpassed that of the former. Protestant traditionalists, such as Toynbee, blamed the interwar crisis on the decline of religion. An Anglican, Toynbee would achieve great fame in the English-speaking world, and *Time* placed his picture on its cover in 1947, a singular distinction for a historian. In 1935 he elaborated his vision of a "dualistic struggle between good and evil as the struggle between fascist tribalism and transcendental Christianity." Both traditionalist and liberal Christians interpreted Nazism as a return to the Dark Ages. The editors of *The Times* and the *Manchester Guardian* closed ranks against the Nazi attack on Christianity, which they defended as the most significant element of Western Civilization. In 1937, Christian circles publicized the regime's imprisonment of hundreds of clergymen, such as Pastor Martin Niemöller, who did not conform to Nazi-approved theology. Traditionalist believers distrusted the "German Christians" who denigrated the Old Testament and parts of the New. Practicing Christians rejected the Nazi conflation of religion and the state, an amalgamation which they considered totalitarian. Roger Lloyd, a Canon of Winchester, observed in 1938 that only Christianity would have the necessary force to fight totalitarianism.[25]

The persecution of the anti-Nazi Confessional Church damaged the regime's reputation in Britain more than its violent and systematic attacks on Jews. Religious critics stressed the anti-Christian rather than anti-Semitic nature of Nazism. This downplaying of anti-Semitism demonstrated a certain blindness to the special plight of the Jews, but it was politically astute because it helped to refute the charge – which continues to this day among pro-Nazi groups – that Jews fomented antifascism and World War II. The British Society of Friends (Quakers) established a Germany Emergency Committee which published regular reports revealing the cruelty of concentration camps. Some churchmen, such as the Anglican vicar John Groser, considered fascism a far greater enemy of Christian civilization than Marxism. In 1939, the British association Friends of Europe published numerous pamphlets that attempted to demonstrate the anti-Christian essence of the Nazi religion. Cardinal Arthur Hinsley, who had supported Franco, sponsored the Sword of the Spirit movement of 1940 that campaigned for Christian values against Nazi "paganism." His interpretation of Nazism was seconded by most British Christians in a nation where Catholicism was growing but remained a minority of approximately 10 percent of the population. Christians offered a revitalized religious response to the challenges of Communism and Nazism.[26]

Churchill's post-Munich parliamentary intervention of 5 October 1938 echoed the traditionalist critique: "There can never be friendship between the British democracy and the Nazi Power, that Power which spurns Christian ethics, which cheers its onward course by a barbarous paganism, which vaunts the spirit of aggression and conquest, which derives strength and perverted pleasure from persecution, and uses, as we have seen, with pitiless brutality the threat of murderous force."[27] Richard Law, the son of the former Conservative leader, pointed out during the same post-Munich debate: "There are . . . enormous numbers of people who regard the Nazi Government in Germany as being the most ruthless, the most cruel, the most inhuman tyranny that the world has ever known, and that is the firm that this country has joined, and, as the Leader of the Opposition [Labour's Clement Attlee] pointed out this afternoon, that is the firm we have joined as a junior partner [at Munich]."[28] These Tory antifascists did not believe that the Third Reich merely repeated the expansionism of the Second. Instead, they saw it as a regression to savagery. Churchill's small troop of dissenters considered Nazism a more immediate danger than European war and its possible Communist aftermath.

Had the Germans not occupied Prague in March 1939, these dissident Conservatives might well have been eliminated by their own party. Immediately after Munich, large sectors of Tory and public opinion rejected the antifascism of the Munich critics which, they thought, would lead to war. In October 1938 Prime Minister Chamberlain enjoyed a 57 percent approval rating. In late 1938, the dissidents' opposition to Germany also implied an alliance with the Soviet Union, a major reason why the Munich critics remained a tiny minority in the Conservative party. The only cabinet member to resign from Chamberlain's government in protest of Munich was First Lord of the Admiralty Duff Cooper, who felt that the Chamberlain's post-Munich slogan "peace in our time" could only impede rearmament and strengthen Germany. Cooper, Churchill, and few more than a dozen Tory deputies concluded that Hitler was neither a "normal" politician nor a "gentleman," as Chamberlain believed. Chamberlain's defenders have excused his commitment to appeasement by citing the unprepared state of British rearmament, the unreliability of France and the Dominions, and the possibility of involvement in a three-front war in Asia, the Mediterranean, and Europe. But pacifism – which meant a commitment to war's avoidance, not merely its postponement – was Chamberlain's first priority in 1938–1939. The strength of pacifism, bolstered by the British elite's desire for normal business with Germany, encouraged Hitler in his belief that the democracies might never declare war on Germany, regardless of its expansionism.[29]

Outside the Conservative party, Munich raised more doubts about the government's appeasement policies and confirmed Churchill's warnings in some sectors of public opinion. The *Manchester Guardian* pointed out that Munich was a tremendous moral defeat for the British and French and would lead to the justified defection of the Soviet Union from an anti-German coalition. Munich induced the Soviet Union to return to its pre–Popular Front position which rejected the distinction between the imperialism of Nazi Germany and that of the capitalist democracies. The Soviet Union concluded that the latter were encouraging the former to expand to the east. In addition, the *Manchester Guardian* argued that Hitler's strengthened security in Eastern Europe would allow him to turn his post-Munich attentions to the west. Other papers – the *News Chronicle* and the formerly very pro-German *Observer* – echoed this analysis of a growing German threat. In Britain, the fallout from the Munich crisis helped to turn an overwhelming majority firmly against the Nazi regime.[30]

The relatively few British Naziphiles acknowledged that Kristallnacht, which closely followed Munich, caused "violent revulsion." The brutal pogrom of 9–10 November made Conservatives who remained sympathetic to the Nazi regime doubt Hitler's commitment to peace. An opinion poll taken shortly after the event showed that 73 percent of the public viewed the persecution of the Jews as an obstacle to a good understanding between the United Kingdom and the Reich. Only 15 percent agreed that the *Reichspogrom* was not a hindrance. According to another poll at the beginning of 1939, 59 percent of the British preferred to see a Russian victory if war erupted between the Soviet Union and Germany and only 10 percent desired a German triumph. However, only after the invasion of Czechoslovakia in March 1939 would public opinion allow the possibility of going to war.[31]

French Hostility to Foreign Fascism

Certain French publications, such as the patriotic but progressive *Europe Nouvelle*, opposed Mussolini immediately after he took power. Its correspondent, Benjamin Crémieux, saw the Italian movement as violently antiparliamentarian and criticized the "excess" and "gratuitous violence" of the Blackshirts. An expert on Italian culture, Crémieux remained skeptical that Fascism would become more moderate since it was composed of "hollow formulas, futile violence, and a total disregard of reality." He harshly criticized its infringements of press freedoms. As a patriotic (Jewish) Frenchman, Crémieux was sensitive to the "insults uttered against France by the major organs of the Fascist press" and the aggressive Italian policy in the Mediterranean, which would alarm the French more than the British. He noted "we cannot follow too closely the fascist experience. This experience of *union sacrée*, reaction, nationalism, and negation of the class struggle raises for Europe the same passionate interest as the complete communist experiment attempted in Russia by the Soviets. In Italy, as in Russia, it is democracy which . . . is accused of all evils. The remedies proposed and implemented are different, but it is the same disease they pretend to cure." Uncannily anticipating the Vichy regime, the weekly feared a French synthesis of Italian Fascism and Action Française that might institute a "provisional dictatorship" in a period of political and economic unrest. During the occupation, Crémieux would join the Resistance; he perished at Buchenwald in 1944.[32]

L'Europe Nouvelle, edited by the Alsatian-Jewish feminist Louise Weiss, exhibited an antifascism which – like the French business publications discussed earlier – was more pragmatic than principled. In fact, Fascism's augmentation of order, discipline, and production led the weekly to equate the Duce's government with that of Napoleon III and to overlook the many differences between the more traditional nineteenth-century French Second Empire and the more radical twentieth-century Italian experience. Even though the review recognized that the Fascist regime ruled through terror, it portrayed Mussolini in the early years of

Fascism in power as a moderate and a "realist." The Duce advanced both national and international stability by restraining his more "extremist" party colleagues.[33]

L'Europe Nouvelle was much more hostile to Hitler. As early as 1923, Gaston Raphaël, a French authority on Germany, predicted that if Hitler took power, the Versailles Treaty would be annulled and "all the Jews in Germany will be killed or expelled. Socialists and Marxists too." When Hitler became chancellor in 1933, the weekly maintained its clairvoyance. It remained committed to the League of Nations, which the French extreme right maligned as a tool of Moscow, and it opposed the Munich Agreement. Its voice on the issue was the perspicacious columnist Pertinax (André Géraud), who had opposed intervention on the side of the Spanish Republic but who demanded a strict application of the French treaties supporting Czechoslovakia. In early 1938, Pertinax correctly perceived – in contrast to the overwhelming majority of analysts on the right – that Italy would prefer to be number two in a dynamic coalition with Germany than number three in a more static alliance with Great Britain and France. He reasoned that once Mussolini had accepted the *Anschluss* on his northern border, he could never be persuaded to join the Franco-British alliance. Pertinax thundered against the intellectual failures of British and French diplomacy which – rather than military weakness – were responsible for appeasement of Hitler. After his American exile during World War II, he would return to his position as a prominent Parisian journalist. It is significant that at the beginning of 1939 the anti-Munich tendency in the Socialist Party launched its own journal, *Agir*. It nurtured some of the most prominent Socialists – including Pierre Brossolette and Daniel Mayer – who would later join the Resistance.[34]

Prominent Christian democrats – such as François Mauriac, Georges Bidault, and Hubert Beuve-Méry – fiercely objected to the *Anschluss* which had reduced Catholic Austria to German control. *Le Temps* journalist Beuve-Méry was critical of Nazism but reluctant to fight it militarily. After the fall of France, he served the Vichy regime for several years, then joined the Resistance and founded the postwar newspaper of record, *Le Monde*, at the end of 1944. Beuve-Méry believed that to defend Czechoslovakia during the Munich crisis was to protect Christian civilization, and he urged readers not to be deceived by Hitler's use of the "Bolshevik scarecrow." He contrasted the right of Sudeten self-determination in Czechoslovakia with the right of Czechs not to live under "National Socialist tyranny." Nostalgic Catholic traditionalists in France and abroad rejected Beuve-Méry's arguments and distrusted the lay Czechoslovak Republic. In 1939 his *Vers la plus grande Allemagne* denounced German expansionism. The attitude of Bidault's newspaper *L'Aube* contrasted with the acceptance of appeasement by most Catholics, including many Christian democrats. Although Bidault, a postwar prime minister, remained reluctant to combat Nazism militarily immediately after Munich, he acutely criticized "realists" who offered little opposition to Germany.[35]

As in Britain, in France too Christians often condemned Nazi paganism. As early as 1934, the *Revue des deux mondes* – a journal of reference for the right – published numerous essays which denounced "the anti-Christianity of the Nazi doctrine," a theme elaborated by the Catholic philosopher Jacques Maritain. He posited that one form of this "revolutionary totalitarianism" was "the depraved paganism of racism, which transforms religion into the idolatry of the 'soul of the people.'" In 1937, Maritain identified anti-Semitism with "Christophobia" and added, "that is why the bitter zeal of anti-Semitism always at the end turns into a bitter zeal against Christianity." Irreligion, which the Enlightenment had encouraged, was allegedly the basis of both fascism and Communism. Maritain accused important sectors of the French right of failing to perceive that "Fascism and Nazism, rooted as they are in the same radical evil as Communism, exist only to supply this evil with more perfected means of destruction." He argued that "the social divinization of the individual, inaugurated by 'bourgeois' liberalism'" inescapably led to the "social divinization of the state" and ultimately to a "Master." The latter was "no longer a normal ruler but a sort of inhuman monster whose omnipotence is based on myths and lies." A similar critique of the dangers of secularization and the decline of traditional religions was voiced by the British Catholic historian Christopher Dawson and the Oxford Conference in 1937. This analysis – which blames totalitarianism on irreligion – remained very abstract, particularly because Christian democratic parties themselves were becoming progressively secular in the interwar years. Yet the inclusion of these anti-secularists shows the ecumenical nature of antifascism.[36]

A post-Munich George Bernanos offered a variation of the thesis that a slippery slope led inevitably from irreligion to fascism. Bernanos charged that the members of Action Française were "as hollow, as empty as their Catholicism without Christ, their Catholic order without grace."[37] The followers of Maurras were not genuine believers but used the Catholic faith as a tool to attract adherents. Bernanos attacked the arguments of so-called realists who presumed to defend the national interest by betraying France's promises to Czechoslovakia. He composed his criticisms in late 1938 when many of his literary colleagues on the left and right – Maritain, Mauriac, Giono, Sartre, Brasillach – were fervent *munichois*.

Bernanos and other non-Communist *anti-munichois* did not compose a movement but acted as individuals. Their isolated voices broke with the consensus of the Catholic right because they concluded that fascism – notably its Nazi form – was more dangerous than Communism. Bernanos attained an audience among a minority of Catholics and clergy. The politicians – Reynaud and Mandel – opposed appeasers in the government and the parliament; the journalists – Pertinax, Bidault, Émile Buré, and Georges Boris – fought in the media; and Kérillis battled in both parliament and the media. These men continued to see Germany as France's main enemy. Like the Churchill group in Britain, they perceived the necessity of a Soviet alliance. They understood that British and French policy makers had delivered Czechoslovakia to the Germans and thus had completed the destruction of the Petite Entente, collective security, and the League of Nations. They also grasped that Munich had opened the door to an *entente* between Germany and the Soviet Union, which understandably became disillusioned with France and the United Kingdom. Three-time prime minister André Tardieu – a follower of Clemenceau like Mandel – was also very critical of Munich. However, unlike Pertinax, Tardieu agreed with the conservative leader Louis Marin that the Soviets should have no place at the table. Both politicians' anti-Communism undermined antifascism. While the French left had condemned the Ethiopian War, which demonstrated to them that the slogan "Fascism means war" was not merely propaganda, only a handful of people on the right – including Buré, Reynaud, and Pertinax – advocated close cooperation with the United Kingdom in 1936 to sanction both Italy and eventually Germany for aggression. Like their Francophile British counterparts, the most lucid non-Communist voices opposing fascism were almost always Atlanticists, who held strong sympathies for the United Kingdom and the United States. They challenged many of their fellow conservatives who were more willing to accept a new European order dominated by Germany.[38]

Pertinax attacked Chamberlain who, instead of appeasing the Germans, should have announced that an unshakable Franco-British alliance would thwart any German aggression in central Europe. He predicted in March 1938 that both France and Britain risked "in a very short time either war or humiliation" over Czechoslovakia since Chamberlain would abandon central Europe. Furthermore, Pertinax correctly forecast that Munich would lead to a Nazi-Soviet agreement. He defended Mandel who – as had Reynaud, Massigli, and a relatively unknown Charles de Gaulle – argued that France should have mobilized in response to the Nazi occupation of the Rhineland and again for the *Anschluss*. Pertinax perceived that the opinion makers and politicians of London and Paris did not understand the youthful dynamism of fascist movements. The industrialist and conservative politician François de Wendel, who was close to Mandel, grew increasingly anti-appeasement in the second half of 1938. At odds with the pro-Germanism of Vallat and Henriot in his own rightist Fédération républicaine, de Wendel concluded during the Munich conference that "the foreign German danger" surpassed "the domestic Bolshevik danger."[39]

Although skeptical of Communism and distrustful of the Popular Front, Buré – Clemenceau's former collaborator – felt that the Soviet Union was a natural geopolitical ally of France and, despite the purges, a reliable military partner. Thus, he opposed Munich because – among other reasons – it excluded the Soviets from the table. His reading of *Mein Kampf* reinforced his belief that Hitler would attempt to implement *Lebensraum*. Buré thought that the anti-Communism of the so-called French nationalists was merely a mask for their defeatism. He attacked those who falsely claimed that the defenders of the Czechs were in the pay of Moscow and accused them of naïveté regarding the intentions of Mussolini and Hitler. According to Buré, the Führer cleverly used his anti-Communism to ruin the Franco-Soviet and the Franco-Czech pacts. Much of the right seemed more determined to assail "the war party" of Communists and neo-Jacobins than to check Nazi aspirations in central Europe.[40]

Buré tartly condemned the pacifism of a large part of the Socialist party. During the Spanish Civil War he had urged the democracies to intervene on the side of the Republic to demonstrate their willingness to stop fascist aggression. Buré recognized that Hitler was not "quite normal" and that by agreeing to British mediation during the Czech crisis, France was forced to follow an appeasing Great Britain. Buré's opinion was seconded by Georges Boris, director of *La Lumière* and a collaborator of Léon Blum. Boris opposed the Munich Agreement much more vehemently than Blum and was more accurate about Nazism, which he asserted could not be assuaged by concessions since it believed that "happiness lies not in well-being, but in the sense of collective power." He was also more critical of the forty-hour week than the Socialist leader.[41]

Kérillis – the deputy of Neuilly, a wealthy Paris suburb – defended the Czechoslovak Republic and its control of the Sudetenland against those who wanted to create a neutral Czech state on the Swiss model. He dismissed the Swiss comparison because, unlike the Sudetenland, the German cantons of Switzerland did not wish to attach themselves to Hitler's Germany. Furthermore, according to Kérillis, the Czech ally was essential for French security since it put major German cities within reach of future French aircraft bases on Czech soil. The defense of the Czechs was the defense of France, and thus he rejected all supposed solutions such as autonomy, plebiscite, and neutralization. Kérillis passionately objected to abandoning an ally to which France was linked by commitments "declared inescapable and sacred." The Munich accord meant that France had renounced its venerable policy of blocking German expansion by bolstering Eastern allies. Munich freed 30 to 40 German divisions for potential use against France, which, he knew from his reading of *Mein Kampf*, Hitler wanted to crush. Kérillis argued that the Führer had violated all agreements and reasoned that an alliance of France, the United Kingdom, and the Soviet Union could defeat the Germans. Furthermore, he also supported de Gaulle's ideas for a more mobile defense. Kérillis asserted that even though the Soviet regime repulsed him, he "would not allow the bourgeois in him to speak louder than the patriot." Munich was "an immense moral and material disaster" which affirmed Nazi hegemony. Nazi anti-Semitism and anti-Communism sowed discord within the democracies, but fascism itself was "a step toward a monstrous communism" rather than a barrier against the latter. Like other conservative antifascists, Kérillis saw fascism as revolutionary. In response, the extreme right – in some ways, his natural political family – accused him of being in the pay of Jews and Communists.[42]

Kérillis, Buré, and Pertinax disputed the argument – shared by Flandin, Bergery, and prominent industrialists, such as Auguste Detoeuf – that Hitler, once dominant in Europe, would permit France to be master of its own empire. Kérillis called the retreat into the empire an "indefensible absurdity," given German-Italian cooperation. He deduced that only a strong France could defend the empire and that the Reich would never renounce its desire for colonies. Kérillis wished to combat the German menace with an authoritarian republic in the Clemenceau tradition that would avoid both communism and fascism.[43]

Colonel Charles de Gaulle became closely associated with the precocious antifascist Paul Reynaud in the late 1930s. Reynaud was an opponent not only of Hitler but also – even rarer for a French rightist – of Mussolini. De Gaulle encountered members of Reynaud's circle in the salon of Émile Mayer, an army colonel of Jewish origin, who greatly influenced de Gaulle's thinking on military and world affairs. Reynaud supported de Gaulle's ideas for a more mobile French army, and both believed that the Maginot line would ultimately prove ineffective against German tanks and artillery. Opposing German expansionism was the only way to protect France and its empire. Thus in 1935 both men supported the Franco-Soviet pact. For de Gaulle, it was "a question of surviving" against rapidly growing German power. He would never forget how Third Republic politicians – including both anti-Communist conservatives and Socialist pacifists – wasted the vital Russian alliance which could have saved Czechoslovakia and perhaps French security in Europe in 1938. De Gaulle detested the Soviet regime, but – unlike many of his fellow officers – he did not think France had the means of refusing Russian help. He understood that "clever" Nazi propaganda had seduced many "worthy" French people into believing that Hitler had no designs on their country and that the Führer would be satisfied with domination of central Europe and the Ukraine. Therefore, he contested Munich: "Without a fight we are surrendering to the insolent demands of the Germans, and we are handing our allies the Czechs to the common enemy." He decried German and Italian propaganda in French "nationalist" publications: "The French, like fools, utter cries of joy [about the Munich Agreement]... Little by little we are growing accustomed to withdrawal and humiliation, so much so that it is becoming second nature to us... France has ceased to be a great nation." He asserted that German and Italian money had corrupted the French press, which terrorized its public. Nor did De Gaulle share the French intelligence community's overestimation of German military strength. To limit the damage from Munich, he wholeheartedly but without illusions supported France's Polish ally in the fall of 1939. Although retaining deep-seated reservations about the Third Republic's parliamentary democracy, as the war approached De Gaulle edged closer to the Christian democracy of the diminutive party Ligue de la Jeune République. During the hostilities, prominent Gaullists and Resistance fighters would emerge from its ranks.[44]

5 Counterrevolutionary Antifascism Alone, 1939–1940

The Consequences of Prague's Fall

France and Great Britain forged the development of a combative counterrevolutionary antifascism that became dominant in those two nations after Germany's invasion of Czechoslovakia in March 1939. The German conquest of Czechoslovakia shattered almost all British and French appeasers' faith in the reasonable intentions of the Nazi regime and undermined their pacifism toward Germany. As long as Nazism was a system for governing only Germans, they tolerated and accepted it. The occupation of Prague showed that Nazi aims were the domination of non-German peoples and neighboring countries, not self-determination for supposedly victimized Germans. The Prague occupation destroyed the faith, voiced continuously by Chamberlain and others, that Hitler's ambitions were limited. In addition, the Prague invasion was a military operation, not a result of negotiations as was the annexation of the Sudetenland. The Western powers were more than willing to concede German expansionism in the east if it were peaceful and limited, but they objected strongly to a *coup de main*. German aggression against Czechoslovakia mobilized – even if hesitantly – many former pacifists. They concluded that fascism had become more repulsive than war and that Hitler had to be stopped. Some of the most committed peace promotors admitted that Nazism in power would produce "a new Dark Age." Partisans of collective security and the League of Nations increased their commitment to an armed antifascism. The advocates of business as usual with Nazi Germany, who had bet on the progressive "moderation" of the regime, were discredited.[1]

The Prague invasion taught many the meaning of fascism and the revolutionary nature of Hitler's foreign policy. The famous war correspondent G. L. Steer – who won an international reputation for his pioneering reporting on the bombing of Guernica – wrote, "the Czech state alone presents in 24 hours more loot than all the [former] African colonies of Germany combined can offer during 10 years of Nazi rule." As both

Communist and non-Communist analysts had predicted, the occupation of Czechoslovakia meant the loss of 35 well-equipped Czech divisions and the German acquisition of large reserves of foreign currency and gold. The Reich's successful short wars against Poland and then France relied significantly on the German seizure in March 1939 of war materials produced by the Czech Skoda works. In the months that followed the Prague coup, a clear majority of the Dominions – Canada, Australia, South Africa, and New Zealand – became more willing to fight the Axis. The Dominions had been strong backers of appeasement and had refused to guarantee Czech security, but after Prague they supported a tougher stance against Germany. The Nazi regime's refusal to accept what an isolationist and pro-appeasement Canada considered Chamberlain's unceasing efforts for peace convinced that country to endorse British firmness. Commonwealth pilots, who often trained in Canada, would volunteer in significant numbers to combat in the RAF.[2]

British newspapers, notably the previously pro-appeasement *The Times* – whose editor had blamed French and British errors for the rise of Hitler – prepared readers for war. British public opinion keenly resisted a second Munich and remained – unlike their stance in World War I – belligerently anti-German until the end of the conflict. A poll taken shortly before Munich showed that 67 percent opposed concessions to dictatorships, and the Prague invasion must have increased that number substantially. After the Munich Agreement was signed, 71 percent of the British public said they would chose to fight Germany rather than return its former colonies. British opinion polls showed that Germany was the least liked country in the world. Labourites – especially Attlee and Dalton – insisted that the government ally with the Soviet Union to defend Eastern Europe. Trade-union leaders – Citrine and Bevin – took a tough line on German, Italian, and Japanese expansionism and, unlike the leaders of the powerful metallurgical unions, were relatively early advocates of rearmament. In contrast to the beginning of World War I, the British prepared themselves for a long war. Pro-German activity, which was often based on a belief in a Jewish conspiracy to secure world domination, was limited to marginal strands of British fascism. Hitler's (and later Mussolini's) regime seemed to have underestimated this overwhelmingly anti-German attitude and mistakenly believed that Britain was unwilling and wholly unprepared for war. The Nazi leadership calculated that the decadent British would not risk losing their empire and Commonwealth in a new conflict with Germany. Chamberlain's refusal to include Churchill in his government until after the war erupted contributed to German misjudgment of British antifascism.[3]

For increasing numbers both in and outside of parliament, Nazi aggression in March 1939 meant the failure of appeasement policies.

The previously anti-Versailles and anti-Czech *Observer* became among the most ardent anti-Nazi papers. It concluded that *Mein Kampf* should be considered as a true blueprint for Nazi policy rather than the Führer's youthful indiscretion. The skilled metallurgical workers' unions that had been reluctant to rearm as late as 1938 cooperated with the government in early 1939 to promote weapons production against fascism. The United Kingdom initiated its first-ever peacetime conscription immediately after the Italian invasion of Albania on 7 April 1939, which aroused the hostility of the whole British press and dispelled the illusions of Tories who hoped that Mussolini could be detached from Hitler. Both Conservatives and Labour agreed that the draft would reassure the French that their army would have an Allied expeditionary force on the continent. British Communists opposed the growing consensus and interpreted conscription not as a sign of stiffening resistance to Nazism but as part of a plan to impose fascist fetters on British citizens. To the Communists, Chamberlain's government was proto-fascist. Like much of the French left (including many Socialists) during its Popular Front, British Communists regarded the domestic right, not the fascists, as the more redoubtable enemy. The CPGB combated capitalism, which could never be truly antifascist.[4]

The firm guarantees given to Poland and Romania in March and April 1939 showed that British policy and opinion had changed. Chamberlain judged the rightist authoritarian states of Poland and Romania (the world's fourth largest oil producer) more deserving of support than leftist revolutionary Russia, and he led his cabinet to protect them and ignore the Soviet Union. Analysts of various political persuasions have customarily considered this guarantee a mistake because it limited the bargaining position of the Western Allies, further alienated the Soviet Union from the democracies, and drove Stalin into Hitler's arms. Hitler himself was surprised by French and British determination to defend Poland. However, the Polish guarantee is understandable in the context of the struggle between revolutionary and counterrevolutionary antifascists. The latter wanted to stop further German aggression and potential Soviet incursions against conservative republics. Defying strategic but not political logic, British and French conservative antifascists, including military leaders, elected reactionary and religious Poland and Romania over revolutionary and anticlerical Russia. Furthermore, Chamberlain – who remained an unenthusiastic antifascist – feared that a Western alliance with the Soviet Union would rule out any last-minute settlement with the Axis powers. The prime minister remained reluctant to include Churchill in the cabinet since his presence might dissuade Hitler from opening future negotiations. Chamberlain rejected Churchill's argument that an agreement with Russia was insurance against a German-Russian alliance and a safeguard against German expansionism. Chamberlain seemed to imagine that Franco's Spain – literally hungry and exhausted by its own civil war – would be a more effective ally than the Soviet Union. The British proved willing to defend the anti-Soviet Polish and Romanian states, not the pro-Western but insufficiently anti-Communist Czech one. For their part, the Soviets suspected that the British guarantee to Poland was an attempt to direct German aggression to the Baltic States and therefore provoke a German-Soviet conflict.[5]

In France, by the beginning of 1939 and certainly after the Prague invasion, Prime Minister Daladier envisaged that the only option was to prepare for war. In early 1939 the cabinet significantly increased defense spending and coordinated military planning with the United Kingdom. The French post-Munich and post–40-hour-week economic recovery was remarkable, and by June 1939 unemployment had nearly disappeared, overcoming the difficulties of the Great Depression. French war preparations of 1938–1940 far surpassed the efforts of the previous prewar period of 1912–1914. In February 1939 over 70 percent of the French public supported resistance to future German or Italian aggression. After the occupation of Prague, the figure rose to 77 percent. Before September 1938, Daladier's correspondence had been equally divided over further resistance to German aggression, but after the occupation of Prague 90 to 100 percent of mail urged resistance. French police reports indicated that as early as September 1938 opinion accepted the idea of an inevitable war and was willing to fight it. After Prague, an overwhelming majority of French politicians on both left and right seconded a policy of firmness against the fascist powers.[6]

Hitler's violation of the Munich Agreement shocked many of those who had supported it, including Blum. Pacifists in the SFIO lost ground to those, such as Blum, more committed to national defense. The entire rural right supported war preparations. Veterans' organizations, which represented large sectors of the lower middle classes, became firmly antifascist. World War II would also be a "Great Patriotic War" in the West. In the spring of 1939, representatives of heavy industry and big business – Comité des Forges and the Confédération du patronat – rejected German demands on Poland. In June 1939, 76 percent of the French polled stated that a German attempt to take Danzig in the disputed Polish Corridor should be halted by force.[7]

A few, usually on the extreme right, maintained their criticism of "warmongers." They were reinforced by the Vatican's silence over the invasion of Prague (and later of Catholic Poland), which showed its conciliatory acceptance of Nazi aggression. The Vatican identified communism with war and tended to ignore the more obvious equation of fascism

and war. Rome largely overlooked the potential of counterrevolutionary antifascism. Despite Vatican neutrality, French antiwar sentiment
remained minimal, and pacifist demonstrations achieved little success.
Even the extreme-right party, Doriot's PPF, sharpened its opposition to
Germany, although it maintained its intransigent and counterproductive
anti-Communism.[8]

After the Prague invasion the French parliament – like its British counterpart – pressured the government to take vigorous anti-German action.
With only a few exceptions, parliamentary deputies agreed that no
more Munichs would be accepted. The Chamber debate on 17 March
1939 showed the nearly universal desire for a French policy of firmness
(*fermeté*). On that day, the Communist deputy, Gabriel Péri, remarked
that the conservative and anti-Communist Czechoslovak Republic had
been crushed. The *munichois* and defender of the forty-hour week,
the Socialist Ludovic-Oscar Frossard, concluded that the right of self-
determination had transformed itself in German hands into *Lebensraum*.
Kérillis charged that during his six months in office Daladier was responsible for "two diplomatic Sedans [the French defeat during the Franco-
Prussian War]" – the Munich accord and the German occupation of
Prague.[9]

As in the United Kingdom, the majority of the working class
remained – to varying degrees – patriotic. Perhaps the gradually improving living standards for workers in the first third of the twentieth century explained their national commitment during both world wars. In
May 1939 the *bellicistes* dominated the pacifists at the SFIO's Nantes
Congress, which supported rearmament and solid alliances with the
United Kingdom and the Soviet Union. French Communists continued to defend "bourgeois democracy" in the spring of 1939 and urged
workers to labor, if necessary, 60 hours per week – the legal norm in
defense industries since March 1939. At the end of 1939 the 60-hour
workweek prevailed in defense industries, where the Sunday holiday was
often eliminated. French armaments production made great strides during the "Phoney War" (*drôle de guerre*) from September 1939 to June
1940. After the signing of the Hitler-Stalin pact in August 1939, the mass
of workers – including many new female wage earners in defense-related
factories – refused to follow Communist revolutionary pacifism.[10]

Until the Hitler-Stalin pact, antifascism revived the *union sacrée* against
an enemy which was both a national and an ideological menace. The
Italian occupation of Albania in April 1939 eliminated any remaining
French hopes for a diplomatic arrangement with Fascist Italy. Both the
United Kingdom and France agreed to guarantee Greek independence
against a possible Italian attack. Nevertheless, between September 1939

and June 1940, the Allies were more anti-Nazi than anti-Fascist since they attempted to encourage Italy's neutrality. Mussolini, though, could not continue to resist the attractions of the Axis, which would offer him many more opportunities for expansion than the Allies. The invasion of Albania bound Italy ever closer to Germany. In September 1939, the Führer wrote to the Duce, "if National Socialist Germany were to be destroyed by the Western Democracies, Fascist Italy also would face a hard future. I personally was aware that the futures of our two regimes were bound up, and I know that you, Duce, are of exactly the same opinion."[11] The Führer proved correct in June 1940 when the easy pickings resulting from the fall of France enticed Italy into the war. If the Duce had not entered the hostilities and had limited his imperialist appetite, he might have survived the conflict, much like his ally Franco, whose regime aided the Axis but remained officially either neutral or nonbelligerent throughout the conflict.

The Hitler-Stalin Pact

The Soviet-German nonaggression treaty of 23 August 1939 was a consequence of the West's estrangement of the Soviet Union. The Soviet Union might have preferred an alliance with Britain and France, but their perceived partiality toward the Third Reich wrecked any deal. During negotiations, foreign minister Halifax decided he was too busy to go to Moscow in person, and Chamberlain's intention may have been less to arrive at an agreement with the Soviet Union than to deflect criticism that he was snubbing a potential ally. In contrast to the Germans, whose foreign minister negotiated personally in Moscow, both France and Britain – disregarding warnings by Churchill, Eden, and Lloyd George that construction of the Soviet alliance should be the highest priority – sent low-ranking delegations to the Kremlin. The democracies' shabby treatment of a great power irritated Stalin. Furthermore, appeasement of Germany was not entirely dead. On 19 March, a few days after the Prague coup, Chamberlain wrote, "I never accept the view that war is inevitable." Despite his guarantee to Poland on 31 March, he still hoped to negotiate with Hitler. In May 1939, he regretted that détente between Germany and Britain would not arrive "as long as the Jews obstinately go on refusing to shoot Hitler." Chamberlain could never surmount his distrust of the Russians and accept Churchill's alternative of a grand antifascist alliance.[12]

Unlike Chamberlain, Daladier and Bonnet believed after the Prague coup that the Soviet alliance was necessary to deter Hitler and preserve peace. Even though Daladier underrated the capabilities of the

Red Army, despite its successes in skirmishes with Japan, high-ranking French officials realized that only a coalition with the Soviet Union could offer the two-front war needed to defend France. France's position as a continental power with Eastern European allies made it more vulnerable than its British ally to a German attack and more willing to negotiate seriously with the Soviet Union. In August 1939, the French were desperate enough to overcome fears of communism and the anti-Soviet attitude of their own general staff to agree to Soviet demands for Red Army passage through Poland, but Britain – once again ignoring the advice of Churchill's anti-appeasement group – vetoed the French concession. The French, of course, were bound to the conservative great power, not the revolutionary one. Even in late August, after the signing of the Hitler-Stalin pact, Daladier and Chamberlain still aspired to negotiate with the Germans over Poland. Yet British ministers rejected an Italian proposal for an early September conference that might have led to a new Munich, a possibility which their parliament and public opinion would have rejected.[13]

Throughout the 1930s, the dominant French and British elites dreaded the mutually reinforcing couple of war and communism. Conservative antifascists who led the Western democracies in 1939 remained halfhearted about a Soviet alliance, although in retrospect it is clear that the Germans could only have been defeated in 1939–1940 by an encirclement which included the Soviet Union. Daladier and Bonnet hated communism as much as war and continued to reason that the latter might allow the former to dominate Europe. Their attitude explains why they ultimately preferred alliances with the weaker but anti-Communist states of Poland and Romania rather than the massive Soviet one. Their anti-revolutionism also illuminates much about the rapid capitulation of France in June 1940 when French elites feared a new Paris Commune, the urban revolution of 1871 that had attempted to prevent Prussian domination of France.

French and British decision makers were correct that a Russian alliance would have meant Communist expansion in Europe since the Soviets demanded assurances that their troops could pass through Poland and Romania. Those nations suspected with reason that the Red Army would remain on their soil, impose a Communist system, and incorporate them into the Soviet empire. Franco-British negotiations in June 1939 to achieve a Soviet alliance against Nazi Germany had failed precisely because both French and particularly British elites, backed by public opinion, had refused to allow the Russians to dominate these neighboring states. The Soviets insisted that they be able to move troops into Poland, regardless of the wishes of the Poles themselves, but in 1939 counterrevolutionary antifascists would not permit this extension of the revolution and vetoed the sacrifice of yet another conservative Republic. France had a full military alliance with Poland and was not prepared to permit Germany to dominate its most important remaining ally in Eastern Europe. The French were satisfied when the British finally committed themselves to Poland. Both nations also agreed to guarantee oil-rich Romania.[14]

Although a boon for the Germans and a bane for the French and British, the Hitler-Stalin pact – like the end of the Spanish Civil War – had the consequence of making antifascism more respectable in the Atlantic democracies. The Nazis lost the argument, which was still being proffered in early 1939, that they were the last bulwark against Communism. Hitler did not conceal his personal admiration for Stalin who – like himself – had no time for potentially rebellious generals. Signing an agreement that permitted the Soviet Union to occupy large parts of Eastern Europe discredited Nazi anti-Communism, which had been its principal appeal to conservatives in the West. Reaction against the pact united all parties in the House of Commons to fulfill Britain's obligations to Poland. The French right was happy to return to its "principled anti-Communism" and its "opportunistic anti-Germanism." The perception of the "totalitarian" identification of the National Socialist and Soviet regimes increased dramatically. The Hitler-Stalin agreement promoted both fascist and Communist expansion and nullified de facto the Anti-Comintern Pact (1936) of Germany, Italy, and Japan.[15]

Stalin calculated that Germany was much more useful as a benevolent neutral than Britain and France as allies and that Hitler might be undermining the capitalist system consciously or unconsciously. Therefore, he rejected Roosevelt's advice not to sign a deal with Hitler. If the Soviets had chosen the Western alliance, they might have been compelled to fight both Germany and Japan, as the United States would do after 1941. The Hitler-Stalin agreement assured them of either peace or a war limited to one front. Furthermore, the pact allowed the German occupation of western Poland, thus tying down Polish troops which could have been deployed against the Red Army and preventing a Polish retreat to the west. The pact had the added benefit of spreading the Soviet model into eastern Poland, Latvia, Estonia, and Bessarabia, an enormous advance for their revolution that, in Communist eyes, was by definition antifascist. Loyal Communists saw Soviet expansion as a great victory for socialism.[16]

Hitler offered the Russians what they could not get from the West. Both the Aryan and Communist revolutions swelled at the expense of the smaller conservative states. Stalin stated to Georgi Dimitrov, secretary-general of the Comintern, "what harm would have been caused if, as a result of the dismemberment of Poland, we had extended the socialist system to new territories and populations?" The Soviets did not separate revolution from territorial security. In their Polish zone they spread "socialism in one country" by abolishing private property, nationalizing businesses, and requiring all former Polish citizens to register as Soviet citizens. Given their vast territorial gains, the Soviets concluded that the Western powers were more of an obstacle to the world revolution than Nazi Germany. The Soviet struggle against fascism was ultimately a fight against capitalism. In 1944–1945, when the Red Army defeated Germany in the East, it would export its revolution even more extensively to Europe.[17]

The Allies remained suspicious of Soviet expansionism but avoided declaring war on the Soviet Union to prevent the further consolidation of a Nazi-Soviet alliance. In effect, they adopted a Germany First strategy. Avoiding war with the Soviet Union made strategic sense and satisfied the opinion of those on the left who were sympathetic to the Soviet experiment. In the first half of 1940 the British public prolonged its hope that the Soviets would switch sides, even though after the signing of the Hitler-Stalin pact, trade between the democracies and the Soviet Union dropped precipitously. To avoid a repetition of the killing on the Western front during World War I, the French were more willing to gamble and extend the conflict to the Soviet Union by bombing Caucasian oil fields, but the more realistic and prudent British ally vetoed these plans.[18]

The Phoney War

Chamberlain waited two days following the German invasion of Poland to declare war. Even after September 3, the date of the British and French entry, the British prime minister proved an unwilling warrior who was hesitant to wage total war and contemplated an armistice if France fell. Hoping that supposed "moderates" within the Nazi regime and (capitalist) economic reason might prevail, he continued to search for an accommodation with Germany until February 1940. The ineffectiveness of the governments of both Britain and France during the "Phoney War" has put their commitment to antifascism into question. Yet both governments sustained the conflict, however ineptly. Much more accommodating to the enemy were Communists, anarchists, pacifists, and extreme rightists who hoped for a peace offer from Hitler. Furthermore, mainstream French parliamentarians – Laval and Flandin – and ministers –

Bonnet and Anatole de Monzie – pushed their desires to revive appease-ment. A number of pacifists from both left and right employed the argu-ment that Jews – such as Blum – were advocating war to save their co-religionists from Nazism. Nonetheless, anti-Semitic pacifists remained a somewhat muzzled minority until the fall of France. In fact, in April 1939 the Daladier government issued a decree-law punishing incitement in the media against Jews.[19]

Following the German invasion of Poland, opposition to the perceived inaction of Chamberlain's government developed quickly. The prime minister was unable to broaden his government to include the left, which not only distrusted him but "regarded him as something evil." In turn, Chamberlain saw Labour as virtual agents of Moscow. Given his reputa-tion as an uncompromising anti-Nazi with close links to the opposition, Churchill was acceptable to Labour, whose press had lionized him in "a Churchill boom." In early May 1940, after Norway came under German control, Chamberlain's conduct of the war disenchanted many MPs – including large numbers of Conservatives. Churchill was then named prime minister and composed the most broadly based government that Britain had ever known. Labourites and trade unionists became powerful ministers and nearly equal partners in a de facto corporatist arrangement which refused a compromise peace. Churchill would also include Cham-berlain and his followers in the cabinet. In June 1940 Churchill told the former prime minister that he had no intention of "seeking scapegoats" since "we must stand or fall together." He nixed anti-Chamberlain cam-paigns in the Commons and in the press. Churchill's antifascism showed an inclusiveness which focused on defeating the enemy.[20]

A similar spirit of unity briefly appeared in France, where the PCF initially participated in the "union of the French nation against Hitler's aggression." Its deputies voted war credits on 2–3 September 1939 and were willing to serve in the armed forces. However, in the second half of September, after the Red Army entered Poland, Daladier banned the party for its close links with the Soviet Union. Following the Moscow line, the PCF then condemned the war as "imperialist, reactionary, and unjust." At the war's beginning, Stalin believed that the conflict would allow the Soviet Union to profit from capitalist infighting and made few distinctions among "counterrevolutionary" belligerent capitalist nations. Fearing arrest, French party leader Maurice Thorez deserted his army unit for Moscow. At the end of October 1939, a clandestine issue of the PCF newspaper, L'Humanité, attempted to "destroy the legend of the alleged antifascist character of the war." It argued that French soldiers would not be dying in combat for their fatherland but rather for bankers and industrialists.[21]

The PCF praised Stalin's ability to split the Soviet Union's capitalist foes and denounced "the imperialist war" between British and German capital. Communists insisted that, unlike the Spanish Civil War, the new conflict was not an antifascist fight. Instead, they frequently circulated the slogan "revolutionary struggle against the imperialist war." The PCF adopted a position of "revolutionary pacifism" and in November 1939 demanded "immediate peace." The latter slogan dismissed the notion of a just war and, curiously, anticipated the Franco-German armistice of June 1940. Like the appeasers of the 1930s and their Vichy successors, the PCF and Comintern leadership prioritized pacifism over antifascism and in October 1939 urged the government to favor Hitler's peace plan. The party encouraged its militants to fraternize with German workers, if not soldiers. The real foe of Communists was Anglo-French capitalism, not Nazism. Repeating the pattern of the Popular Front and Vichy itself, combating the internal enemy – in this case, capitalist reaction – took priority over the more dangerous external one. Leninists returned to their pre–Popular Front position which argued the inseparability of fascism, capitalism, imperialism, and war.[22]

During the *drôle de guerre* the PCF became the most important antiwar organization in France, and its militants – like their Bolshevik mentors – hoped they could eventually turn the war into a revolution. In literature designed for soldiers in February and March 1940, they broadcasted the venerable slogan, "the Soviets everywhere." The French army fought this "revolutionary propaganda" by preparing to punish authors who attacked the army, nation, and Republican institutions. On 9 January 1940 four PCF deputies rejected "*union sacrée*" in a war which was "in the exclusive interest of the mafia of capitalists who fleece the country." "M. Adolf-Édouard Daladier" led this fight to defend capitalism. Socialist pacifists used similar sloganeering to identify "Daladierism" with "Hitlerism." On 16 May 1940, a clandestine issue of *L'Humanité* declared: "When two gangsters are battling each other, honest people do not have to rescue the one who claims that the other one hit him below the belt." The PCF attempted to undermine British antifascism by praising worker strikes in the United Kingdom and its colonies.[23]

Another major consequence of the Hitler-Stalin pact was the Soviet invasion of Finland at the end of November 1939, which the democracies and their public opinion categorically condemned. Allied anti-Communism competed with their antifascism. British Labour and French Socialist leaders proved much more supportive of the conservative but democratic Finnish republic than the revolutionary Spanish one. The British and French governments were more interested in helping the Finns combat Communism than they had been in aiding the Poles against Nazism. Prudently, though, the Allies did not wish to encourage a full-blown Nazi-Soviet alliance and ultimately refused to extend their war to the Russians. Nevertheless, after January 1940, the limited Allied assistance to Finland convinced French and British Communists with some justification that the war had assumed an anti-Soviet character. In February 1940 when French Communists believed that French war materiel might be used in a pro-Finnish campaign against the Soviet Union, they called for industrial sabotage. This subversive appeal had little effect on workers, and after the Soviets successfully concluded the Finnish war in March 1940, the party toned down its antiwar propaganda.[24]

Despite government repression, the PCF's approximately 3,000 to 5,000 militants rooted themselves in French proletarian society by championing popular demands for better wages and benefits. The Communist fight for improvement of material conditions in the factories won a following among wage laborers. Free from the obligations of *union sacrée*, Communists defended workers' struggles more than any other group. They encouraged a revolutionary or pacifist slowdown of arms production and effectively hindered the war effort. In March 1940, French authorities concluded, "[Communist] revolutionary propaganda always plays a role in [military] underproduction."[25] A March 1940 report found a decline of productivity in railroad workshops where Communist influence was formidable, whereas productivity increased in private firms where the PCF presence was weaker. Yet the decrease of worker productivity was just as likely due to dissatisfaction with higher work rhythms and a deterioration of working conditions. Militants opposed the highly unpopular – at least among wage earners – emergency workweek of 60 hours and extra taxes on workers' salaries. Just as Spanish officials politicized the proletarian discontent of the May Days of 1937 as a "fascist" plot against the Republic, French authorities likewise blamed "Communists" for resistance to work during the Phoney War.

French Communists hoped and expected to take power after the exhaustion of the two warring "imperialist" camps. Their enemies were French, British, and German (but not Soviet) imperialism. During the *drôle de guerre* the PCF leadership – like the Soviet Union – combated conservative antifascism more than Nazism. In this period the PCF adopted a position similar to that of the SFIO during the Popular Front: It wanted peace with the Germans and better social and economic conditions for the masses. Also analogous to the Popular Front, PCF antifascism focused on fighting what it considered domestic fascism, which was relatively feeble. The party was less interested in battling the more robust foreign variety. As late as May 1941, it continued to condemn "the imperialist war," and its clandestine *L'Humanité* denounced de Gaulle as a reactionary lackey of London financiers.

Origins of the French Resistance

France's defensive strategy and conventional military expectations rendered it unable to halt the war of movement which Hitler unleashed against Western Europe in May–June 1940. The German army surprised the enemy with the speed of its advance and its uncanny ability to perform the unanticipated. The German "shock and awe" campaign successfully employed tanks and planes to kill and capture French troops and their commanders. As French communications and discipline collapsed, unnerved officers and soldiers – many of whom were inexperienced reservists – fled to attempt to regroup in the panicky rear. Up to 10 million civilians joined them to seek refuge behind the quickly moving fronts. "They shall not pass" accurately described the tenacity of the French army in World War I, but not in World War II. During May–June 1940 the French armed forces suffered 100,000 killed and missing in action compared to only 49,000 for its German enemy. The Germans took more than 1 million French soldiers prisoner during the brief Western campaign, ten times as many as the number of German prisoners captured during the Battle of Stalingrad. Pacifism once again overwhelmed antifascism.[26]

Prominent counterrevolutionary antifascists became as demoralized as their troops. On 16 June their leader, Paul Reynaud, resigned as prime minister. The new government rejected General de Gaulle's plan of continuing the fight with the help of the British – and eventually, it was projected, the Americans – from the French Empire in North Africa. With Allied backing, the still undefeated French fleet and the remaining air force could have attacked Italy and its overseas empire. The Allied assault on the weakest link of the Axis might have forced Germany to defend its Mediterranean ally in a second front which would have diverted resources from the Battle of Britain (and potentially delayed the assault on the Soviet Union). However, the new French rulers refused to remain in the war and establish a government in exile in London, as had other European nations occupied by Germany. Instead, the newly chosen premier, Marshal Pétain, was certain that the French defeat foreshadowed an equally rapid British downfall and rejected joining a counterrevolutionary antifascist coalition. Just as Daladier's government had abandoned a solemn treaty with Czechoslovakia, Pétain decided to ignore the agreement with the United Kingdom and sign an armistice giving Germany direct control of two-thirds of France. His Vichy regime was named after the capital of the southern third of the country left unoccupied by the Germans, who calculated that avoiding the establishment of a French government in exile in London or North Africa was worth granting their former enemy limited autonomy. The terms of the armistice confirmed former Prime Minister Reynaud's 12 June argument against those who sought an agreement with Germany: "You are taking Hitler for Wilhelm I, the old gentleman who took Alsace-Lorraine from us, and that was that. But Hitler is Genghis Khan."[27]

Despite its capitulation, Vichy gained prestige among the rising number of former counterrevolutionary antifascists by preventing a repetition of the Paris Commune and avoiding guerrilla warfare against the Germans, which both de Gaulle and Churchill initially favored. Powerful fears stimulated the demand for an immediate restoration of order. Tall tales of revolution flourished, and at the nadir of the French collapse in mid-June, Supreme Commander Maxime Weygand reported to the French cabinet the bogus story that Communists had seized power in Paris. With the displacement of millions of soldiers and civilians, France seemed to have descended into anarchy. The specter of further physical destruction of the *patrie* and the dissolution of its empire was so disturbing that even those who had felt that negotiating with the Germans meant dishonor nonetheless decided to work for Vichy at its foundation.[28]

Backed by the physical and political force of the defeated military and intact civil administration, Pétain's government restored order and implemented its own counterrevolution, which, like the Spanish Nationalist regime, camouflaged itself as a "National Revolution." The Vichy slogan was "Work, Family, and Fatherland." Assisted by clerical, conservative, and even some center-left forces, it overturned many of the freedoms guaranteed by the Revolution of 1789. At the same time, the Vichy regime rebuffed its former British ally, which wanted France to continue the war from North Africa or London, and embarked on a policy of "collaboration" – a word that Pétain himself coined in this context and which passed into every European language – with the German occupier. Pétain's delusion that war veterans could negotiate an "honorable" peace with Nazism continued to dominate his thinking. The goal of his regime was to destroy internal enemies, not foreign foes.

Convinced of an imminent British defeat, Vichy myopically dismissed the possibility of a conservative antifascism, led by the United Kingdom and joined eventually by the United States. Both Atlantic nations became especially concerned about the fate of the French navy, the world's fourth largest, which possessed some of the biggest and fastest vessels in existence. The Anglo-Saxon powers feared that Axis possession of this fleet would give it dominance in the Atlantic. A US Naval Intelligence report of 17 June 1940 asserted, "the combined naval power of Germany, Italy and France would be about one third greater than that of Britain, and greater also than that of the United States even if the American fleet were to be brought back from the Pacific."[29] In fact, inspired by the British, the Americans warned the French government that before concluding any armistice it should take steps to guarantee that its navy did not fall into enemy hands. If that occurred, the Americans warned, France would forfeit any friendship or goodwill of the United States. Assuming the quick defeat of the United Kingdom, the French navy chief, Admiral François Darlan, refused to sail his fleet to British or American waters, including the French possession of Martinique. In response, on 3–4 July the British destroyed approximately one-third of the tonnage of the French fleet at Mers-el-Kebir (Algeria). The operation, which killed nearly 1,300 French service members, caused the severing of diplomatic relations between the two former allies. However, it rallied the British public behind a determined Churchill and helped convince Americans, including President Roosevelt, that the United Kingdom would not surrender. Subsequently, British and American pressure, plus French willingness to scuttle their ships if the Axis powers attempted to seize them, prevented the shift of naval supremacy to the fascist coalition.

The fall of France profoundly weakened counterrevolutionary antifascism by eliminating one of its major protagonists. Images of the German occupation of Paris shocked and alarmed official and public opinion in the remaining democracies, including the United States. Whereas the Polish defeat was expected, the rapid French collapse was a global earthquake that unleashed philo-fascist counterrevolutions in Europe and the French Empire, while encouraging nationalists in the British Empire. It also raised the prestige of the Nazi model, notably among military officers throughout the world, the United States included. In Western Europe, naked aggression against small neutral nations – Norway, Denmark, Netherlands, Belgium, Luxembourg – and a great power, France, achieved unexpected success in the spring of 1940. As a result, Italy officially and enthusiastically joined the German camp, and Japan became increasingly pro-Axis. Believing fascism to be the wave of the future, the Franco regime was convinced of German victory and asked Hitler, who decided to satisfy Pétain, unsuccessfully for large parts of the French Empire in return for its full participation in the Axis. In September 1940, the Japanese signed the Tripartite Pact, their military alliance with Germany and Italy.[30]

The Germans expected the British to agree to a compromise peace once France had fallen. Yet even after Italy fully allied with Germany in June, the British under Churchill did not abandon their antifascist commitment or their rejection of an agreement with the Reich. The Nazis never comprehended the depth of commitment of British conservative antifascism, which they felt would compromise as had the German, Czech, French, and other conquered elites. The underestimation of the determination of their antifascist foes – first Britain and then the Soviet Union and United States – by the Axis powers and their collaborators was a fatal miscalculation that revealed blind trust in their own dynamism and in democratic decadence as well. Indeed, Hitler's invasion of the Soviet Union in June 1941 was a desperate response to the German inability to conquer Britain or force its antifascists to compromise. The German failure to wage a successful Blitzkrieg in the East in 1941 would allow the transatlantic antifascists at a time of their own choosing to bring their immense resources to bear against the Axis. Despite the fact that the multiple aggressions of Hitler's own regime were the source of the wartime unity of revolutionary and counterrevolutionary antifascists, the Führer never gave up hope of dividing this "unnatural alliance," just as he had divided his opponents on the left and right during his ascent to power.[31]

In Britain, the antifascist coalition remained popular, and during the first year of the war conscientious objection quickly fell to its lowest levels.[32] Official but selective tolerance helped to blunt pacifism as an effective force. Antiwar parties and candidates of the extreme left and right received very little electoral support. After the fall of France, London became the cosmopolitan capital of conservative international antifascism, with the BBC as its multilingual messenger. At the same time, the French withdrawal from the alliance made the war into a British national struggle for survival. The success of the Battle of Britain during the summer and autumn of 1940 ensured a global conflict in which the new European order imposed by the Axis would have no quick or easy final victory. Unlike Vichy, which rejected the continuation of the struggle from abroad after metropolitan France was conquered, the British government prepared to fight, if necessary, from Canada with the sympathy, if not support, of the United States. Even at the height of their conquests, the Axis could not hope to match Anglo-American dominance in the New World, which provided not only inexhaustible resources and reserves for the Allied war effort but also secure space and therefore unlimited time to regroup and recuperate in the face of Axis advances.

Furthermore, after the Depression large and small industrialists and agriculturists in the Dominions, Latin America, Africa, and the Indian subcontinent welcomed the new opportunities and profits that supplying the Allies would offer, even if these came at the cost of inflation that provoked famine in some areas of Africa and Asia. The British Empire with American backing provided multiple means to defeat the Axis in a war of attrition. British imperialists intended to fight the challenges of Germany, Italy, Japan, and possibly Spain to their possessions. These imperialists, who managed to maintain and mobilize their empire throughout the war, were joined by patriots, including large numbers of workers, who opposed the conquest of their country by foreigners, whether fascist or not.

The persistence of transatlantic conservative antifascism provided the window of opportunity for the relatively small number of French officials, including de Gaulle and Mandel, who rejected submission or reconciliation with the German victor. Churchill would have preferred the much better-known Mandel as the leader of French counterrevolutionary antifascism, but this French disciple of Clemenceau was unable to reach London. Unwilling to abandon France – in part because as a Jew he would be accused of desertion – Mandel would offer de Gaulle unconditional support. De Gaulle believed that "Anglo-Saxon" or conservative antifascism would ultimately triumph and escaped to London, where he continued the struggle to liberate France from the Nazi occupier. In addition to his patriotism and commitment to national greatness, de Gaulle also shared Churchill's combativeness and, most significantly, his analysis of World War II as a global conflict which the Axis was destined to lose. The Resistance leader would create his own Gaullist version of counterrevolution which – like Britain's and America's – was much less retrograde than the Vichy alternative. He was aware that French internal resistance could not liberate the nation and insisted on building an imperial state that would draw on the resources of transatlantic antifascism, which included the Dutch and Belgian governments in exile that also possessed their own overseas empires. Although de Gaulle is often considered an irredeemable and narrow nationalist, his desire for his country to stay in the war was so powerful that as France fell he was prepared to join a formal union of his nation with Great Britain.

De Gaulle's antifascism was based on a calculation of forces which transcended the Franco- and Eurocentric worldview of much of the French and, for that matter, continental political and military elites. Like Churchill, he reasoned that the United Kingdom could hold off Nazi Germany and that the United States would back the British. As in World War I, Anglo-American financial, industrial, agricultural, and naval power would eventually seal the fate of the German enemy. This analysis prevented him from accepting French defeat and conceding victory. His insight led him to break with his former sponsor, Reynaud, who like most politicians and military officers throughout the globe, believed that Britain would soon collapse. De Gaulle's deservedly famous declaration of 18 June 1940 on the BBC proclaimed to the French that space and time were on the side of the British, who were backed by the "immense and limitless industry" of the United States. France possessed its own "vast empire" from which it could continue the struggle against its enemies. Victory would be determined not by the political nature of regimes but rather by the application of overwhelming resources. This Gaullist synthesis of imperialism and patriotism launched the French Resistance. In de Gaulle's eyes, by accepting the armistice Pétain was a short-sighted "traitor."[33]

In June 1940, De Gaulle's views resonated with only a tiny number of his compatriots. Most viewed his departure as a sign of cowardice. Communists shared the Vichy perspective that German domination of Western Europe was inevitable and peace the only reasonable option. Socialists were largely passive, and the right commonly followed Pétain's collaborationism. Yet the few early Gaullists often came from the ranks of the traditionalist, if not antidemocratic, Catholic or extreme right, including career military personnel. In fact, some on the left – such as the Radical Pierre Cot, Minister of the Air during the Popular Front – would suspect de Gaulle of fascist tendencies.[34] The Resistance leader chose the Cross of Lorraine as the symbol of his movement to emphasize its fight against the paganism of the swastika. He and his Christian followers saw the battle against fascism in spiritual as much as political terms: "To resist was thus to wish to reestablish the old order with prewar values."[35] Nor were the conservative political tendencies of the Gaullists exceptional among the early leaders of the principal Resistance movements within France itself: "No socialist, syndicalist, or leftist initiated a major resistance movement in the South. Jean-Pierre Lévy of Franc-Tireur was not politically engaged; Henri Frenay, the instigator of Combat – although motivated by debates that agitated the leftist intelligentsia under the Popular Front – remained very marked by his conservative and Catholic environment; . . . and E. d'Astier of Vigerie, a prewar royalist, moved to the left only after he realized the ideological stakes of the conflict."[36]

Captain Frenay was not the only early Resister who approved of the Marshal's war against internal enemies, such as Freemasons. He and others – for instance, the middle-class Resistance group Organisation civile et militaire – also advocated a nonlethal French anti-Semitism which would limit "Jewish" influence less brutally than its German strain. Protesting against persecution of Jews, let alone rescuing them, was not a Resistance priority. In practice, civilian victims of the Axis – Jews, Gypsies, and Poles – were a burden, and very few officials in Allied nations wanted to make sacrifices for their benefit. Furthermore, a competition among victims emerged. At the end of 1942, his superiors discouraged the representative of the Polish government in exile, Jan Karski, from emphasizing the oppression of the Jews, which might distract attention from that of the Poles. Likewise, French Resisters were much more concerned with the deaths of their own comrades than anonymous Jewish sufferers.[37] This indifference was deepened by a wartime culture of heroes that gave more attention to patriotic warriors than to civilian victims.

The early entrance of various traditionalists in the Resistance rested on a simple patriotism: "to overcome the sordidness of defeat" and rid France of German control. The aristocratic former naval officer, Emmanuel d'Astier de la Vigerie – the future head of Libération-Sud, a politically ecumenical resistance movement founded in October–November 1940 – noted on 19 June 1940: "De Gaulle is right. Pétain and Weygand are wrong. Their demand [for an armistice] is ignominious." The sporadically anti-Semitic playwright Jean Giraudoux viewed the armistice as "the act that will make the freest country in the world into the most enslaved." Jacques Maritain, a Gaullist since June 1940, wrote simply, "Armistice = slavery." He and other Gaullists combated what in 1941 Maritain called "pacifist ideology": "Nations that want to survive and live in peace have to understand that neither of these two goals is to be attained without clearly facing the risk of war." Like the Resister and historian Marc Bloch, whom the Gestapo shot in 1944, Maritain attributed the defeat to the failures of both left and right and called for national sacrifice to overcome it. Other Resistance movements and publications – *Petites Ailes* and *Cahiers du Témoignage chrétien* – recruited among the "bourgeoisie of the right and center-right" and labeled the German enemy "anti-Christian" and "neo-pagan."[38]

The antifascism of Philippe de Hauteclocque – who adopted the *nom de guerre* of General Leclerc during and after World War II – resembled de Gaulle's and Churchill's because it too was predicated on patriotism and imperialism. A devout Catholic, Hauteclocque nonetheless continued to read Action Française propaganda despite the Church's ban on its publications. After the fall of France, Captain Leclerc's patriotism superseded his commitment to the ideology of the collaborationist and anti-Semitic league. In the spring of 1940, Leclerc made several astounding escapes from German captivity. When he heard de Gaulle's call to continue the struggle, he worked his way to the south of France, traveled through Spain and Portugal, and joined the Resistance in London.

He termed the armistice the "original sin" of Vichy, rejected Pétain's pacifism, and initially fought the Axis from the French Empire, which he regarded as an integral part of the nation. The ex-Vichyite officers who would eventually join Leclerc in his various African campaigns were as imperialist as their commander. Their goal was to reassert Free French sovereignty over its African Empire even at the price of alienating the irreplaceable British ally. Gaullists were able to keep Chad and Cameroon in their camp as early as 1940, thereby bolstering their legitimacy. With British political and economic backing, these possessions provided a base to assert Free French control over a large region of Equatorial Africa, which could supply conscripts, precious metals, and exports using periodic forced labor. Free French Africa threatened Vichy control of its northern and western African colonies and endangered Italian possession of Libya. The governor of Chad, Félix Éboué, a Freemason and the first Black to achieve the highest rank in the French colonial service, had immediately rallied to the antifascist Free French. In the Pacific and Indian oceans, New Hebrides, Tahiti, New Caledonia, and the small French enclaves of India – all of which were dependent on cooperation with the British Commonwealth – quickly enlarged the imperial footing of the Free French. In the French Antilles, which remained in the Vichy camp until 1943, rumors nonetheless circulated that de Gaulle was Black. Antilleans would enroll in disproportionally high numbers in the Free French. Diversity would constitute the wealth of the Resistance.[39]

The British ability to stymie the Germans weakened support for Vichy and stimulated Anglophilism and Gaullism in French public opinion. Initially marked as a rightist, de Gaulle realized the need to broaden his appeal to enlarge his antifascist coalition and include the growing and sundry Resistance movements within France. He reached out to the left to terminate its suspicions that he was a potential fascist or Bonapartist dictator, and, following the invasion of the Soviet Union, he refused to accept suggestions from either Socialists or Croix-de-Feu members to exclude PCF adherents from the Free French. In turn, Communists dropped their opposition to the imperialism of the Free French and cooperated with Gaullists after June 1941. As in the United Kingdom and the United States, antifascism in France became a comprehensive coalition of left and right or, as de Gaulle put it, "the union of all national forces." In 1942 the Gaullists received the unconditional support of the internal Resistance groups, Combat and Libération, who gathered and organized followers through their eponymous underground newspapers. The circulation of the ecumenical *Combat*, whose collaborators included Camus and Bidault, jumped from 10,000 in late 1941 to 250,000 in

1944. The Resistance brought opposing political forces into a youthful
and overwhelmingly masculine community of risk. As the war endured
and Allied victory became more probable, conservatives and army officers who had supported Vichy joined the Resistance fraternity of combat. The Free French were often Catholic, moderately conservative, and
from comfortable, if not upper-class, families.[40]

A wide range of Resistance tendencies was hostile to a loosely defined
fascism that encompassed not only Hitler and Mussolini but Franco,
Salazar, and Pétain as well. De Gaulle himself considered the Vichy
regime only a "caricature" of fascism and opposed it principally because
of its collaboration with the Germans. He employed a popular antifascist common denominator by asserting that Nazi Germany would
"reduce humanity to the status of robots and slaves." Likewise, Astier
de la Vigerie's Libération regarded Nazism as a renewal of "the most
monstrous traditions of slavery." Unlike a few Resistance movements,
Libération condemned anti-Semitism and defended Jews "strongly and
greatly." It did not claim to "fight for Jews" but for the republican principles of religious freedom and anti-racism. Gaullists would second this
position and place themselves in the Enlightenment tradition of Abbé
Grégoire and others who had emancipated the Jews during the French
Revolution. To ignore freedom of conscience was to negate the legacy
of the Enlightenment and its Christian precursors. Another Resistance
movement, the anti-Communist Franc-Tireur, also proclaimed itself the
heir of the egalitarianism of the French Revolution. Gradually during
1942, de Gaulle would become the defender of "all the freedoms" of the
Third Republic.[41]

Vichyites could not imagine in 1940–1941 that they and their fascist
allies would become incapable of defending Pétain's counterrevolution,
whose regime initially won the backing of a great mass who shared his
pacifism and fears of revolution. In addition, "realists" and opportunists
concurred with the Marshal and benefited from joining what appeared
to be the winning side. In 1940 Pétain's policies and person were so
popular that Resisters were initially reluctant to attack him. The reverse
was not the case, and Vichy immediately and consistently persecuted
Resisters. Even so, against overwhelming evidence, many, if not most,
wished to believe that Pétain was a closet antifascist or a "shield" that
surreptitiously defended French interests.

French and British Communism

Following the signing of the Hitler-Stalin pact in August 1939, until
the spring of 1941, both the British and French Communist parties

preferred peace to confrontation with Nazi Germany. After their light-ning victory, in June–July 1940 German authorities freed from French jails hundreds of Communist cadres. At the same time, Parisian Com-munists sought permission from German occupation authorities to legal-ize their party, and the Parisian PCF leadership attempted to restrain the anti-German activities and gestures of their provincial militants. Only after the Nazi invasion of the Soviet Union in late June 1941 did Com-munist foreign and domestic antifascism completely coalesce. Prior to Operation Barbarossa, the PCF's "semi-legal" strategy achieved some success.

During the early occupation, the PCF acted as a Leninist revolution-ary organization that agitated to gain worker support. By the end of September 1940, the Germans had markedly altered their tolerant atti-tude toward French Communists and jailed more than 300, including 63 trade unionists. During that month Communists began to organize "popular committees" which tried to rally men and especially women over questions of food and fuel supplies, aid to POWs, and other mate-rial demands. Vichy's paternalism made it more difficult for women to engage in wage labor, and it offered only inadequate family subsidies. Given these conditions, the proto-feminist argument that women were the heart of the resistance was not entirely unjustified, and the Com-munists, who theoretically supported female equality, were particularly effective in organizing them.[42] In the Paris region, "Communist agi-tators have repeatedly managed to organize gatherings of women who demonstrated at city halls, food-supply offices ... [and] prisoner-of-war bureaus as well as the German Embassy ... The participation of women is particularly important because it spares the males whom the author-ities repress; whereas, females believe themselves immune to such mea-sures."[43] Similar protests by women also occurred in northern France. The lack of female prison facilities favored short jail sentences that allowed inmates to resume their agitation quickly after release. Women in the Resistance served often as de facto social workers who helped prisoners' families.[44]

Both Gaullists but particularly the better organized Communists ben-efited from the increasing hostility of female and male workers to Vichy's policies of collaboration with the German occupier. The Comintern rec-ognized that its calculation of a war of attrition on the European conti-nent had proven erroneous and that Germany's quick victories made the Reich potentially more dangerous to the Soviet Union. In the summer of 1940, the Third International recommended noncooperation with Ger-man and Vichy authorities. By the spring of 1941, the PCF leadership in Moscow advocated "a broad national front rallying the forces that love the freedom and independence of France."[45] On 1 May the Comintern appealed for the first time for occupied nations to liberate themselves during this still condemnable "imperialist war."[46] During the same month, Germany invaded the Balkans, thereby increasing tensions with the Soviet Union, which now faced German troops near its southwestern border. The PCF wanted to pressure Vichy to restrain closer collaboration with the German war machine. Using French-language broadcasts from Soviet radio, Communists promoted demands for salary increases and better working conditions.

With considerable success, PCF militants continued to encourage females – mainly mothers – to demand increased rations and ration tickets at city halls. On 1 August 1942 on the Parisian rue Daguerre, 500 housewives protested poor provisions. At Asnières 450 females successfully demonstrated at city hall for improved heating in schools and the opening of a school cafeteria. Even French syndicalists who collaborated with the Vichy regime recognized that women were greatly underpaid and demanded – at least in theory – equal pay for equal work. Communists profited from flagrant inequality and turned the regime's traditionalist family discourse – Vichy promoted a national Mother's Day in 1941 – against it. Food protests in Paris markets persisted throughout 1942. Wives of French POWs used the German employment offices to obtain information concerning their husbands, but the women generally refused enticements to enlist as workers for the Reich. The same pro-family sentiment led to the hostility of much Parisian and provincial opinion when in July 1942 during the collaborationist roundup of Jews at Vel d'Hiv stadium, authorities separated Jewish children from their parents. Many French traditionalists accepted the deportation of foreign Jews and even French Jews who were not veterans, but drew the line at the persecution of veterans, children, and the elderly. These acts especially appalled Catholics.[47]

Communists established fighting organizations for immigrants and proudly welcomed foreigners – Jews, Armenians, Spaniards, Italians, and Poles – into Resistance ranks. Zionists and Jewish Communists made considerable contributions to the Resistance and were exceptionally active combating and killing Germans. Yet the PCF refused to acknowledge the centrality of anti-Semitism in the Nazi worldview and regarded Judeophobia as a mere diversion from the class struggle. Like other Resistance movements, the PCF subordinated Jewish interests to its main goal – in this case, defending the Soviet "workers' state." Neither Communist nor, for that matter, Gaullist Resisters – who included a disproportionately high number of French Jews – seldom if ever attempted to prevent the departure of trains carrying Jews from France to the death camps in the East. Communist militants in the Resistance disdained "passive" Jews in the transit and concentration camps. The purely victim status of Jews did not appeal to Resistance fighters, who criticized the supposed absence of antifascism among Jews. In February 1942 at the French transit camp of Compiègne, where Jews – among others – were concentrated for deportation to death camps, a Communist Resistance leader characterized the French camp as "terrible." Yet it was not the ultimate fate of the Jews that really disturbed him but rather their lack of "political leadership or ideals. These people there were not fighters. We were aware of our fight against the occupation, but they were simply victims without hope." The Communist ambivalence toward Jews echoed that of some rightist Resistance movements which maintained suspicions that Jewish interests were incompatible with French ones. Nevertheless, all Resisters regarded Germany and Italy – not the Jews – as the genuine enemy.[48]

Like their French comrades, British Communists also rejected participation in a war among "capitalist" states after the Western powers failed to achieve an antifascist alliance with the Soviet Union in 1939. The CPGB did not wish to follow in the footsteps of European socialists who had supported their respective nations in World War I. Their lack of allegiance to the war effort allowed them to organize workers' dissatisfaction. Until Operation Barbarossa, the CPGB charged that their government and almost all others – except, of course, the Soviet Union – promoted fascism in domestic and foreign policies. Communists imitated fascists and their collaborators by underrating counterrevolutionary antifascism's commitment to defeating Hitler. In the patriotic atmosphere following the Battle of Dunkirk in June 1940, when more than 300,000 Allied troops avoided German capture and were evacuated to England, British party officials toned down the antiwar line, but Communist shop stewards continued to advance workers' demands on the shop floor against employers and the state. By maintaining trade-union activism, Communists expanded their influence among rank-and-file workers. CPGB publications fully supported strikes (euphemistically called "holidays"), backed struggles to increase wages, and resisted appeals to extend working hours. In the summer of 1940, they denounced Minister of Labour Bevin's call for cooperation between workers and management – an essential component of transatlantic antifascism during wartime – as the British equivalent to the German Labour Front, the Nazi regime's official union. Once again, Communists considered social democrats – Bevin, Attlee, and the Labour Party in general – as "social fascists." On 21 January 1941 the Labour leader and Home Secretary, Herbert Morrison, banned the CPGB news-paper, *Daily Worker* for 18 months. Even so, the British government, including Bevin, proved reluctant to crack down on CPGB militants in factories because it feared that repression of Communists would pro-voke more industrial unrest than toleration of their subversive activities. The Communists' inability to damage seriously the British war effort demonstrated their marginality and the strength of broad alliance of UK antifascism.[49]

At first, most politically aware Americans regarded Mussolini as a hard-headed leader who used his Blackshirts to protect property against attacks by leftist revolutionaries. Throughout the 1920s, the Duce consistently attracted more press attention than Stalin. Middle-brow mass magazines (*Saturday Evening Post*) and business periodicals (*Fortune* and the *Wall Street Journal*) admired the Italian dictator. So did conservative dailies, such as the *Chicago Tribune*, which called Fascism "the most striking and successful attempt of the middle classes to meet the tide of revolutionary socialism."[1] Conversely, the relatively high-brow *Atlantic* and *Harper's* remained consistently critical of the regime.

The Nazis' quick consolidation of power in 1933 increased American misgivings concerning Italian Fascism, which now appeared as a dangerous ideological precursor and partner of the National Socialists. The Italian invasion of Ethiopia in 1935 confirmed these qualms. Despite the passage of the Neutrality Acts in the same year, Congress and the administration grew increasingly indignant about Italian actions in Abyssinia. President Roosevelt began to doubt his previous judgment that the Duce was an "admirable Italian gentleman," even if he regarded the Italian dictator as considerably less dangerous than Hitler. The president addressed Congress in January 1936 and condemned Fascism's "twin spirits of autocracy and aggression." To discourage pro-Fascist Italian-American and anti-Fascist African-American volunteers, the administration warned US nationals who volunteered to fight in the Ethiopian conflict that they would be subject to fines, imprisonment, and, in the case of naturalized citizens, possibly forfeiture of their citizenship. By imposing several sanctions against the Italian regime, Roosevelt overruled his own ambassador to Italy, ignored pro-Fascist sentiment among Italian-Americans, and took the risk of provoking nationalist reaction in Italy itself. Italian aggression in Africa also alienated some businessmen who had admired the Fascist experiment. To show his disapproval, Henry Ford cancelled an order prepaid by the Italian government for 800 motor cars. The United Kingdom's proposed recognition of Italian conquests in Ethiopia provoked a direct protest by Roosevelt to Chamberlain. The US government remained nearly alone in refusing recognition of Italy's African victory.[2]

Extensive satire of the Duce did not appear in the American popular press until after 1935, much of it inspired by the Ethiopian invasion. Most Americans strongly sympathized with Haile Selassie's underdog forces, whom the ultranationalist and technologically proficient Italians viciously victimized. By the end of the war, Americans declared themselves "less friendly" to Italy than to the Soviet Union. American Protestants objected more consistently than Catholics to the Italian aggression, which the nondenominational *Christian Century* termed a "most disgraceful" imperialism. African-American pastors launched a vibrant antifascist movement which yielded some funds and several volunteers to fight against the Italian invaders. The National Negro Congress also denounced the Duce. In the summer of 1935 violence between US Blacks and Italian-Americans, many of whom supported their ancestral homeland, erupted in major American cities. The Ethiopian aggression fostered the first major mobilization of the African-American community on a purely foreign policy issue. Yet the democracies ultimately proved reluctant to enforce biting sanctions on Italy. Similarly, the opportunistic Soviet Union ignored them and even increased trade with Italy, thereby alienating many politically conscious Blacks in Africa and the West.[3]

American labor often led the hostility to Fascism, and farmers' groups followed its lead. The academic community, which offered refuge to some of the most prominent opponents of Mussolini, also proved unfriendly to the authoritarian ruler. Scholars objected to the Duce's closed regime and its restrictions on academic freedom. University presses published critical works by exiled Italian and American scholars. Fascist violence, foreign policy, and its frequently successful attempts to influence Italian-Americans troubled mainstream periodicals. The House Un-American Activities Committee of the 1930s was originally conceived to discourage subversion not only by the radical left but also by newer fascist movements. Business opinion toward Fascism became more unfavorable as both the New Deal and the Italian regime adopted more economically interventionist policies. After 1935, American business journals began to equate communism and fascism – in both its Italian and its German forms.[4]

Some positive coverage of the Third Reich on a productivist and anti-Communist basis initially characterized American mainstream publications, such as *Time, Reader's Digest*, and the *Saturday Evening Post*. The perception of Germany and the Germans as a land and people much like

(White) America was a barrier to understanding the Nazi phenomenon. Many Americans viewed the "productive, thrifty and reliable [and clean] Germans" as reflecting their own virtues.[5] Given their potent work ethic, Americans admired a similar legacy in Germany. This common appreciation of labor helped to foster sympathetic treatment and even the whitewashing of German atrocities. Likewise, the rapid decline of German unemployment bolstered the Reich's reputation in the United States. Furthermore, as in Europe, anti-Communists often favored the Nazi state as a barrier to Communism and the Soviet Union. Familiar anti-Semitism – but not European political anti-Semitism – among up to half of the American population reinforced philo-Germanism among large sectors of the public.

Yet despite a certain shared Judeophobia and racism, Nazism was never popular in the United States. In contrast to Mussolini, whose negative image took some time to develop, Hitler immediately aroused grave suspicion in the American media. The Duce had cooperated diplomatically by endorsing the Young and Dawes plans of the 1920s, which rescheduled Versailles reparations. In addition, Mussolini was open to Roosevelt's proposals on disarmament in the 1930s; in contrast, the Führer was consistently obstructionist. In the United States, the Nazi seizure of power bolstered antifascism more than fascism. The brutal aggressions of the party's paramilitary units, the early boycotts of Jews, and in 1934 the Röhm purge (the Night of the Long Knives) brought Nazism into disrepute. Many journalists, politicians, clergymen, and trade unionists denounced the Hitler regime. They saw that Nazism envisaged a "totalitarian state" which would ruthlessly suppress established American "political, religious, and even scientific freedom." Hitlerism had transferred "the doctrine of Divine Right from king to race."[6]

Not surprisingly, American Jews were among the most active anti-Nazis, and many were cognizant of the centrality of anti-Semitism in German fascism. Immediately after the regime took power, Bernard S. Deutsch, the president of the American Jewish Congress, recognized the Nazis' "avowed program of exterminating the Jews." So did Rabbi Stephen S. Wise, who called Hitlerism "a new phenomenon in world history" which refused to tolerate human differences. In 1934 James Wise, the editor of the Jewish journal *Opinion*, offered a sophisticated verdict: "It is impossible to label it [Nazism] as a revolutionary or reactionary movement and thus to pigeon-hole its aims and acts... To dismiss Nazism as a German variant of Fascism and nothing more is to confuse, not clarify the issue. Differences in degree, if they are great enough, become differences in kind." Although supposedly progressive

American opinion was not opposed to the sterilization of "defectives," it rejected the singling out of Jews. As in Britain, Jews provided many of the shock troops for anti-Nazi demonstrations in major cities – New York, Newark, Chicago, and Los Angeles. Municipal authorities often tolerated their attacks on Nazi Bundists.[7]

Like those in Britain and France, American antifascist analyses generally remained captive by the past and interpreted fascism as slavery and regression to barbarism. The "pagan, pre-Christian level" of Nazism led to the "re-subjection of women." "This society of heroes and henchmen, of leaders and blindly obedient warriors is to be an exclusively male society." Its anti-feminism contributed to the construction of "a warrior society committed to national glory." Nazi and Fascist attempts to return women to purely domestic tasks appalled a number of American commentators. Alice Hamilton, the first woman appointed to the Harvard faculty, discerned that "no woman of any prominence in the woman's movement is connected with the Nazi regime." She criticized it for making the "state all-important, not the individual child." Hamilton linked the "enslavement of women" to the Nazi explanation that "sex equality and sex freedom" were "Jewish doctrines." The Nazis limited female enrollment in universities to 10 percent and thus reduced the number of women in higher education from 23,000–30,000 to 15,000. The regime hoped eventually to employ women "only in womanly work, domestic service . . . and welfare work." "Hitler's habit of arresting innocent women for alleged crimes of their husbands and brothers" disturbed British and American feminists.[8]

By the mid-1930s the American public generally condemned dictatorships, and the word "dictator" became as unpopular as "fascist." It was symptomatic that negative attitudes toward Mussolini and Hitler led to automaker Studebaker's 1937 decision to stop producing the vehicle named Dictator. In this context, on 5 October 1937 Roosevelt made his most important foreign policy address since taking office. His "quarantine" speech refuted strict neutrality and appealed for "a concerted effort" to ostracize aggressive dictatorships – Germany, Italy, and Japan. The speech met a mixed reception in the United States, where isolationism remained influential. Nevertheless, the address revealed the growing appeal of antifascism among the press, public, and artists. In the late thirties the fascist threat alarmed prize-winning American authors and poets – Lewis Mumford, Van Wyck Brooks, Carl Sandburg, and Archibald MacLeish. MacLeish, a non-communist antifascist who argued for early intervention in Europe, declared, "a free people cannot fight fascism unless it believes with even greater conviction that freedom is good . . . and that slavery is evil."[9]

Some Republicans, such as the widely read columnist Dorothy Thompson, also embraced antifascism in the 1930s. Thompson, who was expelled from Germany in 1934 and whose image graced the cover of *Time* in June 1939, was likely second only to First Lady Eleanor Roosevelt as the most influential American woman. Thompson alerted conservatives that fascism was a "TOTAL [sic] revolution... pushed forward not by classes but by whole nations" which could be lethal to democracy.[10] Thompson's conservative antifascism allowed her to be "among the first to grasp and publicize the Nazis' murderous intentions toward the Jews of Europe."[11] As early as 1934 she had reported that the Nazis wanted merely "submission" from other groups but aimed "to *eliminate*" the Jews.[12] Yet she usually deemphasized National Socialism's special hatred of Jews to focus on its intolerance of many groups. Her efforts effectively broadened the US antifascist coalition to include all religious and ethnic groups and markedly appealed to the White, Protestant majority, of which she was a member.

Likewise, although American artists were also concerned with Jewish refugees fleeing Germany, they avoided focusing specifically on anti-Semitic racism and emphasized the more general cause of humanitarian assistance to refugees, a theme that encouraged the enlargement of the antifascist coalition. The artists' strategy contributed to the building of a powerful antifascist movement that would eventually triumph over the Nazis. Nevertheless, the ecumenical approach removed the spotlight from the specificity of Jewish persecution. The Nazi problem was viewed through the lens of religious intolerance, not murderous plans. Deemphasizing the targeting of Jews was a concession to Nazi Judeophobia and may have facilitated the extermination of European Jews by limiting public awareness. Rejecting "special pleading" and "reactions from any one group," "the Holocaust seems to have been an irritation for the official American [wartime] propaganda campaign."[13] Americans continued to adhere to their relatively positive image of the German people as victims of Nazism, not its perpetrators. During the war "rescue [of Jews] through victory" remained the dominant slogan. Although it often veiled a leadership that was indifferent to the Jews' fate and invented excuses not to bomb Auschwitz and other extermination camps, the slogan was not entirely empty. Simone Veil – a French Jew and future minister during the Fifth Republic – reported that by the beginning of 1944, when it was clear that the Allies were going to triumph, the willingness of the population and police to assist Jews in France increased dramatically.[14]

Antifascists normally treated Jews as a religious group, not as an ethnicity or race. In fact, anti-racism was a relatively minor component of transatlantic antifascism. Leftists focused on Nazi ties to big business and established German elites, not on its bigotry. Both Marxists and anti-Marxists breezily dismissed Nazi discrimination as demagoguery. The dominant argument was that persecution of Jews was not qualitatively distinct from that of other minority groups. This was especially true of Communist antifascism, but it also characterized elements of conservative antifascism. Both failed to recognize the racial principle that was the basis of the Jews' exclusion and ultimately genocide. In fact, many interpreted Nazi anti-Semitism as simply a cover for extortion of Jews. In the United States as well as in the United Kingdom and France, traditional patriotism – not anti-racism – motivated the antifascist struggle. Indeed, antifascism was compatible with nonlethal varieties of anti-Semitism and violent anti-Black prejudice. After Pearl Harbor, race riots in major American cities cost dozens of, mostly African-American, lives. Many of the one third to one half of the American populace that regarded Jews as greedy and dishonest either worked or fought against the Axis.[15]

Following the 1938 *Reichspogrom*, Roosevelt – who returned Hitler's personal antipathy – recalled the American ambassador. The US president was the only world leader (not excluding the Pope) to condemn the November pogrom, demonstrating the uniqueness – whatever its limitations – of the American concern for persecuted German Jews. American Jews were joined in their protests against anti-Semitism by such conservative veterans' organizations as the American Legion, which firmly opposed Nazism throughout the 1930s. The US armed forces also rejected German anti-Semitism in their publications. In January 1938, an opinion poll revealed that 94 percent of Americans disapproved of Nazism's treatment of Jews. In December 1938, 61 percent of Americans were prepared to participate in a boycott of German-made goods.[16]

Italy's adoption in 1939 of Germany's anti-Semitic policies – a telling example of Fascist deference to Nazi supremacy – angered many American publications. The conservative and pro-Franco *Catholic World* condemned the Duce's "Aryan madness." Generoso Pope, an Italian-American millionaire and press magnate who had steadfastly supported Mussolini, broke with the regime over its recently adopted anti-Semitism. Aping the Nazi line, official Fascist propaganda reacted by conducting a venomous campaign against prominent American Jews and "Hebraized" Gentiles who were allegedly responsible for an antifascist foreign policy. Likewise, the unfavorable American reaction to Kristallnacht confirmed the Nazi belief – shared by others on the US and European extreme right – that Roosevelt was "the mouthpiece of Judah and the instrument of the Comintern."[17]

Despite fascist accusations, philo-Semitism in the United States proved less consequential than Anglophilism. The American East Coast possessed an entrenched current of the latter which surfaced vociferously after the United Kingdom entered the war. The Century Group, composed of several dozen members of the Eastern establishment – businessmen, media executives, and religious leaders – formed in 1940 in New York to aid Britain. All its members were White males, and 22 of 28 were Protestants largely of Anglo-Saxon background. These men were a nearly equal mixture of influential Democrats and Republicans, including magazine (*Time*, *Life*, and *Fortune*) and newsreel (*March of Time*) magnate Henry Luce. A majority were conservative on domestic issues but were willing to risk war with Germany and – during this period when the Hitler-Stalin pact was in effect – with the Soviet Union as well. They viewed Nazism as similar to Communism – a revolutionary phenomenon that endangered private property and traditional religion. This elite feared that a German victory over Britain – the likelihood of which increased after the fall of France – would entail Nazi control of the British fleet and the Atlantic and thus put the United States in direct danger.

On 15 June 1940, as the British government was preparing to demand that the French fleet be sent to British ports, Churchill warned Roosevelt that if the British fleet "were joined to the fleets of Japan, France, and Italy and the great resources of German industry, overwhelming sea power would be in Hitler's hands." If Britain fell, a Quisling government would undoubtedly try to obtain the best terms by using the Royal Navy as their bargaining chip, just as the Vichy regime had done with its fleet. Aware of the danger, American interventionists began to lobby to convince public opinion and Congress to approve trading American destroyers to Britain in return for American bases on British territory throughout the Atlantic, which would be one of the most important territorial acquisitions of the United States since the Louisiana Purchase. They also insisted that the United Kingdom issue a public pledge to never surrender its fleet to the Nazis. In the year before Pearl Harbor, interventionists were particularly successful in gaining the support of organized labor. They counterattacked those who claimed that opposition to Hitler was a Jewish conspiracy by accusing their adversaries of mouthing Nazi propaganda. Interventionists built a multiracial and cross-class antifascist coalition, including African-American leaders such as the Reverend Adam Clayton Powell, Sr., and union president A. Philip Randolph.[18]

American Christian Antifascism

A particular concern of the interventionists was to persuade American Catholics – many of whom were of Irish ancestry and frequently hostile to Britain – to moderate their support for appeasement. The relatively

few Catholic antifascists in the Century Group emphasized Hitler's supposed intention to "exterminate Christianity." Christians in the most
important interventionist groups viewed the Führer as a representative
of the forces of evil and argued that the survival of Christian civilization depended on the endurance of the United Kingdom. In 1939 the
prominent Protestant theologian Reinhold Niebuhr broke with his previous pacifism – which the liberal Protestant review *Christian Century*
had disseminated – and argued for American intervention against Nazi
Germany.[19]

Niebuhr tried to alert the public that Chamberlain's appeasement
policies spelled doom for Europe: "Munich represented a tremendous
shift in the balance of power in Europe . . . it reduced France to impo-
tence, . . . it opened the gates to a German expansion in the whole of
Europe, . . . it isolated Russia and changed the whole course of history."
Niebuhr linked his condemnation of Munich to the misapprehension of
the Versailles Treaty: "The really tragic end of a liberal culture is to be
found in the peace of Munich. What was best in that culture was outraged by the peace of Versailles and what was shallowest in it came to
the conclusion that the horrors of a peace of conquest could be expi-
ated by a peace of capitulation." After the fall of France, Niebuhr criticized the French as "sick" for their quick surrender to the Germans and
embarked on an anti-neutralist campaign to convince Americans to support the United Kingdom. In early 1941 Niebuhr and other prominent
Protestant clergymen – some of whom were members of the Century
Group – established a new "journal of Christian opinion," *Christianity
and Crisis*, to awaken the faithful to the dangers of isolationism and the
necessity of intervention. It identified an Allied victory with "the rescue of Christendom." Niebuhr and his colleagues brought their message
to many audiences, including the conservative, if not racist, Daughters
of the American Revolution. They maintained that pacifists and revolutionary socialists were "utopians" who did not understand the nature of
the Nazi foe. Unlike many other so-called realists in the Atlantic world,
Niebuhr linked the domestic developments of the Reich – notably its
persecution of Jews – with its international aggression. Loving one's enemies did not mean that one could not fight them, but rather that they
were recognized as fellow human beings even in war.[20]

He and his group of Christian realists viewed both fascism and communism as pagan utopias that manufactured false religions that idol-
ized the state. He proposed that Christians imitate the ancient prophets
and engage in worldly activities to counter these "totalitarian" states.
The increasing popularity in the 1930s of the concept of totalitarianism among the right, the center (including American Lutherans), and
also the anti-Stalinist left undermined sympathies for the Third Reich,

even before the Nazi-Soviet nonaggression treaty of 1939 reinforced the identification of both regimes. Niebuhr's assertion that Nazism was a return to "slavery with technical efficiency" provided an insightful twist on the slavery interpretation common to many antifascists by pointing to fascism's dangerous modernity. He might have added that Nazism also propagated a work ethic run amok. Indeed, fascism broke with previous slave systems. Unlike their aristocratic predecessors, who disdained labor and believed it worthy only of slaves, fascist ideology – much like its Communist enemy – glorified the worker and his work. In many ways, this devotion to labor combined with its martial spirit is what made it a powerful and modern ideology, capable of conquering and holding off other great powers for six years. By September 1939 Cardinal Francis Spellman, often considered the leader of American Catholics, joined the antifascist ranks by arguing against a "peace of slavery."[21]

As in Britain and France, in America the interpretation of Nazism as a pagan revolt and a regression to medieval savagery was common. As early as 1934, Roosevelt warned that dictators were preparing a new Dark Age. At the same time, John Haynes Holmes, a Unitarian minister and a pacifist during both world wars, declared, "Hitlerism is a reversion to barbarism." "The Nazis," he claimed, "tested by every standard of modern civilization, are savages" who were replacing God and Christ with Wotan and Siegfried. Like their British counterparts, American Protestants united against Hitler's campaign to create a "German Christianity" which placed churches under state domination. Prominent Protestant and Catholic publications avoided representations of European dictators as humorous or amusing since, they argued, comical portraits risked underestimating the fascist danger to America. The lampooning of the hysterical style of the Führer and the widespread recognition of his intellectual limitations often prevented English-speaking audiences from taking him seriously. Charlie Chaplin's *The Great Dictator* (1940) – one of the most powerful representations of this tradition, which would continue in Hollywood films and cartoons produced during the war – may have contributed to American complacency.[22]

Christian antifascism captivated political leaders in the United States as it had elsewhere. Like Churchill, Roosevelt often tied his antifascism to traditional religion. As Assistant Secretary of the Navy during World War I, the future president had already juxtaposed German paganism with Christianity. As president, he interpreted the fall of France as accelerating the confrontation of democracy and dictatorship and between religion and godlessness. Nearly a year later, in May 1941, in a radio address which attracted a huge audience, the president announced a state of unlimited national emergency: "Today the whole world is divided between human slavery and human freedom – between pagan brutality and the Christian ideal."[23] If Britain were defeated, American workers "would have to compete with slave labor in the rest of the world."[24] This theme connected American and European concerns. The Conservative leader Baldwin expressed himself in similar terms, evoking in March 1934 the existence of "slavery" from the German Rhine to the Russian Pacific. After the German occupation of Czechoslovakia in March 1939, Blum likened Nazi domination to "slavery," as did descendants of Africans in the French Caribbean.[25] Slavery was the metaphor that linked the fight against Nazism to the abolitionist campaigns of Enlightenment thinkers and evangelical Christians, both of whom were especially influential in the developed Atlantic world.

Roosevelt would recall the religious roots of the abolitionist legacy and frequently repeated the message that World War II was a conflict between Christian freedom and Nazi slavery. In his May 1941 radio address, he condemned isolationists who were receiving "sinister support...from the enemies of democracy in our midst – the [German-American] Bundists, the Fascists, and Communists...devoted to racial and religious intolerance."[26] In October 1941 in a Navy Day speech, Roosevelt charged that the Nazis had a plan to "abolish all existing religions," liquidate the clergy, and prohibit the cross. He justified aid to the patriotic "Russians...fighting for their own soil" in the name of the far greater menace of Hitler. A month after Pearl Harbor, on 2 January 1942, he declared in the annual State of the Union address to Congress: "Victory for us means victory for religion...We are fighting, as our fathers have fought, to uphold the doctrine that all men are created equal in the sight of God. Those on the other side are striving to destroy this deep belief and to create a world in their own image – a world of tyranny and cruelty and serfdom."[27] Given American policies of discrimination against minorities, some of this rhetoric was transparently hypocritical, but the Anglo-American rejection of slavery and forced labor clearly contrasted with the massive Axis implementation of both in Europe during the war. In 1944, Roosevelt assured Germans that Allied intentions were not to "enslave" them. He employed against the Axis the word "tyranny" – significantly a term derived from old-regime vocabulary – which had been part of the antifascist lexicon since the 1920s. Roosevelt's conservative antifascism rested on a synthesis of religion and the Enlightenment legacy.

Vice President Henry Wallace's May 1942 speech, "The Century of the Common Man," followed the president's lead and may have been the most celebrated and widely quoted address of the American war effort. Wallace regarded Nazism as a counterrevolution against the "people's march of freedom" exemplified in England's Glorious Revolution, the American Revolution, the French Revolution, the Bolivarian Revolutions, the German Revolution of 1848, and even the Russian Revolution. His address recalled and extended Abraham Lincoln's analysis of the US Civil War to argue that a world "half slave and half free" could not endure. He equated the slave South and Nazi Germany because the elites of both possessed a monopoly of wealth and power. Wallace's challenge to Nazi oppression was faith-based in the abolitionist tradition. He predicted that Americans "would drive the ancient Teutonic Gods back cowering into their caves. The Götterdämmerung has come for Odin and his crew . . . Through the leaders of the Nazi revolution, Satan is now trying to lead the common man of the whole world back into slavery and darkness. For the stark truth is that the violence preached by the Nazis is the devil's own religion of darkness." The vice-president proposed that 'Democratic Christianity' would be the most practical way to unite the postwar world."[28] It is significant that Wallace – a politician who was associated with the left (and even, for some, with Communist fellow-traveling) – employed religious metaphors to help Americans understand the Nazi phenomenon.

Time called the wartime movie series *Why We Fight* "the first impressive attempt in a US film to present the theory and practice of fascism." Its initial movie, *Prelude to War* (1942), repeated the Roosevelt administration's interpretation that the war was a "fight between a free world and a slave world," which included Nazi Germany, Fascist Italy, and Imperial Japan. It enrolled as founders of freedom recognized religious leaders – Mohammed, Confucius, Moses, and Christ. Their principles were put into practice by great men of various ethnicities – Washington, Garibaldi, Lafayette, Kosciuszko, Bolívar, and Lincoln. The last was particularly important given that the war represented "the common man's life and death struggle against those who want to put him back into slavery." Those who did not fight fascism were destined to be either super-exploited workers or savage soldiers. Refuting the still common – but largely erroneous – distinction between the Nazi regime and the German people, the movie indicated a certain level of popular support for the Nazis since it wished to discredit the isolationist position that a negotiated peace with the German military was desirable. The film's anti-German stance both encouraged and reflected a shift in American public opinion that became more critical toward the German people's firm support for the expansionism of their Reich. In contrast to the popular conflation of the Japanese with their government, many Americans had preferred to differentiate between the German people and the regime. The film implied that the conflict had to be resolved by the enemy's unconditional surrender, as the Union had demanded from the Confederacy.[29]

Regional Antifascism

Numerous analysts throughout the world considered fascism as a reactionary movement and a regression to a more backward era. Given these views, the antifascism of the semi-feudal US South was remarkable. The South rejected Italian Fascism because Nativists, right-wing Protestants, and Klansmen regarded Mussolini as an ally of the Pope and an alien anti-Christ. The Ku Klux Klan sent flowers to a New Jersey policeman who had been suspended for removing a Fascist flag from the lead car during a parade of Italian-American Blackshirts. Comparisons that emphasized affinities of the Klan with the Italian movement upset Klansmen, who rhetorically rejected all "isms," including fascism. Their fraternal relations with the German-American Bund deteriorated during the war when the Klan's Imperial Wizard wanted to join the Catholic Knights of Columbus and the Jewish B'nai B'rith in patriotic cooperation.[30] The Klan's antifascism is indeed ironic since it has been viewed as "a remarkable preview of the way fascist movements were to function in interwar Europe."[31] The Klan's uniforms, violence, and alliances with more mainstream conservatives did resemble European fascist movements, but the Klan was too backward-looking to be classified with Fascism and Nazism. Its Protestant exclusiveness circumscribed its national influence, as did its hatred of the omnipotent national state that nearly all European fascisms preferred. Its preference for local control and states' rights harkened back to the Confederacy. The Klan's neo-traditionalism sought a return to the racist traditions of the antebellum South and segregationist North where African-Americans "knew their place" and provided cheap and presumedly compliant labor. It did not envisage building new genocidal empires.

The Southern press denounced Nazi anti-Semitism. Bible Belters and secular Southerners objected to the replacement of Old Testament stories with an Aryanized Jesus and Nordic sagas. African-American newspapers reported Hitler's reference in *Mein Kampf* to Blacks as "half-apes" and called the Führer "the master Ku Kluxer of Germany." A number of African-American journalists perspicaciously reminded their readers that Hitler would abolish all constitutional rights and bring back slavery. Although the Black media and intellectuals – such as W. E. B. Du Bois – condemned anti-Semitism, they often mimicked, as did their White counterparts, the prejudices of the Germans by assuming the Jews' supposed devotion to money, their reluctance to serve in the military, and their domination of certain professions. Black journalists also engaged in a competition for victimhood in which Black suffering in the United States equaled or surpassed any comparable Jewish pain in Germany. Nevertheless, by the end of the 1930s, the southern secular and religious press clearly condemned Nazism. African-American newspapers would rally around the war effort.[32]

During the war, Nazism became so unpopular that some government officials suggested that emphasizing Nazi views on Jews would undermine anti-Semitism in the United States. A Southern conservative intellectual, Richard M. Weaver, argued that the South had retained an antidemocratic conservatism that encouraged its rejection of revolutionary Nazi doctrines. In other words, Southern segregationists were happy to join the antifascist coalition. In fact, the South was the region where polls consistently showed the highest support for anti-Nazi interventionism. Southern martial culture yearned for a fight with a rival militarism. The enlistment of the entire Lepanto, Arkansas, football team in the navy after Pearl Harbor showed deep popular support for antifascism. White southerners and their supporters were enthusiastic participants of a campaign which combated a form of racism even more virulent than their own brand. The racist antifascists of the American South were aggressively anti-German, anti-Italian, and anti-Japanese.[33]

As Weaver suggested, customary racism might have constituted a barrier to fascism. Southern segregationists had no need to adopt newer, more aggressive forms of discrimination since many of the established ones served effectively to suppress African-Americans. Southern racism was traditionalist, based on the Biblical "curse of Ham," not eliminationist as was the Nazi variety. The conservative Democratic senator from North Carolina Josiah W. Bailey opposed Roosevelt's "court packing" in 1937 by claiming that the Supreme Court had protected the South from the evils of "the social equality of the Negro" while preventing in America the sort of persecution that Jews faced in Nazi Germany. Virginia Senator Carter Glass opposed much New Deal legislation and remained a staunch segregationist; yet he became a leader of the interventionist group Fight for Freedom, which formed in early 1941 to promote immediate American entry into the war. According to Southern conservatives, a national government which mandated racial egalitarianism was as "totalitarian" as Communist and fascist states. White Southerners considered federal encroachment as dangerous as an Axis invasion. They fought not for democracy but rather for states' rights.[34]

Furthermore, the South profited greatly from Washington's defense spending, which – unlike welfare spending – generally reinforced conventional political, economic, and cultural hierarchies. The Roosevelt administration was hesitant to use its leverage to threaten Southern segregation; in return, White Southerners overwhelmingly supported it. Many conservative antifascists welcomed increased militarization of society, large defense contracts for big corporations, and continued segregation in the armed forces. Even though American participation in World War II ultimately undermined discrimination against African-Americans, Southern participation in the war effort dampened civil-rights protest and reinforced segregation during the war years.[35] African-Americans were incensed by the preferential treatment given to German prisoners of war in establishments which excluded Blacks. In the immediate postwar period, conservative Republicans and segregationist Democrats strengthened their hold on Congress and blocked civil-rights legislation.[36] Despite raised expectations, African-Americans remained second-class citizens in much of the nation. Nonetheless, by supporting an antifascist war, Southerners strengthened the federal government whose power would eventually eliminate legal racial discrimination.

Southern counterrevolutionary antifascism raises a major interpretive issue. Many, if not most, explanations of the failure of fascism in the Western democracies have rested on the liberal-democratic political culture of the United States, the United Kingdom, and France. Certainly, antifascism was especially potent in nations where abolitionism and feminism were the most powerful. Yet the antidemocratic traditions of these nations and their regions also contributed to the domestic and international failures of fascism. As in Spain in the 1930s, in the United States regionalism was typically antifascist. The American South's own institutional racism and its lack of secularization presented obstacles to fascism that did not exist in much of Weimar Germany or Northern Italy. Segregationist Protestantism obstructed competing ideologies in the fundamentalist South. Fascist racism did not mean that antifascism was not racist.

The internment of Japanese-Americans was another example of US racist antifascism. The state never interned large numbers of either Italian- or German-Americans, whose ancestral homelands were, unlike Japan, truly fascist. Nor did the British ally ever jail any ethnicities who had British nationality. From 1942 to 1944 Secretary of War Henry Stimson, his deputy John McCloy, General Eisenhower's brother Milton, and, of course, President Roosevelt himself implemented and administered the detentions in harsh rural environments of 112,000 American men, women, and children of Japanese ancestry.[37] Their abominable treatment showed that antifascism – whether counterrevolutionary or revolutionary (the Soviet treatment of minorities was far

Figure 6.1 Grant Wood (1891–1942), *Parson Weems' Fable*, 1939. Oil on canvas. Amon Carter Museum of American Art, Fort Worth, Texas.

worse than what occurred in the United States) – was profoundly discriminatory. It was also sexist, even at the cost of the war effort. The principal reason for the American manpower shortage, which became acute after D-Day, was the reluctance to use women on a sufficient scale.

US counterrevolutionary antifascism did continue the established commitment to free expression of the overwhelming majority of intellectuals and artists. It encouraged a big tent artistically as well as politically. Regionalist painters from the Midwest were the closest American equivalent to Nazi *Blut und Boden* style, but the regionalists – Thomas Hart Benton, John Steuart Curry, and Grant Wood – had a sense of irony missing from the dour Nazi canvases. Grant Wood's "humorous streak, demonstrated over and over again in his paintings of the thirties, made him particularly well suited for the task of reviving patriotism without risking the deadly earnest chauvinism of fascist nationalist mythology"[38] (Figure 6.1).

Thomas Hart Benton had engaged in leftist politics in the 1930s, and the fall of France in June 1940 probably convinced him before Pearl Harbor that the United States should join the British. The collapse of a

Figure 6.2 Thomas Hart Benton, *Again*. Art © T.H. Benton Testamentary Trusts/UMB Bank Trustee/Licensed by VAGA, New York, NY.

fellow democratic republic, specifically one that had held off the Germans for four years a generation earlier, challenged American complacency and boosted efforts to strengthen antifascism in the United States. Benton blasted "the naïve isolationists of the middle west" who did not realize that losing the war meant the end of American democracy. His *The Year of Peril—Again* (1942) depicted the three fascist powers – Germany, Italy, and Japan – thrusting a spear into a crucified Christ, thereby identifying antifascism with the defense of Christianity (Figure 6.2). *The Year of Peril* series of eight paintings "may well have been the most famous American antifascist propaganda produced during the Second World War."[39] Government and private industry – such as the Chicago multinational Abbott Laboratories and Hollywood's Paramount Pictures – reproduced it millionfold in pamphlets, newspapers, magazines, cinema, posters, postcards, and exhibits. This more or less spontaneous cooperation between the state and private enterprise obviated the need for a centralized bureau of propaganda on the Nazi or Soviet model.

Benton's *Invasion* (1942) projected the nightmare of a foreign fascist takeover of the United States, forecasting the slaughter of men and the rape of women. *Exterminate* (1942) urged Americans to be as ruthless as the fascists themselves.

The growth and toleration, if not encouragement, of regional consciousness among antifascists has been underemphasized because of subsequent collaboration of Flemish, Breton, and Alsatian nationalists during the Nazi occupation of Belgium and France. Yet the antifascist tent could also accommodate provincial particularisms. Bretons and other Frenchmen from the Atlantic coast joined the Free French in disproportionally high numbers. In Spain, regional movements in Catalonia and the Basque Country benefited from the antifascist consensus of the Republican zone in the civil war. During the world war, the Welsh and Scottish fought foreign fascists and largely ignored their anti-English nationalists and pro-German separatists. Much depressed before the war, Scotland – like the American South – profited from the proliferation of government contracts leading to more than a 250 percent increase in production. Even if a multinational British consciousness began to grow as the antifascist left became more sensitive to Scottish and Welsh traditions, a spirit of national unity reached its summit throughout Britain as the conflict endured.[40]

State Antifascism

Antifascists used state authority to subdue groups whose activities aided potential enemies. As in France and Britain, in America too state antifascism reflected the limited ability of interwar fascist movements to penetrate the centers of power. In 1935 Roosevelt ordered the FBI to investigate pro-Nazi groups and far-right agitators. Similarly, the House Un-American Activities Committee maintained its own scrutiny of varieties of "extremist" politics. The two-party system – or even the one-party system in the US South – limited new entrants. State and local governments employed their repressive apparatus to suppress new movements of the left and right. In 1934, with the cooperation of the federal government, North Carolina prosecuted a potential American Führer – William Dudley Pelley, leader of the Silver Legion – for financial fraud. In 1940, he was jailed for several days. New York acted similarly against Fritz Kuhn, the Führer of the German-American Bund. Despite questionable constitutionality, several states and cities passed legislation – similar to that of Britain's Public Order Act and France's decree-laws – which banned paramilitary regalia and prohibited libel of racial or religious groups. Connecticut authorities dusted off long-established

Blue Laws to prosecute German-American Bund activists who organized
on Sunday. In 1938 New York courts used legislation requiring registra-
tion of adherents of "oath-bound organizations" to convict six members of the Bund. New York City restricted the wearing of the Bund's
uniforms.[41]

At the end of 1939, Roosevelt authorized his attorney general, Frank
Murphy, to probe the subversive activities of both Communists and fascists. Before America was a declared belligerent and in clear violation of
US law, the FBI closely cooperated with British intelligence operatives
against German, Italian, and later Vichy French activities. In 1941 the
Bureau placed taps on the phones of nearly 100 individuals and organizations. As in the United Kingdom, legal prosecution of fascist leaders
and organizations intensified during the war. Convicted of larceny, Fritz
Kuhn spent the first three years of the conflict in several New York state
prisons. In 1942 a federal court convicted Pelley for subversion of the
armed forces and sentenced him to 15 years. In 1942 another would-be
dictator, Gerald B. Winrod, was also indicted, and federal pressure muzzled Father Coughlin. In 1944 the Internal Revenue Service effectively
bankrupted the Klan by filing a lien for back taxes of over $685,000 on
profits which it had earned during the 1920s. From 1934 to the end
of the war, state antifascism trimmed fascist support and dimmed its
potential by raising personal and legal risks for extreme-right activists.[42]

Wars, revolutions, and counterrevolutions awaken fifth-column fears.
Historians have suggested that the fifth-column mania substituted a fic-
titious enemy for a real one. Fifth columnists were a concern to Nobel
prize-winning novelist Sinclair Lewis (and husband of Dorothy Thompson), whose 1935 novel, *It Can't Happen Here*, contributed substantially to American awareness of the fascist threat. During his 1940 election campaign Roosevelt denounced "appeaser fifth columnists" who
had charged him with "war-mongering."[43] Paranoia about spies became
so extensive that by 1941 the Justice Department and the FBI, which
had initially encouraged vigilance against fascist agents, tried to restrain
numerous denunciations. However irrational, this paranoia had the
effect of weakening isolationism and increasing support for the British
war effort.

The Roosevelt administration interpreted the anti-Comintern pact of
1936 as an anticipation of a military alliance of Berlin, Rome, and Tokyo.
By the end of 1938 the president became convinced of the failure of
appeasement. Although he initially supported and even attempted to
share in the credit for Munich, he quickly had second thoughts, particularly after Kristallnacht. The president believed that Hitler would violate
the agreement and that Germany posed a grave threat to US national

security. Roosevelt resolved to contain the Axis, principally the Reich, by methods short of war and without completely alienating isolationist opinion. He embarked on a policy of incipient antifascism, which included rearmament and dividing Italy from Germany. Mussolini's popularity regained a bit of its lost luster because some still considered him a potential counterweight against German expansionism.[44]

In early 1939, the president attempted to deter Germany by providing political and possibly economic backing for Great Britain, France, and Poland. The administration also encouraged an alliance of the Western democracies and the Soviet Union. In early 1939, a Gallup poll showed solid support of the US public to help Britain and France if the Reich attacked them. Sixty-two percent of Americans believed that if Germany defeated the Allies, it would then assault their own nation. As in the other major democracies, the Prague coup allowed Roosevelt to take stronger measures against what was increasingly perceived as the Nazi menace. In late March 1939, duties were imposed on German goods. British and American naval deployments in Europe and Asia were coordinated to discourage both German and Japanese aggression. In July 1939, Roosevelt warned the Soviet ambassador that an agreement between Germany and the Soviet Union would not prevent an eventual German attack on the Soviet Union.[45]

Despite the president's pleas to help the democracies in the months following the German invasion of Prague, in July 1939 a combination of isolationists and anti–New Dealers blocked revision of the Neutrality Act and maintained the arms embargo on belligerents. Isolationists reasoned that the Western hemisphere was secure from attack by any combination of potential enemies. Their vision was similar to that of Halifax in Britain or Flandin in France, who argued before the war that retreat into empire would guarantee national security and preserve peace with a greater Germany. Like British and French appeasers, American isolationists – individuals such as Charles Lindbergh and groups like America First – regarded their internal enemies as more dangerous than external adversaries. European appeasers considered Communists, "warmongers," or Jews as foes, whereas American anti-interventionists focused on the Roosevelt administration, the British, and Communists, usually targeting Jews only privately. Like the left, isolationists charged that their foes were "fascist" or "Hitlerian." Nonetheless, even after the European war began, isolationists continued to argue that a reasonable settlement could be negotiated with Hitler. Isolationists – such as the leader of America First, General Robert Wood, and the anti-Semitic Henry Ford – evoked a guilt similar to the Europeans' Versailles contrition that blamed the aggressed for the aggression, and they would finance pamphlets that posited that the Roosevelt administration had manipulated the Japanese to attack Pearl Harbor.[46]

Only in November 1939, nearly two months after the war erupted in Europe, could the Roosevelt administration convince Congress to modify the neutrality laws to accomplish two complementary goals – the expansion of American business activity and the provisioning of the European democracies. The House approved the revision of the Neutrality Act, 243–172. The support of 110 of 118 Southern congressmen was absolutely essential for passage. Dixie's dependable and overwhelming approval reflected its Wilsonian internationalism and enthusiastic Anglophilia. US public opinion backed the legislation strongly. In October 1939, 59 percent of Americans supported aid to Britain even at the risk of war. The government permitted cash arms sales to France and the United Kingdom. The consequent Cash-and-Carry Bill permitted these nations and other potential allies to buy as many weapons as their resources permitted. While the Soviets were supplying Germany with raw materials and foodstuffs, the United States sold arms to defeat the Axis. Authorization to sell to the antifascist Allies contrasted significantly with the US refusal to vend weapons to the Spanish Republic during its civil war. By the end of the year, 68 percent of Americans thought that facilitating the defeat of Hitler was worth the risks.[47]

Roosevelt's hopes to isolate Germany were destroyed by the fall of France in June 1940, which brought Italy officially into the war on the German side and stimulated Japanese expansionism in Asia. The German conquest of the pacific nations of Belgium, the Netherlands, Denmark, and Norway alienated both official and public opinion of their fellow American neutral. The collapse of conservative republics and constitutional monarchies of Western Europe sparked further American efforts to prepare for war. Britain's coalition government, which included trade unionists, inspired their American counterparts – many of whom had been isolationist – to become actively antifascist. In July 1940 Roosevelt appointed Henry Stimson – a strongly interventionist Republican who had served as President Herbert Hoover's Secretary of State – as Secretary of War to replace an isolationist member of Roosevelt's cabinet. At the same time and for the same reasons, the president named Frank Knox, former Republican vice-presidential candidate in 1936, as Secretary of the Navy. Knox was the publisher of the *Daily News*, the only interventionist Chicago newspaper and a forceful Republican proponent of US military preparedness and aid to the Allies. An Anglophile, Knox criticized his own naval officers for their "defeatism," which was widespread among isolationists. Like Stimson, he had and would lobby influential anti–New Dealers in his own party to support intervention against Germany. Until Pearl Harbor, in Roosevelt's cabinet both present and former Republicans – Knox and Stimson, along with Secretary of the Interior Harold Ickes and Secretary of Agriculture Henry Wallace – were more aggressively interventionist than Secretary of State Hull or even the president himself.[48]

American business executives, who hated to see their machines idle, welcomed fat contracts from any government. The first Cash-and-Carry orders had originated from the United Kingdom and France, whose preparation and commitment to fighting the Germans allowed the American aviation and armaments industry valuable time and resources to prepare for even bigger deals from their own government. After Britain rescued its soldiers at Dunkirk in June 1940, Roosevelt overruled his military advisors – who objected that the United States had no weapons to spare for a United Kingdom uncertain to survive – and ordered the shipment of all possible aid to the British.[49] The action anticipated his own and Churchill's order – which was again disputed by their military chiefs – to send as much assistance as possible to the Soviet Union after the German invasion of June 1941.

The Tripartite Pact of September 1940 announced the development a defensive German-Italian-Japanese alliance that sought to intimidate the United States and discourage it from assisting Britain. The pact estranged a broad base of opinion in the United States and further undermined a declining isolationism. Although the administration still sought to avoid outright war, it advanced plans to supply the United Kingdom on credit and to discourage Axis attacks through the deployment of American naval power.[50] Britain quickly exhausted its cash reserves, and in December 1940 the Republican-Democratic consensus in Congress moved toward approval of British purchases of needed materials on credit.

Effective foreign aid often functions as a system of matching grants, common in American philanthropy, whereby potentially larger donors match the sums of initial donors who demonstrate dedication and sacrifice to the cause. An excellent example of this principle was the British military performance that fortified American interventionists. The combative antifascism displayed by Churchill, the RAF, and the British people during the Battle of Britain in the summer and autumn of 1940 won the admiration of most Americans. If the fall of France was the greatest blow to conservative antifascism, Britain's survival was its greatest triumph. Although less dramatic than the unexpected French collapse, British endurance proved even more consequential by creating a war of attrition which transformed all great powers into belligerents. By September 1940 the American government considered that the production of war material for use by Great Britain was "essential for the national defense of the United States."[51] At that time, the president announced a destroyer deal with Britain which bolstered American strength in the Atlantic. The United States traded fifty to sixty World War I destroyers to the United Kingdom in exchange for the establishment of American military bases on British territory (Newfoundland, Bermuda, Bahamas, Jamaica, etc.) in the Western hemisphere. In addition, the United Kingdom pledged that it would never surrender its fleet.

Many isolationists opposed the deal, despite its obvious value for transatlantic defense, but antifascist Democrats and Republicans – including the Republican presidential candidate in 1940, Wendell Willkie – endorsed it. Like Roosevelt, Willkie believed that the Royal Navy, the most formidable in the world, was essential for American security.[52] Backed by the fervently anti-Nazi and pro-British Willkie, influential labor leaders, and sectors of public opinion stunned by the fall of France, the Roosevelt administration launched a massive expansion of arms production and of the armed forces. American Anglophiles campaigned to institute a draft. Their efforts garnered bipartisan support and culminated in the narrow approval of the first peacetime conscription – again managed through Congress by Southerners – in September 1940. As in the United Kingdom, the peacetime draft gained a legitimacy that it never previously possessed in US history. Hitler's conquests helped the antifascist Roosevelt win reelection to an unprecedented third term in November. In a radio address on 29 December, he insisted that the Axis powers were "an unholy alliance" seeking "to dominate and enslave the human race." In this fireside chat, he asserted, "a nation can have peace with the Nazis only at the price of total surrender." He proposed that the United States become "the great arsenal of democracy" by supplying Britain and its allies.[53]

To carry out his pledges, Roosevelt created new organizations to solve specific industrial problems and invited capitalists to run them. These conservative business executives – called dollar-a-year men because they volunteered their services for that nominal sum – placated corporate America and integrated it directly into the war effort. If the Depression was a major cause of the Nazi takeover of Germany, it was also a reason for American business acceptance of Washington's militarized Keynesianism. In 1940 antifascist Republicans in the administration, such as Stimson, Knox, and William Knudsen, an auto executive and chairman of the Office of Production Management, pushed successfully for large monetary and tax incentives for industrialists. At the same time, the administration won the firm backing of organized labor. In other words, Roosevelt built an American coalition that resembled Churchill's in its corporatist consensus of big business, big labor, and the major political parties. This was particularly important after 1942, when conservative Democrats and Republicans gained control of Congress, but the antifascist coalition held both in Congress and in public opinion.[54]

Isolationists in the Roosevelt administration – Sumner Welles, undersecretary of state, and notably Kennedy, ambassador to the United Kingdom – continued to lose influence. Believing that the injustices of Versailles created Nazi radicalism, both were antagonistic to the British and zealously anti-Soviet. Kennedy shared his friend Lindbergh's defeatism and resigned in November 1940 after warning Jews in Hollywood, some of whom – Fritz Lang, Oscar Hammerstein, and Frederic March – were prominent in the Anti-Nazi League, not to be actively antifascist; whereas Welles abandoned his previous analysis and converted to a policy of containment of fascism. The new ambassador to the United Kingdom, John Winant, a former Republican who had formed close ties to British Labour, was a passionate interventionist. The Lend-Lease Act of March 1941 was a major step toward American belligerency. Supported by the prominent Republicans Willkie and Thomas Dewey, the act allowed Britain to purchase on credit throughout the conflict much of that island's food, fuel, and weapons. Averell Harriman – a wealthy businessman, New Dealer, and deeply committed interventionist – was named its administrator. In effect, the Americans financed the British war effort as the United Kingdom mobilized a greater proportion of its domestic and imperial resources than any other Western ally. American plans for Lend-Lease bolstered the international and domestic confidence of the British government, which took tough measures – namely Essential Work Order 1302 – to reduce worker turnover and absenteeism. The authoritarian law made wage earners work harder in exchange for job protection and a guaranteed weekly wage. Antifascist solidarity among states strengthened Britain's own commitment to the cause.[55]

By 1941, polls demonstrated that 85 to 90 percent of Americans were willing to aid Britain, but nearly an equal percentage opposed US belligerency. In April 1941, 69 percent of Americans believed that Hitler had designs to rule their own country. The growing antifascist consensus further weakened isolationists, some of whom began to accept the need to assist the United Kingdom. Pressure for more aid to the Allies grew as conservative organizations, such as the American Legion, and prominent Republicans, including former presidential candidate Willkie, lobbied for the total abolition of the Neutrality Act in September 1941. At the beginning of that month, Roosevelt proclaimed: "I know I speak for the conscience and determination of the American people when I say that

we shall do everything in our power to crush Hitler and his Nazi forces."
After a difficult battle in Congress, in November the act was revised to
allow American merchant ships to arm and to sail through war zones to
belligerent ports. By the autumn of 1941, Americans were engaged in an
"undeclared naval war" against Axis forces in the Atlantic.[56]

The perception, subsequently confirmed by many scholars, that the
Nazis had long-term plans to attack the Western hemisphere from
bases in the Atlantic and northwest Africa deeply worried the Roosevelt administration. In addition, Washington was concerned that certain Latin American nations might cooperate with the Franco and Hitler
regimes. The administration became anxious about fascist expansion in
Latin America in the mid-1930s and regarded Franco's Spain as a possible spearhead for fascist subversion. By 1936 Germany was the second
biggest exporter to Latin America, and the alleged pro-Nazi tendencies
of the 1 million Germans living on that continent concerned both inter-
nationalists and isolationists.[57] Cordell Hull held that German minorities, as in Czechoslovakia, could destabilize Latin American states from
within. In the mid-1930s, Hull had begun to consider fascism a greater
danger than Communism. The fall of France and the Netherlands in
1940 increased concern that those nations' imperial possessions could be
used as bases for German naval attack or political subversion in the Western hemisphere. To counter this threat, in 1940 Roosevelt named the
wealthy young Republican Nelson Rockefeller as Coordinator of Inter-
American Affairs.

Right and Left Isolationism

Polls showed that Americans were determined to remain formally neutral in 1939. Though eroding during the late 1930s and early 1940s,
isolationist sentiment remained potent in Congress and in public opinion, especially in the Midwest. Isolationist arguments rested on pacifism
and anti-communism and alleged that Hitler's Germany was not dangerous to the United States, and therefore aiding the Allies was unnecessary. Congressman Hamilton Fish, a New York Republican, and others contended that war against Germany would lead both to the end of
American democracy and to Communist domination in Germany and
throughout the world. Colonel Robert R. McCormick, owner of the
Chicago Tribune, endorsed these views, which led him to overlook Nazi
anti-Semitism. He and other newspapermen, including the widely published interventionist Walter Lippmann, shared the common trope which
attributed German Judeophobia to the victimization of Germany by the
Versailles Treaty.[58]

Anti-Semitism and xenophobia often accompanied isolationism. Despite negative reaction toward Kristallnacht, anti-immigrant – if not anti-Semitic – attitudes still dominated US public opinion. In January 1939 66 percent of Americans opposed a plan to allow (Jewish) refugee children into the United States. The United Kingdom eventually accepted 9,000; the United States only hundreds. Pervasive anxiety that Jews would successfully compete with natives for scarce resources and jobs contributed to their exclusion. Except for the activities of Jewish organizations, most American or, as has been seen, European antifascists did not make aiding Jews and other persecuted minorities a priority and generally remained insensitive to their special fate. Revolutionary antifascism demanded Jews' acquiescence to the more egalitarian new order; its counterrevolutionary ally wanted to see the restoration of the old order with Jews as equal citizens. Neither antifascism wished to be seen as fighting for Jews.[59]

Approximately 30 to 60 percent of Americans were susceptible to a range of pacifist and anti-Semitic arguments, among which were that Nazi anti-Semitism was irrelevant, the Axis had no aggressive intentions toward the United States, and finally that UK agents and warmongering Jews were maneuvering Roosevelt into a war against Germany. Philo-German elements in the United States resembled those in Britain. Both were hostile to Germany's enemies, chiefly the Soviet Union, and admired (and exaggerated) the achievements of the Nazi regime. The popular Lindbergh, the most visible spokesperson of America First – one of the largest nonpartisan political movements in American history – openly articulated these arguments. Immediately after the invasion of the Soviet Union on 1 July 1941, he declared to an America First rally: "I would a hundred times rather see my country ally herself with Britain, or even with Germany with all her faults, than the cruelty, the Godlessness and the barbarism that exist in the Soviet Union." On 11 September 1941 in Des Moines, Iowa, Lindbergh answered his own question, "Who Are the War Agitators?" by accusing three groups – "the British, the Jewish, and the Roosevelt Administration" – of manipulating America into the war. His public remarks gave plenty of ammunition to interventionists who claimed that America First mimicked Nazi propaganda. Antifascists promptly accused prominent isolationists of acting as Axis agents. The isolationists' rebuttal that interventionists were British agents lacked the same negative emotional force among the largely Anglophile and anti-Nazi public. Only after the Nazis violated the Hitler-Stalin pact could isolationists charge that interventionists had joined the Communist camp.[60]

Before the invasion of the Soviet Union, American Communists agreed with Lindbergh on the need to avoid war with Germany. Communist-dominated organizations – such as the Veterans of the Abraham Lincoln Brigade – followed the Comintern line and condemned Britain and France while attempting to prevent US intervention on the side of the Allies. The Lincoln Brigade veterans' organizations provided unconditional support for the Hitler-Stalin pact. Stalinists had a de facto alliance with isolationists despite the latter's anti-labor policies. In February 1941, twenty-eight Lincoln veterans led a "Peace Motorcade" to Capitol Hill to lobby against Lend-Lease. Communist union leaders affirmed that by weakening national defense, they helped the cause of peace. Repeating the arguments of British and French Communists during the "Phoney War," Alvah Bessie – one of the most active Spanish Civil War veterans – denied that aid to the Allies was truly antifascist since fascism was "also flourishing here right now." "Our homegrown fascists," he warned, wanted America to enter the conflict. Bessie condemned Lillian Hellman's 1941 play *Watch on the Rhine* for not portraying the Germans as victims of British aggression. At the end of May 1941, the well-known Lincoln Brigade veteran Milton Wolff called Roosevelt a "war-monger." Five weeks later, after the invasion of the Soviet Union, Wolff reversed himself and demanded a "Western Front Now" to relieve German pressure on the Soviet Union. As had occurred among their French, British, and Spanish comrades, Operation Barbarossa gave American Communists an opportunity to participate and advocate an even broader antifascist alliance than during the Spanish Civil War.[61]

Immigrants, Workers, and Artists

An ideology based on self-imposed closure, fascism could not ultimately compete politically, diplomatically, economically, and militarily with its more open enemy. Fascism's exclusiveness explains in large part its violence, since it chose to eliminate many of its real and imagined enemies, not coopt them. Consequently, fascism suffered from a more limited pool of talent than its foes. Furthermore, racism and ultra-nationalism restricted meritocracy. Some recent American literature on World War II has understandably focused on the failure of the US government to grant African-Americans and women full rights, but this commendable attention to counterproductive discrimination has obscured an appreciation of the inclusion of many foreigners. The integration of able immigrant or recently naturalized citizens into the war effort – refugee Italians, Danes, Poles, Germans, and Jews – helped the Allies to win the struggle.

Both the United Kingdom and the United States mobilized the finest civilian minds to develop and produce the most effective ways to wage war. A telling example is William Knudsen, who had arrived in New York at the turn of the century as an impoverished Danish immigrant. Knudsen displayed industrial genius and, with Roosevelt's backing, began in 1940 to prepare American industry for a war "in defense of a democratic political system and free entreprise."[62] A dollar-a-year man, Knudsen rose to head the National Defense Advisory Commission. In 1942 he was commissioned a lieutenant general in the US Army, the only civilian ever to join the Army at such a high initial rank. His rapid success in converting the auto industry into massive arms production astonished his trade-union critics as well as the Axis enemy.

Foreigners also took prominent roles in such diverse activities as promoting antifascism in the media, developing cryptanalysis, and the atomic bomb. In Britain the foreign scientists – many of whom were young and relatively unknown – focused their energies on the conception and production of atomic weaponry, since they lacked security clearances which would have allowed them to work on existing top-secret projects, such as radar.[63] To inspire their problem solving, the British scientists who did develop radar posted a picture of their immediate enemy – Nazi air force chief Göring – in their main seminar room. Although many of the atomic scientists – including a good number of refugee Jews – dreaded the use of the bomb, they created it because they feared that Nazi Germany might get it first. If the initial advances in the design of atomic weapons occurred in the United Kingdom, only the United States – spurred by the initial British lead – had the geographical and financial resources to spend more than $2 billion and employ 200,000 people on the Manhattan Project to develop the first nuclear bombs.

Well-known Italian anti-Fascists Count Carlo Sforza and Don Luigi Sturzo – both of whom immigrated to the United Kingdom and then to the United States – provided a transatlantic antifascist perspective. Sturzo's influence was limited to progressive Catholic circles until the Italian attack on nearly defeated France in June 1940 alienated many even in the largely philo-Fascist Italian-American community. In New York alone 122 Italian groups condemned the invasion of France and agreed with Roosevelt's characterization of Mussolini as a "backstabber" who knifed a neighbor from behind. Mussolini's image in the United States became that of a "jackal." Americans and their government might have (barely) tolerated the Duce – as they did Franco – if he had not wholly linked his fate with that of Hitler. When Italy declared war on the United States three days after Pearl Harbor, Italian-Americans denounced the Duce and demonstrated solid loyalty to their adopted nation. The power of American assimilation was also evident in the failure of the German-American Bund to attract a significant membership of German-Americans, perhaps a fifth of the population, a massive majority of whom showed a firm commitment to the US war effort. They rejected the Bund's appeal, which was based on both Aryan brotherhood and resentment of anti-German hysteria in the United States during World War I.[64]

Organized labor composed an integral component of the antifascist alliance. In the United States, the United Kingdom, and France, union rights were correctly seen as barriers to fascism and, in many cases, communism. Like their British and French counterparts, American trade unionists were often reluctant to support antifascist military measures but nonetheless led the rhetorical fight against fascism in the 1920s and throughout the 1930s. In 1934 the relatively conservative William Green, the president (1924–1952) of the American Federation of Labor, wrote that "the working people of the United States cannot understand how it has been possible for the German working people to submit to such [Nazi] enslavement and such autocratic control." The German Reich had completely subordinated the workforce "to the dictatorial power of its industrial masters." Fascist restriction of worker turnover and Nazi concentration camps for the work-shy terrified wage earners and trade unionists. Many American volunteers who fought for the Spanish Republic did so to defend the labor movement from fascism.[65]

If the antifascism of organized labor was predictable, the absence of fascist art, specifically in the United States and the United Kingdom, was more surprising. *New Verse*, a nonpartisan literary journal, mailed forty questionnaires to individual American and British poets; twenty-two were returned.[66] No respondent advocated Fascism or National Socialism, and only one – Marianne Moore – called herself a conservative. Although Soviet styles influenced American aesthetics during the Popular Front period, Anglo-American artists and writers defended individual conscience against the claims of mass movements. Stylistic innovation, surrealistic effects, and numerous historical references broke with socialist realism. As in Spain, the pluralism of aesthetic antifascism was reflected in the complex iconography of antifascist artists, such as Stuart Davis. His representations – *Artists against War and Fascism* (1936) – dismissed simple messages, often conveyed through clenched fists, of workers' victory. Like Picasso's work, Davis' paintings were vivid appeals for artistic freedom. An urban artist, he conveyed the light, speed, and spaces of American cities. His paintings could match the dynamism of Italian Futurism and overwhelm Nazi neoclassicism. His call for liberty

Figure 6.3 Stuart Davis, *Ultramarine* (1943). Courtesy of the Pennsylvania Academy of the Fine Arts, Joseph E. Temple Fund.

met a positive response from conservatives at the World's Fair of 1939. The central theme exhibit of the fair entitled itself "Democracity" which emphasized the democratic values of freedom and independence. The anti-Communist and anti-modernist art critic Peyton Boswell contrasted "the blessings of free breathing" at the New York fair with Europe's "chained brothers."[67]

It was symptomatic that Davis, who had been close to the Communist Party during the Popular Front period, broke with it over the Hitler-Stalin pact in 1939 and the invasion of Finland three months later. Concurrently, he returned to a more individualist perspective in his work and aesthetic theory. Like Dorothy Thompson who wrote of the "general persecution in Germany of *all* individualism," Davis argued that individualism – which was perfectly compatible with conservative antifascism – distinguished democracy from totalitarianism, whether fascist or communist. Individuality within universality was central to counterrevolutionary antifascism and opposed the collectivism and racism of totalitarianism. British artists, critics, and cultural establishment justified their own pluralist creations with identical arguments that emphasized individual and creative freedom. Anglo-American pluralism contrasted with the conventional heroism of Nazi and Soviet art. Davis' *Ultramarine* "affirmed the universality and order that Davis felt were necessary to preserve the democratic state"[68] (Figure 6.3).

In the late war years, regionalists – such as Benton – lost influence to more abstract painters – Davis, Mark Rothko, and Adolph Gottlieb. The latter insisted that antifascism meant a broad freedom to explore themes

Figure 6.4 Robert Motherwell, *Elegy to the Spanish Republic, no. 126* (1965–1975). Getty Images.

that the state and public would find difficult to understand and accept. In other words, antifascism meant being nonconformist, experimental, and challenging. Abstract paintings were not explicitly antifascist. Instead, their apparent apoliticism merely implied anti-totalitarianism. They developed mythical themes which had been re-introduced by Surrealists, enemies of the Nazis. As the transatlantic Surrealist Nicolas Calas wrote in 1940: "Hitlerism... fights not only against all Surrealism fights against but also against all Surrealism fights for."[69] Unlike Fascist myths, Surrealist myths were not regional, national, or racial, but rather universal. The more obvious antifascist responses of the social realists were quickly forgotten, and the abstract explorations of Davis, Rothko, and Gottlieb became hegemonic after the war. Accordingly, Robert Motherwell's *Elegies to the Spanish Republic* mourned the death of the hopes of revolutionary antifascism (Figure 6.4).

7 Antifascisms United: 1941–1944

Democrats may have failed to understand fascism, but fascists failed to understand democrats and never realized the depth of the commitment of counterrevolutionary antifascists to reverse the expansionism of Germany and its allies. The Nazis and Fascists assumed that their domestic successes against antifascists would be repeated internationally. Marxist revolutionary antifascists might offer resistance, but they would collapse after a short struggle. Conservative antifascists – whether bourgeois or workers – would eventually collaborate to protect their own property and positions. Throughout the 1930s, both Hitler and Mussolini were contemptuous of British and French leadership. Fascists and their allies, who often saw both revolutionary and counterrevolutionary antifascism as a result of transparent Jewish scheming, could not imagine that the subsequent unity of antifascist forces with their massive economic and military power would totally defeat them. In short, they utterly misjudged their enemies.

Hitler hoped that divisions among antifascists, which had allowed him to take power in Germany, would reoccur abroad. After the fall of France, his hopes were constantly denied. The Führer's provincialism and ignorance – which diplomats, historians, and journalists documented in the early 1930s – contrasted strikingly with the sophistication of both Roosevelt and Churchill. Whereas Hitler never understood the sea, Roosevelt and Churchill had great experience in naval warfare. Churchill's main concern during and after the fall of France was to avoid the French fleet falling into German hands, and Roosevelt made great efforts to prevent the British fleet from becoming a German weapon to gain hegemony over the oceans. Both men united in their resolve to win the Battle of the Atlantic, a prerequisite for victory, which allowed American aid to Great Britain and the Soviet Union in 1941, the invasion of North Africa in 1942, and finally the invasion of France in 1944.

Except for his cousin Theodore, Franklin Roosevelt was the most cosmopolitan American president since John Quincy Adams in 1825. Roosevelt was an internationalist who recognized neither the Japanese takeover of Manchuria in 1931 nor the Italian conquest of Ethiopia in 1935–1936. In 1928 he labeled Hitler "a madman," and in 1933 yearned for a return of "that German sanity that existed in the Bismarck days." The president was aware that even though Imperial Germany was relatively healthy compared to its Nazi successor, militarism and authoritarianism characterized both regimes. Churchill's cosmopolitanism surpassed that of his American partner. Not only did he have extensive experience in the British Empire, but also a deep knowledge of the United States. His mother was American, and he frequently visited that nation, where he contributed dozens of articles for the US press.[1]

Antifascist Collaboration

The Allies cooperated much more closely than the Axis. British survival depended on this collaboration, and Churchill calculated that the United States must come to Britain's aid financially and ultimately militarily in a war of attrition. His private correspondence with Roosevelt bypassed their diplomats and forged the Anglo-American alliance. Churchill ruthlessly mobilized industry, which within six months transformed Britain into a fortress bristling with modern weapons but, at the same time, bankrupted the United Kingdom. His attitude toward financial matters differed distinctly from the financial appeasers – such as Neville Chamberlain and Georges Bonnet – who placed a higher value on protecting the pound or the franc than fighting fascism. Churchill made the bankruptcy which he deliberately accepted a transatlantic weapon of war. He deduced that the Americans would either have to continue to supply Britain and its empire on credit [Lend-Lease], thereby siding with her, or they would lose all they had provided previously, let the United Kingdom go under, and make Hitler master of the Atlantic. Churchill never tired of insisting to Roosevelt that the Führer's domination of the ocean would extend to America's eastern seaboard. The prime minister, who became one of America's most popular radio personalities, appealed successfully to his audiences by demonstrating antifascist combativeness. "His classic tribute to the Battle of Britain fighter pilots in August 1940 – *Never in the field of human conflict was so much owed by so many to so few* – was directed mainly at the United States."[2]

By the summer of 1941 the United States had made an unprecedented peacetime commitment to the United Kingdom. Anglo-American staff talks exchanged significant technical information, and the Americans incorporated large parts of the North Atlantic, such as Greenland, into their hemispheric defense system. The United States patrolled its waters (including Iceland) to warn the British of German submarines. In effect, the United States had become an antifascist power. Churchill and Roosevelt culminated this process by signing the Atlantic Charter in August 1941. At that time – less than two months after the initially successful German invasion of Russia – neither leader could be certain of the survival of the Soviet regime. In response to the Axis campaign to build enormous self-sufficient empires, they called for freedom of the seas and free trade. The American nation's commitment to open markets made both Republicans and Democrats adverse to fascist autarchy but would also create tensions with their British imperial ally and, of course, the Soviet Union. The president believed that free trade would revive the world economy, an American vision that would persist into the postwar period.[3]

The Atlantic Charter offered restoration of "sovereign rights and self-government," giving hope to those who had been forcibly deprived of them in the new Axis order. Yet the expressed right of self-determination was limited to Europe, since Churchill did not intend to relinquish the British overseas empire. Likewise, the Americans did not plan an immediate challenge to segregation and White supremacy in the US South. Instead, the Atlantic Charter articulated basic tenets of counterrevolutionary antifascism. Both leaders condemned "Nazi tyranny" and desired a return to conservative governments which could protect the achievement of the democratic revolutions of the eighteenth and nineteenth centuries – i.e., constitutionalism, separation of powers, civic equality for the great majority of citizens, generally fair elections, and robust protections for private property.

Attacks on Jewish property demonstrated to American diplomats in Germany and conservative businessmen at home the revolutionary and aggressive intentions of the Nazis. As had their predecessors in the French Revolution and in the American Civil War, fascists determined what forms of private property were legitimate and what forms illegitimate. Instead of declaring seigneurial dues and slavery illegal, fascists condemned "parasitic" private ownership, particularly that by Jews. This aspect of Nazism and later Italian Fascism revealed their revolutionary nature to those who were devoted to bourgeois order.[4]

To cement the Anglo-American relationship, on Sunday morning, 10 August 1941, the two leaders celebrated a "divine service" aboard the HMS *Prince of Wales*, where participants sang the hymn "Onward, Christian Soldiers" (Figure 7.1). Counterrevolutionary Atlantic antifascism ecumenically appealed to Christians of nearly all denominations. In this context, it is not surprising that a large proportion of paintings of buildings damaged in the Blitz against Britain focused on churches, as did the classic wartime Hollywood film *Mrs. Miniver* (1942). The Nazi

Figure 7.1 Churchill and Roosevelt at divine service, 10 August 1941, during Atlantic Conference. Getty Images.

assault on British houses of worship aroused a shared Anglo-American indignation.[5]

The United States realized that European fascism was their most dangerous foe and adopted a Europe First strategy even before the nation officially entered the war in December 1941. In January 1942, British and American military leaders concluded, "Germany is still the prime enemy and her defeat is the key to victory. Once Germany is defeated, the collapse of Italy and the defeat of Japan must follow."[6] American aid to the British helped to convince the Führer to declare war on the United States and forced him to open the campaign against Russia earlier than he would have wished. Although Reich Marshal Hermann Göring felt that Germany needed time to digest its gains in Western and Eastern Europe, Hitler believed that it was better to invade the Soviet Union before American support for Great Britain became overwhelming.[7] The German invasion of the Soviet Union in June 1941 forged temporary unity between revolutionary and counterrevolutionary antifascisms across Europe. The Soviets declared a day after the

German invasion that the conflict had become their "Great Patriotic War," and Communists returned to their Popular Front policy of broad antifascist unity. Patriotism and nationalism motivated both revolutionary and counterrevolutionary antifascists.

Over the objections of their own chiefs of staff, who argued that their nation's resources were insufficient to aid the Soviet Union, Roosevelt and Churchill insisted on the absolute priority of assistance to Russia, no matter what the cost. Neither leader was as pessimistic as their military advisors concerning the chances of Soviet survival, which – like those of the Western Allies – controlled enormous resources even in retreat. As had occurred during the Battle of Britain, combative antifascism – this time of the Red Army and the Russian people – aroused American and British admiration. The ability of the Soviet Union to withstand the Nazi assault became, after the quick collapse of France and the standoff during the Battle of Britain, the third great surprise of World War II. In October and November of 1941 – with the strong support of public opinion, which was increasingly rejecting neutralism – the United States expanded and accelerated Lend-Lease to Russia, at the expense of British and even American needs. Roosevelt quickly comprehended that the Red Army was taking and inflicting casualties and thus relieving British and, he projected, subsequently American forces. At the same time, American anti-Communist interventionists proposed "to clean up the Atlantic" while the "two gangsters" – Stalin and Hitler – were fighting in the East.[8]

Yet Soviet expansionism seemed less dangerous than Hitler's variety. In 1942 Churchill was willing to risk the sinking of half of British Arctic convoys to contribute to the Russian war effort. The Western Allied aid demonstrated to Stalin that the United Kingdom and the United States were committed to the defeat of Nazi Germany and discouraged him from seeking another agreement with Hitler. By the war's end, the Soviet Union possessed 665,000 motor vehicles, 400,000 of which were American-made, while US food shipments helped to prevent greater Soviet starvation. Just as the Soviet Union would deprioritize revolution from 1941 to 1944, the Western Allies relinquished elements of their own counterrevolutionary project. Not only did they help the Soviet Union to survive, but they also provided aid to revolutionary antifascists, such as the Communist Yugoslav Resistance chief, Tito, a former recruiter for the Spanish Republic, and Ho Chi Minh, the leader of the Indochinese Communists.[9]

The Axis invasion forced the Soviet "workers' state" to abandon provisionally its revolutionary goals and to cooperate, however reluctantly, with the capitalist powers. Stalin widened his antifascist coalition to resemble – at least superficially – that of the West. On 3 July 1940 he reiterated the call for a "Great Patriotic War," tolerated a resurgence of religious worship, but nonetheless kept property in the hands of the state. To reassure his new allies, he officially dissolved the Comintern in May 1943, although it remained quite active even if more discreet. The Soviets advocated not pan-leftist Popular Fronts – as had occurred in Spain – but more inclusive national fronts of all forces, including conservatives and traditionalists, willing to oppose the Axis. Thus, Communists were able to recruit those who had an extreme-right past that they wished to erase as the tide turned against the Axis.[10]

Red Army soldiers revealed a willingness to fight and die that surprised their German enemy. The Soviet sacrifice of millions of lives destroyed the Wehrmacht and lent the Soviet Union an antifascist legitimacy that its non-revolutionary partners lacked. The Russians killed more than 4.5 million German soldiers; the Western Allies about 500,000. Russian participation in World War II also possessed characteristics of a civil war, because more than 1 million Soviet citizens enlisted in the German army by late 1943. Still, revolutionary antifascism in Russia proved much more vigorous and more committed than its Spanish precursor. When attacked, neither Madrid nor Barcelona proved willing to martyr itself like Leningrad or Stalingrad. As Jan Karski put it for the case of the Poles: "Where did Polish sacrifice rank next to the immeasurable heroism, sacrifice and sufferings of the Russian people?" The deaths of dozens of "anti-Nazis," i.e., Resistance fighters who were often Communists, received more attention in many major American newspapers than the murders of noncombatants. In the United States, it was the massacre of nearly 100 American soldiers at Malmédy by German SS in December 1944 – not the slaughter of millions of Jews and Poles – that aroused American public opinion.[11]

The Western Allies were reluctant to take the human losses that the defeat of the Nazi (and Japanese) warrior machines demanded. American and British "citizen-soldiers" were not expendable. "The Western Allies' manner of fighting, hampered by bourgeois sensitivity about casualties, was a chronic impediment to overcoming the Wehrmacht."[12] Compared to both the Soviets and the Germans, the Western Allies were relatively indulgent with their deserters. Instead of shooting them, they returned most to their units, where many performed satisfactorily thereafter. The Germans executed 15,000 of their own soldiers for desertion and other disciplinary violations, and the Soviets at least ten times that number, but the United States put to death only one deserter.[13] National Socialism and Soviet Communism showed no such leniency and produced millions of Communist and fascist "new men" – detached from conventional morality – who quickly became dead men. Some British commanders concluded that their troops were too soft to fight the Axis successfully, and Churchill worried about the surrender of substantial British forces to a sometimes much smaller enemy in Crete, Singapore, and Tobruk in 1941–1942. These defeats damaged his own position as prime minister, but public opinion continued to support him. In percentage terms, British and American actual fighting forces were much smaller and their noncombatant support troops much larger than in the Russian and German armies.

Ultimately, though, the Western Allies did not have to match the Nazis in military ruthlessness and brutality, since their Soviet partner performed that function. Indeed, only because of the willingness of the Soviet Union to sacrifice its own citizens more massively than Germany was Nazism vanquished as quickly as it was. None of the Allies, including the Soviet Union, had to seek – as the Germans and Japanese did – the "decisive battle" to defeat their enemies. The logistically superior antifascist coalition rendered fruitless the many victories of the Axis. The Blitzkrieg against the vast spaces of the Soviet Union and the aircraft assault on distant Pearl Harbor demonstrated the folly of German and Japanese militarism. Both grave miscalculations were related, since the Japanese would not have attacked Hawaii if they had not assumed that Hitler would win the European war. Japanese belief in an ultimate German victory persisted into 1942. Guided by their parochial leaderships, Japanese, Italians, and Germans underestimated British, Soviet, and American abilities to produce and to fight.

Similarly, from June 1940 to late 1942, the highest Spanish officials, including Franco himself, believed in German victory. In June 1941 the Spanish Nationalist government decided to continue its war on revolutionary antifascism and dispatched the Blue Division of nearly 20,000 fascist volunteers to the Russian front to fight Communism. Given its faith and desire for the ultimate triumph of the Axis, the Franco regime sneered at the "plutocratic democracies" (read the United Kingdom and United States) even if it remained officially nonbelligerent toward them. The insults directed at the counterrevolutionary antifascists and the regime's suspected transfer of US petroleum shipments to Germany provoked a temporary suspension of American oil deliveries in November 1941, prior to the US entry into the war. Again in the autumn of 1942, the Roosevelt administration threatened to suspend petroleum shipments unless Spain stopped sending to Germany wolfram (tungsten), which was used to produce armor-piercing metals. Allied control of the Atlantic would eventually make the Franco regime, which was dependent on food and fuel imports, grudgingly compliant.[14]

Figure 7.2 Giraud, Roosevelt, de Gaulle, and Churchill (left to right), Casablanca Conference, January 1943. Getty Images.

Roosevelt insisted on an early military engagement in Europe to bolster what he saw as lagging American morale. North Africa was considered relatively easy prey, and Operation *Torch* was launched in November 1942. The Western Allies offered assurances to the counterrevolutionary regimes of Franco and Pétain that their vital interests on the continent and in North Africa would not be adversely affected, even though such concessions to these two collaborationist dictatorships provoked an adverse reaction from liberal opinion in the United States. Both authoritarian regimes remained suspicious of Allied intentions, and Vichy warned the Americans that France would defend its empire, if necessary, with German assistance. Following the successful Western Allied penetration of North Africa, at the Casablanca Conference in January 1943 Roosevelt and Churchill demanded the unconditional surrender of the Axis powers (Figure 7.2). Their goals were to reassure their own public opinion and the Soviet Union that they would not return to the policies of appeasement and conduct separate peace negotiations with the Axis or its most notorious collaborators. They reasoned that their position would dissuade Stalin from negotiating a new pact with Hitler. Unconditional surrender also expressed British and American determination to destroy the fascist leaderships and their hold on their societies. It reflected a consensus among the Western Allies that domestic German resistance would be unable to overthrow Hitler. Finally, unconditional surrender ensured that another postwar "stab in the back legend" would not be resurrected. The common German belief in this myth after World War I greatly contributed to the weakness of counterrevolutionary antifascism in that nation. Most of the German right and sectors of the left subscribed to the legend that the Allies had not really defeated the German military in World War I. Furthermore, the right often added that Socialists and Jews were the backstabbers and that without their subversion of the war effort, Germany could have achieved victory. The logical corollary of this belief was that Germany would win the next war if it eliminated the internal "traitors." The Third Reich executed the final part of this program.[15]

The downside of the demand for unconditional surrender was that the ultimatum for total capitulation might have solidified the German resistance to Allied conquest by uniting the regime and the people in a "community of fate." Aware of the atrocities committed by the Reich in the name of the German people, the German public knew that defeat would bring retribution, and it fought to the fiery end. In March 1943 the Minister of Propaganda, Joseph Goebbels, related to Göring: "Above all as regards the Jewish Question, we are in it so deeply that there is no getting out any longer. And that's good. A Movement and a people that have burnt their boats fight, from experience, with fewer constraints than those that still have a chance of retreat." As psychoanalyst Eric Erikson has suggested, the shrewdness of the Nazis was involving the population in crimes that bound them to their leaders.[16]

Furthermore, the insistence on unconditional surrender reflected a hardening of US public opinion toward Germany. One third of Americans were willing to make a separate peace with the Reich in mid-1942. After the German murder and abduction of nearly the entire population of the Czech town of Lidice in June 1942, opinion began to question the widely accepted distinction between the Nazi leadership and the German people. By the summer of 1942, between 88 and 95 percent believed that in the event of a Germany victory, the Nazis would occupy the United States, make it pay for the cost of the war, kill its leadership, and implement forced labor. Americans acknowledged that the German people had supported the regime as long as it seemed to succeed. Formerly isolationist conservatives, such as Herbert Hoover, who had identified Nazism and Communism since the 1930s, recognized the special nature of Nazi crimes and called for punishment of Germans who had violated treaties and pursued imperialistic designs.[17]

British diplomat Robert Vansittart influenced the American discussion of the German problem. The Society for the Prevention of World War III – headed by popular mystery writer Rex Stout – propagated Vansittart's beliefs. In the early 1930s Vansittart had voiced his suspicions of revived German militarism and during the war acquired reliable information on the mass murder of Jews. He held that Nazism had deep roots in German history and unassailable popular support. The German people were thus not merely victims of the regime but its perpetrators. Therefore, he demanded the re-education of the population. Vansittart was outraged by those who asked that "we pray for our enemies" and instead demanded compassion (and compensation) for the Germans' victims. During the war Vansittart's analysis of Nazi Germany was often dismissed as prejudiced and emotional, but his willingness to see Nazism as popular, barbaric, and irrational provided insights that few contemporaries could match: "The strength or advantage of the Vansittartist position in World War II was that believing the worst and accepting fanatical statements at face value got one closer to the truth."[18] The same analysis allowed anti-appeasers like Churchill to be much more accurate about Nazism than "realists" such as Chamberlain. As Emil Ludwig, a celebrated biographer and a member of the Society for the Prevention of World War III, stated, "other nations have been cruel in their wars ... but they did not make a religion of barbarity."[19]

French Resistance

The Vichy minister Admiral Darlan initially decided to fight against the Western Allies during their November 1942 landings in North Africa. In other words, the Vichy regime took up arms against counterrevolutionary antifascism but not against the Germans when they invaded the so-called Free Zone of southern France at the same time. After the loss of 1,368 French and 453 Allied soldiers' lives, the opportunistic Darlan then switched sides and signed an agreement with the United States that allowed him to become head of French North Africa. The deal with Darlan, an enthusiastic supporter of Pétain's personal rule, stretched the credibility of the democratic claims of counterrevolutionary antifascism. The admiral had earned a well-merited reputation as an anti-Republican and anti-Semitic collaborator who had firmly believed – at least until the Allied invasion of North Africa and the subsequent German occupation of the Free Zone – that France should be part of a German-dominated Europe. Opposition to Darlan placed Churchill on the defensive, and he responded to his critics by disassociating himself from the Darlan deal: "Since 1776 we [the United Kingdom] have not been in the position of being able to decide the policy of the United States."[20] Given Anglo-American opinion's adverse reaction to the Darlan agreement, Roosevelt felt compelled to publicly justify it by stating that it was only a temporary but necessary expedient to save American lives. The assassination of Darlan in December 1942 by a Resister resolved, at least momentarily, conservative antifascism's crisis of democratic credibility.

The somewhat less compromised US-backed General Henri Giraud then took Darlan's place. Giraud had gained a hero's reputation for escaping POW captivity in a German fortress and reaching French soil in April 1942. Although Giraud – unlike Darlan – had never collaborated with the Germans or served the Vichy regime, he shared much of its ideology, principally its authoritarianism and anti-Semitism. Giraud's support of Pétain's National Revolution allowed the Gaullists – backed by nearly all currents of the internal Resistance – to offer an alternative which was more democratic than that of their rivals. Ironically enough – much like Churchill and also Roosevelt, who often opposed de Gaulle – the leader of the Free French constructed a broad coalition of left and right. Official US support for both Darlan and Giraud revealed the counterrevolutionary tendencies of US antifascism, which – as it had in some Caribbean and Central American republics – opportunistically promoted antidemocratic, but nonetheless anti-German, reactionaries. Churchill adhered to a similar conservative pragmatism, which curiously echoed Hitler's preference to support reactionary leaders like Pétain rather than more purely fascist elements. The Conservative prime minister assumed that the established constitutional monarchy would be a successful bulwark against both fascism and communism in Allied-dominated Italy in 1943. Thus, he sustained as successors to the Mussolini regime the highly compromised House of Savoy and the Fascist General Pietro Badoglio – the former conqueror of Ethiopia. By 1943 the pressures of Allied public opinion would push for more democratic and steadfast antifascist alternatives to Badoglio, Darlan, and Giraud.[21]

In contrast to Giraud, de Gaulle had proven his commitment to the antifascist struggle and remained much more popular among the Anglo-American public and French Resistance fighters than his rivals. His Free French flotilla had seized the North Atlantic islands of Saint Pierre and Miquelon from Vichy in December 1941. The Free French's heroic contribution to the Allied victory at Bir Hakeim (Libya) in May–June 1942 bolstered its visibility and standing. The British and American press acclaimed the French feat, and de Gaulle used this opportunity to change the name of his movement from the Free French to the Fighting French (la France Combattante) on 14 July 1942. De Gaulle understood the wartime popular appeal of victorious antifascist combatants. His movement juxtaposed its military victories with Vichy's subservience to the Axis. Eisenhower and other American commanders, who had initially cooperated in Algeria with Darlan and numerous other Vichy officials, learned that it was more effective politically and militarily to work with Gaullists. In North Africa, the latter restored civilian control over the military, allowed union organizing, and abolished discriminatory legislation against Jews, while avoiding major purges of Vichy administrators and military officers. De Gaulle quickly outmaneuvered the politically naïve and militaristic Giraud, whose former supporters joined the Gaullist camp and reinforced its conservative tendencies. In 1943 the Americans, whose major press organs continued to praise the Fighting French, began providing large amounts of war material to the Gaullist forces. In Tunisia during the first half of 1943, 75,000 French troops performed admirably, and their military victories helped to bolster French antifascism.[22] Allied and French opinion would provide crucial support for de Gaulle's Fighting French when both Churchill and Roosevelt wanted to replace the French leader with someone more pliable.

Following the North African landings, in a letter to Roosevelt and Churchill Léon Blum endorsed the democratic credentials of de Gaulle, thus boosting the latter's legitimacy. His fellow Socialist Georges Boris, who had joined the Free French immediately after the fall of France, had warned Blum that by not joining de Gaulle's movement, Socialists would commit the same error as had the right when it refused to rally to Blum's call for antifascist unity in March 1938. Boris' and Blum's endorsements helped de Gaulle overcome Giraud's challenge by showing that the Socialist party, a pillar of the Third Republic, had moved into the camp of the Fighting French. The official Socialist presence in the Resistance had lagged, even though by the summer of 1940 Blum shared the Gaullist analysis of an ultimate Allied victory. The Socialists' pacifist and parliamentarian culture typically hindered militants from joining Resistance movements willing to fight the occupiers. Unlike the PCF, which had always been prepared to go underground and had members who had acquired military experience in Spain, the SFIO was often unable to adapt rapidly to the clandestine struggle against the occupier.[23]

Throughout the conflict the support of Resistance fighters within France was invaluable to sustain the Gaullist position. By the summer of 1940 internal Resistance movements shared de Gaulle's analysis of the war as a global one in which France should and must be on the side of the eventual victors – the economically powerful "Anglo-Saxons" who could defeat the Germans on the seas and, after the Battle of Britain, in the air as well. At the same time, the Resistance insisted that national honor required that France participate in its own liberation. The movement, Libération, was representative when it charged that Vichy engaged in "fascist treason" by collaborating with the Germans and therefore resembled all other European regimes associated with "international fascism."[24] In its rejection of fascism, Libération and other Resistance groups also insisted on the Republican values of liberty, equality, and fraternity, which became an official slogan of the Free French only in the autumn of 1941, even though it was used as early as July 1940.

Resistance leaders in the south of France – Astier de la Vigerie of Libération and Frenay of Combat – were initially hostile to the PCF and any revolutionary line. In the spring of 1943, Combat asserted that it fought "against Hitlerism and against Marxism," a position which alienated both Communists and Socialists. At the end of 1942 Libération viewed de Gaulle as the "incarnation of Republican continuity" that Pétain had abolished. In March 1943 its newspaper, *Libération*, envisaged a return after the war to a new republic which would adopt a constitution based on the Atlantic Charter, guaranteeing workers' rights but rejecting a "statist dictatorship." In July 1943 *Libération* affirmed, "our mystique is republican and democratic, that is to say Jacobin. Our national tradition inspires us." Like its Jacobin predecessors, it regularly publicized the names of "traitors." During the first half of the war, *Libération* rejected a close association with Communists and attempted to engage the non-Communist left – Christian democrats, Socialists, trade unionists, and Masons.[25]

Unlike most Communists who entered the Resistance *en masse* after the invasion of the Soviet Union, Masons joined as individuals. Some of the most prominent Masons – for example, Jean Moulin, the unifier of diverse Resistance groups into the Mouvements Unis de la Résistance (MUR) and Pierre Mendès France, a French Jew and future prime minister – played central roles in the Gaullist Resistance. Many Masons, including Moulin and Mendès France, who were close respectively to the Socialist and Radical parties, distrusted Communism as "totalitarian." By 1943 Masons had regained influence in such non-revolutionary bureaucracies as the Marseilles police, where the Gaullist leadership of Combat found followers.[26]

For their part, Communists remained suspicious of Masonry, and the Soviets banned it throughout Eastern Europe after the war. Likewise, Nationalist Spain and Vichy France persecuted Masons. The latter regimes considered them symbols of republican and Enlightenment tenets of equality, tolerance, and secularism. Franco and Pétain rejected the "Masonic" principles of popular sovereignty and representative government. Spanish Nationalists and French Vichyites adopted established Catholic hostility toward Masons, who were identified with Jews as anticlerical, secretive, cosmopolitan, and disloyal. Vichy Interior Minister Pierre Pucheu assimilated Masons to Jews, both of whom connived in the "synagogue of Satan." Pétain declared, "Freemasonry is the main cause of our current woes. It taught the French lies." His regime's anti-Masonic exhibition, which was seen by more than 1 million persons in Paris and provinces, reinforced this hostility. Pétain and Franco connected anti-Masonry to their own counterrevolutionary agendas, which viewed – without evidence – the Revolution of 1789 as a product of a Masonic conspiracy.[27]

Anti-Semites multiplied the power of Jews by identifying them with Masons, and anti-Masons similarly fantasized that their alleged enemies dominated their societies. They explained their nation's and often their own personal failures as well by imagining that both groups conspired against them to preserve a monopoly on power. Anti-Semites and anti-Masons fancied that Masons and Jews secretly plotted to fight fascism to serve the interests of both capitalism and – illogically enough – Communism. Anti-Masons argued that Bolsheviks machinated with Freemasonry. They held that four great Internationals – Jewish, Bolshevik, capitalist, and Masonic – were arrayed against France, tellingly omitting Germany from their list of enemies. Anti-Semites and anti-Masons adhered to the conspiratorial theories of history that fascists promulgated. The Masonic membership of both Roosevelt and Churchill reinforced their beliefs, even if Churchill hardly ever attended meetings. Fellow Masons pleaded – usually unsuccessfully – with Roosevelt to intervene on the side of the Resistance.[28]

While always open to Masons, Libération's attitude toward Communists altered during the war. Until the summer of 1943 it retained its initial reluctance to cooperate closely with the PCF and did not have any "Communist or fellow-traveling officials." Even during that year it refused "overly sectarian Marxism." However, like many other conservatives and centrists in the Atlantic world, "the overwhelming victories of the heroic Red Army" convinced it to adopt a more sympathetic attitude toward Communist militants. While Frenay of Combat remained the PCF's bête noire, by the end of the war Astier of Libération had become a PCF fellow traveler.[29]

As had its Soviet mentor after Operation Barbarossa, the PCF subordinated any revolutionary conquest of power to a broad antifascist alliance with Gaullist and other Resistance forces. Following Moscow's line, French Communists supported the extension of the Popular Front coalition to include all those opposed to the Vichy government and its collaboration with Germans. Both its supporters and its opponents often exaggerated PCF power in the Resistance, but there was little doubt of increasing Communist activism and mounting prestige. As had occurred in the Spanish Republic during its civil war, the multiple contributions of Communist militants made antifascists increasingly philo-Communist. However, in contrast to the Spanish Republic, conservatives, led by de Gaulle, retained dominant authority and influence in the French Resistance. From a position of relative strength, Gaullists had no hesitation allying with the Soviet Union and its followers inside France. Gaullism had neither revolutionary origins nor goals. Despite the fears of *pétainistes*, restorationist antifascism maintained hegemony within the French Resistance.

During the occupation, the anti-Communism of most French conservatives continued to exceed their anti-Germanism, as it had during the period from the Spanish Civil War to the Prague coup. Approximately 12,000 Frenchmen would volunteer to fight against the Soviet Union after the German invasion. The fear of Bolshevism, even among Socialist and syndicalist pacifists, was so potent that in late 1943 collaborators and their sympathizers viewed the hand of Moscow as dominant not only in de Gaulle's Algerian government but also in Britain and America.[30] The arrest in Algeria in 1943 and eventual execution of Pucheu, the minister who had participated in the selection of Communist hostages whom the Germans had shot, confirmed to intransigent rightists that the Resistance government in exile – Comité français de libération nationale (CFLN), founded in 4 June 1943 in Algiers – and de Gaulle himself were under growing Soviet influence.[31] They ignored that the entire Resistance demanded the death of Pucheu who – unlike other prominent Vichyites, such as Flandin, who had also tried to switch sides as Axis fortunes dimmed – lacked high-ranking Allied protectors. Like their Nazi patrons, the Anglophobes Pétain and Laval continued to underestimate conservative antifascism and believed in the spring of 1944 that the Germans remained the only defense against a Bolshevized Europe.[32] Others who were better informed trusted that the Anglo-Americans and the Gaullist Resistance would prevent a revolutionary France.[33]

At first, the Gaullist movement had rejected Communist and other political parties of the Third Republic. Disappointed that few members of the traditional elites – high-level civil servants, business executives, and provincial notables – enrolled in the Free French, by November 1941 de Gaulle affirmed his fidelity to the Republican tradition inherited

from the French Revolution. He eventually decided that the best solution
would be "the return of the Third Republic freed from its flaws." This
"bitter enemy of Hitlero-fascist system" replaced the original traditionalist slogan of the Free French, "Honor and Fatherland," with the republican "Liberty, Equality, Fraternity." Even if the former motto did not
completely disappear from Free French propaganda, Gaullists shifted
from an authoritarian nationalist to a more democratic stance that, like
most of his antifascist allies, accepted political pluralism. In November
1942, the Socialists too were insisting on the return of the multiparty
political regime "that ranges from [nationalist] Marin to [Communist]
Thorez." The embrace of the Republican tradition allowed Socialists
and Communists to join with the Gaullist resistance. In February 1943
the Conseil National de la Résistance (CNR), which coordinated Resistance movements within France, granted official recognition to anti-
Vichy trade unions and political parties, including the SFIO and the
PCF.[34]

The CFLN, which officially supervised the CNR, would achieve a
legitimacy and control of territory that no other European government
in exile could match. The CFLN comprised all factions of the Resistance – from Communists to conservatives (including former *giraudistes*
and *ex-vichystes*). It pledged solemnly to restore traditional French liberties, the republican form of government, and its laws. In November
1943 the CFLN was the only government in exile which was recognized
by numerous nations, including the Soviet Union. Its tax base throughout Africa allowed it to free itself from dependence on British subsidies. Although it made good on its promise to restore the rights of Jews,
many of whom had joined the ranks of the Fighting French to neutral-
ize Vichy troops, the CFLN's imperialism and colonialism made it less
forthcoming about Muslim rights. Its Constituent Assembly in Algiers
contained many Third Republican politicians, some of whom became
CFLN ministers. The establishment of a parliamentary assembly offered
the Socialists "their natural environment." In effect, the regime of parties – once so detested by de Gaulle – had returned and would ensure
that his own power as well as that of the Communists was circumscribed.
The restoration of traditional French democracy further improved de
Gaulle's position in Anglo-American public opinion, even if their governments remained reluctant to completely cut ties with Vichy and officially recognize the CFLN.[35]

In 1943 the Resistance began to reproduce the conservative parliamentary republic which had dramatically failed in 1940 but which both
French democrats and the Western Allies favored. In de Gaulle's analysis, the French defeat was essentially military and intellectual, not

social or economic. His argument coincides with recent literature that attributes the fall of France to short-term military and political failures, not to errors intrinsic to the French republican tradition or the decadence of the Third Republic.[36] At the end of World War II with Allied help, as at the close of World War I, the French maintained and consolidated their republic. Given its overall positive evaluation of republican institutions, the Resistance would not revolutionize society or the economy.

In early 1944 the military breakthrough of General Alphonse Juin's Free French fighters in Italy reinforced de Gaulle's position. So, in the spring of that year, did the presence in Great Britain of General Pierre Koenig, the hero of Bir Hakeim. By early 1944 domestic support for Resistance movements in France was majoritarian.[37] *The Times* and the *Economist* demanded that the British government officially recognize the CFLN. The support offered to de Gaulle as early as 1942 by the centrist president of the Third Republic's Senate, Jules Jeanneney – who had abstained from supporting Pétain – reassured the Western Allies. Eisenhower told a skeptical Roosevelt, who in May 1944 remained suspicious that de Gaulle did not represent the French people and would act as a dictator, that the CFLN was the only body in France that could assist the Allies in the fight against Germany. Eisenhower and his aide-de-camp, Walter Bedell Smith, contended that de Gaulle alone was best suited to prevent domestic chaos behind the lines when Allied forces engaged the German army in France because he enjoyed popular support and was prepared to take power. In May 1944, voices were raised in the House of Commons questioning the government's reluctance to recognize the Fighting French, who had performed so admirably in Italy. In addition to Harold Macmillan and Duff Cooper, Francophile members of Churchill's own cabinet – Eden, Attlee, and Bevin – were also vigorous advocates of the CFLN. These men – backed by the BBC and much of the Conservative establishment – acknowledged that only de Gaulle had sufficient prestige and authority among the French to restore an antifascist state, prevent anarchy, and keep a leftist revolution in check. British support for the CFLN also expressed a common Anglo-French determination to defend their respective empires against a variety of anti-imperialists.[38]

In their own manner, the Soviets agreed. In February 1944, a perceptive Soviet diplomat informed Moscow, "De Gaulle is afraid of the revolution," which would be a disaster for "imperialist" France. The Russians continued to stress de Gaulle's "profound anti-revolutionary instinct" which helped to rally to his side the "bourgeoisie which is half the population of the country." French Communists – such as the

Spanish Civil War veteran André Marty – confidentially told the Russians that de Gaulle was a bourgeois enemy. The Soviets considered Gaullist advisors – Massigli, Pierre Billotte, René Pleven, Gaston Palewski, and even d'Astier de la Vigerie, who would become a Communist sympathizer – "a band of neo-fascists." PCF leaders predicted that antifascist unity would dissolve. The Russians displayed little respect for the French nation that aided Nazi Germany during the war. Stalin was especially disappointed in the 1940 performance of the French army, which he had expected to hold off the Germans as in World War I. The Soviets were much more solicitous of American and British power, which had directly aided their efforts to defeat the Germans, than concerned with assisting the French.[39]

Despite Soviet hostility, the Fighting French attempted to win support from Moscow in order to strengthen their bargaining position with the Western Allies, whose leaders hesitated to recognize them as the official government of France. In fact, following Operation Barbarossa, de Gaulle was ready to send French troops into southern Russia to help the Soviet Union, a gesture that pleased the Soviets but aroused suspicion among the Western Allies. Yet well before the Liberation, his movement planned from its headquarters in London and Algiers to prevent Communist domination of a liberated France. Gaullists distrusted the Communist hegemony on the island of Corsica, which had been freed in the summer of 1943 after nearly a year of Italian and German control. Communists had profited greatly from their reputation – which was partially true but often highly exaggerated – of being the most combative antifascists. De Gaulle was aware that growing PCF strength had to be controlled and channeled. Indeed, he wished to make himself the only viable alternative to the Communists. He acted quickly to impose his authority over Communists in Corsica, thereby reassuring the Anglo-American Allies of his counterrevolutionary intentions and providing a model for the liberation of the metropole. From the summer of 1943 de Gaulle was determined not to be a French Kerensky.[40]

The mutual assistance that the Resistance and the Western Allies provided each other during the Allied invasion in June 1944 strengthened the hand of the leader of the Fighting French. During the reconquest of Normandy, the British cooperated thoroughly with Gaullist civil authorities. De Gaulle's headquarters in London used its Commission d'Action Militaire, which coordinated the parachuting of supplies, to hinder Communist hegemony. By August 1944, anti-revolutionary Gaullists decided to nationalize the *maquisards* (underground) and Resistance fighters, with the goal of integrating and moderating revolutionaries. The maneuver was successful: one-third to one-half abandoned their arms, and the others joined the regular army. Moscow loyalists in the PCF cooperated by suppressing those dissident communists who wanted to seize power in the name of a working-class or popular revolution. Despite the revolutionary rhetoric of many in the Resistance, France's Liberation would be integrated into an Atlantic counterrevolution that would restore or continue democratic government domestically and empire internationally.[41]

The weight of Communists in the Resistance disturbed both Washington and London, which acted to strengthen its non-Communist elements. They supplied weapons only to non-Communist French Resistance movements, and as early as December 1943, Eisenhower pledged that Free French troops would be among the first to enter Paris. The Second Armored Division, whose diversity represented the Fighting French, led the march into the capital on 24–25 August 1944. In April 1944, it counted 14,490 officers and men, including 3,600 North Africans. Fighters who had escaped from France to battle the Germans numbered 4,000, including perhaps several hundred Spanish Civil War veterans. These Spanish Republicans – commanded by the conservative, if not reactionary, General Leclerc – emerged on the winning side in Western Europe only when they became part of a non-revolutionary coalition. Despite his independent and sometimes anti-American pretentions, de Gaulle solicited US troops to ensure that revolutionaries would not dominate the Liberation. At his request, Eisenhower also stationed two American divisions in the capital to reinforce Gaullist authority and discourage revolutionary activity. Evoking not only the events of 1871 but also the fears of 1940, the leader of the Resistance stated, "we cannot have another Commune." Many conservatives and former *pétainistes* rallied to de Gaulle, whom they finally recognized as a formidable barrier to the revolutionary left. French Communists realized the impossibility of launching an immediate "proletarian" revolution. Furthermore, Stalin had little desire to break with his Western Allies, including de Gaulle, at least until the war was won on both the Eastern and Western Fronts. Ultimately, the PCF was outnumbered by the non-Communist Resistance in a nation occupied, not by Soviet, but by Anglo-American forces.[42]

Yet the situation was fluid, and "no bookmaker would have given odds against a people's democracy in France."[43] The Communist intention was to govern large sectors of the capital, and their militants controlled nine town halls of the twenty *arrondissements* (municipal districts).[44] Without the constraining presence of Allied troops, the Communist-led Forces françaises de l'intérieur (FFI), which headed the internal Parisian insurrection, would have exerted more influence on the national government than Gaullists wished. The Anglo-American presence bolstered their position and undermined that of the PCF, which had counted on domestic revolt to boost its standing. In sum, the Western Allies – not the Resistance, whether Communist or Gaullist – liberated France. Of 212 cities surveyed, only in 5 did residents mobilize to emancipate themselves.[45] After the liberation of Paris, de Gaulle toured the south – where he reestablished "republican legality" in Communist-controlled cities such as Bordeaux, Limoges, Montpellier, and Toulouse. In this task, he was immensely assisted by the presence of the Free French Army, the great majority of whom entered France, not from Normandy, but from the Mediterranean. They would help disarm the Communist-dominated units.[46]

Reflecting the belief of much of the non-Communist Resistance, de Gaulle thought that collaboration with Communists would last no longer than the war itself. He had grown suspicious of the Soviet Union, above all during 1945 because of its increasing dominance in Eastern Europe, where France had traditionally exercised influence. To balance the pro-Soviet left, the Catholic general desired to further strengthen Christian democracy, which had become an important current in the Resistance. The higher-ranking Catholic clergy had generally been *pétainistes* who misunderstood Gaullism and counterrevolutionary antifascism. Georges Bernanos criticized his church and its upper clergy when he stated that the Catholic embrace of a neutral position with respect to the defeat of Hitler and Mussolini revealed not only its moral bankruptcy but also its analytical failure. As the German military position worsened, many ordinary churchgoers realized that continued collaboration with "pagan" Nazism would discredit their church and nation. They reinforced small Catholic Resistance groups, such as *Témoignage Chrétien*, which warned as early as November 1941 that collaboration risked losing the "soul" of France. Country priests came to solidly oppose German National Socialism. De Gaulle's goal of restoring a state which could protect freedom of conscience and private property appealed to antifascist Christians. The commitment to private property was fundamental to win support in rural France.[47]

Despite Churchill's desire not to challenge Roosevelt's anti-Gaullist policy, the British press and public opinion pressured the prime minister to allow de Gaulle – who had initially been kept in the dark about the Allied invasion of his country – to make a triumphal journey to Normandy in mid-June. The successful visit compelled even American anti-Gaullists, such as Secretary of War Stimson, to admit that the general represented French opinion, although Roosevelt continued to question de Gaulle's democratic credentials. In essence, the US president remained doubtful whether the general was the best representative of the French democratic restoration that Roosevelt desired.[48] Like Churchill, Roosevelt wanted to assure continuity between pre- and post-war France. The president insisted on the elimination of all forms of fascism in France – as in Italy and Germany. He also supported a purge of French collaborators from the immediate postwar civil administration. At the same time, Roosevelt feared that Gaullists would join Communists in a civil war against rightists. He miscalculated, because Gaullists attempted to limit violence against internal enemies whom they often wished to coopt. The Gaullist counterrevolution would need the assistance of former *pétainistes*.

De Gaulle's followers insisted that the new regime reestablish confiscated republican liberties. The Resistance rebel of the war years became a man of order, who reinstated a rights-bearing republic. Like Adolphe Thiers after the Paris Commune, de Gaulle realized that the republic was the best regime to guarantee order based on private property. He refused to formally acknowledge Vichy because recognition would have meant that his own government was revolutionary rather than restorationist. In fact, for de Gaulle and much of the internal Resistance, Vichy was illegitimate and the republic had never ceased to exist. He had been one of the last ministers of the Third Republic and claimed credibly that if its leaders had continued the war, he would have never started his own movement. This insistence on continuity placed him squarely in the counterrevolutionary camp, which he led to victory much more quickly than his predecessors, who only succeeded in 1815, 26 years after the outbreak of the revolution of 1789. Like Clemenceau, whom de Gaulle (and Churchill) so admired, the general proved himself to be a republican of order who tamed or integrated the left during wartime. His government sustained the republican tradition that the Resistance had revived not only in Paris but also in early June and then in August 1944 in the Resistance-dominated Vercors and Burgundy counter-states, which rejected revolutionary violence and reassured those who feared a new Commune.[49] De Gaulle recovered the national state with the long-term goal of reestablishing French hegemony in its empire and on the European continent.

No revolutionary versus counterrevolutionary civil war materialized in France that was similar in scale and duration to Spain in the late 1930s, let alone Russia after World War I or Greece during and after World War II. Nor did the bloodshed of the Liberation equal the Vendée or the Commune. Justice may have suffered because more Vichy supporters were not punished, but toleration meant that retribution was considerably less than in Soviet-controlled Eastern Europe. High-ranking Vichyites, such as Maurice Papon – who was convicted in 1998 of crimes against humanity involving his instrumental role in deportations of hundreds of Jews – were welcomed if they could aid the return of a conservative republic. At the end of 1945, de Gaulle became more inclined to pardon collaborators and commute death sentences. Unlike Franco, the French general dreaded issuing the ultimate penalty. The Resistance vanquished the Vichy counterrevolution, which favored regression to an Old Regime, and replaced it with a republican variety founded on Enlightenment values. As in the United Kingdom and the United States, in France a broad-based antifascist consensus assumed power.[50]

As the US presidential campaign began at the end of 1944, American opinion – unwavering in support of the war once it began – obliged Roosevelt to adopt a more favorable position toward the Free French. Thomas Dewey, his Republican opponent, advocated prompt recognition of de Gaulle's government.[51] Furthermore, de Gaulle won the support of the influential columnists Walter Lippmann and Dorothy Thompson, New York mayor Fiorello La Guardia, Ambassador Winant, and countless others. Demonstrations on his behalf showed that he had more backing than any other French public figure. Under the pressure of the favorable verdict of the voting public, the United States recognized the multiparty French provisional government on 25 October 1944. Defying Roosevelt's and others' expectations, he never became a dictator. On 20 January 1946 he resigned as head of the provisional government because he could not get the executive authority that he wished. Paradoxically, he helped to create a new republic quite similar to the old parliamentary Third Republic, which had been his bête noire.

8   Beyond Fascism and Antifascism
Working and Not Working

Although organized labor throughout the Atlantic world would become staunchly antifascist, the position of rank-and-file workers was much more ambiguous. As has been seen, wage laborers in Barcelona did not always sacrifice for the antifascist cause, and, regardless of the political circumstances, their resistance to wage labor prefigured that of British and American workers in World War II. During that conflict, French workers operated in a different context where their refusal to work – flight, strikes, absenteeism, lateness, slowdowns, and, less frequently, sabotage – was implicitly antifascist. Yet in France and throughout Axis-occupied Europe, social dissidence – whether resistance to wage labor, black marketeering, or theft – was unable to defeat wartime fascism. Only the massive state power of the Allies could accomplish that goal.

Forced Labor in France

Until 1942, the largely opportunistic French were waiting on events (*attentisme*), and the Resistance remained marginal to most workers' lives. However, in the second half of that year German attempts to directly exploit French labor brought a significant number of apolitical workers into the Resistance. On the first anniversary of the German invasion of the Soviet Union, 22 June 1942, Pierre Laval – the head of the Vichy government and an enthusiastic collaborator – announced the *Relève* program, a labor exchange with Germany. France would send three workers to the Reich, which promised to return one French POW. The *Relève* marked the first time the Vichy regime encouraged the French to work in Germany. At the same time, Laval notoriously declared, "I wish for German victory, because, without it, tomorrow Bolshevism will be installed everywhere." In December 1943, Laval continued egregiously to misjudge counterrevolutionary antifascism, which he regarded as subservient to Jewish Bolshevism: "The victory of Germany will prevent our civilization collapsing into communism. The victory of the Americans would be the triumph of the Jew and of communism."[1]

Vichy once again reiterated its preference for fascism over communism or even conservative antifascism. The collaborationist regime associated the latter with the defeated Third Republic and did not understand its transatlantic potency.

Approximately 250,000 French volunteered to labor in Germany during the occupation.[2] Once assured of the freedom of Catholic workers to practice their faith, significant numbers of confessional trade-union militants supported Laval's appeal for workers to go to the Reich.[3] Gabriel Lafaye, president of the collaborationist Comité d'Information ouvrière et sociale, justified the departures of French workers by appealing in the name of the POWs to "French solidarity" and stated, "today's battles are to defend civilization and build a new Europe where work will be sovereign." Equally productivist, syndicalist supporters of Vichy argued that "the law of compulsory social labor commits France to a really revolutionary path . . . We must now demonstrate to French youth the necessity of work, its grandeur and nobility."[4]

The overwhelming majority of workers rejected the regime's call for volunteers for Germany. Wage earners – particularly skilled labor in metallurgy – dreaded compulsory contracts that would send them to the Reich. However, they also worried that their ration cards would be withdrawn if they did not "volunteer." Their employers were understandably alarmed by the prospect – and sometimes the reality – that the Germans would follow the labor draft of irreplaceable French workers with the confiscation of their machinery. In certain cases, the Germans shipped to the Reich equipment from public transport and modern factories, such as Gnôme et Rhône, which made airplane motors. In others, they requisitioned and directly "occupied" important firms – Simca at Nanterre, L'Arsenal de Puteaux, Blériot at Suresnes, Construction Mécanique (Amiot) at Colombes, Matford at Asnières, Société Alsacienne de Construction Mécanique at Clichy, la Cartoucherie at Vincennes, and certain workshops at Renault which repaired German tanks. Workers cursed Laval, who pushed them to labor in and for what he saw as a victorious Reich. From London, the Fighting French mounted a clamorous campaign to urge workers not to go to Germany.[5]

Even before Allied military victories at the end of 1942, police observers viewed Parisian workers as "Germanophobic," "anti-fascist," "committed to democracy," and favorable to the Anglo-Saxon powers. Throughout 1942 wage earners were more skeptical about an eventual German victory than governing elites. Rank-and-file attitudes differed greatly from those of Vichy union leaders, who were either enthusiastic about Laval's proposals or saw at least some good in them. A majority of workers and even "certain syndicalists" objected that Vichy's Comité d'Information ouvrière et sociale, which workers believed represented the interests of management, aimed to place French workers under German authority. By July 1942 many non-Communist trade unionists favored an Anglo-American victory which, they believed, would prevent the spread of Communism. These trade unionists anticipated public opinion in 1943 when fears of a Communist takeover had decreased after the Anglo-American invasions of North Africa and Italy. The increasingly successful antifascist coalition of transatlantic conservatives and social democrats boosted the confidence of French persons who desired the restoration of Western-style democracy.[6]

Vichy's law of 4 September 1942 allowed the government to assign a job to all those of working age, 18–50 for men, 21–35 for unmarried women, and thus made many more women eligible for conscription than even in the United Kingdom. In effect, "useful employment" of at least 30 hours per week would usually exempt the individual from the labor draft for the Reich but, if necessary, employed workers could be conscripted at random. Workers regarded the law of 4 September as "further evidence of the[ir] enslavement." This "obligation to work" introduced into metropolitan France forced labor – which was widely used in the empire – and thus completely broke with all previous French labor legislation. Although Communist plans for a general work stoppage and a public demonstration in Paris to protest the September law failed, conscription to work in Germany aroused great opposition among workers who felt it constituted "the beginning of an era of servitude." In a number of factories, wage earners engaged in slowdown strikes and work stoppages to protest the new decree. Strikes affecting 12,000 workers erupted in Lyons in October 1942 and spread to unoccupied France when authorities began to draft skilled workers for compulsory labor in the Reich. In the Peugeot automobile plants at Sochaux in February and March 1943, the attempt to round up workers for labor in Germany provoked violent work stoppages.[7]

Despite the encouragement of the occupation authorities, who attempted to attract unemployed workers – especially skilled metalworkers – to go to Germany, only 400 of 305,000 unemployed in the Paris region, an unspecified number of whom were foreigners, accepted the offer. The proffered higher wages, bonuses, and free transportation attracted very few. Notwithstanding relatively low rent, generous vacation benefits of 4 weeks per year, and the right to remit most of their pay to France, the German workweek of 50–60 hours discouraged potential recruits. Workers referred to recruiters as "slavers" and those drafted to work in the Reich as "slaves." At the major weapons-maker, Hotchkiss in the Paris suburb of Saint-Denis, three strikes occurred to protest proposed departures for Germany, and the overwhelming majority (78 of 90) of those workers who were automatically designated (*d'office*) refused to board trains heading toward the Reich. Similar actions prevented the 75 designated workers of MATRA (Mécanique, Aviation, Traction) in La Courneuve from leaving.[8] Workers preferred capitalist wage labor to its more coercive collaborationist alternative.

Workers remained unconvinced – as it turned out correctly – that Germany would repatriate French prisoners of war as Laval had promised since the Reich needed the prisoners' labor. The POWs who did return were frequently sick or unable to work and therefore a burden to the Germans. Urban/rural tensions exacerbated workers' suspicions. Wage earners assumed that peasant POWs whom the *Relève* allowed to return to France would engage in black marketeering. Furthermore, unlike World War I when peasants paid the nation's blood tax, in World War II wage earners felt that the tax had fallen on them. Thus, urban workers were generally more antifascist than peasants. Workers believed that the *Relève* "in no case serves our fellow prisoners of war and should be considered an outright deportation in the service of the German war industry." Wage laborers knew how to read between the lines of a controlled media: "Some wonder why the Parisian press, full of pictures of workers going to work in Germany and the feats of German hiring offices, has nothing on repatriation of a corresponding number of French prisoners."[9]

Although during the war 221,000 French POWs returned because of Vichy's efforts, Parisian workers proved their perspicacity: Nazi labor czar Fritz Sauckel, who earned the nickname "the slave-trader of Europe," arbitrarily extended the contracts of French labor volunteers in 1942. French wage earners worried that all workers between 16 and 60 would be requisitioned in the near future. They became apprehensive that Frenchmen would find themselves digging fortifications for the Germans on the Russian front. During the Battle of Stalingrad in 1942–1943, also a winter of cold and urban hunger in France, fears of laboring in Germany surpassed salary demands as the workers' main concern. Those who departed for the Reich generally did so only "from fear of repression." Resigned to their fate, they were informed of neither their salaries nor their destination. Reports of deaths of French workers during the Anglo-American bombings of Berlin and the Ruhr region reinforced the reluctance to leave.[10]

Declining German fortunes after 1942 emboldened more persons to resist government orders. The Allied landings in North Africa and, even more consequentially, neighboring Italy in 1943 increased unwillingness to labor in the Reich. A few educated elites – even high-ranking Vichy personnel such as Flandin – began to see by the end of 1942 that Allied victory was inevitable. Still, the North African campaign of 1942–1943 reinforced the "Americanophilia" of wage earners much more than the bourgeoisie. The failure to raise enough volunteers led in February 1943 to Vichy's introduction of an extensive labor draft for the Reich, the Service du travail obligatoire (STO). While the Fighting French sustained their vociferous campaign against working in Germany, Vichy ministers urged their sons to set an example by toiling in and for the Reich. STO workers who left for Germany generally refused to sacrifice for the antifascist cause. To a certain extent, they identified with the victimization of Germans by Allied bombing and took a more critical stance toward the Anglo-Americans and Russians. In turn, many of their compatriots ostracized them upon return.[11]

The STO measure of 16 February 1943 affected those born in 1920 through 1923 and aroused wide-ranging opposition among the population. Wage earners had multiple reasons not to labor in an increasingly defensive and devastated Germany. Many workers described the STO as they had the *Relève* – the return of "slavery" by German "slavers" – and 20 percent refused their conscription. Public opinion viewed Vichy as intensifying collaboration with the Germans without receiving much in return, and the STO became a symbol of Vichy submission to the Reich. In the universities, numerous students – who, as a rule, originated from middle- or upper-class families – resisted the census which attempted to list young people and to select "social parasites" for forced labor campaigns. In early 1943, the mobilization of skilled or young French workers to labor in German factories generated bottlenecks in French production. Employers ignored Vichy's initial sexism and, as in World War I, often replaced missing men with women.[12]

In the face of an escalating sense of class injustice and massive refusals, Laval proposed retaliatory measures against family members of the *réfractaires* – those who avoided compulsory labor in Germany – but trade unionists close to the regime protested this measure. Laval and his successors were saddled with the popular suspicion that they wished to keep French salaries low and hours long to incentivize workers to depart for the Reich. Potential draftees believed that employers had a decisive voice on the composition of the lists that determined the individuals who would be subject to forced labor. They objected that forty-year-old workers were drafted for labor service before much younger ones. Wage earners considered Vichy's extension of the workweek to 54 hours and the reduction of rations for high-intensity laborers as ways to help the German war effort at the expense of French workers. As shall be seen, strikes erupted over demands for extra rations for hard physical labor.[13]

A certain Payannet, secretary of the Syndicat des Terrassiers, recycled the *pétainiste* family argument to protest working in Germany. He asserted, "French workers do not like to leave their families, even when they are offered higher salaries than those in France." Workers resisted the *Relève* and the STO by proclaiming that they would be unable to assist their hungry wives and children if they toiled in Germany. Threats were often powerless to convince them, and many fled or even joined the French army. Authorities suspected that these newly enlisted soldiers would be reluctant to combat the "Anglo-Saxons." Wage earners became angry over the refusal of officials to tolerate *réfractaires* and fugitives from the Organization Todt, whose major task in France was to construct the Atlantic Wall. Much to the chagrin of Paris police, the public tolerated, if not supported, the refusal of the *réfractaires* to work and disassociated them from the "terrorist" activities of the Resistance.[14]

Resistance to the labor draft intensified as the war endured. Young people ignored the requirement to collect their work cards at town halls. French workers on leave from Germany painted a somber picture of their lives in the Reich, and wage earners disbelieved the more positive image of life in Germany portrayed by the official media. French workers found incredible the press' assertion that the Reich treated French and German workers equally. Indeed, a large number of wage earners on leave from Germany – perhaps more than 100,000 or about a third of the *réfractaires* – avoided returning to the Reich and remained in France without permission. The Reich authorities responded by suspending all leave until 15 October 1943. German officials continually pressed their French counterparts to find fugitives on leave and return them to the Reich. The extension on 1 February 1944 of the labor-draft age to 16 to 60 for men and 18 to 45 for childless women deepened the unpopularity of the regime. Opinion contested the support for these measures by the anti-communist Vichy propagandist Philippe Henriot and feared that new groups of French workers would be dispatched to help a progressively desperate Germany. The increasingly "massive" Anglo-American bombing campaign against the industries of the Reich remained a further deterrent for those subject to the labor draft.[15]

Hiding to avoid the STO was common. Although two thirds of *réfractaires* intended to join the Resistance, only 10 to 20 percent did so. Peasants seemed particularly reluctant to become engaged. Thus, even in the case of those compelled to labor for the Reich, very few were what can be called committed antifascists, who wanted to both fight and work against the Axis. Yet the denial of labor for the Reich was perhaps the first important act of mass antifascism in France since its defeat in June 1940, and it anticipated the Liberation's restoration of wage labor. The withdrawal of labor power for the German war machine constituted a serious act of resistance that was legally punishable. Furthermore, it fostered an outlaw culture which defied Vichy and the occupier. Even if relatively few *réfractaires* found refuge in the Resistance, the presence of the Resistance encouraged *réfractaires* to repudiate the draft and to remain in France. Chances of escaping the STO grew as the Resistance became more popular. Avoidance of the STO might be the first step toward joining the Free French or the PCF, whose affiliated organizations were willing and able to supply false identity papers and ration cards. The refusal to work in Germany aroused sympathies from some church officials.[16]

Whether or not formally in the Resistance, *réfractaires* declined to become, in their words, "the slaves of the Reich." Fifty-nine percent of *réfractaires* avoided their conscription and their departure by train; 33 percent evaded their obligation to return at the end of their leave; and 8 percent deserted. Three quarters of *réfractaires* hid on farms, although only one third had agricultural experience. Despite the law of 11 June 1943 that threatened jail for those helping *réfractaires*, the population either actively or passively protected them. State officials proved reluctant to report or arrest them. Of course, peasants were happy to have access to their (cheap) labor and, for that matter, the labor of fugitive Jews, who had a reputation in the countryside for working hard and paying rent. In comparison, Gypsies and "nomads" who refused regular wage labor remained unpopular in rural France. Nonetheless, steady Gypsy opposition to the Vichy slogan, "Travail, Famille, Patrie," anticipated and supplemented proletarian refusals of labor. The resistance of *réfractaires* was conditional. After the Franco-German agreement of 17 September 1943, some regularized their situation by working for French firms that produced for the German war effort. By January 1944, more than a million French workers were laboring in these exempted firms.[17]

Even if 8.5 million foreign workers toiled in German industries, laboring for the Germans was considered a form of collaboration frequently during and certainly after the war. In fact, most French workers in Germany accommodated themselves to laboring – with various degrees of foot-dragging – for the Nazi regime. This was also true of French POWs who, after some time in captivity, left their prison camps to work in German factories and farms. Germans encouraged this toil since it allowed them to economize on camp guards and provided more labor. In this context, it is interesting to note that 90 percent of legal charges against French prisoners involved sexual offenses, i.e., relations with German women, not avoiding work. Defying sexual prohibitions may be termed "resistance" (*Resistenz*) if an ecumenical definition is used, but it was not an act of active antifascism (*Widerstand*). This does not mean that only collective and conscious actions to combat the occupier and collaborators were antifascist. Antifascism included either individual or group activities that either fought fascists or worked against them.[18]

Despite many refusals, the STO eventually supplied 600,000 French laborers, the third largest contingent of foreign workers to the Reich, after Russia and Poland. It appears that a good number of Communists – who composed perhaps a quarter of all French workers in Germany in 1942 – abandoned antifascism to toil for the Reich, thus implementing their own individual Hitler-Stalin pacts. As the war ended, French workers in Germany became afraid that they might be denounced as collaborators. To prevent patriotic condemnation or punishment, those who had toiled in the Reich later claimed that they had been victims of forced labor and asserted – with varying credibility – that they had no choice. These arguments failed to convince doubters who recalled the many STO evaders. Recent historiography has modified the perception that STO workers were enthusiastic collaborators but has indicated that French workers laboring in Germany were usually more productive than their counterparts in France. Closer surveillance and more brutal repression of workers in the Reich may have offered fewer opportunities to refuse work than there were for wage earners in France.[19]

If STO draftees employed their exemptions as policemen or miners to remain in France, they were often producing for the Germans or their direct collaborators. Additionally, wage earners in any enterprise where 75 percent of output was destined for the Reich were released from labor requisition. So were the thousands who toiled on the construction of the Atlantic Wall. The occupation authorities encouraged low salaries in France to attract labor to Germany; nevertheless, authorities allowed considerable wage flexibility for those firms producing for the Germans. Employers could also raise salaries by offering bonuses and other incentives, in a context where workers suffered from a salary freeze and increasing inflation. Germans and their collaborators also made sure that enterprises that produced for the Reich had priority for fuel and transportation.[20]

French Workers' Resistance to Work

During the Phoney War, Communist militants – following the Comintern condemnation of a "capitalist and imperialist" war – often encouraged resistance to work. At Renault at the end of December 1939, the absentee rate was 10 percent, twice as high as the same period during previous years. "A wave of industrial absenteeism" began in December 1939 and lasted until March 1940, a winter of discouragement for wage earners – notably women – who faced deteriorating working conditions and sharpened discipline. Absenteeism among railroad workers was higher in 1940 than in 1941. To diminish it, employers and the state collaborated to require that absentees produce a medical certificate from a military physician.[21]

Slowdowns (*freinage*) were also common, especially when the workweek extended beyond forty hours. After the dismantling at the end of 1938 of the social and economic legislation of the Popular Front, many workers viewed a workweek of more than forty hours as hyperexploitative. Individual resistance against workspace and worktime replaced collective action in a period when the state and employers augmented their powers of repression. Nevertheless, during the *drôle de guerre* resistance to work never reached the level of the Popular Front. In this situation, extra taxes – a 15 percent deduction imposed in October 1939 – on workers' salaries and obligatory overtime infuriated Parisian metallurgists, who engaged in slowdown strikes and work stoppages in large suburban aircraft factories – Caudron at Issy-les-Moulineaux, Bréguet at Aubervilliers, SNCM of Argenteuil, and Capra at La Courneuve. Heavy taxes on overtime provoked a feeling of estrangement from the war effort. On 8 May 1940, 700 workers – a third of the workforce at the Capra factory, which made airplane fuselages – struck "under the influence of the many communists in the company." Police arrested 140 strikers.[22]

In decrees of May 1940 and November 1941, German occupation authorities outlawed work stoppages, and penalties for violators included capital punishment. Yet miners under occupation engaged from August to October 1940 in carefully prepared strikes of one or two days over diverse bread-and-butter issues. German officials reminded miners' delegates that they would not tolerate work stoppages but promised to seriously study their grievances. Given the Reich's need for energy supplies, the Germans recommended that employers satisfy certain "legitimate" demands and pledged to improve food provisions for this high-calorie-consuming profession. Relations between miners and occupiers quickly deteriorated after the arrest of a Communist militant, Michel Brulé. His detention on 7 October provoked solidarity among the miners of Dourges where young people shouted in the streets of Montigny-en-Gohelle (Pas-de-Calais), "Long live the strike! Long live the revolution!" On 11 October Brulé's release demonstrated the vacillation of the Germans and their desire not to provoke work stoppages. The occupation authorities were not interested in arresting Communists per se, but rather in detaining "troublemakers" who could arouse the miners. Instead of strikes that would invite repression, miners arrived late, departed early, took long breaks, and produced slowly. Throughout the occupation, they were known for their high rates of absenteeism. Older miners, in particular, withdrew their labor from the German war machine and its French collaborators.[23]

In January 1941 miners of Aniche (Pas-de-Calais) refused to descend into the pits to protest impoverished rations. The latter – although large in comparison with other classes of wage earners – were half of what workers consumed before the war, despite German food favoritism toward workers in heavy war-related industries. In May–June 1941, strikes erupted in both Belgium and northern France, which involved 70,000 Belgian workers and 100,000 French coal miners. In the Nord and the Pas-de-Calais, Communists carefully prepared the work stoppages of the "great strike" which began on 27 May and lasted until 9 June, affecting tens of thousands of workers. The strike originated at Dourges as a dispute over concrete issues, principally food supplies, but simultaneously expressed French nationalism. The slogan "No coal for the enemy" emphasized the latter.[24]

Communist propaganda in this work stoppage stressed material demands and opposed the class collaboration of the German occupiers and French capitalists, even if the PCF – like the Comintern – continued to emphasize its desire for peace and the "imperialist" nature of the war. The strike occurred as the Germans completed their conquest of the Balkans, thereby alarming the Soviet Union about Nazi intentions. The stoppage spread rapidly, and intimidation of "scabs" by both strikers and their female supporters contributed to its remarkable longevity. Strikes momentarily overcame the tendency – reinforced by the occupation – of every person for herself. Despite exceedingly ruthless repression – perhaps 50 strikers were shot, 450 arrested, and 244 deported, of whom 130 never returned – the Germans lost 500,000 tons of coal. The stoppage dramatically reduced the Parisian energy supply. After the invasion of the Soviet Union, Communists promoted the miners' strike of May–June 1941 as a model for the disruption of the German war machine. Another series of stoppages erupted in the mines of the Nord and Pas-de-Calais in September–October 1943 over wages, working hours, discipline, clothing, food distribution, and Sunday labor. The last became highly unpopular in the context of miners' reliance on gardening and hunting for food. More strikes in Northern France would accompany Allied successes in 1944.[25]

The Vichy regime favored agricultural over industrial France. Like its German partner, Vichy was in many ways hostile to the city, which it viewed as a tangle of the impure and a source of social instability. Similar to Franco's rule, Pétain's regime was rooted in the countryside, whose residents ate better (and had more babies) than those of urban areas. Rural dwellers were less likely to participate in either the Resistance or the Liberation. Yet in contrast to Spain, where the majority of the population was still rural in the 1940s, by 1931 French town and city dwellers outnumbered rural residents. Thus, Vichy's social base was narrower than that of its Spanish counterpart, and it was not surprising that the Resistance was largely urban. French wages did not keep up with price increases, unlike in the United States and the United Kingdom, where average real wages for workers rose respectively 20 and 25 percent during the war. French wage earners' standard of living descended to the level of the 1860s. For the first time since the nineteenth century, food expenses consumed as much as 70 to 80 percent of the French workers' family budget. By June 1942 the average worker in nationalized aviation had lost at least 33 pounds. Real income in Paris at the end of 1943 was half that of 1939. In contrast to the Third Republic during World War I, the Vichy regime during World War II lost legitimacy because of its inability to ensure basic provisioning to large parts of the urban population. The dearth of fuel and winter clothing compromised public health.[26]

Parisian police noted that food shortages, long queues, and perceived inequalities rendered "the laboring classes" hostile to the government and its collaborationist policies. In May 1941, "working families are undernourished; factory workers can no longer maintain the production rhythms imposed on them. It is impossible for the unemployed to buy what they need to live. Moreover, many people cannot procure the foodstuffs that their ration cards entitle them since supplies are unavailable . . . For the worker, collaboration represents – besides the presence on our territory of the German army – the organized requisitioning by the Reich of commodities or products, which, as a result, the French population cannot obtain. Furthermore, the workers believe that the leaders of the Third Reich want to be surrounded by de-industrialized vassal countries that will serve as outlets for Germany." In striking contrast to Britain, food shortages for workers, low-paid white-collar workers, *fonctionnaires*, and modest *rentiers* worsened as the war endured.[27]

The Vichy regime maintained the wartime ban on strikes and stressed discipline and order in the workplace. Nonetheless, strikes in French cities, notably Paris, developed quickly. Little information survives on early work stoppages, but they were probably short and centered on salary issues. During the entire war French Communists were comfortable leading and participating in strikes which extended their position as wage earners' tribunes. Communists called on the 70,000 metalworkers in the major Paris factories – most of which were producing for the German war effort – to labor deficiently: "For poor wages, work poorly . . . For bad food supplies, work badly."[28] They challenged the productivism of both the Vichy regime and its German partners.

Workers used the threat of strikes to obtain more food. Throughout the occupation, movements to demand greater access to canteen meals were reported at the major metallurgical firms, Citroën, Farman, Chenard et Walcker, and Sauter-Harlé. Many wage earners and their families were dependent on canteens and other group kitchens for sustenance. The priority given to large collectivities (canteens, cafeterias, and cooperatives) effectively deprived the elderly, children, and women – the majority of whom were not employed by large establishments – of access to supplies. Adding to their burdens, female wage earners were often the first to be laid off in the factories of the Paris region. In July 1940 Renault was planning to hire 5,000 part-time workers but would not employ foreigners, men over 50, or married women. As early as October 1940, women were dismissed from department stores and many other workplaces, including public services, if these employed their husbands. Housewives from all classes who could not participate in collective kitchens demanded a higher priority for family consumption. Mothers accentuated the contradiction between the Pétainist defense of the family and their inability to feed their own. Female and male workers contrasted the meager rations of their families with the scandalous abundance in the "deluxe restaurants."[29]

In the autumn of 1941 the night shift of Gnôme et Rhône – 1,000 workers producing airplane motors for the Germans – stopped work for three hours, "despite threats from the German management" and won greater provisions for their canteen. On 19 October 1943 at the Chaudronnerie Général in Ivry-sur-Seine, 45 of 50 workers, "busy producing field kitchens for the occupying armies," stopped working at 5:00 instead of 6:00 pm and demanded a salary increase, a family ration of potatoes, and improvement of canteen food. The following day, they began work several hours late and only after the intervention of the police. On 23 November at a boiler works in Saint-Denis, 450 workers struck to protest sanctions – the deduction of a half day's pay and the elimination for a week of the wine ration served during meals in the canteen – that German authorities imposed after wage earners had stopped working on 11 November, Armistice Day, which had become an ordinary working day during the occupation. The Germans randomly arrested 50 workers whom they imprisoned at Romainville, notorious as a holding station for hundreds of soon-to-be executed hostages and a transit prison for the thousands deported to the Reich's concentration or death camps. Thus, even brief work stoppages could be extremely risky, particularly compared to the situation of strikers in the democracies. Work resumed the following day, and repression seemed effective since "no incident" was reported "in the various workshops." At the factory Compteurs de Montrouge and at La Lorraine, workers also struck briefly on 11 November, an indication of their patriotism.[30]

Insufficiency of rations provoked protests and strikes among factory and transport workers. In early 1942 at Gnôme et Rhône, night workers again struck for three hours to demand meat and dairy products. On 28 April 1944 at the Cristallerie de Courbevoie, 300 of 458 stopped work for an hour to protest the poor quality of food served at the canteen. On 28 June at the large nationalized aviation company, SNCASO, at Issy-les-Moulineaux, 281 workers of the night shift ceased labor for a half hour because of the cafeteria's inferior meals. On 30 June a similar strike erupted at Chausson, where 1,000 of the 1,300 workers on the night shift stopped labor for two hours to protest against the inadequate food served in the factory. As supplies for factory dining rooms decreased, day and especially night workers were subject to increasing physical exhaustion, illness, and blackouts. Also on 13 July, 316 of 1,530 métro workers in the 18th district stopped work for a half hour to demand higher salaries and better food. On 25 July at the métro workshops rue Championnet, 300 of 1,500 workers ceased labor for an hour to demand more pay, retirement benefits, and improved food. They were seconded by 140 of 150 métro workers at the workshops in the 15th, who stopped laboring for five hours. Striking métro workers had the power to delay the commute of countless others and thereby deprive the Germans of thousands of hours of labor.[31]

Renault workers seemed content with the meals provided by their company canteen, which were often the most nutritious of their day. Furthermore, company gardens maintained by workers multiplied rapidly and furnished increasing amounts of potatoes, peas, and beans. The overwhelming majority of Renault workers – whose numbers could reach nearly 30,000 – found that the *comités sociaux d'entreprise* that provided them with garden plots, health insurance, and other benefits were useful in their struggle to survive. In fact, the committees transformed the firms into essential providers ("enterprise-providence") which was the reason for their multiplication during the war.[32]

Yet according to police, the *comités sociaux* never sparked enthusiasm among workers or even collaborationist militants, who disliked their paternalist ethic. Workers viewed the committees as an attempt by the government and employers to control their social lives. Many wage earners were skeptical of the value of cooperation with employers when the latter rejected workers' choices for the *comités sociaux* because their

picks were "too combative." "These committees too often operate without input from the personnel, in other words at the pleasure of the
boss." High levels of abstention prevailed during elections of committees, and workers suspected that employers manipulated committees to
increase profits. The intervention of Hubert Lagardelle, Secrétaire de
l'État au Travail, who provided for more union representation on the
committees, assuaged some militants' grievances. However, in June 1942
news of the appointment of Georges Dumoulin as Inspecteur Général
des Comités Sociaux alienated many rank-and-file workers who distrusted Dumoulin's "pro-German" attitudes and his very public collaborationism. Many assumed that the delegates of the committees employed
their positions to protect themselves from forced labor in Germany. As
the war endured, the advocates of the comités became rarer, and workers'
antagonism greater. Wage earners disdained delegates who were unable
to achieve substantial pay hikes.[33]

The distrust of the committees extended to the law from which they
emerged, the Labor Charter of 4 October 1941. The Charter aimed to
eliminate the class struggle through the corporatist organization of producers. Thus, as in other fascist and authoritarian regimes, it prohibited
independent unions, lockouts, and strikes. Workers, including barbers
and butchers, considered the Charter "a form of fascism." Postal workers were particularly upset by the "sidelining of the former leaders of
the union and their replacement by Christian activists and others who
have been only a small minority." Construction workers suspected that
the imposition of a monopolistic union on workers and the inclusion
of employers was a betrayal of workers' interests. Wage earners constantly feared the domination of this single union (syndicat unique) by
employers and politicians. In general, "the great mass of workers [of the
Paris region] is not interested during the current period in unions and
their activities." Wage earners – notably metallurgists – objected to the
mandatory dues required by the syndicats uniques whose leadership they
distrusted.[34]

The Charter's denial of the right to strike confiscated wage earners' best weapon and constituted "the most serious infringement on
the freedom of wage earners." By the summer of 1942, Parisian workers looked back at the Popular Front social reforms with considerable
nostalgia. Many workers yearned for a return to 40 hours, instead of
the legal wartime workweek of up to 60 hours. Supervisory personnel
(maîtrise), who had opposed work stoppages during the Popular Front,
favored them during the occupation because of their low salaries and
the subordination of French industry to the Reich. By early 1943, police
thought the collaborationist trade unionists – who included Dumoulin,

Lafaye, and ex-CGT official René Belin – had lost considerable influence over wage earners in favor of CGT leaders, such as Léon Jouhaux of the "semi-légal" Comité d'études économiques et syndicales that had entered the Resistance in December 1940 and the Communist Benoît Frachon of the clandestine *Vie Ouvrière*. In August 1943 the underground CGT called for the "re-establishment of the social legislation of 1936." Workers desired the "abolition of the Paul Reynaud decrees [of November 1938]" which had ended the forty-hour week.[35]

As the war endured and the popularity of Vichy declined, defenders of the Charter – who were never particularly numerous – dwindled. Workers yearned for the unions of the Third Republic: "We want...only the trade unionism that existed before the war." Former trade-union militants often objected that the Charter had eliminated their positions. These activists – whether CGT or Christian – insisted that they be able to regain their influence, and clandestine CGT membership rose impressively during 1943. Former CGT activists were sometimes willing to work within Vichy's *syndicats uniques* to preserve their own authority, and they would seize the opportunity to reassert a more independent unionism once the war terminated.[36]

In the summer and autumn of 1943, the collapse of the Italian Fascist government, Soviet successes on the battlefield, Anglo-American bombings, and – most importantly – the steadily worsening food provisioning encouraged Parisian workers to increasingly defy occupation authorities. Workers' thefts from factories, shops, and gardens of food products and other items that could be used for barter multiplied during early 1943 and lasted until the end of the war. In a coal company at Boulogne-Billancourt, 22 of 32 workers refused to labor to protest the arrest of 6 of their colleagues for theft of coal and the levy of a fine of 10 francs for continual violations of the time limit allotted for breaks in a nearby café.[37]

Deteriorating working conditions – especially the lack of heat – also provoked work stoppages. Protests against insufficient warmth reveal much about wage earners' everyday lives and their reluctance to collaborate. Workers viewed coal shortages as a result of occupation priorities. Some thought that the energy shortage indicated that the Germans were preparing the closure of all factories that did not produce directly for them and feared that the occupiers would send the redundant and unemployed workers to the Reich. Those who were laid off due to the lack of coal and other raw materials often blamed their reduced income on the Germans and their French collaborators, who – they accurately believed – monopolized access to essential resources. During March 1944, the scarcity of coal caused production slowdowns in major chemical firms of the Paris region. Shortages of electricity and gas meant shorter hours and lower take-home salaries. To mitigate electric outages, the Ministry of Industrial Production encouraged continual night work, but workers – particularly in metallurgy – were reluctant to obey not only because of the unavailability of nocturnal public transportation but also since employers did not provide them with a hot meal but only a cold snack.[38]

Strikes erupted at several factories in the suburbs to demand more heating in the workshops. In December 1943 at a bottle-recycling firm at Gennevilliers, five of nine female workers halted labor at 10:00 am to protest the lack of heat. One striker returned to work at 1:00 pm, another the next day, but three promised not to reappear until warm weather resumed. On 14 February at the much larger Société de Constructions Aéronautiques du Sud-Ouest at Suresnes, 1,200 workers and employees of the nearly 2,000-person workforce halted labor for 3 hours to protest the frigidness of the factory. After management borrowed 4 tons of coal from nearby establishments and restarted the heaters, work resumed. On 5 January at Suresnes at the firm Farman, which made aviation equipment and parts for the Germans, 600 workers and employees of a workforce of 1,350 stopped for 15 minutes to protest the lack of heat. On 7 March at the metalworking firm Rateau in Pre-Saint-Gervais, thirty-six refused to begin work because of the low temperature in their workshop. They returned to work after several hours when the director assured them that they would regularly receive a hot beverage.[39]

The inadequate supply of clothing aggravated individual chilliness. By the autumn of 1942, wage earners' "clothing stocks" were very exhausted. The availability of footwear waned throughout the war. The lack of shoes adversely affected not only wage earners but also their children, who attended school in unheated classrooms. In 1944 most 16-, 17-, and 18-year-olds, who were subject to conscription by the Service Civique Rural, were little better than barefoot and hoped that the government would be able to provide them with "adequate footwear." In the summer, the thermal logic of protest reversed. On 13 July at a gas factory in Saint-Denis, 60 stokers stopped work for a half hour in solidarity with their apprentices who, they felt, deserved the same job security and benefits because of the intense heat that both categories of workers endured.[40]

A few examples will suffice to show that throughout the war salary issues, particularly piecework pay, provoked dissatisfaction among male and female workers. On 14 September 1943, 800 male and female foundry workers in a firm located at Noisy-le-Sec stopped work for a half day over salary issues. A delegate designated by German authorities intervened to negotiate a solution. On Friday, 1 October, six workers at an aviation subcontractor at Courbevoie departed at 5:00 instead of 6:00 pm to demand the complete payment of a special productivity bonus, which was based on a 60-hour workweek. They refused Saturday labor and arrived on Monday at 7:30 instead of 6:00 am, but then resumed the normal schedule. On 12 October at a firm producing insulating materials at Vitry-sur-Seine, 232 men and 438 women in a workforce of 1,222 workers and employees stopped working at 9:00 am to demand an hourly increase of 2 francs and a bonus for regular attendance. Negotiations between the *comité social* and management quickly resolved the dispute, and the following day male workers returned to work at 6:00 am and female workers at 11:00 am.[41]

A strike over piecework rates erupted in October 1943 among 23 of the 240 female workers who were laboring in the textile workshops of the department store Belle Jardinière. The 23 stopped laboring at 3:00 pm and left with non-strikers at 5:00 pm, the normal time of departure. The following day the 23 came to work at the usual time of 8:00 am, and management negotiated with their delegates. However, it asked that they labor during the deliberations. The strikers refused and visited the Ministry of Labor. Police then intervened, and workers resumed work the next morning. On 14 and 15 April 1944, 50 female workers in a male and female workforce of 350 at SKF (Compagnie d'Applications Mécaniques at Bois-Colombes) – which made ball-bearings vital for the German war effort and thus was targeted by Allied bombings – stopped work for several hours each day to demand a salary increase of 13 percent. On 5 and 6 April 1944 at a foundry in La Courneuve, 83 of 148 male and female workers halted labor for several hours to protest against management's refusal of a piecework incentive. They returned to work when they received a new piecework rate that granted higher hourly pay.[42]

These kinds of strikes showed dramatically the ambiguity of stoppages over salary issues. On the one hand, the refusals of work exhibited antifascism by denying labor to the German war machine; on the other, the return to work continued everyday economic collaborationism. The complexity of the situation was clearly revealed when in early 1942 French wage earners struck for an hour at the factory manufacturing Heinkel aircraft at Nantes (Loire-Atlantique), demanded a wage increase of 1 franc per hour, and won the support of their German colleagues. In other words, this and other work stoppages did not directly challenge Nazism or the occupation. Short strikes exhibited the vast gray area which defined the relations of resistance and accommodation between occupier and occupied.[43]

Nonetheless, French wage earners risked severe repression to stop work. On 7 April 1941, at Issy-les-Moulineaux at the Incombustibilité ("Le Raphia") with 3,000 (majority female) workers, who made camouflage net for the German army, wage earners struck, and the Germans arrested 17 of them. Short work stoppages – usually not more than an hour – put pressure on the regime to raise salaries and were successful in the Paris region in May 1941. In August 1943 Gnôme et Rhône was the scene of apparently brief but victorious strikes concerning wage issues, despite arrests and direct intervention of German authorities. On 15 November in Ivry-sur-Seine at the Établissements Louis Lemoine, a metalworking firm, 238 of 900 workers halted work to demand a 3-franc-per-hour pay increase. The following day, German authorities and French police arrested 69 strikers. A day later, on 17 November, work resumed. Direct state intervention was frequent, if not nearly constant, in work disputes, a major change from the pre-Vichy period.[44]

Repression limited the length of strikes, especially in industries producing for the German war effort, but it did not eliminate work stoppages. On 20 October 1943 at La Courneuve in the Rateau plant, which produced artillery parts for the Germans, 1,600 workers ceased laboring for one hour to protest the refusal to increase salaries. Work resumed when management promised to study the issue with the *comité social*. On October 25 at Panhard et Levassor where 3,000 workers made trucks and parts for the German army, 150 workers stopped laboring at 1:30 pm to demand a salary increase. Police intervened, and workers returned to their workshop at 4:30 pm. In the afternoon of 26 October at Roche in Saint-Denis, which fabricated auto bodies and airplane parts for the Germans, all of its 302 workers stopped production to demand a 3-franc-per-hour raise. In consultation with the police commissioner, the manager closed the factory. It reopened the following day on schedule at 7:30 am, and 100 workers resumed their tasks. However, given the continuation of the strike by their colleagues, they ceased ten minutes later. A representative of the Ministry of Information reminded strikers of possible punishments and promised to consider their demands. All workers resumed work at 8:40 am. On October 29 at Ford in Ivry, 470 of 629 workers stopped work at 1:30 pm to demand a 2.5-franc hourly increase. Work resumed fifteen minutes after the police intervened. Also on 29 October in an aviation factory in Gentilly, 170 of 210 halted work at 4:00 pm and continued to strike for several days despite the attempt of the work inspector to negotiate a solution.[45]

It should be noted that almost all aviation companies produced for the Germans. By the end of 1941, 80 percent of the aeronautical sector was destined for the Reich. By 1944 the French supplied over 10 percent of the German military's aircraft and nearly half of Germany's transport planes. By 1944, 14,000 French businesses and more than 2 million workers were producing directly for the Germans, whose demands became the driving force of the French economy. Sixty-five percent of the French labor force was engaged in the German war effort, which consumed 93 percent of France's industrial goods. Seldom did French firms turn down German production requests, which were usually accompanied by priority access to food and raw materials. Nevertheless, workers' absenteeism remained elevated, and shop-floor theft was frequent.[46]

Political strikes were rare but did occur. On 22 October 1941, the Germans retaliated for the assassination of one of their officers at Nantes by executing 48 hostages in what became known as "the massacre of Châteaubriant." A Communist source reports that a number of sympathy strikes erupted immediately after the executions. PCF militants claimed that many of the major metallurgical enterprises of the Paris region engaged in a five-minute work stoppage to protest the killing of Jean-Pierre Timbaud, a CGT metalworkers' leader shot at Châteaubriant. On the second anniversary of the massacre as Axis fortunes declined, workers throughout the suburbs apparently followed the Communist watchword. For example, 900 workers of the Société Nationale de Constructions Aéronautiques du Sud-Ouest stopped working for a half hour and demanded a salary increase. Similar strikes – combining political and economic protest – occurred at MATRA, involving 1,000 strikers, and at four smaller enterprises where hundreds of workers refused to labor for short periods. At Morane-Saulnier at Puteaux, 200 workers observed three minutes of silence for the martyred trade unionist; 1,800 wage earners in the métro workshops in the 18th extended their afternoon break an additional 45 minutes and shouted "Our wages." Several other factories and workshops also reported brief work stoppages involving hundreds of workers.[47]

Le Carbone-Lorraine (nationalized as SNCM after 1937) at Gennevilliers, which employed more than 1,300 workers who produced aviation motors, experienced a brief strike in the afternoon of 21 January 1943. Police claimed that the work stoppage was not "political" but purely over salary issues. Yet, as in many nationalized aviation firms, the factory had possessed an influential Communist presence in the late 1930s and a reputation for resisting work and refusing overtime. Communists claimed that sabotage, which Socialists also encouraged, was widely practiced in large metallurgical factories. For example, at La Lorraine in Argenteuil, three machines were sabotaged, as was other equipment about to be shipped to Germany. A mysterious fire destroyed a tire workshop at Bas-Meudon. From June to December 1941, historians have counted

107 incidents of sabotage, 41 attacks with explosives, 8 derailments, and several burned harvests. Communists claimed other incidents of derailments and purposeful delays. In November–December 1941, the largely Jewish sweater makers sabotaged 375,000 pullovers destined for the Germans.[48]

By November 1943, much of the underground CGT called openly for noncooperation with the regime. On 13 December 1943, Communists promoted "a day of demands." At the Société de Constructions Aéronautiques du Sud-Ouest at Châtillon, 1,493 of 2,447 workers stopped work for a half hour to claim a more egalitarian salary structure. The German authorities arrested 15 strikers, 10 of whom were members of the *comité social*, and sent them to the fearsome Romainville prison. At an auto-body maker at Ivry-sur-Seine, 230 workers struck for three hours to support the list of demands presented by their nine-man delegation. Germans seized three strikers and shipped them to Romainville. At MATRA in La Courneuve, 250 of 950 workers halted work for an hour and only resumed after the intervention of the police. Germans apprehended ten strikers and sent them to Romainville. We remain ignorant of their fate.[49]

By February 1944 employers concluded that the influence of political and military events, i.e., the progress of Allied forces and the strengthening of the Resistance, led most "wage earners" to possess "a silent desire to fight." "Many industrialists complain... of the poor attendance of their employees as well as their many harmful thefts. Employers regret that they remain powerless over this situation due to shortage of male workers." The employers feared that the "bad attitude" of the workers would grow in the near future. Police confirmed, "the food situation dangerously affects the mood of the workers who suffer growing hardships of all sorts." On 1 May "the Communist watchword" to strike from 11:00 to 12:00 am was followed at the Landry workshops by 1,016 workers; at the Montrouge workshops by 160 workers; and at the Charolais workshops by 600 workers.[50]

By May 1944, the workweek in most major metallurgical firms decreased from 48 to 40 hours, in part because bombardments reduced the distribution of raw materials. Shortages of electricity and gas caused fewer hours, layoffs, and lower take-home pay. An increase in the fares on public transportation, including the train, métro, and bus services, added to these deteriorating conditions. Those who worked less than 40 hours typically did not receive additional pay to compensate for hours missed due to power outages or air raid alerts, notably in small and medium firms that were unable to reimburse workers. Wage earners in larger firms were more fortunate. Gnôme et Rhône workers struck for two hours to receive pay for air-raid alert time. Although the Ministry of Industrial Production encouraged night shifts, casualties from Allied night bombing restrained the employment of nocturnal labor. In addition, workers suspected that the government would silence air-raid sirens since it wanted production to continue regardless of danger.[51]

Truncated income, the threat of forced labor, and dismal food consumption probably increased Communist influence among wage earners in the war's final year. On 2 May 1944 at Willème, a truck maker at Nanterre, 750 workers followed the PCF line to strike and stopped production for a half hour while providing a list of demands to management. Likewise, at Rateau in La Courneuve, 250 of 1,850 workers also struck for 45 minutes and submitted their demands. At a firm in the 3rd district making clothes for the Germans, male and female workers claimed they were exhausted and protested by beginning work at 10:00 pm instead of 9:00 pm. After the intervention of the work inspector and a German officer, it was decided to maintain the 48-hour workweek, which was their weekly norm, but to start work at 9:30 pm instead of 9:00 and to forgive lateness up to 15 minutes.[52]

Yet wage earners largely ignored Communist, CGT, and Gaullist appeals and did not engage in ostensibly political strikes during the Normandy invasion and the month that followed. Work stoppages in the Paris region continued to revolve around issues of rations and salaries. In a number of working-class suburbs, demonstrators shouted the supposedly Communist-inspired slogan, "We're hungry." They claimed that workers were the only category of the population that had nothing to eat. Yet months earlier, even middle-class families complained that their sons did not have sufficient strength to engage in construction or agricultural labor. In July 1944 wage earners protested that public transportation was inadequate since so much space on trains was devoted to care packages that no room remained for passengers.[53]

Workers may not have consistently followed Communists, but a month after the Normandy invasion, they expressed a patriotic antifascism by halting work. Perhaps 100,000 participated in protests on Bastille Day. At a gas equipment maker in Montrouge, "obeying the orders given on the occasion of July 14," 1,400 workers of the night shift stopped work for two hours. For the same reason, 60 workers of the Grands Moulins de Paris completed a day-long strike. So did 60 of the 200 workers at the SNCF (Société Nationale des Chemins de Fer français) depot in the 18th district. Communists reported other strikes in major metallurgical plants and the métro. Work stoppages lasting an entire day were unusual and demonstrated the renewed appeal of patriotism among antifascist wage earners. On 19 July at the SNCF workshops in the 13th, 1,430 workers stopped laboring two hours to protest the arrest of 7 employees at the Vitry depot who had been seized by German authorities on 14 July.

For the same reason, on 21 July 1,350 SNCF workers at Vitry-sur-Seine stopped work for an hour. On 27 July at the SNCF depot at Noisy-le-Sec, 100 of 3,000 workers began a strike in late afternoon that lasted until 1:30 pm the following day because their ration tickets were not honored. "In reality, this movement followed the watchword from the clandestine Communist Party to protest against the tragedy of Oradour-sur-Glane," where the SS massacred 642 men, women, and children.[54]

Railroad workers, who had a tradition of close contact with Communists, were supposedly a bastion of the Resistance. PCF activists claimed to have carried out dozens of acts of sabotage and strikes in the Paris region to mark the assassination of Pierre Semard, a Communist railroad man executed on 6 March 1942. A PCF source reports that in August 1943, 1,263 SNCF workers were dismissed or interned, 184 arrested by the Germans, and 53 shot. Those working in repair shops were particularly active in strikes. On 31 March 1944 at the SNCF's Batignolles depot in the 17th, the entire workforce of 350 stopped work for 40 minutes to demand a salary increase and better work clothes. On 4 April workers at four SNCF depots – one in the 18th, two at Saint-Denis, one at Bobigny – ceased labor for one hour in the afternoon to protest the executions at Ascq (Nord) of 120 hostages, of whom 20 were *cheminots*. The Germans had shot them in retaliation for a train derailment, a specialty of the antifascist *cheminots*. On 18 April the SNCASO workforce of 1,028 stopped work for five minutes to observe a moment of silence in memory of the executed hostages of Ascq. In contrast to most other occupational groups, transportation workers seized the initiative during the Normandy invasion. From 6 to 25 June 1944, Communists claimed that there were 296 incidents of sabotage, causing 1,193 hours of traffic interruption. In June 1944, 230 bus drivers of the Paris transportation authority went underground rather than work for the Germans. Dozens of buses destined to move German troops were sabotaged. Police reports are missing from August to October 1944; however, according to a PCF source, after 15 August stoppages occurred in the Paris region among train, métro, postal, and metallurgical workers, a good number of whom were Communists. The authority of Vichy and the Germans collapsed. Faced with massive uncertainty, employers often closed their firms. The Liberation also meant liberation from labor.[55]

The contrast between state antifascism, whose bombardments of Parisian industry cancelled millions of hours of labor for the Reich, and the work stoppages and even sabotage of wage earners that annulled thousands, is telling. The operational gap between bombings and strikes does not entirely mesh with recent historiography, which has claimed that "ordinary people were resisting fascism all along, albeit in different forms and through different channels from the political."[56] In that vein,

French Communists have asserted that sabotage was more effective in hindering production than Allied bombing. If so, the German war effort in France was only marginally affected, and the output of the French aeronautical industry destined for the German military increased substantially from 1942 to 1944. There is no doubt that examination of popular resistance – including workers' resistance to work – has enlarged our knowledge of fascist and collaborationist regimes and the reactions they provoked among wage earners and others; however, the efficacy of this resistance seems to have been limited. Its negation of exploitation through individual or small-group rejection of wage and forced labor was similar to French peasants' refusals to meet the German quotas of meat, milk, potatoes, and other produce. In no case were peaceful or violent forms of popular resistance – even in the very combative Yugoslavian case – able to bring down fascist or collaborationist regimes. That task was accomplished by antifascist armies and economies mobilized by national states.[57]

Strikes delayed output destined for the Axis for hours or days; air assaults for weeks. The bombardments of March 1942 seriously disrupted production at Renault, Société Nationale de Constructions Aéronautiques du Centre (SNAC), Usines Salmson, Ford SAF, and others. Despite the destruction of industrial plants, French public opinion nevertheless continued to favor the Allies. Communists hoped that these factories would be unable to produce their "criminal manufactures," and they persisted in urging workers to stop producing for the German war effort. At Renault in March 1942 after the aerial attacks, 4,000 workers were laid off, and 14,000 of the remaining 16,500 workers were assigned cleanup jobs. At the SNAC, 1,200 of 1,700 workers were also designated for cleanup and clearing tasks. At Salmson the numbers were similar to the SNAC. The majority or a high percentage of workers in these firms continued to be assigned repair chores well into April. In late April, Colombes and Gennevilliers were hit, and most workers of the Société de Téléphones Ericson, employing 660 workers, found themselves performing cleanup duties in the damaged workshops. Gnôme et Rhône and Alsthom also suffered severe damages which halted or hindered production. It took several months for certain factories that received heavy bombing – such as Goodrich at Colombes – to recover, and a large percentage of their workers were laid off during the repair period. British attacks on power plants also disrupted the operation of surrounding factories.[58]

Allied bombardments intensified in 1943. After the aerial assaults of 4 April, nearly all of the male workers at Renault, SNAC, and Salmson were unable to produce vehicles, aircraft, or engines for several weeks because their efforts were devoted to cleaning up debris and fixing equipment. During this repair period, which was even more extensive at Renault than at the other firms, their female colleagues were often discharged. The Anglo-American air attacks of 15 September 1943 on the Parisian industrial suburbs of Boulogne-Billancourt, Bois-Colombes, and Courbevoie temporarily eliminated nearly 28,000 workers from production. Renault at Boulogne-Billancourt took several months to resume full output, and the raids forced occupation authorities to take measures to decentralize the Renault plant into four different locations throughout the Paris region. The bombings of that area on 31 December 1943 were particularly devastating for "the major metallurgical plants," which needed several months to restore output. Many Parisians believed that the Allies chose the New Year's Eve holiday to minimize casualties among workers. The bombardments of 19–21 April 1944 forced 5,000 metallurgical workers out of production and into repair duties. Another raid on the night of 9–10 May rendered jobless 6,000 metal and chemical workers. Allied bombardment destroyed approximately 70 percent of the aircraft industry's factory space.[59]

The Allied destruction of eight railroad yards in May 1944 in the Paris region, where 70 percent of French war industries were concentrated, paralyzed transportation and deprived factories of coal and other indispensable raw materials, forcing many firms to close for extended periods. Renault was obligated to halt production from 2 to 7 and again from 9 to 15 May. For its workers in Boulogne-Billancourt, the air attacks meant not only layoffs but also the increased possibility of being sent to work in Germany. The four Citroën factories in the Paris region closed for an even greater length of time than Renault. Gnôme et Rhône's shutdown was briefer (from 14 to 18 May). The SNCF formed teams to repair the damage, and they continued to labor well into June when another bombing raid on 22 June damaged several firms and left 2,800 metal and chemical workers without work. In early July 1944, raw material and energy shortages compelled Gnôme et Rhône, SNCASO, and another major metallurgical enterprise to lay off nearly their entire workforces, totaling 14,400 people. In early August 1944 Renault was employing only 10,000 workers, when it usually engaged 20,000.[60]

Repeated Allied bombing divided French public opinion. Sectors of the population resented the British and American attacks, which resulted in numerous victims and heavy damage, but others understood – as the United Kingdom had repeatedly cautioned in 1940 – that collaboration exposed France to RAF assaults against industrial sites laboring for the German military. Pro-Allied French sympathizers hoped that the destruction of their industrial plant would hasten the moment of

Liberation. The collaborationist trade unionists gathered around *L'Atelier* condemned the attacks as typical examples of British "barbarism," even though the United Kingdom had attempted to warn the affected population through leaflets and radio broadcasts. French opinion was more critical toward inaccurate US bombing, but even in this case it often excused their notorious imprecision. Many persisted in blaming the air assaults on the Germans who converted factories in populated areas to war production, placed anti-aircraft weapons in dense neighborhoods, and failed to alert the population in time. In the provinces locals assisted downed Allied pilots or gave them proper burial.[61]

Metallurgical workers at the affected firms became resigned to the inevitable bombardments.[62] The prospect of being forced to work in Germany continued to frighten wage earners more than the Allied air attacks. Despite official efforts to blame shortages on the Anglo-American bombings of transportation facilities and the "terrorist" acts of the Resistance, "workers continue to declare that only the occupiers and the government are responsible for this situation."[63] Bombing provided an argument, which the Resistance employed without much effect, that producing for the Germans would cause casualties and destruction from the air. Prior to the Normandy invasion, Churchill had objected to the intensified bombing of French rail links, which he believed would injure too many civilians; however, Roosevelt, Eisenhower, and US Army Chief of Staff General George Marshall overruled him. The Allies devoted a quarter of their European bombing to France and killed 60,000 French civilians, one-third more than the Luftwaffe's assaults on Britain. By disrupting the French transportation network, the air assaults significantly hindered German defenses and ability to bring up reserves. If Allied restorationist antifascists benefited from the considerable goodwill of French workers, the latter were nonetheless disillusioned when shortages of certain foods and fuel continued to occur months after the Liberation. For many, "the subsistence minimum" for an active life remained unattainable. Thus strikes, whose length may have been greater than those during the occupation, persisted into the autumn of 1944.[64] At the same time, the lack of basic supplies made the French dependent on the Western Allies and circumscribed revolution.

British Workers' Resistance to Work

In contrast to France, where the Third Republic and its Vichy successor had banned the PCF, His Majesty's Government – fearing the potential subversion of the Communist underground – wisely refused to dissolve the CPGB. This did not stop British Communists from using the occasion of the passage of the American Lend-Lease Act in March 1941, which guaranteed US aid to the United Kingdom on a massive scale, to argue that the "imperialist" war had forced Britain to choose subordination to either German or American big business. Communists concluded that regardless of the choice, homegrown fascism would progress unless workers revolted against it. In other words, as had the French Popular Front, British Communists put the fight against domestic "fascism" ahead of the foreign one. During the year prior to Operation Barbarossa, the CPGB wanted to wage only what it called a "People's War" and win a "People's Peace," in which British and German progressives would join to end the threats of both foreign and domestic fascism. The Communists completed their fantasy by demanding a new Popular Front government, precisely the same sort of government that had proven ineffective against fascism in both Spain and France.[65]

CPGB promoted workers' grievances until the Germans invaded the Soviet Union. At that moment, the party became fully committed to the antifascist war effort, even though it remained critical of Churchill's government as overly conservative. Post-Barbarossa British Communists revived popular patriotism that emphasized the national tradition of resistance to foreign oppression. They demanded the end of strikes, maximum output in war factories, and an immediate second front to relieve pressure on the Red Army.[66] CPGB shop stewards became "the most energetic and potent peacemakers, which is in direct contradistinction to their previous attitude."[67] This rapid shift to Stakhanovism with its "insistence upon uninterrupted work at the highest standard of intensity" caused the loss of Communist influence on "those who were previously willing to follow their leadership, although far from being converted to their doctrines."[68] In fact, Scottish Communists became so intent on "the maintenance of maximum production" that "a kind of vendetta" developed between them and some who had left the party and objected to their former comrades' transition "from agitators into upholders of continuity of work." They denounced Arthur Horner, the Communist leader of the South Wales miners, as a class traitor because "I [Horner] refused to support strike action to remedy every grievance."[69]

As in the United States and France, in Britain the hostility against the Soviet Union aroused by the Hitler-Stalin pact, the German-Russian division of Poland, and the Soviet invasion of Finland was replaced by admiration for the heroic Red Army, specifically in contrast to the weak performance of its British counterpart. The admirers included not only Labour leaders but, surprisingly, prominent Conservatives, such as Lord

Beaverbrook, Minister of Supply. As CPGB members marched in Anglo-Soviet solidarity parades with banners showing Churchill's photograph, Tory MPs responded by praising Stalin to enthusiastic crowds. Philo-Russian opinions in the West – including occupied France – grew as the Red Army resisted in 1941–1942 and intensified with its victories in 1943–1945. This appreciation of the Russian war effort was accompanied by the popular delusion that the Soviet Union represented a form of democratic socialism. Nonetheless, the tripling of membership in the year after the attack on the socialist motherland was insufficient for the CPGB to become a mass party. Labour remained the preference for workers and the progressive middle classes.[70]

In a democracy, workers' grievances will find a voice, and Communist pro-war belligerency after June 1941 permitted leftist but non-Communist shop stewards to represent the protests of the rank and file. These sometimes revolutionary stewards became capable of leading strikes of thousands of workers. Revolutionary or not, stewards found themselves caught between a disgruntled rank and file – whose power was strengthened by the skyrocketing demand for labor – and their bosses, who were backed by the state and often by the trade-union leadership that wanted more output. "Important employers were afraid of a recrudescence of the National Shop Stewards Movement" which, centered in Scotland during World War I, spurred strikes and eventually a demand for the forty-hour week. Particularly in the Scottish shipbuilding industry, employers feared shop stewards more than union organizers. Yet the corporatist commitment to antifascism by the unions, Labour Party, and Communists ensured that a shop stewards' movement in World War II would not be as powerful as its predecessor and would not take an antiwar direction. Experienced state mediators preferred to let the trade-union leadership – rather than the police or the courts – weaken rank-and-file strike movements and discipline workers. The extent to which the unions cooperated in this repressive enterprise surprised even veteran mediators, whose job during the war was "to do everything possible to bring about a resumption of work."[71]

Without the cooperation of the trade-union leadership, the war might have been lost on the industrial front. A combination of union persuasion and state power often ended rank-and-file strikes: "In a large proportion of cases where a stoppage of work occurs a resumption can be secured within two or three days, as the result of action limited to bringing the responsible Officials of Trade Unions concerned into the picture, and securing their cooperation in disciplining their members. As things now stand, such co-operation is obtained without question and is accepted Trade Union policy."[72] The consensus of both union and government authorities was that enforcement of a blanket prohibition of strikes caused more harm than good. Officials concluded that repression would also be counterproductive. Only in cases where workers engaged in illegal "subversive activities" and defied "union discipline" would the state prosecute them. "Lightning" or what Americans called wildcat strikes – which were spontaneous escapes from wage labor – were particularly apt to draw judges' attention. Union officials frequently acted as firefighters whose intervention extinguished disputes, and their absence or nonintervention encouraged walkouts and stoppages. The nearly complete collaboration of trade-union officials resulted in the elimination of "official strikes, i.e. strikes which are recognized or supported by executives of Trade Unions."[73]

State regulation rapidly expanded. In fact, Britain may have mobilized its people more quickly and efficiently than either Germany or Italy.[74] Authorities used Order 1305 – issued in 1940 – to prohibit strikes and lockouts. In addition, Minister of Labor Bevin gained power to conscript workers to perform war work. By March 1941 he also had the authority to exempt them from military service and to discipline them for absenteeism and turnover. In return, workers received job security and higher pay. Indeed, one Birmingham shop steward admitted confidentially that piecework rates were so high that they discouraged hard work and effort.[75] Various firms, particularly in the mining industry, seconded his conclusions. The strike menace by the dissatisfied rank-and-file made managements reluctant to lower wages. Well-paid workers threatened to withdraw their labor if not immediately awarded promised bonuses. Foremen and other supervisory personnel came to resent their own salaries' failure to keep pace with wage earners stimulated by piece-work incentives and overtime.

De facto union control could also allow a relaxed shop-floor atmosphere where workers ignored and even insulted foremen without fear of dismissal. The demand for labor and the growth of union power forced supervisors to treat their subordinates with – for many – previously unaccustomed tact. When too overbearing, workers accused them of acting like "little Hitlers." Rank-and-file wage earners protected their mates who were redundant or who were accused of pilfering – which some employers charged was endemic (especially on the docks) – or other transgressions. Likewise, the popularity of certain shop stewards prevented their dismissal even though they allegedly committed a multiplicity of violations – playing games (often darts) in the workshops, assaulting a security officer, spending an inordinate number of hours on union activities, arriving late and leaving early. Solidarity of hundreds, if not thousands, who were willing to strike forced management to retreat from disciplinary sanctions. At the beginning of 1944, during preparations for the invasion of France, the imprisonment by the Northern Ireland government of five shop stewards aroused the work stoppage of 30,000 Belfast engineers and shipyard workers. In April 1944 as strikes were increasing, the government prepared legislation, which nearly split the Labour Party, which severely punished instigators of "unofficial" strikes with a maximum of five years imprisonment. In tense situations, management had to rely on union cooperation to restore order.[76]

Yet union leaders could not always control their men. For example, officials of the powerful Boilermakers Union (metalworkers) were unable to prevent "irregular stoppages," which were "a reaction to wartime conditions accentuated by strain and fatigue." In the first eight months of 1941, the number of illegal work stoppages in the shipbuilding and ship-repairing industries more than doubled compared to the corresponding period in 1940 when the patriotic "Dunkirk Spirit" and the fear of German invasion combined to generate a severe but temporary decline of strikes, absenteeism, and lateness. The Dunkirk effect disappeared over the course of the war, even if the common national cause helped to encourage a reduction of the suicide rate from 12.9 per thousand in 1938 to 8.9 in 1944. In the first eight months of 1941, the number of workers involved in disputes increased fourfold to 71,000 and working days lost to stoppages multiplied fivefold, reaching 336,000 in shipbuilding. Although the number of days lost to strikes was half that of World War I, which was shorter by two years, the total number of strikes was considerably higher, even though an executive order had banned them. Wartime censorship limited the publicity given to strikes, thereby helping to preserve the unions' (and workers') popularity among the public.[77]

The state solicited shop stewards to curb absenteeism, but workers' representatives that were reluctant to protect chronic absentees could lose the support of their constituents. Unions were unable to completely disregard their role as defenders of the rank and file without losing all credibility among their members. Penalties for absenteeism and lateness caused severe discontent and provoked strikes of workers who lost additional pay and bonuses. Absenteeism in shipbuilding seemed minimal but apparently increased in early 1942 when workers refused mandatory overtime and skipped work to enjoy "the end of a rather grim winter." Employers insisted, "payment on Friday was a useful influence in getting people to attend on that day." Nevertheless, absenteeism rose steadily during the conflict. In two of three cases, workers had "no good reason," at least in the minds of the authorities, for evading wage labor.[78]

Throughout the war absenteeism averaged 12 to 15 percent of hours worked. Male colleagues refused to substitute for female bus drivers and conductors when they protected their free time through absenteeism, which affected nearly a third of conductresses during the winter months. Absenteeism was twice as high among women as men, and it was greater among single than married women. Therefore, the "double burden" of wage labor and housework cannot entirely explain female absenteeism. Young women also gained a reputation for lateness and a tendency to chat in the workplace rather than devote themselves to the task. In several cases women were jailed for missing work. Females were prone to extend their weekends by skipping work on Saturdays and Mondays. As in France, women seemed to be particularly resistant to working in factories without heat; yet males too would stop labor to protest unheated workshops, even if they could be enticed to continue if paid double time. Given female refusals of work, their very high rate of turnover, and low wages, it is not surprising that most women did not wish to stay at their jobs when the war ended.[79]

Unions, state mediators, and management collaborated to diminish absenteeism and lateness in the mines, but they remained major issues in mining, one of the most masculine professions. Young miners between the ages of 20 and 35 or miners whose wives worked had among the highest rates of absenteeism. Inversely, in stark contrast to France, male miners over 50 had the best attendance records. In this pre-consumerist society – at least for most workers and notably miners – the "persistent problem of absenteeism in this coalmining industry" was partially attributed to the unavailability or high cost of alarm clocks. Thus, miners' wives stayed awake "at nights to ensure that their men catch the very early shifts."[80]

The war's underground in the mines and elsewhere were stunningly depicted by Henry Moore. Moore, a dedicated antifascist who had devoted several works to the Spanish Republican cause, became one of Britain's most illustrious "Official War Artists." The son of a mine manager, Moore sketched in 1941 a series of drawings of miners, Britain's "underground army." These illustrations returned to the literally dark themes of the late 1930s, whose obscurity defied the capacities of the camera (Figure 8.1). Moore's portrait of colliers presented a new and violent kineticism. Their pictorial productivism was a foil to their high rates of absenteeism and contrasted with the war's destructiveness. Moore's portraits of working miners differed strikingly from his more celebrated Shelter Drawings of the same year. Turning from the depiction of male miners' ceaseless activity to wrench coal from its natural home, Moore showed the stoicism of Londoners of various classes displaced during the Blitz. Commissioned by the War Artists' Advisory Committee, the drawings of citizens resting in the tube revisited his most

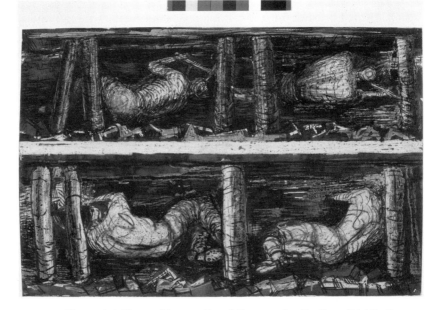

Figure 8.1 Henry Moore, *Four Miners at the Coalface* (1942). Reproduced by permission of The Henry Moore Foundation.

prominent sculptural theme of reclining females. The Shelter Drawings greatly expanded Moore's public, who admired his images of the dignified sacrifice of groups who periodically inhabited the underground. Like *Guernica*, the Shelter Drawings were soon displayed in New York and enhanced, if not created, the artist's transatlantic and antifascist reputation.[81]

As in France, UK strikes were concentrated in mining and metallurgical sectors where unrest was sometimes accompanied by "lack of discipline." High-ranking state officials urged the Boilermakers' leaders "to terminate this deplorable state of affairs" where both adult skilled workers – who, as in France, were usually in short supply – and apprentices each engaged in several dozen strikes. Metallurgical union officials and veteran employers remained reluctant to prosecute strikers, whose work stoppages were often spontaneous. Instead, they concluded that the best solution from a productivist perspective was to use the threat of prosecution to intimidate strikers. In various industries young workers, who received relatively low wages, tended to engage in "numerous" "interruptions of production" sometimes in defiance of older union men, state mediators, and public opinion. The youths were largely unorganized and thus immune to trade-union discipline.[82]

A mediator considered that young miners were responsible for low coal output in the Durham pits. The Durham Miners' Association condemned "lightning" strikes as "sabotage" and demanded "less disrespect for obligations and agreements." In July 1943 during the Allied invasion of Italy, the union posted "an appeal for 100 per cent effort now that 'the attack on the European fortress of fascism has begun.'" Thousands of Durham miners and ship workers, particularly young wage earners, ignored this antifascist plea. Management-labor relations in the pits were unusually tense since wages composed nearly two thirds of the cost of producing coal. Miners, many of whom would eventually leave the pits for better jobs, even though their underground labor was increasingly remunerated during the war, had the highest strike rate in all British industry. Furthermore, they earned the reputation of being among the most recalcitrant at the workplace.[83]

Other groups of "most indisciplined workers" were "inexperienced operatives" ignorant of trade union tradition. One group of relatively new steel workers "simply walked out because a demand for improved conditions was refused." Some quit the union, refusing to pay dues in order to be transferred to another, possibly better, job. In other words, workers used the closed-shop rules for their personal benefit, not union solidarity. Given the jump in days lost in 1941, the state – notably in shipbuilding – felt compelled to increase prosecutions of workers for violating no-strike decrees. The First Lord of the Admiralty – A. V. Alexander, a veteran Labour MP – complained to Bevin: "The Riveters and Platers have been the men chiefly affected, and their stoppages naturally affect all the rest of our shipbuilding operations. I am therefore continually faced with retardation of building programmes." Churchill apparently supported the Admiralty's anti-strike position, and Bevin – against his own judgment – was obliged to accept more prosecutions. Experienced officials charged that the riveters continuously engaged in work stoppages and were "quite beyond control." However, "a large number of workpeople cannot be sent to prison and it is undesirable to make martyrs by selecting a few for prosecution."[84]

Authorities made many threats of prosecution but carried out few. "Well over 1,000 illegal strikes have occurred since Order 1305 was made, but proceedings have been taken in only six cases." Nonetheless, at the end of 1942, labor ministry commissioners reluctantly concluded that workers' refusals of work made "prosecution . . . necessary to a larger extent than one would have anticipated." "The readiness of some classes of workpeople to cease work at the slightest provocation was displayed in

a dispute at a Drop Forging works in Dudley area . . . One of the work-
men, who was the Trade Union representative at the work, was requested
to change over from a 27 cwt. [hundredweight] to a 15 cwt. hammer
owing to faulty work. He refused to comply with the request and asked
for his release . . . As a result of this action about 100 workpeople struck
work in sympathy. Work was resumed within a few hours, pending negotiations. The man was eventually reinstated and given another chance."
Strikes in aircraft production in the first nine months of 1943 – when
mobilization and labor demand reached its maximum – resulted in the
loss of approximately 60 bombers and 15 fighters, which led to some
slackening in the air offensive against Germany. Nevertheless, resistance
to work was always done in the name of antifascism, which meant that
workers accused the bosses – rather implausibly – of favoring fascism by
hindering production. The employers, wage earners asserted, "would be
just as happy under Hitler."[85]

When prosecution was used, its effects could be widespread. In October 1942, 70 male and female toolroom workers and machine operators
struck at Searchlight Ltd. (Halesowen), which fulfilled Admiralty contracts. The employer took the strikers to court for several illegal stoppages, and the overwhelming majority was fined. The judge declared,
"Even if some of the complaints against the firm were justified[,] they
were only trivial when they came to think what our men were doing in
Egypt and the Russians in Stalingrad." In this case, the judge's criticisms – which, like those of Communists, politicized resistance to work
as anti-antifascist – were widely publicized. During the same period, an
industrial commissioner concluded, "it is rather surprising to find that
the war situation has not had the anticipated quietening [sic] effect upon
the labour situation in this area [Scotland]." He mentioned "a wave of
dissatisfaction" which had developed into more than a dozen strikes over
wage and disciplinary issues, involving over 4,000 union and nonunion
workers at important shipyards and defense factories. Despite workers'
recognition of the significance of "events abroad . . . disputes on issues
which are of a petty kind still continue and are rather numerous. The
outstanding feature is that not infrequently an impulsive stoppage of
work takes place without any reference to available procedure. Indeed,
in many cases Managements profess ignorance of the causes of the trouble . . . This feature is most marked in shipbuilding."[86]

As in France, wage disputes provoked most stoppages, particularly
among women, who were often paid considerably less than men for a
similar job. A multiplicity of motives sparked wage disputes. For example, at the Caledon Shipbuilding and Engineering Company, 29 appren-
tice riveters stopped work for several days at the end of September 1941

to demand a week's wages that had been lost on account of the absence of the heater boy. Although alternative work had been offered during the week, they had refused to accept it. Apparently, these strikers – and other wage earners who skipped work in sympathy – were not sanctioned. An exception to the general preference for persuasion rather than prosecution was the Durham coalfields, where illegal stoppages were numerous, and 1,300 prosecutions of violations occurred in the first eleven months of 1943. Yet the Durham exception proved the rule, since arrests of striking workers in that coalfield provoked strikes of thousands.[87]

It must also be recognized that dedication to the cause along with wage incentives drove workers to labor under hazardous conditions. The inspectors judged that "the constant alerts [over flying bombs] might have been expected to retard production but only three cases have come to our notice where workers have been unwilling to continue work except during 'imminent danger' periods. Only a small number of workers are involved in each of the three cases, and there is no reason to doubt that the vast majority of people will be prepared to take a risk." "In general, workers appear to be responding well to appeals by the Unions to give the fullest support to the fighting forces." Munitions workers – notably those employed producing radar equipment – made especially impressive sacrifices.[88]

Yet as in Spain during its civil war, UK workers in the final years of the war used air raids "to subvert managerial control over work" by engaging in many activities – playing cards, reading newspapers, talking, sleeping – except wage labor. "More than one trade Union Official has told us this week that he is having to deal with complaints that workers are refusing to work after the public siren [warning of rockets] has sounded, even in factories where an internal warning system is in operation, and has had to indulge in some straight talking to persuade his members that such action is not calculated to assist the troops fighting on their behalf in Normandy . . . Undoubtedly a good deal of time is being lost and production is suffering. It is difficult to understand . . . why a body of workers, who are quite prepared to spend their lunchtime in the canteen whilst a public alert is on, should feel impelled to go to ground on resumption of work, until the all clear sounds or finishing time arrives. It is perhaps brought about by a feeling of apathy engendered by war weariness." Contributing to this exhaustion was an increase of accidents "arising from war conditions." "It seems that workers find it hard to take a long view of the progress of the war and are apt to become restive and irritable." Instead of working on company-assigned tasks, metalworkers pursued their own personal projects – making cigarette lighters, jewelry, and other knick-knacks. Like their Catalan and French counterparts, British workers demanded compensation for wages lost during air raids.[89]

As in Paris, but much less frequently, inadequate or poor-quality meals could provoke agitation: "Finding that they could not be served immediately with their midday meal at the canteen, a number of foundry workers walked out with the remark 'no dinner, no work' and despite the explanation of the delay in the cooking arrangements the men declined to resume work after the break." Yet, over the course of the war, British workers' diets improved while infant mortality and tuberculosis declined. Higher wages allowed increased consumption of alcohol and tobacco. Notably in the latter years of the war, UK workers received plentiful calories, vitamins, and a good deal of protein from US shipments of dried eggs, evaporated milk, cheese, bacon, lard, and canned meat. Canteens, which had expanded in numbers from 1,500 prewar to 11,800 in 1944, ranked highest among the different types of welfare matters discussed by worker-management production committees. These new eateries – which became compulsory in firms employing more than 250 workers – supplemented the diet of many manual laborers with meat, cheese, butter, and sugar.[90]

Unions were undoubtedly a force for stability, and both employers and workers experienced increased union power. The closed shop, an "unwritten rule" "connived at" in wartime by most employers to avoid stoppages, sometimes hindered important war production when newly transferred workers could not prove that they were union members. Unionized colleagues engaged in strikes involving thousands of wage earners to protest the presence of nonunion colleagues. These strikes were effective by forcing state mediators – supported by employers who were determined to produce – to convince the recalcitrant workers to join the union to avoid provoking stoppages. Union control as well as employer traditionalism did not allow the British to build ships and planes nearly as quickly as the Americans. The Boilermakers' Society waged an effective struggle against the fabrication of standardized ships. Boilermakers were "fonder of stoppages both than they ought to be and than most other classes of workpeople." Dilution – the deskilling of manufacturing processes which allowed faster and less expensive (often female) labor – was absolutely crucial given the immense demand for wartime production. However, skilled men feared women's "cheap labor" and frequently opposed their employment in ship repairing, aircraft construction, and many other industries. State mediators confirmed that employers used women "to break up the highest prices [sic] and employ women on them." Sheet metal unions opposed "any measure of dilution by female labour." Strikes against dilution were frequently effective.[91]

Nevertheless, by the autumn of 1942, many men – particularly younger trade unionists – accepted female employment in their own industries as inevitable during wartime, if only to prevent the transfer of their own girlfriends and relatives to other regions. They had little choice since – as Bevin's biographer noted – the British conscription of women for labor "was one of the boldest acts of policy ever carried out by a democratic Government . . . [It was] a drastic act of total war . . . more drastic than even Hitler could contemplate." In mid-1943, the proportion of women who were in the military, munitions work, and essential industries was approximately double that in 1918. Although dilution caused tensions, unionized males commonly expressed solidarity with unorganized female colleagues. The Amalgamated Engineering Union (AEU), whose membership doubled during the war, reaching over 900,000, finally admitted women at the end of 1942. Still, many female wage earners in Britain and elsewhere lacked interest in militant or work-based organizations, including trade unions. A few women refused to accept discrimination passively and formed "a somewhat mysterious body, known as the Glasgow and West of Scotland Women's Parliament," which fought for a national female minimum wage and daycare for children. Government officials reported that male trade unionists dismissed the "Women's Parliament . . . with a measure of contempt." In the spring of 1944 Churchill's veto of a proposal to grant female teachers pay equal to that of their male colleagues demonstrated the extent to which female inequality was assumed.[92]

Whatever their gender, wage earners possessed a progressively more powerful bargaining position as the war created full employment. In one case, workers – led by their shop stewards – defied the wishes of their own union by refusing all overtime. The availability of overtime signified the heightened demand for labor as well as greater income for both male and especially female workers. Wage earners' struggles against overtime – which was sometimes combined with an "embargo" on piecework – were particularly acute in northern England and Scotland. With or without overtime, better-paid workers – like their French counterparts during the Phoney War – came to resent newly imposed tax deductions from their wages. Anti-tax protesters on the Clyde contrasted unfavorably their own government's position with that of Nazi Germany, where authorities supposedly exempted overtime from taxation. Non-Communist but leftist shop stewards pressed this issue by demanding no income tax on overtime.[93]

Average weekly hours worked by men over 21 were 47.7 in 1938 and 52.9 in 1943. Long 12-hour shifts severely strained women workers, and management of one firm responded by reducing hours from 60 to 55 per week on the day shift and from 55 to 50 on the night shift. Production incentives remained in place, and output in this firm increased 10 to 15 percent. This augmentation was attributed to workers' improved "vitality." As in France, the night shift was usually unpopular among workers not only for its unnatural schedule but also because of the danger of a nighttime air raid, in this case by German aircraft. Workers' strike threats reinforced their demands for a more equal sharing of nighttime burdens.[94]

Both women and men vigorously defended their weekend and holiday schedules. As in France during the Popular Front, paid holidays were a newly won right in UK industries. Workers with union support began to insist – sometimes with no legal standing – on compliance for bank and statutory holidays, even at the cost of delaying urgent war work. Married women laboring in industrial jobs objected that they had only one week of vacation while single women in offices and shops received more. Sunday and holiday labor remained unpopular even during war emergencies, unless highly compensated, i.e., awarded double time. When this condition was met, workers preferred to labor on Sunday rather than less remunerated normal working days. To avoid paying higher wages, some employers preferred to close on weekends and holidays. In response, in one southwestern town more than 1,000 workers demonstrated against factories which proposed to restrict work on weekends.[95]

One employer demanded that the Industrial Relations Department immediately prosecute absentees if he operated his factory on the Saturday before Easter. His complaint was not isolated. Absenteeism on the weekends at the William Beardmore Company at Parkhead was very high, a consequence of long hours and 12-hour shifts totaling 69 to 74 hours per week for several years. Toward the end of the war, nearly 100 female bus conductors, joined by hundreds of their male colleagues, stopped work to protest against the introduction of a Saturday winter schedule. Likewise, several thousand bus drivers and conductors struck to protest the introduction of summer schedules. The ongoing strike led authorities to employ military personnel to drive the buses. If the state judged workers' "defiance" to be "inexcusable," the military could replace them. Mondays saw the desire to extend the weekend or what was called the "Monday morning blues," "the most fertile day for producing strikes."[96]

Employers had to restrain workers' attempts to leave before the recognized finishing time, a widespread desire among wage earners of many, if not all, nations. It is significant that a strike at the important Briggs Motor Bodies Limited to protest the demotion of a union militant took the form of 90 percent of workers at the company's three factories stopping work at 5:15 pm instead of the normal time of 6:45 pm. The following day, sixty shop stewards extended their lunch hour to discuss the case and refused to return to work. The shop stewards' action was followed by a complete stoppage at the 3:15 pm tea break at the main factory where 8,000 workers labored. Faced with similar cases of refusal to work, an aircraft company banned "premature clocking-off" in fall 1942. At the aircraft works of Cornercroft Ltd. Coventry, "some 150–200 people left work at 4:00 pm on Christmas Eve [of 1941] in spite of very definite warnings by the employer that such action would be punished by dismissal." By carrying out its pledge and firing 72 wage earners, management provoked a strike and resolute determination by four trade unions to fight for the dismissed men's rehiring. In addition to struggles over early departure, lunch breaks became conflictual when workers extended their dining beyond the standard hour or half-hour.[97]

Management and state officials lamented workers' disinterest in increasing productivity. A curious event illustrated the problems of *autogestion* or workers' control, which was advocated by Jack Tanner, president of the powerful AEU. State mediators noticed "an instance of the running of a 'successful' Works Advisory Committee ... A London engineering firm arranged for its Committee to meet once a month on Saturday afternoons after normal work had ceased. In course of time the workers' representatives suggested that it would, perhaps, be advantageous if the Committee were to meet more frequently – say on alternate Saturday afternoons. The management agreed to this suggestion and they then found that other workers were desirous of being co-opted on the Committee so that, eventually, its members swelled considerably. The Managing Director was very gratified but, being a student of human nature, a little perplexed at the workers' sustained and diligent application to the problems of production. Enlightenment came when he discovered that his cashier had unwittingly been paying the workers double time for all their attendances at the meetings." Consequently, it is understandable that although some enthusiasts called for the British equivalent of the Soviet "shock worker," there was little grassroots enthusiasm for this proposal. Instead, wage earners continued to produce at their own pace. Workers' resistance to work shows the conditional nature of wage earners' and, for that matter, nearly all antifascism.[98]

Postwar periods always raise the prospect of relaxation, and like their French counterparts, both male and female wage earners looked forward after the cessation of hostilities to the replacement of the standard wartime working week of at least 47 hours by the 40-hour week. Given the unions' growing power and the proliferation of strikes in 1944, the prospect of a 40-hour week divided into 5 days of 8 hours frightened employers, most of whom had confronted workers' and union opposition to extending the working day beyond 8 hours without the pledge of considerable overtime compensation. After the war, it was acknowledged that workers would continue to press for holiday pay.[99]

American Workers' Resistance to Work

In contrast to its European Allies, the United States remained out of reach of Axis invasion and, with the major exception of Pearl Harbor, from enemy bombers. Its enormous demographic, agricultural, financial, and industrial resources made it the arsenal of democracy or, more precisely, antifascism. Its unparalleled productive capacities encouraged allies and discouraged nonbelligerents from aiding or joining the Axis. The American military-industrial complex supplied two-thirds of all Allied military equipment used in World War II. Seventy percent of these defense contracts went to 100 of the nation's largest corporations. Notwithstanding its founder's pro-German isolationism and its sales of thousands of trucks to Franco's Nationalists during the Spanish Civil War, the Ford Company would eventually produce more war materiel than Mussolini's Italy. General Motors, which had also done business with Franco and maintained its overseas operations in Germany and Japan despite the anti-American politics of those nations, made 10 percent of everything the United States produced to fight World War II. "Victory is our Business" became the company's wartime slogan. The profits of antifascism altered the priorities even of Texaco. Its board had had no objection to sales of oil on credit to the Spanish Nationalists, but in July 1940 it forced its philo-Nazi chairman, Torkild Rieber, to resign. Large companies gained greatly when in 1942 President Roosevelt jettisoned antitrust laws for the benefit of the war effort. For example, Henry Kaiser made between $60,000 and $110,000 on each of the several thousand Liberty ships he built from an originally British design.[100]

While big business profited, the government's war effort won the loyalty of trade-union federations, who advertised their detestation of what they regarded as their principal foe, Hitlerism. To facilitate smooth production, Washington intervened in the setting of labor policy as never before in American history. Only ten days after Pearl Harbor, Roosevelt summoned business and labor leaders who agreed to a no-strike pledge as long as the war endured and to a tripartite (labor, management, and government) National War Labor Board (NWLB), which would arbitrate labor disputes that affected the war effort. In return for a no-strike commitment and union cooperation to make workers work, the government through the NWLB encouraged workers in unionized plants to remain or become trade-union members. As in Britain, closed shops would dominate the industrial landscape. Union membership rose from 8.7 million in 1940 to 14.3 million in 1945.[101]

The surrender of the strike weapon diminished the loss of days from 23,000,000 in 1941, a near record, to 4,180,000 in 1942, in what could be termed the Pearl Harbor effect that was similar to the United Kingdom's 1940 Dunkirk effect. Unions quickly recognized "the vital importance to the war effort of uninterrupted production . . . Devotion to country and the cause of liberation was a powerful deterrent of strikes." So was the prospect of higher take-home pay through longer hours in a society much more consumerist than either its allies or enemies. Furthermore, US conservatives often attributed the fall of France to its shortened workweek and were reluctant to limit working hours. By the end of 1941 an officially neutral America was manufacturing nearly as much for defense as Nazi Germany. A year later, the United States produced more war materiel than the three major Axis powers together. In 1943 American war production was twice that of Germany and Japan combined.[102]

However, it was not always easy making workers labor as productively as the corporatist trio of labor, management, and the state hoped. A pro-business historian calculated that unions slowed war production as much as 25 percent before Pearl Harbor. Thomas DeLorenzo, an official of the United Auto Workers (UAW), the nation's most important and largest union, proclaimed, "Our policy is not to win the war at any cost . . . [but] to win the war without sacrificing too many of [our] rights," including the right to strike. In other words, even an antifascist war could not serve as an excuse to overexploit wage earners who – like their comrades in other nations – identified fascism with insufficient wages and rigorous supervisory control. Like African-Americans, who desired the defeat of both foreign fascism and domestic racism, trade unionists also had the goal of a "double victory" – the defeat of both international and internal "fascism," i.e., strict managerial control on the shop floor. In 1941, 4,228 walkouts involved 2.4 million workers, making it the biggest strike year since 1919. In early April 1941, thousands stopped work for over a week in a union-supported walkout in the Detroit area, including Ford's huge River Rouge plant, which employed approximately 80,000, causing "serious delay" of production of airplane engines and considerable impairment of defense programs. One of the most important strikes, involving 12,000 workers, occurred in May–June 1941 in southern California at North American Aviation, which possessed 25 percent of the nation's fighter aircraft manufacturing capacity. The Roosevelt administration attempted but failed to isolate the Communist leaders of the walkout, who led the influential UAW local at the plant. Before the invasion of the Soviet Union, American Communists – like their comrades in other nations – were notably unconcerned with efforts to help Britain. On 9 June Roosevelt ordered 2,500 army troops with fixed bayonets to occupy North American and told local draft boards to cancel deferments of those who failed to return to work. State antifascism effectively ended this stoppage and discouraged others. The administration's strikebreaking and prosecution of rebellious union leaders displayed its determination to combat resistance to national defense in a period when Communists opposed the "imperialist" war. As in the United Kingdom and France, counterrevolutionary antifascism in the United States curbed strikes.[103]

Once the United States became an ally of the Soviet Union, Communists viewed strikers no longer as heroes but as villains. The change was exceptionally dramatic at North American Aviation, where union and management agreed, "our country and the democratic people of the world are engaged in a life and death struggle against the fascist powers" and pledged "to work together to a successful conclusion of the war." Nevertheless, rank-and-file wage earners maintained their battle to loosen the tight discipline of the workplace. The percentage of wage laborers participating in undeclared strikes jumped substantially from 1942 to 1944. Conflicts over working conditions and particularly discipline sparked the great majority of these stoppages. Workers sometimes violently attacked supervisory personnel who opposed them. In a special American twist, racist opposition to employing Blacks also motivated walkouts. The relatively tiny number of strikes for better rations demonstrated the greater standard of living of American workers compared to their European counterparts, a huge advantage for the Allies. High wages, which increased by almost 20 percent in the 20 months after Pearl Harbor, offered workers an income cushion and encouraged them to engage in wildcats. Some strikes defied union officials, but many were led by local union activists, whom management fired whenever possible. Dismissal might be the first step toward induction into the military, in which almost 30 percent of the Detroit workforce served. In other words, antifascist governments gave wage earners a choice – either work or fight. States such as Florida proposed prison terms for strikers in war work.[104]

In 1943 workers increasingly ignored the no-strike pledge, and days lost to stoppages rose to 13.5 million, triple the number in 1942, although proportionally less than in the United Kingdom. The antifascist war revived a sluggish American capitalism, but, as in Britain, it also augmented workers' bargaining power by increasing employment possibilities. US workers took advantage of the opportunities to leave agricultural regions for industrial ones, and wages rose more than business profits. Furthermore, American companies could pass the cost of almost all new plants and at least part of higher wages of their defense contracts to the government. Generally, unions in the United Kingdom and United States greatly benefited from the war since their membership and dues – including those of millions of recent female adherents – expanded rapidly. The give-and-take of interest-group politics and the longer working week in Britain and America was ultimately more effective in raising wage earners' wartime standard of living than the authoritarianism of the Axis and its collaborationist partners. Anglo-American union power emboldened workers' refusals of work. US union representatives defended their members, who were fired for various violations – gambling on factory premises, insulting a supervisor, leaving early or arriving late, and unexcused absences. It was easier to protect workers with seniority since the arbitrators of the NWLB were less willing to punish older wage earners who had proven to be reliable producers.[105]

"Idleness" proliferated, and toilets and locker rooms became refuges from wage labor. At Ford's monstrous Willow Run, one of the largest factories in the world, management posted in the women's restrooms "matrons" who made sure that female wage earners did not dawdle. Union committeemen used their position "for loafing in the lunch rooms" and to "absent themselves for excessive periods." Newspaper reading occurred on company time. Workers slept on the job, above all during the night shift. The complicity of their peers allowed them to avoid detection by the "Gestapo," the workers' sobriquet for Ford's factory guards. Card playing was common during working hours. Employers sometimes objected to vacation demands "because the war effort is too important," but, as in the United Kingdom, vacations – often justified by custom and by their apparent reduction of absenteeism and elevation of productivity – were common and were usually approved by the NWLB.[106]

Brief wildcats interrupted production throughout the war. As in France and Britain, lightning strikes spontaneously and simultaneously achieved two goals – to press specific demands and to avoid work. Labor walkouts declined to 8.7 million man-days lost in 1944, but nonetheless a week before D-day 70,000 workers were on strike in the Detroit area. In the winter and spring of 1944–1945, it is estimated that a majority of autoworkers engaged in wildcats. During those years, more strikes occurred and more wage earners stopped work than in any similar period in the United States since 1919. In early 1945 auto industry executives complained of a 39 percent decline of unit productivity. Well-paid piecework workers did not exert their maximum efforts. As labor shortages sharpened, industrialists – usually with the support of the NWLB – successfully introduced incentive systems to heighten productivity, which increased workers' wages but threatened to unleash inflation. The government reduced the latter by heavily taxing workers' income.[107]

Management hopes that cooperation with unions would restrain disobedience were disappointed. Although the UAW, its Ford local, and the Communist Party endorsed "patriotic productionism" and often refused to authorize work stoppages, 773 strikes of all kinds erupted during the war at the Rouge plant alone. From June 1942 to April 1944, 303 wildcats occurred, costing 932,000 hours of work. During one in January 1943, the NWLB accused strikers of "giving aid and comfort to our enemies." Despite no-strike pledges, in 1943 the most significant stoppages occurred in coal mining, which in the second half of that year led to the loss of two weeks' worth of coal production. The length of the miners' strike matched that which occurred under much more repressive conditions in northern France during May–June 1941, but most other "unauthorized work stoppages" remained brief walkouts that halted one shift or less, thereby reducing loss of income and dodging the retaliation that longer strikes invited. Antifascists, such as Dorothy Thompson, regarded Roosevelt as a hero for breaking the strike by putting the mines under military protection and thus alienating his own labor base. An angry Congress enacted legislation – over Roosevelt's veto – to allow the federal government to imprison strike leaders and seize mines or plants whose strikes disrupted war production.[108] The state disregarded labor's charges that the legislation was "fascist" and resolved to make workers work.

In theory, the "impartial" grievance procedures, not worker strikes, settled disputes. Wage labor was expected to continue even as grievances were decided. The UAW-Ford umpire – the Yale University law professor Harry Shulman, the most influential arbitrator during the war – articulated corporatist productivism. Shulman recognized that union representatives could not override management authority since "production must go on." Wage earners must respect the industrial chain of command by not stopping work at will. He believed that management had the right and duty to discipline workers who disrupted output. "A Union and its members can choose, if they like, to settle each day-to-day dispute by strike action. They could stop work every time a supervisor or other representative of management did something that they deemed improper. But union men long ago recognized that this method of protest would destroy the Union and their own economy. For this method would necessitate a stoppage nearly every day. Now workers live by production. Strikes are costly to workers as they are to management.

In normal times an occasional, deliberate test of strength on matters of major importance may be necessary and desirable. The anticipated victory is then deemed to be worthy of the cost. But wanton and needless use of the strike weapon weakens the weapon itself, casts undue burden on the workers, and threatens to destroy their organization." Shulman articulated the needs of the union bureaucracy, management, and the government, not necessarily those of workers. By avoiding regular wage labor and seizing time for their personal projects, workers may have benefited more from strikes than management or even the union, which was more committed to wage labor than the rank and file who avoided it.[109]

A case in point occurred at the end of September and the beginning of October 1944, when workers struck to protest a two-week disciplinary layoff of an influential union official, the chairman of the plant committee. The strike violated the contract, the union constitution, and the no-strike pledge. The umpire Shulman concluded: "There is no reason for imposing an economic loss [through a strike] on hundreds of employees for the purpose of securing illegally to one of them [the union chairman] that which he can get in an orderly, legal manner without loss to any employee." In this case, workers preferred to halt work rather than follow procedures established by management, state, and their own union since they believed that the immediate benefits of the avoidance of wage labor offered greater satisfaction than procedures that required its continuation. As in the United Kingdom, local union leadership was willing to tolerate or even provoke stoppages to prevent companies from punishing members and local officials for contract violations, such as flight from regular wage labor by unauthorized exits from the shop floor. Corporatist antifascism could not overcome the rank-and-file rejection of work.[110]

According to the NWLB, the goal of all parties throughout the war was continuous and uninterrupted production. It insisted that unions act "with responsible care" to avoid "slowdowns, work stoppages, and strikes." In one firm, it reported with disillusion "16 work stoppages and 29 separate slowdowns during thirteen months" and concluded that during 1944 "the local leadership of this union [Local 759, UAW-CIO] has been utterly unable to control its members." The NWLB recommended that union preference in hiring and retention ("maintenance of membership") be made contingent on the union's good behavior in preventing strikes and slowdowns. The NWLB concluded, "the principal contribution of labor to the prosecution of the war under the no-strike agreement is its willingness to refrain from work stoppages despite the existence of grievances and even of provocations." In other words, the union should make its members labor and allow bureaucratic procedures to resolve grievances. The union local admitted that when it acted to prevent wildcats or what it called "interruption of production," its leaders risked putting "themselves in an anomolous [sic] position in the eyes of large sections of their constituency." The union local defended itself by citing the many strikes that it had prevented and its agreements with the company to dismiss or lay off undisciplined workers, including union officials.[111]

The role of unions was more ambivalent than management within the productivist framework of wartime corporatism. On the one hand, like management, unions depended on the workplace and wage labor for their organizational existence. On the other, union members and even officials continued to violate rules that limited work stoppages. For example, on 25 and 26 August 1944, they defied the contract that prevented strikes and "other curtailment of production" until the initiation of grievance procedures. They also ignored their own union's constitution which stipulated that representatives of the International UAW authorize stoppages. Instead, union officials at the mammoth Ford Highland Park plant joined "hundreds" of supposedly disgusted workers who decided to leave the shop floor. "No one of the employees seemed to know what incident, if any, ... brought on the stoppage." One union committeeman who participated in the walkout explained that although he was opposed to all wildcats and tried to dissuade employees from engaging in them, he felt compelled to respect a picket line. For their refusal to work and their leadership of the wildcat, twelve strike leaders were dismissed. This case showed the allure of the wildcat for many rank-and-file workers.[112]

As in Britain, supervisors could no longer exercise control over the workforce as they had in the 1930s. Known for their company loyalty and imposition of harsh discipline prior to the war, during the hostilities Ford foremen became willing to strike against their employer if they felt their interests were endangered. Workers and union officials expressed their defiance of supervisors – often recently appointed novices who earned little more than the workers they were directing – with "obscene" or "vulgar" language during disputes. "Insubordination" – along with drunkenness, "chronic loafing," and persistent absenteeism – remained a legitimate reason for dismissal. Workers also massively violated safety rules by smoking, chiefly in the toilets, those spaces of ephemeral factory freedom. To combat what it considered laziness in its large Ohio plant, Curtiss-Wright – the major American aircraft producer – placed transparent glass doors in the men's rest rooms, a decision which helped to prolong a strike. Dismissals for smoking could produce stoppages and even "riots" which destroyed company property and injured supervisory personnel, demonstrating both the addictive power of tobacco and worker defiance of regulations. Women were reluctant to abide by dress codes and wear the caps, shoes, and clothing that management provided in the interest of reducing the frequency of accidents. With the approval of their colleagues, women selected by their peers would exit the factory before their shift ended to shop for their families and colleagues. Wage earners expropriated the machines and materials of the workplace to produce objects for their own use or amusement.[113]

One of the major justifications of collective bargaining was its alleged ability to improve production through labor-management collaboration. Contracts "expressly recognized . . . [the obligation] to provide a fair day's work for a fair day's pay." The unions signed collective bargaining procedures in which umpires and arbitrators supported the right of the company to discipline and even dismiss workers who were habitual absentees. These decisions disappointed union members who expected their locals could protect them from sanctions. Absenteeism doubled in auto plants and tripled in the new airframe factories that employed a large proportion of women, teenagers, and rural migrants. At Willow Run, absenteeism ranged from 8 percent to 17 percent each day, and 10 percent of the workforce quit every month. The plant's elevated figures are partially explained by its long distance from workers' residences and the rationing of both tires and gasoline. Seventy-five percent of Detroit-area workers commuted to their jobs in private automobiles, and the percentage was even higher for Willow Run. However, workers were willing to commute to receive training at Willow Run and then sell their new skills to a higher paying or more conveniently located employer. Two investigating sociologists concluded that "plain old factory fatigue . . . probably accounted for most of the absenteeism." As in other plants throughout the country, the beginning of hunting season fostered more absentees, as did "draftitis" or skipping work as induction neared. Relatively good pay and de facto job security motivated some workers to take short and unauthorized vacations. The impulsive walkout of thousands of workers at the Rouge for four days (14–18 August) when the victory over Japan (V-J Day) was announced confirmed the popularity of both impulsive and planned holidays. It is significant – but little remarked – that states decide to celebrate major events by allowing the withdrawal of wage labor and wisely do not attempt to impose its continuation. The spontaneous celebration of V-J Day announced the greatest 12 months of strikes in US history.[114]

Major corporations made sure to pay workers at their place of work – usually Friday but sometimes Saturday – to avoid "day after payday absenteeism." Absenteeism was lowest on paydays and highest on

Mondays and Saturdays. Like their British and French counterparts, American workers fashioned their own individual weekends even during wartime. Regional War Labor Boards granted bonuses to reduce absenteeism if they were effective and non-inflationary. As in the United Kingdom, absences – accompanied by some heavy drinking on the job – swelled during the Christmas–New Year's period. The class struggle expressed itself in contested medical judgments. Company physicians tended to support conclusions of "malingering," whereas wage earners' doctors confirmed the "sickness" of the absentee.[115]

As in other nations, the female expression of class consciousness was absenteeism, not union participation or strikes. Corporations justified wage discrimination against women with the argument that their high rates of absenteeism warranted their lower pay. General Motors claimed the absenteeism rate for men was 5.3% and for women 11.5%, and, as in Britain, other studies showed the female rate approximately two times greater than the male. Married women – who, of course, often had childcare responsibility – were most often absent, followed by single men and single women. The massive propagation of Stakhanovist images, however feminized, of Rosie the Riveter attempted to diminish female absenteeism (Figure 8.2). Nevertheless, many women felt the factory to be a hostile domain and avoided it during and after the war. Newly employed and lower-paid workers also missed work more frequently than the average. The National Association of Manufacturers estimated that absenteeism jumped from a prewar 3.48 percent to 5.42 percent during the conflict. Senator (and future president) Harry Truman emphasized "reducing absenteeism" as one of the keys to Allied victory. "Unnecessary absenteeism" cut output as much as 10 percent. Almost half of the public demanded conscription of regular absentees.[116]

Workers switched from lower-paying jobs to more highly remunerated positions, often in the defense industry. Strictly speaking, unlike absenteeism, turnover is not an expression of refusal of wage labor, but in the context of a global war, it indicates that workers' desires for personal promotion or convenience motivated them as much or more than the antifascist cause. According to a confidential analysis by a number of federal agencies, "Some of it [turnover] is necessary ... resulting from curtailed industries or non-essential occupations to war work, but the bulk of it is wasteful in a Nation at war and cannot be permitted." In 1939 layoffs accounted for 71 percent of workers' separation from their jobs, whereas in 1943 voluntary resignations accounted for 72 percent of turnover. The War Manpower Commission attempted to reduce turnover – which was particularly acute in the major industrial states of Texas, California, and Michigan – by issuing a series of restrictions

Figure 8.2 *Rosie the Riveter* (1942). Courtesy of the National Archives. Getty Images.

on workers' job mobility and employers' pirating of labor. Local Manpower Committees – which were corporatist bodies composed of government, labor, and company representatives – enforced these restrictions and effectively reduced job shopping.[117]

The attraction of war industries created new problems of housing, transportation, and adaptation to the workplace. The Associated Shipbuilders of Seattle, which constructed minesweepers for the Navy, had an average employment of 8,000 but lost 6,900 workers from September 1944 to March 1945. Only 11 percent were due to the military draft or enlistment. During the same period, it could hire only 5,130. Thus, the company suffered a net loss of 1,800. The inability of the Federal Shipbuilding Company at Kearny, New Jersey, to replace the loss of 11,000 workers during five months delayed the production of destroyers and light cruisers. The factory of one Pontiac plant, which made most of the castings for the jeeps produced in the Detroit area, was threatened with a shutdown by the exit of a mass of low-wage earners who quit for new higher paying jobs.[118]

The employment of large numbers of women created special problems of child- and eldercare. Turnover remained especially high, even "excessive," among female workers, who often prioritized personal and familial needs over factory wage labor. One shipyard, subject to high levels of turnover, interviewed hundreds of women who had quit. It found that over 50 percent left after only one month or less and 90 percent within the first 6 months. Forty-nine quit because the work was harder than they expected; 45 said it was too hot (or, in the winter, too cold) to work outside; 35 left when the military transferred their husbands; 35 departed to care for children or a family member; 32 moved to another area; 23 could get no one to perform their housework; 20 asserted they were tired of working; 13 got married; 11 stated that working conditions were unacceptable; 11 left without giving a reason.[119]

As in Britain, women workers' participation in the workplace sometimes increased tension with their male counterparts, who were often uncomfortable with the female presence. Men who performed lighter jobs were reassigned to heavier tasks which women were thought to be incapable of performing. According to Shulman, "very considerable resistance to this program [employment of women for lighter physical tasks] was encountered among many male employees – a resistance that was overcome only by careful planning, long negotiations, the country's need, and the pressure of union leaders and official union opinion." In numerous cases, NWLB arbitrators attempted to protect female workers against blatant discrimination in pay, harassment, and insults. Nonetheless, strikes by thousands of disgruntled female workers, who were eventually joined by their male colleagues in many firms in early 1944, defied both the NWLB and management. Similar problems of prejudice arose against those of Mexican ancestry and particularly African-Americans. On 20–21 June 1943, a notorious race riot in central Detroit left 34 dead (25 of whom were Black), and 1,250,000 hours of labor lost. NWLB also fought discrimination against both minorities and union officers, since the latter were especially essential – at least in theory – for keeping production running smoothly. Like other wage earners, both racists who protested the presence of Black workers and anti-racists who struggled against discrimination expressed their grievances by skipping work, sometimes for at least a week.[120]

Regardless of their mutual antifascist commitment to produce, management and labor often disputed the pace of wage labor. Trade unionists would defend workers who were laboring too slowly in the judgment of both employers and arbitrators. In early 1944, in one well-publicized case at Ford, the union dismissed from its ranks two test drivers of Army trucks who had caused friction in their team of approximately ten men because the two performed their tasks much too rapidly in the opinion of their fellow workers. The union claimed that, according to the contract signed by both parties, Ford was obligated to dismiss the two test drivers, whom the other workers in their team considered ratebusters who made them look either incompetent or lazy. The team, a number of whom had solid military records, ostracized and threatened the two go-getters. Of course, unionized and even nonunionized workers in many countries during both peace and wartime have harassed workers who produced beyond a de facto quota. The incident revealed everyday limits to patriotism, since the small group of work companions took precedence over larger national and antifascist goals.[121]

In judging this case of a team-enforced slowdown, umpire Shulman found that the company could not be compelled to dismiss productive workers who adhered to the agreed-upon practice of "a fair day's work for a fair day's pay." Furthermore, the union had pledged to "use its best efforts in behalf of the Company" to prevent its members from participating in any "slow down, curtailment of work, restriction of production, interference with work." The Ford Company, Shulman ruled, had the right to discipline an employee who violated these obligations. He concluded that "Optimum production" was in the best interest of both management and labor, and he justified the closed union shop by arguing that the latter should contribute to maximum output. For that reason, the NWLB encouraged provisions in contracts – for example, the 1942 agreement between General Motors and the UAW – which stipulated that a closed shop would promote heightened production because of greater harmony between workers and employers. "It follows that a use of the union shop provision to slow-down or interfere with production is a perversion of its agreed upon function and a betrayal of its promised objectives." Shulman called on the union to eliminate unjustified slowdowns and stoppages in return for management's acceptance of the closed shop. The two ratebusting drivers were reinstated over the strong objections of the union local.[122]

Resistance to workspace and worktime showed the limits of both fascism and antifascism to entice workers to work. Denials of labor revealed that workers defied the fascist or antifascist productivism that promoted devotion to labor. Workers' rejection of wage labor demonstrated their detachment from revolution and counterrevolution, both of which shared a common belief in hard work and patriotism. Spanish workers refused the collectivist revolution's productivist priorities, and French workers defied the "Travail" of the counterrevolutionary Vichy slogan, "Family, Fatherland, and Work." British and American wage earners distanced themselves from the Protestant and patriotic work ethic. Workers defended their individual and collective rights but offered no clear alternative to the various religious and secular, left and right work ideologies.

Short strikes and other refusals were not – as a number of historians have interpreted them – merely "symbolic" or "primitive." Instead, they reveal two potentialities. One is akin to black marketeering and reflects an asocial or hedonistic individualism, which leisure industries can commercialize and exploit. The other is a more collectivist, but perhaps utopian, project that was familiar to the French Popular Front. It aimed to diminish working hours, share limited wage labor with the unemployed, and devote leisure time to improving the health and culture of wage earners. The cultural revolution of the 1960s would revive and articulate this anti-work utopia, but wars and postwar reconstructions prevented its fulfillment.

The antifascist victory generated the reconfiguration of the conflict between revolutionary antifascism, dominant in the East, and counter-revolutionary antifascism, hegemonic in the West. After the war, these quite different antifascist coalitions confronted each other for the first time.

Revolutionary Antifascism

Much postwar controversy revolved around whether the Western Allies could have imposed their own democratic model on Eastern Europe if they had adopted a strategy which would have invaded the European continent earlier and campaigned there more aggressively. This is not the place to settle the issue, but by adopting a Europe First strategy, the Roosevelt administration committed itself to a counterrevolutionary antifascism that would express immediate solidarity with the United Kingdom and eventually would limit – as vast as they were – Soviet gains in Eastern and Central Europe. Making the defeat of Japan the top US priority would have opened Western Europe to a more extensive penetration of Communist revolution and might have split the Western Allies. Nevertheless, to combat the Japanese effort in the Pacific, the British and Americans diverted massive resources, which may have delayed an attack on Nazi-occupied Europe.

Furthermore, Soviet domination of Eastern Europe – the Baltics, Finland, Poland, and Bessarabia – was the price paid for the democracies' appeasement of Germany in the 1930s and their reluctance or inability to successfully invade the continent until relatively late. Churchill's peripheral strategy in North Africa, which Roosevelt approved, allowed the Soviets time to conquer the east. The strategy responded to reasonable British fears that an early frontal assault against the continental Nazi fortress would have resulted in enormous Western Allied casualties similar to those of World War I. In addition, the Americans – who were uncertain throughout the conflict that their atomic weaponry would be

Figure 9.1 Churchill, Roosevelt, and Stalin at Yalta Conference, February 1945. Getty Images.

effective – did not wish to antagonize their Soviet ally, whose help, it was thought, would be needed to subdue Japan. In the end, the Soviets took what they could not be stopped from seizing. Their enormous casualties – which, unlike those of the Western Allies, far surpassed those of World War I – quickened the defeat of the Reich. Even ardent US anti-Communists, such as Herbert Hoover and John Foster Dulles, praised the Yalta conference of February 1945 that acknowledged Soviet and Western spheres of influence (Figure 9.1). Yalta acquiesced to Soviet control over much of Germany, the Baltic States, the Kurile Islands, and the southern half of Sakhalin, as well as recognizing Mongolia – the first People's Republic.

At the end of the war, the Red Army broke with the inclusive antifascism decreed in 1941 and with the help of local Communists imposed its version of "people's democracy" and revolution on Eastern Europe. In April 1944 Stalin famously stated: "This war is not as in the past: whoever occupies a territory also imposes on it his own social system.

Everyone imposes his own system as far as his army can reach. It cannot be otherwise." The Russians recognized their major allies' interest in continuing capitalism in Western Europe and expected Britain and France to sanction their "revolutionary-imperial paradigm" in Eastern Europe. The latter included Poland, Romania, and Bulgaria in 1944, the Soviet zone in eastern Germany in 1945, Hungary in 1945–1946, and Czechoslovakia in 1948. Revolutionary Stalinism feared capitalist encirclement while Western antifascists increasingly dreaded Soviet expansionism. In his "Iron Curtain" speech of 5 March 1946, the leading conservative antifascist, Churchill, recognized that "Communist parties, which were very small in all these Eastern States of Europe, have been raised to pre-eminence and power far beyond their numbers and are seeking everywhere to obtain *totalitarian* control. Police governments are prevailing in nearly every case, and so far, except in Czechoslovakia, there is no true democracy ... the Communist parties or fifth columns constitute a growing challenge and peril to Christian civilization." Suspicion of a growing Soviet empire devoted to anti-capitalist and anticlerical revolution began to supplant the admiration and gratitude for the Soviet role in the defeat of Nazi Germany.[1]

Communists would regard those who refused their hegemony as capitalist and thus potentially fascist. After the Axis defeat, they employed the specter of a resurrected fascism – paradoxically enough, by counterrevolutionary antifascists – to strengthen their appeal to the entire left. Thus, in Eastern Europe revolutionary antifascism resurfaced, and it became a fundamental part of the official ideology of the Eastern bloc and offered it legitimacy against the "fascist" West. By insisting on their shared antifascism, the Soviets and their satellites in Eastern Europe continued to benefit from fascism's unpopularity. Postwar antifascism in the Soviet Union and Eastern Europe provided an alternative to liberal democracy.[2]

Through a revolution from above, antifascism in Eastern Europe attempted to create a unity of state and society that did not exist in the liberal capitalist West. Cooperation among the occupying Red Army, Soviet secret police, and local Communists imposed socialist conformity on national politics and society in an environment less spontaneous and more controlled than Republican Spain, with its powerful anarchist and significant dissident communist movements. Unlike Spain, whose revolution was not immediately preceded by a global conflict, World War II had brought several revolutionary changes to the East. It had displaced one third of the prewar population, discredited the collaborationist right, and eliminated broad components of the national bourgeoisie, including its important Jewish component, while putting large amounts of private property under state control. Nevertheless, the Spanish Republic became a prototype of the model developed in Eastern Europe from 1944 to 1948, where a minority Communist party developed a mass base by dominating key bureaucracies. The Soviet victory bolstered revolutionary antifascism among significant sectors of the population – notably youth and workers. The new regimes led a cross-class antifascist coalition which carried out radical social-economic measures. As in revolutionary Spain, postwar Eastern European "democracies of a new type" completed land reform at the expense of the aristocracy and wealthier peasantry.[3]

The new authorities often equated "fascism" with anti-Soviet behavior, and the regimes crushed independent organizations. So-called free elections were limited to "antifascist parties." As in Republican Spain during the civil war, politics in Soviet-occupied Europe would quickly exclude and then arrest members of the right and the center. Following the Bolshevik model, the socialist states imposed a cultural revolution through limits on traditional religions, control of education, and manipulation of the mass media, especially the radio. Revolutionary antifascists were hostile to parliamentary democracy, political pluralism, and private property. In the East, fear of counterrevolution rejuvenated the usage of "fascist" to designate political and social opposition to socialism. In the West, anxiety about the triumph of revolutionary antifascism revived the critical concept of totalitarianism among counterrevolutionary antifascists. The Communist argument that fascism was merely another form of capitalism crudely equated different phenomena. Likewise, cold warriors simplistically identified fascism and communism as varieties of totalitarianism. Each side feared its rival's imperialism.[4]

Counterrevolutionary Antifascism

In the area of Europe where the Western powers dominated, constitutional monarchies or conservative republics were either established or restored. In this case, "conservative" meant a republic willing and capable – unlike the Spanish Republic from 1936 to 1939 – of protecting private property, religious freedom, media pluralism, freedom of assembly, and multiparty democracy. It did not imply the refusal of an incipient welfare state. The shift from warfare to welfare had begun during World War I, continued in the interwar period, and culminated in both Western and Eastern Europe at the end of World War II, which intensified the leveling tendencies of the first war. Many antifascists – Christian democrats as well as Socialists – held that the state had to play a greater role in organizing and planning the economies of liberal democracies, while respecting the electoral process and the rule of law. In the postwar period, the social democracies of Western Europe opposed the authoritarian popular democracies of Eastern Europe.[5]

Faced with what they perceived as an aggressive Soviet threat, counterrevolutionary antifascists constructed an inclusive anti-Communist coalition. Western antifascists replaced Nazism with Communism as their number one enemy. Social democrats were a key part of this coalition, and their role in 1945 paralleled their opposition to Bolshevism in 1918. At that time, German Social Democrats, who had allied with the forces of the old regime to support the fatherland in World War I, participated in a broad counterrevolutionary coalition. Social democratic and trade-union leaders coalesced with conservative forces and even the extreme right to establish an anti-revolutionary Weimar Republic. This alliance crushed an incipient workers' revolution of the radical left.[6] The result was the conservative and parliamentary Weimar Republic, similar in many ways to the Third French Republic, which had eliminated the revolutionary Paris Commune. More globally, Socialist parties – such as British Labour and the French SFIO – refused Lenin's revolutionary Third International and maintained membership in the "old house" of the reformist Second International.

As in 1918–1919, in 1945–1946 French and British social democrats engaged in a "disguised counterrevolution" to battle Communism and restore liberal democracy in Europe. At the same time, they continued to support and extend their nations' empires abroad. Bevin had fought Communists in the trade unions at home, and as Foreign Secretary in the postwar Labour government he combated them abroad. The British government maintained aid to the anti-Communist resistance in Greece, where local Communists were attempting to imitate Lenin's victory during the Russian Civil War. British officials also tried to restore the Dutch colonial empire in Java and assist the reestablishment of the French Empire in Indochina. Moscow reacted to the revival of counterrevolutionary activity and Western imperialism by regarding the British Labour Party as "the main enemy." French Christian democrats seconded the anti-Soviet and imperialist orientation. All parties of the French Resistance, including the Communists, wanted to reform the empire, not abandon it.[7]

Unlike Vichy, which was nostalgic for the pre-1789 Old Regime, both the Third Republic and its successor, the Fourth, were rooted in the Atlantic revolutions of the eighteenth century. In many crucial domestic domains, the postwar Fourth Republic returned to the democratic traditions of the Third. The growing negative perception of the French toward Vichy throughout the war helped the Republic to regain its former luster. At the end of the conflict the quick transition from a brief "insurgent period to the stage of stringent republican legality" reflected "the majority of public opinion" which desired "a return to republican institutions." The public supported the Resistance majority, which demanded the restoration of the parliamentary regime. The old parties of the Third Republic and many former state functionaries resumed positions of responsibility. Resistance fighters came from various political organizations, but they all insisted on the revival of "the freedoms of the Republic."[8]

Approaching history "from above," American historians of France have often minimized the modernity of the Third Republic and have emphasized the technocratic and institutional innovations of Vichy. Yet the Third Republic was in essential ways less archaic than Vichy. The latter effectively favored rural immobility over urban dynamism. The dramatic decline of urban workers' purchasing power reimposed a nineteenth-century living standard by reducing their consumption of calories, clothing, and footwear. Spending on the leisure industry, which had expanded greatly during the Popular Front, collapsed. In contrast, higher wages in the United States and the United Kingdom provided incentives for both work and play.

Major firms during the occupation abandoned a money economy and regressed to barter in order to avoid strikes and feed their workers. Vichy's ban on strikes– which was not merely a wartime expedient, as it was in the democracies, but an intrinsic part of its corporatist project – was another regression to the nineteenth century. Strikes and refusals of work made labor more expensive and stimulated capitalists in a dynamic market economy to invest in the development of machinery that could replace costly wage labor. Furthermore, Vichy's "single and compulsory trade unions" transformed the union card into the nineteenth-century *livret*, which – along with sexist employment legislation – restricted labor mobility that is a prerequisite for a vibrant economy. In July 1944, following the pressure and actions of the workers themselves, the provisional Republic abolished Vichy's Labor Charter and monopolistic unionism, while restoring union and worker rights, including the right to strike. In the empire, the Free French insisted less than Vichy on European racial supremacy, recognized trade unions, and pledged to abolish forced labor.[9] Their greater commitment to wage labor encouraged the development of a postwar consumer society in France.

The renewed republic also reinstated key elements of the Atlantic Revolutions – freedom of assembly, religious tolerance, separation between church and state, and secular education. Despite the church's collusion with Vichy, the massive waves of iconoclasm and violent persecution of the clergy – as had occurred in Republican Spain – were absent in France during the Liberation. The purge of clerical collaborators was minimal. The understanding with the church, which played an important role in legitimizing the Liberation's republican restoration among Catholics, distinguished French republican antifascism from that of its Spanish counterpart. Even if anticlericals and Christian democrats remained divided over state subsidies to confessional schools, shared participation in the Resistance and the Gaullist desire to avoid a religious war encouraged reconciliation between believers and skeptics. Therefore, it is not surprising that the Christian democratic left, which represented the Catholic Resistance, played a larger role at the Liberation and in the Fourth Republic than it had during the Third Republic.[10]

The Liberation and the Fourth Republic (1946–1958) returned to the tradition of assimilation based on the individual. It rejected the exclusionist communitarianism of Vichy, which mimicked that of the Old Regime. Liberation France abolished all anti-Semitic legislation. Even if Jews took a back seat to Resistance fighters, the broad postwar antifascist family included them. Liberated France accepted as individuals Jews whom Vichy had rejected as a group and encouraged once again careers open to talent. Unlike Soviet-occupied Eastern Europe, France gradually but systematically returned expropriated property to its Jewish owners. It also reinstated their citizenship and reintegrated dismissed Jewish civil servants. Likewise, as early as October 1943 in recently liberated North Africa, Masons were permitted to resume their activities. The Masonic revival in France contrasts with their persecution in the Soviet-dominated East.[11]

Egalitarian French republicans reinvigorated parliamentary democracy by giving the vote to women in March 1944, thus extending the mass suffrage which had been the basis of the Third Republic and deepening the commitment to female participation in government which had first occurred during the Popular Front. More women were elected in local and national political seats during the Liberation than any prior period. The state promoted more wage equality of men and women, whom it encouraged to bear more children for a supposedly demographically deficient nation. The female vote was also considered a clerical and conservative counterweight to the potential power of the Communists.[12]

In certain departments, municipal councils retained the majority that had been elected before the war, a direct link to the Republic. The local notables who had supported and served both the Third Republic and Vichy conserved their grip on power in many villages and towns. The CFLN, which by D-Day had prepared a full slate of prefects for all departments, sustained the Jacobin centralization that characterized the previous republic. In early 1944, the CFLN carefully prepared to replace Vichy's "super-prefects," who administered several departments, with

Gaullist-appointed *commissaires régionaux* who rapidly reinforced their centralized and civilian authority.[13]

Gaullist antifascists maneuvered politically to reinforce their supremacy over Communists. On 15 November 1944, an anti-Communist coalition, led by de Gaulle, refused to award the PCF – which elections of October 1944 had shown was the largest party – the most powerful and prestigious ministries. De Gaulle made sure that his state apparatus, including the courts, dominated the Resistance and not vice versa. The restoration of republican legality meant that the state maintained its monopoly of force, and at the end of October and beginning of November 1944 its police disarmed the leftist Gardes and PCF paramilitary Milices Patriotiques, despite demonstrations against their dissolution by hundreds of leftists. In the Jacobin tradition of national unity, much of the Resistance supported their disbanding since it reinforced the central government's authority. The Communist Resistance abandoned its goal of replacing the French military with its own battle-hardened militants. Resisters with revolutionary inclinations sensed the return of the capitalist old regime, even in supposedly "red cities" such as Toulouse. The country that invented revolution in the eighteenth and nineteenth century would remain a counterrevolutionary power in the twentieth.[14]

The limitations of the postwar purge demonstrated the hegemony of restorationist antifascism. Gaullists, Christian democrats, and many Socialists defended a purge that complemented a conservative Republic. Collaborators were judged less on their fascist or philo-Nazi ideology than as traitors to the fatherland. Purges affected those who had voluntarily worked or fought for the enemy. Immediately after the Liberation, the French executed 10,000 persons with or without judicial sanction. According to historian Stanley Hoffmann, "The executions of collaborators in the summer and autumn of the Liberation were examples of ritual murders far more than evidence of civil war." Purges did not convey a social revolution. Instead, the Republican state consolidated a generally capitalist economy. The largely *pétainiste* armed forces were mostly spared because Gaullists wished to enroll them in the final push against the Axis. Nor did a thorough purge of the civil service occur. De Gaulle declared paternalistically, "France needs all her sons." To that could be added "her daughters," whom the general systematically pardoned, even if "popular justice" scandalously shaved the heads of thousands of women engaged in "horizontal collaboration." However disgraceful, this public humiliation sometimes saved them from the terminal punishment of lynching. Compromised right-wingers were spared as much as possible so that their parties would have representation in postwar France. According to the historian/philosopher Grégoire Madjarian, "The failure of the purge was, somehow, the corollary of the success of the Restoration, not in the sense that the Restoration led to gradual limits on the extent and severity of the purge, but in the sense that one of the first successes of the Restoration was to restrict the purge to revenge against *individuals*."[15]

After surviving deportees returned from German camps in the spring of 1945, anger mounted against those who had participated, in Mauriac's words, "in the cruelest and most comprehensive attack ever made on human dignity." Nevertheless, the percentage of French collaborators who were imprisoned was considerably lower than in other occupied nations of Western Europe. Although leniency did not always serve justice, it escaped the full-scale conflict and twentyfold more executions that had ensued during the Spanish Civil War, a possibility that terrified many French citizens. French justice also avoided the "consistently revolutionary" courts in Eastern Europe under Soviet supervision. Like de Gaulle, neither Roosevelt nor Churchill encouraged enormous antifascist cleansings in areas which their troops occupied. Rather they wished to reconstruct in Allied-occupied nations the broad antifascist alliances with conservative elements that had proved so effective in their own wartime coalitions. Throughout Western Europe local conservatives – most of whom had accommodated fascist regimes and their partners – were delighted to cooperate with the triumphant democracies that would act as a barrier against social upheaval. Popular support in France for the revolutionary aims of many Resisters proved limited. French purges broadly mirrored those of Germany. During 1945 a consensus began to emerge that certain elites of the Nazi regime needed to be punished but that Germany should be rapidly rebuilt and rehabilitated. Like Germany, France would eventually be integrated into the European market economy and a new system of collective transatlantic security.[16]

The victory of conservative antifascism in Western Europe pressured the Franco regime to change. Shorn of its German and Italian backers, it devoted all its efforts to self-preservation. The regime played on genuine and perhaps justified suspicions of Spaniards themselves and the Western Allies that its collapse might lead to revolutionary outbursts and civil war, as had occurred from 1936 to 1939. In the second half of 1944, when the Red Army was conquering Eastern Europe, Churchill feared that a revolutionary Spain might encourage communism in France and Italy. He preferred a reactionary, non-expansionist Spain to a leftist alternative. Franco's official neutrality – even if highly tilted toward the Axis – during World War II prevented an Allied invasion that would have placed Anglo-American soldiers on Spanish soil to bolster democratic alternatives to fascist and authoritarian rule. Without a substantial military and economic effort by the Allies, which would have opened another theater and continued the war, democratic antifascism was unlikely in Spain. The failure of leftist guerrillas in Pyrenees (Val d'Aran) in October 1944 demonstrated the difficulty of overthrowing the regime without much more extensive foreign support that was not forthcoming. At the end of 1944, with Allied encouragement, de Gaulle disarmed the Spanish guerrillas and began the process of the reestablishment of full diplomatic relations with his southern neighbor. In 1945 the Spanish Republican government in exile disappointed the Western Allies by demonstrating its inability – as had occurred during its civil war – to achieve a broad coalition with the center-right opposition. The monarchist option of the Spanish Pretender, Don Juan de Borbón, was deeply compromised by his dealings with German, Italian, and, most of all, Spanish fascists. Spanish generals other than Franco were as venal and as authoritarian as their Caudillo. Eden concluded that "a monarchy with the same corrupt gang of generals would be no improvement."[17]

The United States was particularly concerned with the role of the Spanish fascist party – the Falange – and, as the war concluded, warned Franco to dissolve it. Ambassador Carlton Hayes, a devout Catholic who was somewhat sympathetic to the regime, told the Spanish foreign minister in November 1944: "The antifascist campaign we have waged is so powerful and important that sincere cooperation cannot occur while this obstacle [the Falange] is in the way." Hayes reminded high-level Spanish officials that Spain – which was dependent on Allied control of the seas for its petroleum, raw materials, and much of its food supply – would be subjected to sanctions if it did not dissolve the Falange. He added that President Roosevelt would take into account American public opinion, which judged that Spain was a fascist power. The Spanish ambassador in Washington, Juan Francisco de Cárdenas, confirmed the US public's hostility to Franco's regime. In the spring of 1945, 49 percent of the American public believed – essentially correctly – that Spain had not cooperated with the Allies during the war, and 23 percent wanted to sever diplomatic relations with the Iberian nation.[18]

Given these pressures and the triumph of antifascism, it is not surprising that during the postwar period Franco gradually reinvented himself as a combative Catholic anti-Communist, which many of his Western supporters argued that he was even during the civil war. His regime eventually integrated itself into the Western bloc. However, the Caudillo could never fully disassociate himself from fascism, nor did he ever restore a democratic form of government. American liberals and European social democrats vociferously opposed his distinctive counterrevolution.

European Social Democracy

The sacrifices made by the British during the war against the Axis aroused popular desires for social democratic reform. Given intense state intervention into everyday lives during the conflict, workers and rank-and-file soldiers developed a claim for government entitlements – such as housing, employment, minimum wage, and health care. In November 1942, when the British were celebrating their victory at El Alamein, the government – pressured by its Labour members – published William Beveridge's report that laid the foundations for the postwar welfare state. In Victorian language, Beveridge advocated the slaying of "five giants": Want, Disease, Ignorance, Squalor, and Idleness. The elimination of the last would abolish the great interwar "scourge" of unemployment, which wasted and decayed lives. Beveridge gave priority to present and future producers, at a time when workers' dissatisfaction and resistance to work was widespread. Although he wanted a minimum level of assistance, he never argued that people were entitled to welfare merely because they were citizens. Instead, his Victorian values promoted individual incentives to create a society where every male adult worked and women furthered the British race. Following in the footsteps of interwar social democrats, Beveridge united pro-natalism and progressive family legislation. His demands often took on a moral and Christian tone, which moderates, Labourites, and Conservatives (including Churchill) could support. The report proved wildly popular and sold 635,000 copies. The government gave it worldwide publicity as a social or Christian democratic alternative to Nazi propaganda, which boasted of a revolutionary "New Order" or what the British called the "warfare state."[19]

Increased trade-union membership during the war and the aspiration for full employment were important factors in Labour's overwhelming electoral victory of 1945, the first time the party won an absolute majority. Most observers expected the Conservatives, led by the war hero Churchill – whose radio addresses had attracted an astounding two thirds of British adults – to win easily. Yet his success as a warrior stamped him as man inappropriate for peace. Voters, including an estimated one third of middle-class electorate, appreciated Labour's loyal participation as nearly equal partners in governments which had triumphed over fascism. The electorate rewarded its patriotic and centrist collectivism. Although the Labour victory was a surprise, the results were recognized without hesitation. In contrast to Spain in 1934 and 1936 or Soviet-occupied Eastern Europe from 1945 onward, both left and right accepted the electoral verdict – a result of a solid turnout – without violence or chicanery. Labour rejected a Popular Front strategy of electoral alliance with Communists, who remained a marginal force, despite the CPGB tactic which deemphasized revolution in favor of a peaceful parliamentary transition to socialism. The composition of Labour's delegation in the House of Commons became much more middle-class than it had been before the war. Post-1945 Labour governments enacted parts of Beveridge's 1942 report by creating socialized medicine (National Health Service) and building public housing. Along with virtual full employment, these reforms were indirectly financed by American loans, a continuation of the wartime alliance by the capitalist United States.[20]

The postwar Atlantic regimes demonstrated their reforming capacity. In the victorious European antifascist nations, the demand for social welfare was much greater than after World War I. Pierre Laroque, the chief architect of postwar French social security, drew much inspiration from the Beveridge Report. In France, new social security regulations issued in October–November 1945, which both the left and right supported, completed those of the interwar period. The Popular Front had extended family allowances to wider, more rural sectors of the population, and the Liberation legislation built upon Third Republic and Vichy precedents. As in the United Kingdom, the working and especially the middle classes profited from the new reforms, which provided them and their children with greater access to both public and private health care and postsecondary education. Postwar social security reinforced "the bourgeois character of the French welfare state" in which employers and state planners retained considerable power.[21]

The immediate postwar wave of nationalizations in France and Britain was the greatest achievement of the left, which offered a social and Christian democratic alternative to revolutionary communism. Nationalizations rewarded British and French socialists and trade unionists who had proven to be among the most dedicated and consistent antifascists. The question of public ownership reopened contentious political issues that UK wartime unity had temporarily muted. Nationalizations confirmed increased confidence in the efficacy of the British antifascist state, which had begun and won the protracted fight to defeat the Axis. Furthermore, the appointment of Labour Party and the trade-union officials to highest responsibility for the war effort legitimized state control. During the war Labour ministers had improved social services, augmented wages, strengthened collective bargaining, and taxed high incomes and profits, but they had postponed their demands for nationalizations to prevent divisions in the coalition government. Labour contributions to victory on the home front – where Attlee served as deputy prime minister, Bevin directed labor, and Herbert Morrison engineered reconstruction – gained public confidence.

With the war concluded and their own enormous electoral victory of May achieved, these "social patriots" embarked on their long-delayed nationalization programs, to which Conservative-dominated investigating committees had contributed constructive suggestions. Public ownership of specific industries – coal, gas, electricity, inland transport, iron and steel, and the Bank of England – bolstered trade-union power but was usually defended on the grounds of economic efficiency, not workers' control. Wartime planning and antifascist cooperation prepared one fifth of the British economy to be placed under public ownership from 1945 to 1948 with less opposition than expected. Advocates of the new nationalizations cited the BBC and other public corporations as successful prewar precedents. Bank nationalization was "a great non-event," a limited and technical change given that the government had already managed the currency since 1932. The consolidation of the electric grid under state control also generated little controversy. Conservatives offered only token opposition to the nationalization of the coal mines. Miners were enthusiastic about their new and shorter five-day week, even as their rates of absenteeism and turnover remained high. In contrast to the collectivizations of the Spanish Revolution and the Soviet imposition of socialism in Eastern Europe, the British transition was peaceful, moderate, and democratic. Unlike in Spain or Eastern Europe, compensation to private shareholders was – according to one specialist – "remarkably generous," and most of the previous management remained in place. Nationalizations won the support of large numbers of civil servants and, more generally, the middle classes. Attlee reassured the nation that workers had more to lose than their chains and that property rights would be protected. Untidy British pluralism robustly persisted.[22]

Likewise, the Liberation of France augmented state intervention and management of the economy. In contrast to the United Kingdom and the United States, where employers were at least as antifascist as their workers, in France nationalizations punished certain capitalists who were notorious collaborators. In January 1945, the Communist leader Jacques Duclos referred to "confiscations," not "nationalizations," of the property of "traitors." As in Britain, shareholders and owners whose property was nationalized were almost always compensated, even if the indemnity varied in timeliness and generosity. Despite its popularity among Resisters and workers, public ownership was generally confined to industries that had earned the reputation for outright collaboration with the Germans or were necessary for immediate reconstruction. The principle of these confiscations looked back toward the "bourgeois" French Revolution of 1789–1794 more than the Russian Soviets of 1917. Expropriations did not represent an attack on 1789's "sacred right of man" to possess private property but were a Jacobin method to punish enemies of the country, whether individuals or "trusts." The state sanctioned and requisitioned certain French employers who had labored too conscientiously for the occupiers. For instance, the major automobile producer Peugeot was left in private hands because Jean-Pierre Peugeot – unlike his competitors, Louis Renault and Marius Berliet – had an acceptable Resistance record. During the war Peugeot was complicit in workers' sabotage of production destined for Germany. In contrast, the firms of the collaborators Renault and Berliet were confiscated in 1945. In Camus' words: "It is just that the property [of a traitor] . . . returns to the nation he abandoned."[23]

Usually, punishment for economic collaboration was quite restrained on the grounds that a more extensive purge would hinder national reconstruction. According to the Resistance publisher Jean Paulhan, "The engineers, contractors, and masons who built the Atlantic fortifications [against the Western Allied invasion] walk among us without fear . . . They are building walls for new prisons for journalists who made the mistake of writing that the Atlantic fortifications were well-made." As in West Germany, the rebuilding of the nation took precedence over justice. The purges pursued wage earners who were notoriously collaborationist but spared employers and technicians whose expertise would be useful for reconstruction. Big businessmen were usually punished less severely than small traders and black marketeers who claimed unconvincingly that their price gouging of the Germans was a form of resistance. The Christian democratic Minister of Justice, Pierre-Henri Teitgen, told parliament, "I do not have the right to use the purge to make structural reforms."[24] The French purge thus diverged deeply from those carried out in Eastern Europe, where the Soviets and their collaborators promoted those of working-class origin and eliminated the bourgeoisie as the owners of the means of production. Instead of eradicating economic elites, the French purge often cleared their reputation and allowed them to maintain their managerial roles. In other cases, bosses lost the power to direct their businesses but retained their shares and investment. Public ownership, which was in the statist (*dirigiste*) tradition, gathered a solid consensus, even from the right. Nationalizations remained perhaps the most important economic legacy of the Resistance coalition and revealed the adaptive ability of restorationist antifascism.

Although local Communists and CGT members encouraged further confiscations of private property, the national PCF and CGT leaderships feared that extensive expropriations would alienate middle-class voters and property-owning peasants whose support they were trying to attract. Unlike in Southern or Eastern Europe, peasants or landless agricultural laborers were not a driving force for sweeping change, and land reform – i.e., the confiscation of large estates – was not a major issue in France. The state needed to earn the confidence of the propertied and generally conservative peasantry – which was willing to tolerate and profit from the ambient inflation – in order to feed a hungry nation. Conservative rural elites cooperated with the new regime by successfully distancing themselves from Vichy and promoting a republican counterrevolution that replaced the more reactionary Vichy variety. De Gaulle's government refused to confiscate widely before legislative elections were held. In addition, the need for American loans clipped the left's demand for more nationalizations. Forces absent or ineffective during the Spanish Republic and in postwar Eastern Europe, such as Christian democrats grouped in the Bidault's MRP (Mouvement républicain populaire), successfully limited the scale of nationalizations and insisted on adequate compensation for shareholders. As early as August 1942, in a letter to Socialist leaders, Blum envisaged postwar nationalizations in the same circumscribed manner as those of 1936–1937. His moderation was followed by his party, which agreed to respect republican legality, universal suffrage, and parliamentary pluralism. Concerning the last, the prominent Socialist Resister Daniel Mayer stated, "we fought in the Resistance for the right to disagree today." In the immediate postwar period the SFIO became the Fourth Republic's key party and attracted anti-Communists who refused unity with the PCF. It ensured both the Enlightenment legacy and cautious social reforms.[25]

As in Britain, nationalizations in France were also technocratic means to overcome perceived stagnation ("Malthusianism") and to modernize certain economic sectors such as coal mines and electricity that were indispensable to economic rebuilding. Public ownership also had the political goal of limiting the influence on governments of large private companies, the justification that the Popular Front employed for the nationalization of private weapons makers. De Gaulle targeted powerful "monopolies" for state control. In 1936 during the Popular Front, the Bank of France had come under government direction, and further nationalization of banks in 1945 had the goal of capitalizing and rationalizing the coal, gas, and electric branches. At Crédit Lyonnais – which, like all French banks, had been regulated during the war – state ownership after 1945 meant little change: "the modification was purely legal."[26] The banks saw slight alteration of their boards of directors. Nationalized insurance companies experienced a greater restructuring. Ultimately, though, the nationalizations of 1944–1945 were surprisingly "timid."[27] In the long term, management of nationalized firms differed little from that of large private ones. Unions did participate in management councils, but they were always in a minority. Attempts at workers' control or *autogestion* were relatively rare and ephemeral. The comparatively tiny number of anarcho-syndicalists and Trotskyists proved incapable of arousing interest for workers' councils.

The PCF supported the new republican government, despite the fact that it was not a "popular democracy." At the end of November 1944, after the dissolution of Communist militias, de Gaulle finally authorized the return from Moscow of Maurice Thorez, who, ordered by the Comintern, had deserted from the French army in 1939. Thorez helped to contain remaining revolutionary designs and supported government reforms, the same position that he had advocated during the Popular Front. Thorez, Duclos, and other PCF leaders addressed numerous meetings in January and February 1945. In all of them, "the desire for the union of all the French . . . seems to constitute the essence of all the present activity of this party." The PCF revived its Popular Front policy of the "outstretched hand" toward Socialists and Catholics to facilitate the "rapid return to work" and the victorious conclusion of the war.[28]

French Communists desired to be part of the restored republican state and, after the Liberation of Paris, sent some of their most dedicated militants not to make revolution but to finish the fight against the Germans. The PCF consented without much protest to the exclusion of France from the Yalta conference of the "big three" (the United States, the United Kingdom, and the Soviet Union) in February 1945. As has been seen, the PCF advanced counterrevolutionary republican continuity by cooperating in disbanding its armed militias, despite protests from its own militants. It profited from its moderation by becoming the largest party (26 percent of the vote) in the legislative elections of October 1945, which marked the return of parliamentary democracy that had disappeared during Vichy. The SFIO won 24 percent, and centrist and rightist parties gained perhaps 40 percent of the vote. As in the United Kingdom and unlike the Soviet-occupied East, the results were accepted without attempts at falsification.

The dominant patriotic antifascism convinced Communists to appeal for increased discipline in the workplace, which had the added advantage of pacifying and pleasing employers. Despite the official reestablishment of the 40-hour week in February 1946, the Liberation was productivist, and – unlike during the Popular Front – the CGT and other unions accepted 48 hours. Economic recovery depended on increased output of miners, but, undernourished and cold, they often proved reluctant to make an extra effort in their newly nationalized pits. They registered high rates of absenteeism and struck sporadically, provoking from

Thorez multiple Stakhanovist appeals for sacrifice. Local union leaders discouraged work stoppages. At a meeting in Paris on 29 October, a leader of the Syndicat des Terrassiers admonished that "workers should not call a strike without checking with the union leadership because this is no longer the moment for disorder."[29] Other union and PCF officials repeated the same message urging hard work and condemning "sabotage." By 1946, Communists charged that strikers had become "anti-Communist," anticipating their critique of workers' revolts in East Germany in 1953 and Hungary in 1956. Nevertheless, since wage earners maintained their identification of rigorous work discipline with "fascism" and "collaboration," absenteeism and short work stoppages increased in several regions. Furthermore, from 1945 to 1947 the PCF and the CGT had difficulty recruiting new working-class members. Despite militant pleas, workers displayed indifference and apathy that, in effect, hampered schemes of national or European reconstruction. For many workers, reconstruction meant excessive wage labor.[30]

A Different American Model

Although allegedly anti-imperialist, Roosevelt refused to articulate a global New Deal and proposed the restoration of non-revolutionary democracy in Western Europe. His administration preferred maintaining good relations with its Western European allies (and Southern Democrats) rather than raising contentious colonial and racial issues. After Roosevelt's death in April 1945, President Truman largely acquiesced to the restoration of European empires and opposed Communist revolution throughout the globe. In the postwar period the American government prolonged its interventionism by restraining revolutionary antifascism or what was labeled "totalitarianism."

In the immediate postwar period, US voters gave little indication that they wished to see drastic change beyond the defeat of fascism. Furthermore, trade unionists and socialists were less influential in high US government circles than in either France or the United Kingdom. There were no American equivalents to Attlee and Bevin, let alone the PCF ministers in the French government. Instead, conservative Republicans and powerful businessmen continued to hold considerable sway in the American government. Thus, unlike other Atlantic nations, in 1945–1946 the United States dismantled wartime price controls and rejected national health insurance and full employment legislation. No equivalent to the French and British nationalizations and state planning occurred. Instead, the savings accumulated during the war initially fueled postwar expansion. The federal government's generous funding of veterans' benefits and – in cooperation with large corporations – research and development proved a successful formula for the growth of corporate capitalism. A coalition of government, big business, and labor unions encouraged an affluent consumer society – i.e., mass consumption of inexpensive food, energy, single-family homes, automobiles, household appliances, and commercialized leisure. Given their high rates of absenteeism and turnover during the war, it was not surprising that large numbers of American women – like their British counterparts – withdrew from the workplace to manage their households in peacetime. Labor unions, whose right to strike was limited by federal legislation in 1947 following massive postwar work stoppages, nonetheless pushed successfully for higher wages and better benefits for their members. Large employers fought to maintain or strengthen managerial prerogatives, despite pressure from labor, which attempted to erode them in contract negotiations and by resistance to work on the shop floor.

The rejection of the European welfare state did not stop a growing number of Americans from experiencing what the French called "the 30 glorious years" of economic and demographic growth from 1945 to 1975 when mean and family incomes doubled. White male breadwinners – especially veterans of the antifascist war who benefited from government largesse in the form of the GI Bill – profited most from this rising tide, but minorities and women also participated in the mounting prosperity. The United States exported its model of mass production and consumption to former allies and enemies. Postwar economic growth throughout the Atlantic world provided the basis of political stability lacking in the 1930s.[31]

10   Conclusion and Epilogue

The antifascisms of the 1930s and 1940s were opportunistic. Very few individuals and no major nation demonstrated principled and consistent antifascism. The transatlantic powers and the Soviet Union sporadically courted the governments of Hitler and Mussolini. Both Communists and anti-Communists adopted appeasement policies. Working-class organizations realized sooner than most the dangers of fascism, but their rank and file frequently used the heightened demand for wage labor during wartime to push their own agenda for less work and better pay, regardless of the political circumstances. Most workers knew that whether fascism or antifascism prevailed, they would continue to work for wages. Their resistance to work suggested an individualistic escape from wage labor and its radical reduction. Fascists and antifascists politicized workers' refusals to labor. In turn, resisters of work felt exploited by both capitalist and communist states. In Spain during the civil war and France during the occupation, refusers of wage labor might find themselves in a labor or concentration camp. In the less repressive United Kingdom and United States, refusers might be disciplined, dismissed, or drafted. Counterrevolutionary antifascists, including trade unionists, proved more committed to wage labor than their Communist allies and fascist enemies, who reintroduced mass slavery and forced labor throughout the European continent.

The Spanish Civil War divided revolutionary antifascists from counterrevolutionary ones. Revolutionary antifascism became hegemonic in a relatively backward country whose bourgeoisie had not created a modern nation. Given violent attacks against property and religion, potentially antifascist conservatives and Catholics in Europe and America refused to aid the Republic and either assisted or accepted the fascist victory in the Iberian Peninsula. The French left and center during the putatively antifascist Popular Front unwisely devoted more effort to defeating their own relatively weak domestic fascism than battling the more dangerous foreign, specifically German, variety. The leftist Popular Front prefigured the rightist Vichy regime of World War II by fighting much more against the internal than the external enemy.

Versailles guilt pervaded nearly the entire French and British political spectrum and led many to attribute the excesses of Nazism to the supposed faults of the postwar treaty. Pacifism and anti-Communism of the majority of the left and the right combined to permit the expansionism of the fascist powers until the Nazi regime's conquest of the non-revolutionary republic of Czechoslovakia in March 1939 and conservative Poland in September pushed the reluctant democracies to abandon appeasement. The German invasion of the revolutionary Soviet republic in June 1941 created a coalition of the great powers to defeat Nazism, their most dangerous enemy. The struggle and ultimate victory against Hitlerism and its collaborators revived the Western Allies economically and politically and allowed them to restore the old regimes of liberal democracy in Western Europe. Simultaneously, the Soviet victory permitted it to establish revolutionary antifascist regimes in Eastern Europe whose social and political structures resembled in many essential ways the Spanish Republic during its civil war. Only in the late 1960s and 1970s when the specter of revolution in Spain had disappeared did that country complete its transition to democracy.

The Allied victory in World War II has often concealed the division between the two antifascisms that fought concurrently a war among nations and civil wars of different dimensions in Spain and France. Revolutionary antifascism pioneered a combative antifascism during the Popular Fronts and, after the invasion of the Soviet Union, made an unparalleled contribution to the antifascist triumph of 1945; however, from August 1939 to June 1941, Communist revolutionaries were complicit with Axis domination of the European continent. Given this spotty record, the most consistent antifascists were counterrevolutionaries. Their conservatism has been obscured by a certain historiographical consensus that fascism was ultimately a reactionary phenomenon. The fascist counterrevolution has hidden the antifascist one. In particular, the conservative, if not reactionary, Churchill pioneered the separation of antifascism from communism. He, Roosevelt, and de Gaulle constructed broad national and international coalitions against fascist foes. Their antifascism brought together both states and resistance movements that crushed the adversary. In contrast to the exclusiveness of fascist and Communist regimes which desired to unify state and society, the Western Allies expressed conventional democratic pluralism. The presence of the left in the antifascist coalition stimulated reformist projects in Europe and Asia that offered an alternative to communist revolution and its variant of "popular democracy."

Although the fascist threat died in 1945, postwar national liberation struggles revived rhetorical antifascism. Revolutionary antifascists supported Third-World nationalist movements. Echoing the antiwar Ethiopian campaign, anti-imperialists often viewed those who fought against national liberation in Vietnam and Algeria as fascists, once again demonstrating the ideologically expansive nature of antifascism. The Algerian War (c. 1954–1962), the most consequential decolonialization struggle of the French Empire, again generated two kinds of antifascism. The first posited that national liberation movements were a legitimate and desirable revolutionary response to racist and colonialist imperialism. The second, once more championed by de Gaulle, concluded that the continuation of the French presence in Algeria destabilized the conservative French Republic. Therefore, the leader of French counterrevolutionary antifascism ceded Algerian independence in 1962. Likewise, for similar reasons, a decade later President Richard Nixon ordered an American withdrawal from Vietnam – a war ignited in 1945 by Gaullist imperialists – to prevent further international unrest and domestic instability.

Revolutionary anti-imperialism and antifascism provided a powerful inspiration for the radical political movements of the 1960s.[1] Strands of the New Left – Trotskyism, Maoism, and anarchism – revived and expanded in the Atlantic world and beyond. Once more, revolutionary antifascism attempted to undermine "imperialist" Western democracies. Yet during this decade, radical movements proved completely unable to overthrow the regimes in France, the United Kingdom, and the United States, all of which derived a substantial part of their legitimacy from their victorious counterrevolutionary antifascism. Instead, the cultural revolution of the "long 1960s," which advanced multiculturalism, gender equality, and expansion of personal freedoms (including sexual ones), challenged both revolutionary and counterrevolutionary antifascisms. In this period, anti-work ideologies – articulated by intellectuals such as Guy Debord, Henri Lefebvre, and Herbert Marcuse – gained popularity and unprecedented public exposure. Countercultural anti-work movements revived the critique of wage labor voiced by nineteenth-century critics of capitalism and attempted to synthesize the New Left's desire for immediate personal and social liberation. Anti-work ideology attracted a large and public mass of followers that included both students and young workers who regarded resistance to work as revolutionary, thereby politicizing refusals to labor. They imagined a cybernetic and hedonistic utopia. From the 1970s onward, the growing scarcity of wage labor undermined the popularity of anti-work theorists and movements while propelling the rebirth of the extreme right.

The victory of antifascism in 1945 and the continuing memory of fascist crimes have obliged the contemporary extreme right to reformulate its doctrines into "national populisms" which have abandoned the expansionism, totalitarianism, and much of the violence of their fascist predecessors.[2] At the end of the twentieth and beginning of the twenty-first century, the renaissance of a populist radical right provoked a new antifascist reaction. Contemporary Western "antifa" movements are directed against political parties that express prejudices that were common among antifascist leaders and their supporters during the era of World War II. The patriotic and even nationalist antifascism during the 1930s and 1940s has little in common with the pacifist and multicultural antifascism of today. Contemporary pacifism and multiculturalism would have been totally unconvincing to many, if not most, of their antifascist predecessors, who aggressively believed that their culture, nation, (Christian) religion, civilization, gender, and even race were superior to others. Contemporary antifascism ignores these differences and justifies itself by combating what it sees as the continuation of the fascism of the interwar period.

The differences between the fascism of the 1930s and European and American extreme-right movements – such as the French National Front, United Kingdom Independence Party, or the Trump presidential campaign – are more important than the similarities. Unlike the fascist movements in the interwar period, the contemporary extreme right largely plays by the democratic rules and has abandoned the paramilitary violence of its predecessors. Current "national-populists" have integrated women and gays into their leadership in ways unknown to their forerunners. They have maintained the racism and xenophobia – bolstered by reactions to the new phenomenon of Muslim immigration and Islamist terrorism in Europe and North America – of the fascist past, but not its totalitarian aspirations. Finally, they are hyper-nationalist but not expansionist. Allied occupations largely eliminated the rural roots of militarism in Germany, Italy, and Japan. Thus, the emergence of national-populists has stimulated less international anxiety than in the 1930s.[3] The era of fascism ended in 1945, even if antifascism – legitimized by its complete victory in World War II – has demonstrated more resilience by enduring until today.

Notes

1 INTRODUCTION

1 Robert O. Paxton, *The Anatomy of Fascism* (New York, 2004), 77; Wolfgang Schivelbusch, *Three New Deals: Reflections on Roosevelt's America, Mussolini's Italy, and Hitler's Germany, 1933–1939* (New York, 2006), 120.

2 Cf. Gilles Vergnon, *L'antifascisme en France de Mussolini à Le Pen* (Rennes, 2009), 94–98: "Antifascism is certainly . . . a discourse and a mobilizing myth belonging to the left." Cf. also Jean Vigreux, *Le front populaire, 1934–1938* (Paris, 2011), 117; François Marcot, ed., *Dictionnaire Historique de la Résistance: Résistance intérieure et France Libre* (Paris, 2006), 12, 639, 850; Geoff Eley, "The Legacies of Antifascism: Constructing Democracy in Postwar Europe," *New German Critique*, no. 67 (Winter, 1996), 75; Christopher Vials, *Haunted by Hitler: Liberals, the Left, and the Fight against Fascism in the United States* (Amherst, MA, 2014), 8.

3 Tim Kirk and Anthony McElligot, "Introduction," in Tim Kirk and Anthony McElligot, eds. *Opposing Fascism: Community, Authority, and Resistance in Europe* (Cambridge, UK, 1999), 6; Enzo Traverso, *À feu et à sang: De la guerre civile européenne 1914–1945* (Paris, 2007), 21: "In this book, antifascism will be analyzed primarily as part of a process of radicalization and politicization of intellectuals." See also Dave Renton, *Fascism, Anti-Fascism and Britain in the 1940s* (Basingstoke, 2000), 4.

4 Cf. Nigel Copsey, "Towards a New Anti-Fascist 'Minimum'" in Nigel Copsey and Andrzej Olechnowicz, eds. *Varieties of Anti-Fascism: Britain in the Inter-War Period* (Basingstoke, 2010), xv, and Nigel Copsey, *Anti-Fascism in Britain* (Basingstoke, 2000), 4, which makes a distinction between "active" and "passive" antifascism. The former involves "actions" which oppose fascism; the latter a "hostile attitude." This definition may be appropriate for an analysis of British antifascism but is less useful for understanding international antifascism. Supporters of Francisco Franco and Philippe Pétain, including high-ranking Catholic clerics, often held hostile attitudes toward fascists who played important roles in these regimes. Depending on the period, even Franco and Pétain made statements and gestures hostile to fascism. So did a good number of upper-class Germans who went into "internal exile" but nevertheless never lifted a finger to oppose Nazism until its defeat was certain.

5 Arno J. Mayer, *Dynamics of Counterrevolution in Europe, 1870–1956: An Analytic Framework* (New York, 1971), 115 [italics in original]. See also James H. Meisel, *Counter-Revolution: How Revolutions Die* (New York, 1966).
6 These and following citations from Paxton, *Anatomy of Fascism*, 22, 71, 114, 219.
7 Daniel Hucker, *Public Opinion and the End of Appeasement in Britain and France* (Surrey, 2011), 15, 30.
8 Emilio Gentile, *Politics as Religion*, trans. George Staunton (Princeton, 2006), 33.
9 Piers Brendon, *The Dark Valley: A Panorama of the 1930s* (New York, 2000), 319–320, 425; Joseph Fronczak, "Local People's Global Politics: A Transnational History of the Hands Off Ethiopia Movement of 1935," *Diplomatic History*, vol. 39, no. 2 (2015), 245–274.
10 I use "isolationists" in preference to "neutralists" to underline the similarities between the former and European appeasers. Furthermore, substitutes for "isolationism" usually raise as many problems as they solve. Cf. Brooke L. Blower, "From Isolationism to Neutrality: A New Framework for Understanding American Political Culture, 1919–1941," *Diplomatic History*, vol. 38, no. 2 (April 2014), 345, and Andrew Johnstone, "Isolationism and Internationalism in American Foreign Relations," *Journal of Transatlantic Studies*, vol. 9, no. 1 (March 2011), 14; For African-American opposition to American involvement in World War II, see Brenda Gayle Plummer, *Rising Wind: Black Americans and U.S. Foreign Affairs, 1935–1960* (Chapel Hill, NC, 1996), 70–73, 81. Claude Bourdet, *L'Aventure incertaine: De la Résistance à la Restauration* (Paris, 1975), 98, 182, 397.

2 REVOLUTIONARY ANTIFASCISM IN THE SPANISH CIVIL WAR, 1936–1939

1 Stanley G. Payne, *Spain's First Democracy: The Second Republic, 1931–1936* (Madison, WI, 1993), 34.
2 Mary Vincent, *Catholicism in the Second Spanish Republic: Religion and Politics in Salamanca, 1930–1936* (Oxford, 1996), 258–259.
3 Francisca Rosique Navarro, *La Reforma agraria en Badajoz durante la IIa República* (Badajoz, 1988), 241.
4 Manuel Álvarez Tardío and Roberto Villa García, *El precio de la exclusión: La política durante la Segunda República* (Madrid, 2010), 203–241; Mercedes Vilanova, *Les majories invisibles* (Barcelona, 1995), 18.
5 Fernando del Rey, *Paisanos en lucha: Exclusión política y violencia en la Segunda República española* (Madrid, 2009), 439–447.
6 Quoted in Stanley G. Payne, *Civil War in Europe, 1905–1949* (New York, 2011), 112.
7 Álvarez Tardío, *El Precio*, 250–283.
8 Gabriele Ranzato, *La grande paura del 1936: Come la Spagna precipitò nella Guerra civile* (Rome-Bari, 2011), 86–91.
9 Justo Vila Izquierdo, *Extremadura: La Guerra Civil* (Badajoz, 1984), 18; Rosique Navarro, *Reforma agraria*, 226.

10 Rafael Cruz, *En el nombre del pueblo: República, rebelión y guerra en la España de 1936* (Madrid, 2006), 149; Aurora Bosch, *Miedo a la democracia: Estados Unidos ante la Segunda República y la Guerra civil española* (Barcelona, 2012), 100–108; General Motors, 2 July 1936, Barcelona 1329, Archivo Histórico Nacional-Sección Guerra Civil [hereafter AHN-SGC].

11 Clara Campoamor, *La revolución española vista por una republicana* (Barcelona, 2002), 72; Santa Cruz de Tenerife, Memoria, 1938, 44/2792, Archivo General de la Administración, Madrid [hereafter AGA]; Juan Ortiz Villalba, *Sevilla 1936: del golpe militar a la guerra civil* (Seville, 1998), 261; *La Provincia*, 12 June 1936; Ian Gibson, *The Death of Lorca* (Chicago, 1973), 27–33; Gabriele Ranzato, *El Eclipse de la democracia: La guerra civil española y sus orígenes, 1931–1939*, trans. Fernando Borrajo (Madrid, 2006), 245; José Llordés Badía, *Al dejar el fusil: Memorias de un soldado raso en la Guerra de España* (Barcelona, 1968), 33–35.

12 Payne, *Spain's First Democracy*, 357.

13 Ranzato, *La grande paura*, 271; Manuel Álvarez Tardío and Roberto Villa García, "El impacto de la violencia anticlerical en la primavera de 1936 y la respuesta de las autoridades," *Hispania Sacra*, LXV, 132 (July–December 2013), 685.

14 Julio de la Cueva, "Religious Persecution, Anticlerical Tradition, and Revolution," *Journal of Contemporary History*, vol. 33, no. 3 (1998), 357.

15 Narración, 21 December 1936, Extremadura 24, AHN-SGC.

16 Chris Ealham, *Anarchism and the City: Revolution and Counter-Revolution in Barcelona, 1898–1937* (Oakland, 2010), 175–180; Julius Ruiz, *El Terror rojo: Madrid 1936* (Barcelona, 2012); Francisco Alía Miranda, *La agonía de la República: El final de la guerra civil española (1938–1939)* (Barcelona, 2015), 46, 65; Stanley G. Payne, *The Spanish Civil War, the Soviet Union, and Communism* (New Haven, CT, 2004), 117.

17 Cited in Andrés Trapiello, *Las armas y las letras: Literatura y guerra civil (1936–1939)* (Barcelona, 1994), 45.

18 Salvador de Madariaga, *Spain: A Modern History* (New York, 1963), 692–693.

19 Javier Zamora Bonilla, *Ortega y Gasset* (Barcelona, 2002), 410–411; José María Carrascal, *Autobiografía apócrifa de José Ortega y Gasset* (Madrid, 2010), 259–263; Chaves cited in Trapiello, *Las armas y las letras*, 132.

20 Tom Buchanan, "Anti-fascism and Democracy in the 1930s," *European History Quarterly*, vol. 32, no. 1 (2002), 43; Payne, *Spanish Civil War*, 150; Geoffrey Roberts, "Soviet Foreign Policy and the Spanish Civil War," in Christian Leitz and David J. Dunthorn, eds. *Spain in an International Context, 1936–1939* (New York, 1999), 93–96; Fernando Hernández Sánchez, *Guerra o Revolución: El Partido Comunista de España en la guerra civil* (Barcelona, 2010), 325–331, 373–374, 454, 471; Hugh Ragsdale, *The Soviets, the Munich Crisis, and the Coming of World War II* (New York, 2004), 189; Lisa A. Kirschenbaum, *International Communism and the Spanish Civil War: Solidarity and Suspicion* (New York, 2015), 78–79, 109–112, 120–125.

21 Cited in Buchanan, "Anti-fascism and Democracy," 46.

22 The following is from the libro de actas, 1936–1937, PS Lérida, AHN-SGC.

23 George Orwell, *Homage to Catalonia* (New York, 1980), 6.
24 Informe confidencial, 1 January 1938, 855, AHN-SGC.
25 Rémi Skoutelsky, "Les volontaires français des Brigades internationales: patriotisme et/ou internationalisme," in Serge Wolikow and Annie Bleton-Ruget, eds. *Antifascisme et nation: les gauches européennes au temps du Front populaire* (Dijon, 1998), 87; Dubinsky quoted in Peter N. Carroll, *The Odyssey of the Abraham Lincoln Brigade: Americans in the Spanish Civil War* (Stanford, CA, 1994), 61; Michaela Hoenicke Moore, *Know Your Enemy: The American Debate on Nazism, 1933–1945* (New York, 2010), 141; Martin Glaberman, *Wartime Strikes: The Struggle against the No-Strike Pledge in the UAW during World War II* (Detroit, 1980), 104; Tom Buchanan, *The Spanish Civil War and the British Labour Movement* (Cambridge, UK, 1991), 51, 92.
26 Carroll, *Lincoln Brigade*, 199.
27 Tom Buchanan, *Britain and the Spanish Civil War* (New York, 1997), 132; Sygmunt Stein, *Ma Guerre d'Espagne: Brigades internationales la fin d'un mythe*, trans. Marina Alexeeva-Antipov (Paris, 2012), 23–83.
28 Silvio Pons, "La diplomatie soviétique, l'antifascisme et la guerre civile espagnole," *Antifascisme et nation*, 63–66.
29 Carroll, *Lincoln Brigade*, 159.
30 Dominic Tierney, *FDR and the Spanish Civil War: Neutrality and Commitment in the Struggle that divided America* (Durham, NC, 2007), 74; Glyn Stone, "The European Great Powers and the Spanish Civil War," in Robert Boyce and Esmonde M. Robertson, eds. *Paths to War: New Essays on the Origins of the Second World War* (New York, 1989), 214; David Wingeate Pike, *Les Français et la guerre d'Espagne* (Paris, 1975), 101.
31 Vigreux, *Le front populaire*, 38; Yves Denéchère, *Jean Herbette (1878–1960): Journaliste et ambassadeur* (Paris, 2003), 302; Pike, *Les Français*, 55, 174.
32 Antonio Manuel Moral Roncal, *Diplomacia, humanitarismo y espionaje en la Guerra Civil española* (Madrid, 2008), 324, 330, 354; Javier Rubio, *Asilos y canjes durante la guerra civil española* (Barcelona, 1979), 29–39, 87–95; Denéchère, *Herbette*, 269, 281.
33 Anthony Adamthwaite, *France and the Coming of the Second World War 1936–1939* (London, 1977), 256.
34 Peter Jackson, *France and the Nazi Menace: Intelligence and Policy Making, 1933–1939* (Oxford, 2000), 308; Denis Mack Smith, "Appeasement as a Factor in Mussolini's Foreign Policy," in Wolfgang J. Mommsen and Lothar Kettenacker, eds. *The Fascist Challenge and the Policy of Appeasement* (London, 1983), 263; Anne-Aurore Inquimbert, "Monsieur Blum...un roi de France ferait la guerre," *Guerres mondiales et conflits contemporains*, no. 215, 2004, 35–45; Jill Edwards, *The British Government and the Spanish Civil War, 1936–1939* (London, 1979), 139; Adamthwaite, *France*, 262.
35 Serge Berstein, *Léon Blum* (Paris, 2006), 517; Martin Thomas, *Britain, France and Appeasement: Anglo-French Relations in the Popular Front Era* (Oxford, 1996), 91; Buchanan, *Britain and the Spanish Civil War*, 45; Stone, "The European Great Powers," 214; Pike, *Les Français*, 83, 195; Maurice Cowling, *The Impact of Hitler: British Politics and British Policy, 1933–1940* (Chicago, 1977), 130–131; Tom Buchanan, *The Impact of the Spanish Civil*

War on Britain: War, Loss and Memory (Portland, OR, 2007), 2, 13; Richard Griffiths, *Fellow Travellers of the Right: British Enthusiasts for Nazi Germany 1933–9* (London, 1980), 264.

36 Neville Thompson, *The Anti-Appeasers: Conservative Opposition to Appeasement in the 1930s* (Oxford, 1971), 124; Cowling, *Impact of Hitler*, 131, 135; Zara Steiner, *The Triumph of the Dark: European International History 1933–1939* (Oxford, 2011), 206.

37 Robert Graves and Alan Hodge, *The Long Week-End: A Social History of Great Britain 1918–1939* (New York, 1940), 337; K. W. Watkins, *Britain Divided: The Effect of the Spanish Civil War on British Political Opinion* (London, 1963), 4, 77; Hugo García, *Mentiras necesarias: La batalla por la opinión británica durante la Guerra Civil* (Madrid, 2008), 210; Buchanan, *Britain and the Spanish Civil War*, 51–59.

38 Roy Jenkins, *Churchill: A Biography* (New York, 2001), 493; Winston S. Churchill, *Step by Step, 1936–1939* (New York, 1939), 294; Winston S. Churchill, *The Gathering Storm* (New York, 1948), 192.

39 Poets cited in Richard Overy, *The Twilight Years: The Paradox of Britain between the Wars* (New York, 2009), 339–340; Stanley Weintraub, *The Last Great Cause: The Intellectuals and the Spanish Civil War* (New York, 1968), 18, 53; Steiner, *Triumph of the Dark*, 221; Buchanan, *British Labour*, 39, 74, 106, 111.

40 Duchess of Atholl, *Searchlight on Spain* (Harmondsworth, 1938); Overy, *Twilight Years*, 327.

41 Nigel Copsey, "'Every time they made a Communist, they made a Fascist': The Labour Party and Popular Anti-Fascism in the 1930s," *Varieties of Anti-Fascism*, 63; Jim Fyrth, "Introduction: In the Thirties," in Jim Fyrth, ed. *Britain, Fascism and the Popular Front* (London, 1985), 19; Copsey, *Anti-Fascism*, 16.

42 Mary Vincent, "The Spanish Civil War as a War of Religion," in Martin Baumeister and Stefanie Schüler-Springorum, eds. *"If You Tolerate This . . .": The Spanish Civil War in the Age of Total War* (New York, 2008), 74–89; Wolfram Kaiser, *Christian Democracy and the Origins of European Union* (Cambridge, UK, 2007), 45; Tom Lawson, "'I was following the lead of Jesus Christ,' Christian Anti-Fascism in 1930s Britain," *Varieties of Anti-Fascism*, 127; Buchanan, *Britain and the Spanish Civil War*, 162.

43 Edwards, *British Government*, 199; Buchanan, *British Labour Movement*, 79, 173.

44 Allen Guttmann, *The Wound in the Heart: America and the Spanish Civil War* (New York, 1962), 56, 62; Steven Casey, *Cautious Crusade: Franklin D. Roosevelt, American Public Opinion, and the War against Nazi Germany* (New York, 2001), 16; Marta Rey García, *Stars for Spain: La Guerra Civil Española en los Estados Unidos* (La Coruña, 1997), 56.

45 Kaiser, *Christian Democracy*, 131–136; Wayne S. Cole, *Roosevelt and the Isolationists, 1932–1945* (Lincoln, NE, 1983), 8, 235; Leo V. Kanawada, *Franklin D. Roosevelt's Diplomacy and American Catholics, Italians, and Jews* (Ann Arbor, 1982), 55, 64–67; *Commonweal*, 3 March 1939.

46 The following citations are from *Catholic World*, April to October 1938.

47 Joseph B. Code, *The Spanish War and Lying Propaganda*, (New York, 1938).
48 *Catholic World*, March, April, and May 1939. For Vatican figures, see Paul Christophe, *1936: Les Catholiques et le Front Populaire* (Paris, 1986), 216; Code, *Lying Propaganda*, 22.
49 Pike, *Les Français*, 346; Hugh Thomas, *Spanish Civil War* (New York, 1961), 536; Rey García, *Stars for Spain*, 464–466; Michael E. Chapman, *Franco Lobbyists, Roosevelt's Foreign Policy, and the Spanish Civil War* (Kent, OH, 2011), 95–106.
50 René Rémond, *Les crises du catholicisme en France dans les années trente* (Paris, 1996), 172–192; Kaiser, *Christian Democracy*, 97.
51 Xuan Cándano, *El Pacto de Santoña (1937): La rendición del nacionalismo vasco al fascismo* (Madrid, 2006), 59.
52 Manifesto reproduced in Rémond, *Catholicisme*, 179. See also Javier Tusell and Genoveva García Queipo de Llano, *El catolicismo mundial y la guerra de España* (Madrid, 1993), 81, 93.
53 Christophe, *1936*, 121, 215.
54 John P. Diggins, *Mussolini and Fascism: The View from America* (Princeton, NJ, 1972), 202; Tierney, *FDR*, 63; Kaiser, *Christian Democracy*, 134; Guttmann, *Wound*, 94.
55 Tierney, *FDR*, 61; Tusell, *El catolicismo mundial*, 322; Cole, *Isolationists*, 224, 236; Cecil D. Eby, *Comrades and Commissars: The Lincoln Battalion in the Spanish Civil War* (University Park, PA, 2007), 138; Chapman, *Franco Lobbyists*, 15; Bosch, *Estados Unidos ante la Segunda República*, 9, 215.
56 Citation from Trapiello, *Las armas y las letras*, 122; William Carlos Williams, "Federico García Lorca," *The Kenyon Review*, vol. 1, no. 2 (Spring 1939), 58; Nicole Racine, "Les Unions internationales d'écrivains pendant l'entre-deux-guerres," *Antifascisme et nation*, 42.
57 Cécile Whiting, *Antifascism in American Art* (New Haven, CT, 1989), 40.
58 Quoted in Carroll, *Lincoln Brigade*, 267.
59 Abraham Ascher, *Was Hitler a Riddle?: Western Democracies and National Socialism* (Stanford, CA, 2012), 157; Buchanan, *Britain and the Spanish Civil War*, 163–164.
60 Hernández quoted in José Hinojosa Durán, *Tropas en un Frente olvidado: El ejército republicano en Extremadura durante la Guerra Civil* (Mérida, 2009), 115–116, 177.
61 Cited in Trapiello, *Las armas y las letras*, 165–166; Carl-Henrik Bjerström, *Josep Renau and the Politics of Culture in Republican Spain, 1931–1939: Reimagining the Nation* (Brighton, UK, 2016), 119.
62 Russell Martin, *Picasso's War: The Destruction of Guernica and the Masterpiece That Changed the World* (New York, 2003), 136.
63 Overy, *Twilight Years*, 335; Buchanan, *Britain and the Spanish Civil War*, 170; Guttmann, *Wound*, 107.
64 Guttmann, *Wound*, 131; Rey García, *Stars for Spain*, 340.
65 Thomas, *Britain, France and Appeasement*, 216, 234; Steiner, *Triumph of the Dark*, 242.
66 Buchanan, *Britain and the Spanish Civil War*, 91

67 Louis Stein, *Beyond Death and Exile: The Spanish Republicans in France, 1939–1955* (Cambridge, MA, 1979), 29, 45, 95; Scott Soo, *The routes to exile: France and the Spanish Civil War refugees, 1939–2009* (Manchester, 2013), 40, 78; Denéchère, *Herbette*, 151; Rubio, *Asilos*, 353: France's asylum policy toward Spaniards of both camps was "a noble humanitarian gesture without precedent."

68 Geneviève Dreyfus-Armand and Émile Temime, *Les camps sur la plage, un exil espagnol* (Paris, 1995), 110; Joseph Parello, "Los republicanos españoles en la Francia Libre," *Memòria antifranquista del Baix Llobregat*, no. 16 (2016), 6–10.

69 Stein, *Spanish Republicans*, 130–137; Bernd Zielenski, "Le chômage et la politique de la main-d'oeuvre de Vichy (1940–1942)," in Denis Peschanski and Jean-Louis Robert, eds. *Les ouvriers en France pendant la seconde guerre mondiale* (Paris, 1992), 300, reduces the number of Spaniards to 11,000 building Atlantic fortifications in November 1941.

3 THE ANTIFASCIST DEFICIT DURING THE FRENCH POPULAR FRONT

1 Stanley G. Payne, "Soviet Anti-Fascism: Theory and Practice, 1921–45," *Totalitarian Movements and Political Religions*, vol. 4, no. 2 (Autumn, 2003), 6; Vergnon, *L'antifascisme*, 19–36; Payne, *Civil War in Europe*, 98.

2 Jacques Droz, *Histoire de l'antifascisme en Europe, 1923–1939* (Paris, 1985), 10, 100; Vergnon, *L'antifascisme*, 63, 83; Michel Dreyfus, "Les socialistes européens et les Front populaires: un internationalisme déclinant," *Antifascisme et nation*, 24; Mona L. Siegel, *The Moral Disarmament of France: Education, Pacifism, and Patriotism, 1914–1940* (New York, 2004), 196.

3 Vigreux, *Le front populaire*, 33; Yvon Lacaze, *L'opinion publique française et la crise de Munich* (Berne, 1991), 606.

4 Berstein, *Blum*, 391, 407.

5 Xavier Vigna, *Histoire des ouvriers en France au XXe siècle* (Paris, 2012), 121; Berstein, *Blum*, 400.

6 André Combes, *La franc-maçonnerie sous l'Occupation: Persécution et résistance (1939–1945)* (Monaco, 2001), 289.

7 Berstein, *Blum*, 554.

8 Ibid., 549; James P. Levy, *Appeasement and Rearmament: Britain, 1936–1939* (Lanham, MD, 2006), 100.

9 Raymond Aron, "Réflexions sur les problèmes économiques français," *Revue de Métaphysique et de Morale*, vol. 44, no. 4 (October 1937), 803; Raymond Aron, *The Committed Observer: Interviews with Jean-Louis Missika and Dominique Wolton*, trans. James and Marie McIntosh (Chicago, 1983), 42; Jean-Louis Crémieux Brilhac, *Georges Boris: Trente Ans d'Influence: Blum, de Gaulle, Mendès France* (Paris, 2010), 68; Thomas, *Britain, France and Appeasement*, 152, 165, 230; Robert Frankenstein, *Le prix du réarmement français, 1935–39* (Paris, 1982), 235; R. A. C. Parker, "British rearmament 1936–9: Treasury, trade unions and skilled labour," *The English Historical*

Review, vol. 96, no. 379 (April 1981), 317–320; Vigna, *Histoire des ouvriers*, 139–140.

10 Pierre Birnbaum, *Léon Blum: Prime Minister, Socialist, Zionist*, trans. Arthur Goldhammer (New Haven, CT, 2015), 112; Herrick Chapman, *State Capitalism and Working-Class Radicalism in the French Aircraft Industry* (Berkeley, CA, 1991), 110, 190.

11 Lacaze, *L'opinion*, 108; Philippe Burrin, *France under the Germans: Collaboration and Compromise*, trans. Janet Lloyd (New York, 1996), 82; Jacques Maritain, *France My Country: Through the Disaster* (New York, 1941), 20.

12 Ascher, *Riddle*, 101; Jackson, *France and the Nazi Menace*, 69.

13 Maurice Lecerf, "Encore une tentative pour comprendre l'Allemagne," *L'Économie nouvelle*, no. 327, June, 1933, 316; Martin-Dumesnil, "L'Allemagne et son unité," *L'Économie nouvelle*, no. 328–329, July–August 1933, 376; "Hitler et l'économie allemande," *L'Économie nouvelle*, no. 326, May 1933, 239–246; Maurice Lecerf, "Hitler et les paysans allemands," *L'Économie nouvelle*, no. 330–331, September–October 1933, 442.

14 "L'Inconnue Hitlerienne," 2 February 1933; "L'Étatisation," "Hitler et les syndicats," 4 May 1933; "Nuages," "M. Hitler," 9 May 1933; "L'Allemagne Hitlerienne," 9, 11–12 June 1933, all in *La Journée industrielle*. Sylvain Schirmann, *Les relations économiques et financières franco-allemandes, 24 décembre 1932–1 septembre 1939* (Paris, 1995), 216.

15 Blum cited in Pike, *Les Français*, 87; Lacaze, *L'opinion*, 384; Richard Gombin, *Les socialistes et la guerre: La S.F.I.O. et la politique étrangère française entre les deux guerres mondiales* (Paris, 1970), 178; Berstein, *Blum*, 511; Talbot Imlay, *Facing the Second World War: Strategy, Politics, and Economics in Britain and France 1938–1940* (Oxford, 2003), 315.

16 Berstein, *Blum*, 412, 510; Frankenstein, *Réarmement*, 51; Gombin, *Les socialistes*, 178–179, 189, 207.

17 Thomas, *Britain, France and Appeasement*, 178; Michel Margairaz, *L'État, les finances et l'économie: Histoire d'une conversion 1932–1952* (Paris, 1991), 204; Berstein, *Blum*, 482; Ludovine Broch, *Ordinary Workers, Vichy and the Holocaust: French Railwaymen and the Second World War* (Cambridge, UK, 2016), 36.

18 Gombin, *Les socialistes*, 230; André Tollet, *La classe ouvrière dans la résistance* (Paris, 1984), 32; Jacques Rancière, *Staging the People: The Proletarian and His Double*, trans. David Fernbach (London, 2011), 130.

19 Lacaze, *L'opinion*, 446, 478, 580.

20 Franklin Reid Gannon, *The British Press and Germany 1936–1939* (Oxford, 1971), 4–6, 12; Ritchie Ovendale, "Why the British Dominions Declared War," *Paths to War*, 271–280; Anthony Adamthwaite, *Grandeur and Misery: France's Bid for Power in Europe 1914–1940* (London, 1995), 189.

21 Norman Ingram, *The Politics of Dissent: Pacifism in France, 1919–1939* (Oxford, 1991), 201; Julie Gottlieb, "Varieties of Feminist Responses to Fascism in Inter-War Britain," *Varieties of Anti-Fascism*, 113.

22 Lacaze, *L'opinion*, 384; Ascher, *Riddle*, 141; Julian Jackson, *The Politics of Depression in France, 1932–1936* (Cambridge, UK, 1982), 2; Nicole Jordan, "The Cut Price War on the Peripheries: The French General Staff, the Rhineland, and Czechoslovakia," *Paths to War*, 137.

23 Robert Boyce, "René Massigli and Germany, 1919–1938," in Robert Boyce, ed. *French Foreign and Defence Policy, 1918–1940: The Decline and Fall of a Great Power* (London, 1998), 143; Raphäelle Ulrich-Pier, *René Massigli (1888–1988): Une vie de diplomate*, 2 vols. (Paris, 2006), 385–392; Thomas, *Britain, France and Appeasement*, 42, 71; Stephen A. Schuker, "France and the Remilitarization of the Rhineland, 1936," *French Historical Studies*, vol. 14, no. 3 (Spring 1986), 330–335; Adam Tooze, *The Wages of Destruction: The Making and Breaking of the Nazi Economy* (New York, 2006), 606; Pike, *Les Français*, 372.

24 *Le Canard* cited in Ingram, *Pacifism*, 213; Jean Plumyène and Raymond Lasierra, *Les fascismes français, 1923–63* (Paris, 1963), 7, 10; Werth cited in Adamthwaite, *Grandeur*, 179.

25 Ragsdale, *Soviets*, 15.

26 Elizabeth Wiskemann, *The Europe I Saw* (New York, 1968), 40; Baldwin cited in Adamthwaite, *France*, 38; Gannon, *British Press*, 13; MacDonald cited in Schuker, "Remilitarization of the Rhineland," 314.

27 Gannon, *British Press*, 78; Lawson, "Lead of Jesus Christ," *Varieties of Anti-Fascism*, 135.

28 Lloyd George cited in Griffiths, *Fellow Travellers*, 208–210, 223; Gannon, *British Press*, 104.

29 Blum cited in Joel Colton, *Léon Blum: Humanist in Politics* (Cambridge, MA, 1974), 203; Robert Boyce, "World Depression, World War: Some Economic Origins of the Second World War," *Paths to War*, 74; Bernd-Jürgen Wendt, "Economic Appeasement – A Crisis Strategy," *The Fascist Challenge*, 162–165.

30 Griffiths, *Fellow Travellers*, 192, 212.

31 Ibid., 230.

32 Adamthwaite, *France*, 68; Sidney Aster, "Guilty Men: The Case of Neville Chamberlain," *Paths to War*, 245; Churchill quoted in Eugen Spier, *Focus: A Footnote to the History of the Thirties* (London, 1963), 11; Callum A. MacDonald, "The United States, Appeasement and the Open Door," *The Fascist Challenge*, 403; David Dutton, *Anthony Eden: A Life and Reputation* (London, 1997), 85–110.

33 Lacaze, *L'opinion*, 223.

34 Aster, "Guilty Men," 242; Robert Paul Shay, *British Rearmament in the Thirties: Politics and Profits* (Princeton, NJ, 1977), 190, 228; Gustav Schmidt, "The Domestic Background to British Appeasement Policy," *The Fascist Challenge*, 103.

35 Berstein, *Blum*, 482; Frankenstein, *Réarmement*, 22, 31–32, 110, 122; Jackson, *Nazi Menace*, 158; Crémieux Brilhac, *Georges Boris*, 70; Christine Levisse-Touzé, *L'Afrique du Nord dans la guerre, 1939–1945* (Paris, 1998), 42; Philippe Garraud, "La politique française de réarmement de 1936 à 1940: priorités et contraintes," *Guerres mondiales et conflits contemporains*, no. 219 (July 2005), 94; Adamthwaite, *Grandeur*, 142–144; Imlay, *Facing the Second World War*, 263; Robert J. Young, *France and the Origins of the Second World War* (New York, 1996), 104.

36 Angus Calder, *The People's War: Britain 1939–1945* (New York, 1969), 143; Lynne Olson, *Citizens of London: The Americans Who Stood with Britain in*

Its Darkest, Finest Hour (New York, 2010), 127, 130; Steiner, *Triumph of the Dark*, 1045.

37 Adamthwaite, *France*, 243.

38 Richard Cockett, *Twilight of Truth: Chamberlain, Appeasement and the Manipulation of the Press* (New York, 1989), 8; R. B. Cockett, "Ball, Chamberlain and Truth," *The Historical Journal*, vol. 33, no. 1 (March 1990), 136–140; Brendon, *Dark Valley*, 611; Martin Pugh, *Hurrah for the Blackshirts: Fascists and Fascism in Britain between the Wars* (London, 2006), 273; Chamberlain cited in Thompson, *Anti-Appeasers*, 210.

39 Gannon, *British Press*, 166; Thompson, *Anti-Appeasers*, 21, 42.

40 Julian Jackson, *The Popular Front in France: Defending Democracy, 1934–38* (Cambridge, UK, 1988), 195; Thomas, *Appeasement*, 134; Annie Lacroix-Riz, *Le choix de la défaite: Les élites françaises dans les années 1930* (Paris, 2010), 388; Adamthwaite, *France*, 237, 242.

41 Gombin, *Les socialistes*, 180; Adamthwaite, *France*, 84–87.

42 Ingram, *Pacifism*, 210; Blum cited in Gombin, *Les socialistes*, 234; Blum cited in Lacaze, *L'opinion*, 394, 396; *Le Populaire*, 20 September 1938; Berstein, *Blum*, 604.

43 See Philip Nord, *France 1940: Defending the Republic* (New Haven, CT, 2015), 146; cf. Vigreux, *Front populaire*, 94; Jean Vigreux, *Histoire du Front populaire: L'échappée belle* (Paris, 2016), 198, and Jackson, *Defending Democracy*.

44 Mussolini cited in Brendon, *Dark Valley*, 571; Dan Stone, "Anti-Fascist Europe Comes to Britain: Theorising Fascism as a Contribution to Defeating It," *Varieties of Anti-Fascism*, 196–198; Arnold A. Offner, *The Origins of the Second World War* (New York, 1975), 126.

45 Michel Winock, *Histoire politique de la revue "Esprit," 1930–1950* (Paris, 1975), 178; Michel Winock and Nora Benkorich, *La trahison de Munich: Emmanuel Mounier et la grande débâcle des intellectuels* (Paris, 2008), 11; Lacaze, *L'opinion*, 473.

46 Marc Sadoun, *Les socialistes sous l'Occupation: Résistance et collaboration* (Paris, 1982), 50; Lacroix-Riz, *Le choix de la défaite*, 538.

47 Lacaze, *L'opinion*, 90, 444.

48 Ibid., 397.

49 Ingram, *Pacifism*, 230.

50 Lacaze, *L'opinion*, 444. The following paragraphs are largely based on this thorough study.

51 Antoine Prost, *Les Anciens Combattants* (Paris, 2014), 10, 100; Lacaze, *L'opinion*, 110, 279–336, 453–500.

52 Steiner, *Triumph of the Dark*, 987; Lacaze, *L'opinion*, 329, 464.

53 Lacaze, *L'opinion*, 226, 287, 317; Frédéric Vitoux, *Céline: A Biography*, trans. Jesse Browner (New York, 1992), 349–362.

54 Jouvenel cited in Lacaze, *L'opinion*, 321; Pétain cited in Burrin, *France under the Germans*, 60.

55 Combes, *La franc-maçonnerie*, 33, 91, 373; Pierre Chevallier, *Histoire de la Franc-Maçonnerie française*, 3 vols. (Paris, 1975), 3:303.

56 Lacaze, *L'opinion*, 254–255, 325–326, 578; Lacroix-Riz, *Le choix de la défaite*, 538.

57 Roche and Caillaux cited in Lacaze, *L'opinion*, 373–374.
58 Adamthwaite, *France*, 194, 198, 210, 358; Jackson, *France and the Nazi Menace*, 321, offers a different interpretation. See also Ragsdale, *Soviets*, 101–102; Geoffrey Adams, *Political Ecumenism: Catholics, Jews, and Protestants in de Gaulle's Free France, 1940–1945* (Montreal, 2006), 227.
59 Blum cited in Berstein, *Blum*, 592–594.
60 *La Bataille Socialiste* cited in Sadoun, *Socialistes*, 16.
61 *Le Populaire*, 15 August and 23 August 1938.
62 This is also the historiographic case. Cf. Lacroix-Riz, *Le choix de la défaite*, 556–566.
63 Cf. Jackson, *Defending Democracy*, 212.
64 Robert Frank, "La gauche sait-elle gérer la France? (1936–1937/ 1981–1984)," *Vingtième siècle*, no. 6 (April–June 1985), 15.
65 Droz, *Antifascisme*, 61.
66 Cited in Pike, *Les Français*, 329.

4 BRITISH AND FRENCH COUNTERREVOLUTIONARY ANTIFASCISM

1 Shay, *British Rearmament*, 16; Overy, *Twilight Years*, 268; Pugh, *Blackshirts*, 195–197; Neil Barrett, "The anti-fascist movement in south-east Lancashire, 1933–1940: The divergent experiences of Manchester and Nelson," *Opposing Fascism*, 59–60; Bruce Coleman, "The Conservative Party and the Frustration of the Extreme Right," and Richard Thurlow, "The Failure of British Fascism 1932–40," in Andrew Thorpe, ed. *The Failure of Political Extremism in Inter-War Britain* (Exeter, 1989), 51, 73.
2 Pugh, *Blackshirts*, 246–252.
3 Griffiths, *Fellow Travellers*, 56; Janet Dack, "It certainly isn't cricket!: Media Responses to Mosley and the BUF," *Varieties of Anti-Fascism*, 155; Andrzej Olechnowicz, "Historians and the Study of Anti-Fascism in Britain," *Varieties of Anti-Fascism*, 5–11; Philip Williamson, "The Conservative Party, Fascism and Anti-Fascism, 1918–1939," *Varieties of Anti-Fascism*, 73.
4 Nigel Copsey, "Every time they made a Communist, they made a Fascist," *Varieties of Anti-Fascism*, 58; letter cited in Barrett, "Manchester and Nelson," *Opposing Fascism*, 58.
5 Richard Thurlow, "Passive and Active Anti-Fascism: The State and National Security, 1923–45," *Varieties of Anti-Fascism*, 168; Copsey, "Popular Anti-Fascism," *Varieties of Anti-Fascism*, 60; Kaiser, *Christian Democracy*, 129; Tom Buchanan, "'Beyond Cable Street': New Approaches to the Historiography of Antifascism in Britain in the 1930s," in Hugo García, Mercedes Yusta, Xavier Tabet, and Cristina Clímaco, eds. *Rethinking Antifascism: History, Memory and Politics, 1922 to the Present* (New York, 2016), 63; Pugh, *Blackshirts*, 167.
6 Keith Hodgson, *Fighting Fascism: The British Left and the Rise of Fascism, 1919–39* (Manchester, 2010), 136; Pugh, *Blackshirts*, 227.
7 Coleman, "Conservative Party," *The Failure of Political Extremism*, 65; Copsey, *Anti-Fascism*, 75; Pugh, *Blackshirts*, 174–176, 230.
8 Cited in Gannon, *British Press*, 83.

9 Ibid., 46; Overy, *Twilight Years*, 272.
10 Cited in Griffiths, *Fellow Travellers*, 226.
11 Overy, *Twilight Years*, 279; Pugh, *Blackshirts*, 233; Jean Medawar and David Pyke, *Hitler's Gift: The True Story of the Scientists Expelled by the Nazi Regime* (New York, 2001), xiii, 56.
12 Overy, *Twilight Years*, 300.
13 Ibid., 303; Cowling, *Impact of Hitler*, 246.
14 Overy, *Twilight Years*, 307.
15 Thompson, *Anti-Appeasers*, 195.
16 Spier, *Focus*, 42. Historians have largely ignored Focus, which remains without a monograph. Thompson, *Anti-Appeasers*, 137, 146, 210; Andre Liebich, "The Anti-Semitism of Henry Wickham Steed," *Patterns of Prejudice*, vol. 46, no. 2 (2012), 197; Sadoun, *Socialistes*, 28; Jean-Louis Crémieux Brilhac, *Les français de l'an 40* (2 vols.) (Paris, 1990), 1:48–52; Burrin, *France under the Germans*, 62.
17 Overy, *Twilight Years*, 267.
18 Hodgson, *Fighting Fascism*, 4; Paul Addison, *The Road to 1945: British Politics and the Second World War* (London, 1975), 54; Droz, *Antifascisme*, 217; Neil Riddell, "Walter Citrine and the British Labour Movement, 1925–1935," *History*, vol. 85, no. 278 (April 2000), 302; Sabine Wichert, "The British Left and Appeasement: Political Tactics or Alternative Policies," *The Fascist Challenge*, 135.
19 Copsey, "Popular Anti-Fascism," *Varieties of Anti-Fascism*, 55; Kevin Morgan, *Against Fascism and War: Ruptures and Continuities in British Communist Politics, 1935–41* (Manchester, 1989), 36.
20 Overy, *Twilight Years*, 271–286; Roger Moorhouse, *The Devils' Alliance: Hitler's Pact with Stalin, 1939–1941* (New York, 2014), 134; Shay, *British Rearmament*, 278, 285. Cf. G. C. Peden, "Keynes, the Economics of Rearmament and Appeasement," *The Fascist Challenge*, 148–154.
21 Betty Reid, "The Left Book Club in the Thirties," in Jon Clark, Margot Heinemann, David Margolies, and Carole Snee, eds. *Culture and Crisis in Britain in the Thirties* (London, 1979), 193–194; Webb cited in Overy, *Twilight Years*, 291; Calder, *People's War*, 350.
22 Gannon, *British Press*, 154, 226; Thompson, *Anti-Appeasers*, 158.
23 Griffiths, *Fellow Travellers*, 40; N. J. Crowson, *Facing Fascism: The Conservative Party and the European Dictators, 1935–1940* (London, 1997), 47; Thompson, *Anti-Appeasers*, 67.
24 Brendon, *Dark Valley*, 319–320, 425.
25 Overy, *Twilight Years*, 44; Donald C. Watt, "The European Civil War," *The Fascist Challenge*, 17; Gannon, *British Press*, 119; Stanley High, "The War on Religious Freedom," in Pierre van Paassen and James Waterman Wise, eds. *Nazism: An Assault on Civilization* (New York, 1934), 35; Serge Wolikow, "Table Ronde: Front Populaire et antifascisme en débat," *Antifascisme et nation*, 253; Gentile, *Politics as Religion*, 89.
26 Griffiths, *Fellow Travellers*, 251; Lawson, "Lead of Jesus Christ," *Varieties of Anti-Fascism*, 134; Joe Jacobs, *Out of the Ghetto: My Youth in the East End Communism and Fascism 1913–1939* (London, 1978), 207; Calder, *People's War*, 57, 478; Tusell, *El catolicismo mundial*, 243.

27 W. S. Churchill, *Winston S. Churchill: His Complete Speeches, 1897–1963*, vol. 5 (New York, 1974), 6011.
28 Cited in Thompson, *Anti-Appeasers*, 185.
29 Levy, *Appeasement*, 121; Shay, *British Rearmament*, 231; Aster, "Guilty Men," 250–253.
30 Gannon, *British Press*, 202–203; Cowling, *Impact of Hitler*, 123–126, 252.
31 Griffiths, *Fellow Travellers*, 292–342; Gannon, *British Press*, 28, 205–226.
32 Crémieux, "La crise gouvernementale italienne et le fascisme," 4 November 1922; Crémieux, "La situation en Italie," 11 November 1922; Paul Bruzon, "Le fascisme et la question tunisienne," 9 December 1922; Crémieux, "La deuxième révolution fasciste" 30 December 1922; [No author], "Fascisme et Action Française," 18 June 1923, all in *L'Europe Nouvelle*.
33 Italicus, "Où en est le fascisme?" 5 May 1923; Marcel Ray, "Don Luigi Sturzo," 21 July 1923; Italicus, "La politique de M. Mussolini" 23 June 1923; Philippe Millet, "Les relations franco-italiennes," and Emmanuel Audisio, "M. Mussolini et ses collaborateurs," 6 October 1923, all in *L'Europe Nouvelle*.
34 Gaston Raphaël, "Le socialisme national et Adolf Hitler," 24 February 1923; Maurice Pernot, "L'Allemagne va voter: pour la dernière fois?" 4 March 1933; "Triomphe du nationalisme en Allemagne," 11 March 1933, all in *L'Europe Nouvelle*. Lacaze, *L'opinion*, 52.
35 Lacaze, *L'opinion*, 52–55, 464–470; Kaiser, *Christian Democracy*, 112.
36 Jacques Maritain, *The Social and Political Philosophy of Jacques Maritain: Selected Readings*, Joseph W. Evans and Leo R. Ward, eds. (Notre Dame, IN, 1976), 24; Maritain, *My Country*, 48; Gentile, *Politics as Religion*, 73–106.
37 Cited in Lacaze, *L'opinion*, 90.
38 Ibid., 127–128, 301, 329, 514.
39 Ibid., 491.
40 Ibid., 270.
41 Pike, *Les Français*, 274, 293, 322; Lacaze, *L'opinion*, 216, 370; Pierre Mendès France, "La portée de ce témoignage," *Les Cahiers de la République* (September–October 1960), 14.
42 Lacaze, *L'opinion*, 345, 286, 524.
43 Kérillis cited in ibid., 581.
44 Éric Roussel, *Charles de Gaulle* (Paris, 2002), 64; cited in Jean Lacouture, *De Gaulle: The Rebel 1890–1944*, trans. Patrick O'Brian (New York, 1990), 128, 154; Antonio Varsori, "Reflections on the Origins of the Cold War," in Odd Arne Westad, ed. *Reviewing the Cold War: Approaches, Interpretations, Theory* (London, 2000), 289; Peter Jackson, "Intelligence and the End of Appeasement," *French Foreign and Defence Policy*, 237.

5 COUNTERREVOLUTIONARY ANTIFASCISM ALONE, 1939–1940

1 Overy, *Twilight Years*, 352; Vergnon, *L'antifascisme*, 112.
2 Gannon, *British Press*, 240; On Steer's politics, see Buchanan, *Impact*, 23–42; Esmonde M. Robertson, "German Mobilisation Preparations and

the Treaties between Germany and the Soviet Union of August and September 1939," *Paths to War*, 345; Ovendale, "British Dominions," 288; David Edgerton, *Britain's War Machine: Weapons, Resources, and Experts in the Second World War* (New York, 2011), 56, 149.

3 Crowson, *Facing Fascism*, 118–119; Cowling, *Impact of Hitler*, 219–220; Imlay, *Facing the Second World War*, 303, 306; Ian Kershaw, *Hitler, 1936–1945: Nemesis* (New York, 2000), 213, 229; Denis Mack Smith, "Appeasement as a Factor in Mussolini's Foreign Policy," *The Fascist Challenge*, 261.

4 Gannon, *British Press*, 261; Christopher Seton-Watson, "The Anglo-Italian Gentleman's Agreement of January 1937 and Its Aftermath," *The Fascist Challenge*, 278; Morgan, *British Communist Politics*, 77.

5 Steiner, *Triumph of the Dark*, 738, 750; Jackson, *France and the Nazi Menace*, 363–364; Aron, *Committed Observer*, 48; Kershaw, *Hitler*, 213–228; John Dunbabin, "The British Military Establishment and the Policy of Appeasement," *The Fascist Challenge*, 190; Payne, *Spanish Civil War*, 148; James S. Herndon, "British Perceptions of Soviet Military Capability," *The Fascist Challenge*, 310.

6 Cf. Annie Lacroix-Riz, *De Munich à Vichy: L'assassinat de la Troisième République* (Paris, 2008), which denies any possibility of a significant current of conservative antifascism. Young, *France*, 121; Crémieux Brilhac, *Les français*, 2:350; Jackson, "Intelligence," 251; Adamthwaite, *France*, 318.

7 Lacaze, *L'opinion*, 501, 506; Adamthwaite, *Grandeur*, 179.

8 Steiner, *Triumph of the Dark*, 1003; Lacaze, *L'opinion*, 323, 608–609.

9 Steiner, *Triumph of the Dark*, 768; Lacaze, *L'opinion*, 537–543.

10 Crémieux Brilhac, *Les français*, 2:142, 234–235. For Britain, Geoffrey G. Field, *Blood, Sweat, and Toil: Remaking the British Working Class, 1939–1945* (New York, 2011), 8; Sadoun, *Socialistes*, 19; Vigna, *Histoire des ouvriers*, 57; Frankenstein, *Réarmement*, 284, 297; Talbot Imlay, "Democracy and War: Political Regime, Industrial Relations, and Economic Preparations for War in France and Britain up to 1940," *Journal of Modern History*, vol. 79, no. 1 (March 2007), 24.

11 Cited in Steiner, *Triumph of the Dark*, 1015.

12 Brendon, *Dark Valley*, 674; Moorhouse, *Devils' Alliance*, 13; Shay, *British Rearmament*, 231–232; Chamberlain cited in Aster, "Guilty Men," 252–253.

13 Steiner, *Triumph of the Dark*, 777; Imlay, *Facing*, 45; Adamthwaite, *France*, 160.

14 Steiner, *Triumph of the Dark*, 895–896, 1057; Moorhouse, *Devils' Alliance*, 22.

15 Robertson, "German Mobilisation Preparations," 354; Lacaze, *L'opinion*, 608.

16 Moorhouse, *Devils' Alliance*, 14; Callum MacDonald, "Deterrent Diplomacy: Roosevelt and the Containment of Germany, 1938–1940," *Paths to War*, 322; Annette Wieviorka, *Ils étaient juifs, résistants, communistes* (Paris, 1986), 66–67.

17 Stalin cited in Steiner, *Triumph of the Dark*, 913; Moorhouse, *Devils' Alliance*, 43.

18 Moorhouse, *Devils' Alliance*, 187; Gerhard L. Weinberg, *A World at Arms: A Global History of World War II* (New York, 1994), 73, 104.
19 Imlay, *Facing the Second World War*, 187; Jerry H. Brookshire, "Speak for England, Act for England: Labour's Leadership and the Threat of War in the Late 1930s," *European History Quarterly*, vol. 29, no. 2 (1999), 267; On weak antifascism, see Lacroix-Riz, *Le choix de la défaite*; Cowling, *The Impact of Hitler*, 352–355; cf. Jackson, *France and the Nazi Menace*, 379–380, who insists on Daladier's commitment to the war effort; Berstein, *Blum*, 626.
20 Cited in Thompson, *Anti-Appeasers*, 232; Addison, *Road to 1945*, 79; Churchill cited in Aster, "Guilty Men," 259.
21 PCF cited in Jean-Louis Crémieux-Brilhac, "Les Communistes et l'armée pendant la drôle de guerre," in Jean-Pierre Rioux, Antoine Prost, and Jean-Pierre Azéma, eds. *Les communistes français de Munich à Châteaubriant, 1938–1941* (Paris, 1987), 98, 102; Mikhail Narinski, "Le Komintern et le Parti Communiste français," *Communisme*, vol. 32–4 (1992–1993), 13, 17.
22 Hernández Sánchez, *El Partido Comunista*, 458; Jean-Pierre Rioux, "Présentation," *Les communistes français*, 11; Nicole Racine-Furlaud, "Université libre," *Les communistes français*, 140–141; Wieviorka, *Ils étaient juifs*, 49, 64; Henri Michel, *Les courants de pensée de la Résistance* (Paris, 1962), 557, 559.
23 Crémieux-Brilhac, "Les Communistes," *Les communistes français*, 99, 102; Sadoun, *Socialistes*, 31; *La Vie Ouvrière*, May 1941, reproduced in Gustave Allyn, *Le mouvement syndical dans la résistance* (Paris, 1975), 24; Michel, *Courants de pensée*, 570.
24 Buchanan, *Impact of the Spanish Civil War*, 181; Imlay, *Facing the Second World War*, 225; Calder, *People's War*, 75; Philippe Buton, "Les communistes dans les entreprises travaillant pour la défense nationale en 1939–1940," *Les communistes français*, 125–127.
25 Cited in Buton, "Les communistes dans les entreprises," 129. See also Talbot Imlay, "Mind the Gap: The Perception and Reality of Communist Sabotage of French War Production during the Phoney War 1939–1940," *Past and Present*, no. 189 (November 2005), 181.
26 Eugenia C. Kiesling, *Arming against Hitler: France and the Limits of Military Planning* (Lawrence, KS, 1996), 82–85, 173; Karl-Heinz Frieser with John T. Greenwood, *The Blitzkrieg Legend: The 1940 Campaign in the West* (Annapolis, MD, 2005), 150, 177, 195, 268, 270, 318.
27 Eleanor M. Gates, *The End of the Affair: The Collapse of the Anglo-French Alliance, 1939–40* (Berkeley, CA, 1981), 303; Norman J. W. Goda, *Tomorrow the World: Hitler, Northwest Africa, and the Path toward America* (College Station, TX, 1998), 10; Reynaud cited in Julian Jackson, *The Fall of France: The Nazi Invasion of 1940* (Oxford, 2003), 104.
28 Andrew Buchanan, *American Grand Strategy in the Mediterranean during World War II* (New York, 2014), 15; François Kersaudy, *De Gaulle et Churchill: La mésentente cordiale* (Paris, 2003), 55, 57; Gates, *Collapse of the Anglo-French Alliance*, 202; Arthur Koestler, *Scum of the Earth* (London, 1941), 186.
29 Report cited in Gates, *Collapse of the Anglo-French Alliance*, 259–260.

30 Lynne Olson, *Those Angry Days: Roosevelt, Lindbergh, and America's Fight over World War II, 1939–1941* (New York, 2013), 209–210; David Reynolds, "1940: Fulcrum of the Twentieth Century?" *International Affairs*, 66:2 (April 1990), 338; Srinath Raghavan, *India's War: World War II and the Making of Modern South Asia* (New York, 2016), 53.

31 Kershaw, *Hitler: Nemesis*, 388, 642, 730.

32 Calder, *People's War*, 52, 495.

33 Roussel, *de Gaulle*, 110, 126.

34 Alain Griotteray, *1940: La droite était au rendez-vous* (Paris, 1985), 26; Adams, *Political Ecumenism*, 54; Michel, *Résistance*, 15–16, 120; "Cot, Pierre," Claire Andrieu, Philippe Braud, Guillaume Piketty, eds. *Dictionnaire de Gaulle* (Paris, 2006), 286.

35 Jacques Semelin, *Unarmed against Hitler: Civilian Resistance in Europe, 1939–1943*, trans. Suzan Husserl-Kapit (Westport, CT, 1993), 34.

36 Sadoun, *Socialistes*, 164.

37 Renée Poznanski, "French Apprehensions, Jewish Expectations: From a Social Imaginary to a Political Practice," in David Bankier, ed. *The Jews Are Coming Back* (Jerusalem, 2005), 29; Max Hastings, *Inferno: The World at War, 1939–1945* (New York, 2011), 500; Crémieux Brilhac, *Georges Boris*, 271.

38 Laurent Douzou, *La Désobéissance: Histoire d'un mouvement et d'un journal clandestins: Libération-Sud (1940–1944)* (Paris, 1995), 36, 77, 193, 323; Laurent Douzou, *Lucie Aubrac* (Paris, 2012), 174; Michel, *Résistance*, 154; Maritain, *France*, 17; Jean-François Muracciole, *Histoire de la France libre* (Paris, 1996), 26; Marc Bloch, *Strange Defeat: A Statement of Evidence Written in 1940*, trans. Gerard Hopkins (New York, 1968); Robert Gildea, *Fighters in the Shadows: A New History of the French Resistance* (Cambridge, MA, 2015), 27–43.

39 André Martel, "Philippe Leclerc de Hauteclocque: Maréchal de France, 1902–1947," and Jean-Louis Crémieux-Brilhac, "Leclerc et la France Libre," in Christine Levisse-Touzé, ed. *Du capitaine de Hauteclocque au général Leclerc* (Brussels, 2000), 24, 143; Martin Thomas, *The French Empire at War, 1940–45* (Manchester, 1998), 58–60; Levisse-Touzé, *L'Afrique du Nord*, 129; H. R. Kedward, *Occupied France: Collaboration and Resistance 1940–1944* (Oxford, 1985), 37; Eric T. Jennings, "La dissidence aux Antilles (1940–1943)," *Vingtième Siècle*, 68, October–November, 2000), 65.

40 Roussel, *de Gaulle*, 242, 284; Buchanan, *American Grand Strategy*, 83; István Deák, *Europe on Trial: The Story of Collaboration, Resistance and Retribution during World War II* (Boulder, CO, 2015), 116; Tollet, *La classe ouvrière*, 4; Tzvetan Todorov, *Une tragédie française: Été 44: scènes de guerre civile* (Paris, 2004), 19; Jean-François Muracciole, *Les Français libres: L'autre Résistance* (Paris, 2009), 72, 95, 162, 174.

41 De Gaulle cited in Roussel, *de Gaulle*, 113; Douzou, *La Désobéissance*, 270; Perez Zagorin, *How the Idea of Religious Toleration Came to the West* (Princeton, NJ, 2003), 293.

42 Stéphane Courtois, "Les Communistes et l'action syndicale," *Les communistes français*, 94; Donald Reid, *Germaine Tillion, Lucie Aubrac, and the Politics of Memories of the French Resistance* (Newcastle, 2008), 126. Cf. Olivier

Wieviorka, *Histoire de la Résistance, 1940–1945* (Paris, 2013), 429–434.
Women composed 7 to 17 percent of Resisters. See Muracciole, *Français libres*, 45.

43 L'état d'esprit de la population et la propagande communiste, May 1941, GB 140–161, Archives de la Préfecture de Police [hereafter APP].

44 Lynne Taylor, *Between Resistance and Collaboration: Popular Protest in Northern France, 1940–45* (New York, 2000), 98; Bourdet, *De la Résistance à la Restauration*, 101.

45 Narinski, "Komintern," 25–26.

46 Courtois, "Action," 62; Wieviorka, *Ils étaient juifs*, 80, 95.

47 Situation à Paris, 2 March 1942, 2 November 1942, 2 May 1944, APP; Henri Amouroux, *La vie des français sous l'Occupation*, 2 vols. (Paris, 1961), 2:303; Danielle Tartakowsky, *Les manifestations de rue en France, 1918–1968* (Paris, 1997), 461–467; Tollet, *La classe ouvrière*, 77; Paula Schwartz, "Redefining Resistance: Women's Activism in Wartime France," in Margaret Randolph Higonnet, ed. *Behind the Lines: Gender and the Two World Wars* (New Haven, CT, 1987), 149; K. H. Adler, *Jews and Gender in Liberation France* (New York, 2003), 37, 49; On Jews, Situation à Paris, 27 July 1942, 22 February 1943, APP.

48 Wieviorka, *Ils étaient juifs*, 77; Erwan Le Gall, "L'engagement des France Libre: une mise en perspective," in Patrick Harismendy and Erwan Le Gall, eds. *Pour une histoire de la France Libre* (Rennes, 2012), 43; Henry Rousso, "Où en est l'histoire de la Résistance," in Jean-Charles Asselain, *Études sur la France de 1939 à nos jours* (Paris, 1985), 132; Cited in Tollet, *La classe ouvrière*, 107; Wieviorka, *Histoire de la Résistance*, 239. A good number of Jews reacted to the popular accusation of "Jewish passivity" by joining the Resistance. See Michel Pigenet, "Jeunes, ouvriers et combattants: Les volontaires parisiens de la colonne Fabien (septembre–décembre 1944)," *Les ouvriers*, 487.

49 Morgan, *British Communist politics*, 22–30; Field, *British Working Class*, 315; Calder, *People's War*, 246; Richard Croucher, *Engineers at War* (London, 1982), 115.

6 AMERICAN COUNTERREVOLUTIONARY ANTIFASCISM

1 Diggins, *Mussolini*, 17, 31.

2 Tierney, *FDR*, 29; Diggins, *Mussolini*, 291, 303–312, 352.

3 Whiting, *Antifascism*, 59; Diggins, *Mussolini*, 292–293; Joseph E. Harris, *African-American Reactions to War in Ethiopia, 1936–1941* (Baton Rouge, LA, 1994), 157–158; Thomas Sugrue, "Hillburn, Hattiesburg, and Hitler," in Kevin M. Kruse and Stephen Tuck, eds. *Fog of War: The Second World War and the Civil Rights Movement* (New York, 2012), 89; Plummer, *Rising Wind* 48–55; Kanawada, *Roosevelt's Diplomacy*, 77.

4 Diggins, *Mussolini*, 174; Benjamin L. Alpers, *Dictators, Democracy, and American Public Culture: Envisioning the Totalitarian Enemy, 1920s–1950s* (Chapel Hill, NC, 2003), 35.

5 Moore, *American Debate on Nazism*, 18, 105.

6 James Waterman Wise, "Introduction," *Nazism: An Assault on Civilization*, xii; Charles H. Tuttle, "The American Reaction," *Nazism: An Assault on Civilization*, 253.
7 Wise, "Introduction," xi; Bernard S. Deutsch, "The Disfranchisement of the Jew," *Nazism: An Assault on Civilization*, 44; Stephen S. Wise, "The War upon World Jewry," *Nazism: An Assault on Civilization*, 207; Johnpeter Horst Grill, "The American South and Nazi Racism," in Alan E. Steinweis and Daniel F. Rogers, eds. *The Impact of Nazism: New Perspectives on the Third Reich and its Legacy* (Lincoln, NE, 2003), 23; Arnie Bernstein, *Swastika Nation: Fritz Kuhn and the Rise and Fall of the German-American Bund* (New York, 2013), 127.
8 Ludwig Lewisohn, "The Revolt against Civilization," *Nazism: An Assault on Civilization*, 149–150; Hastings, *Inferno*, 11; Hew Strachan, "The Soldier's Experience in Two World Wars: Some Historiographic Comparisons," in Paul Addison and Angus Calder, eds. *Time to Kill: The Soldier's Experience of War in the West, 1939–1945* (London, 1997), 375–376; Alice Hamilton, "The Enslavement of Women," *Nazism: An Assault on Civilization*, 78, 83; Julie Gottlieb, "Varieties of Feminist Responses," *Varieties of Anti-Fascism*, 108.
9 Alpers, *Dictators*, 16; MacLeish cited in Whiting, *Antifascism*, 108.
10 Bosch, *Estados Unidos*, 230; Marion K. Sanders, *Dorothy Thompson: A Legend in Her Time* (Boston, 1973), 218, 225, 253; *Washington Post*, 31 March 1939, 17.
11 Moore, *American Debate on Nazism*, 57
12 Dorothy Thompson, "The Record of Persecution," *Nazism: An Assault on Civilization*, 12 [italics in original].
13 Moore, *American Debate on Nazism*, 152.
14 Deborah E. Lipstadt, *Beyond Belief: The American Press and the Coming of the Holocaust 1933–1945* (New York, 1986), 199, 210, 224; Simone Veil, *Une Vie* (Paris, 2007), 39, 81.
15 Lipstadt, *Beyond Belief*, 62, 250; Jean-Michel Chaumont, *La concurrence des victimes: Génocide, identité, reconnaissance* (Paris, 1997), 231; Gannon, *British Press*, 228; Paul Yonnet, *Voyage au centre du malaise français: L'Antiracisme et le roman national* (Paris, 1993), 41; Michel, *Résistance*, 427; James T. Sparrow, *Warfare State: World War II, Americans, and the Age of Big Government* (New York, 2011), 76.
16 Ascher, *Riddle*, 194; Moore, *American Debate on Nazism*, 76; Richard Seelye Johns, *A History of the American Legion* (Indianapolis, 1946), 281, 292.
17 *Catholic World* cited in Diggins, *Mussolini*, 319; German propaganda cited in MacDonald, "Deterrent Diplomacy," 306.
18 Mark Lincoln, *American Interventionists before Pearl Harbor* (New York, 1970), 71, 84, 269; Churchill cited in Gates, *Collapse of the Anglo-French Alliance*, 437; Susan Dunn, *FDR, Willkie, Lindbergh, Hitler – the Election amid the Storm* (New Haven, CT, 2013), 182.
19 Chadwin, *Warhawks*, 147; Richard Crouter, *Reinhold Niebuhr: On Politics, Religion, and Christian Faith* (New York, 2010), 6; Richard Wightman Fox, *Reinhold Niebuhr: A Biography* (New York, 1985), 186–191.

20 Niebuhr cited in William C. Inboden, "The Prophetic Conflict: Reinhold Niebuhr, Christian Realism, and World War II," *Diplomatic History*, vol. 38, no. 1 (January 2014), 71–72; Mark Thomas Edwards, *The Right of the Protestant Left: God's Totalitarianism* (New York, 2012), 83.

21 Niebuhr quoted in Fox, *Niebuhr*, 195; Spellman cited in David Zietsma, "Sin Has No History: Religion, National Identity, and U.S. Intervention, 1937–1941," *Diplomatic History*, vol. 31, no. 3 (June 2007), 563.

22 Brendon, *Dark Valley*, 513; John Haynes Holmes, "The Threat to Freedom," *Nazism: An Assault on Civilization*, 128–132; Alpers, *Dictators*, 86.

23 Cited in Moore, *American Debate on Nazism*, 34.

24 Cited in Olson, *Roosevelt, Lindbergh*, 306.

25 Gombin, *Les socialistes*, 237; Jennings, "La dissidence aux Antilles," 64.

26 Zietsma, "Sin," 563.

27 Cited in Gentile, *Politics as Religion*, 110; Moore, *American Debate on Nazism*, 318.

28 Henry A. Wallace, *Christian Bases of World Order* (Freeport, NY, 1971), 18.

29 Film script cited in Moore, *American Debate on Nazism*, 58, 158.

30 Diggins, *Mussolini*, 19, 207; Nancy MacLean, *Behind the Mask of Chivalry: The Making of the Second Ku Klux Klan* (New York, 1995), 183; David M. Chalmers, *Hooded Americanism: The History of the Ku Klux Klan* (New York, 1965), 274, 323, 234.

31 Cf. Paxton, *Anatomy*, 49, and MacLean, *Second Ku Klux Klan*, 180–181.

32 Grill, "American South," *The Impact of Nazism*, 20–32; Blower, "From Isolationism to Neutrality," 335; Chadwin, *Warhawks*, 186; Plummer, *Black Americans*, 67.

33 Grill, "American South," *The Impact of Nazism*, 32; William L. O'Neill, *A Democracy at War: America's Fight at Home and Abroad in World War II* (New York, 1993), 129; Joseph A. Fry, *Dixie Looks Abroad: The South and U.S. Foreign Relations, 1789–1973* (Baton Rouge, LA, 2002), 205.

34 Bailey quoted in Alpers, *Dictators*, 80; Jason Morgan Ward, "A War for States' Rights," *Fog of War*, 136–140.

35 Talk, 13 November 1942, War Policy Division, Box 14, Reuther Library, Detroit [hereafter RL].

36 Julian E. Zelizer, "Confronting the Roadblock: Congress, Civil Rights, and World War II," *Fog of War*, 44.

37 O'Neill, *Democracy at War*, 232–235.

38 Romy Golan, *Modernity and Nostalgia: Art and Politics in France between the Wars* (New Haven, CT, 1995), 119–136; Whiting, *Antifascism*, 106.

39 Whiting, *Antifascism*, 116, 124.

40 Christian Bougeard, "Éléments d'une approche de l'histoire de la France Libre," *Pour une histoire de la France Libre*, 27; Muracciole, *Français libres*, 78; Antonio Elorza, "La nation éclatée: Front populaire et question nationale en Espagne," *Antifascisme et nation*, 114; Calder, *People's War*, 58, 135, 243; Kevin Morgan, "Une toute petite différence entre La Marseillaise et God Save the King: La gauche britannique et le problème de la nation dans les années trente," *Antifascisme et nation*, 207.

41 Leo P. Ribuffo, *The Old Christian Right: The Protestant Far Right from the Great Depression to the Cold War* (Philadelphia, 1983), 184; Bernstein, *German-American Bund*, 173, 206, 261.
42 Carroll, *Lincoln Brigade*, 230; Olson, *Roosevelt, Lindbergh*, 118; Ribuffo, *Old Christian Right*, 79; Alan Clive, *State of War: Michigan in World War II* (Ann Arbor, MI, 1979), 140; Chalmers, *Hooded Americanism*, 323.
43 Cole, *Isolationists*, 397; Lipstadt, *Beyond Belief*, 121.
44 Tierney, *FDR*, 70; Casey, *Cautious Crusade*, 9; Brendon, *Dark Valley*, 515; MacDonald, "Deterrent Diplomacy," 297–298.
45 MacDonald, "Deterrent Diplomacy," 312–322; Steiner, *Triumph of the Dark*, 814.
46 Cole, *Isolationists*, 537–548.
47 Fry, *Dixie Looks Abroad*, 189, 203; Chadwin, *Warhawks*, 197. Dunn, *FDR*, 35, downplays pro-Allied public opinion.
48 Reynolds, "1940," 334; Offner, *Origins*, 177; Olson, *Citizens of London*, 68; Nelson Lichtenstein, *Labor's War at Home: The CIO in World War II* (New York, 1982), 42; Cole, *Isolationists*, 368, 441, 482.
49 Arthur Herman, *Freedom's Forge: How American Business Produced Victory in World War II* (New York, 2012), 87; O'Neill, *Democracy at War*, 18; Dunn, *FDR*, 40.
50 MacDonald, "Deterrent Diplomacy," 323.
51 Herman, *American Business*, 100.
52 Cole, *Isolationists*, 395.
53 Offner, *Origins*, 193; Sparrow, *Warfare State*, 205; Cole, *Isolationists*, 412.
54 Adam J. Berinsky, "Assuming the Costs of War: Events, Elites, and American Public Support for Military Conduct," *The Journal of Politics*, vol. 69, no. 4 (November 2007), 988.
55 MacDonald, "Deterrent Diplomacy," 300–306; Dunn, *FDR*, 287; Olson, *Citizens of London*, 23, 55; Raghavan, *India's War*, 87; Yasmin Khan, *India at War: The Subcontinent and the Second World War* (New York, 2015), 84–85, 170–174, 308.
56 Lipstadt, *Beyond Belief*, 131; Moore, *American Debate on Nazism*, 101; Cole, *Isolationists*, 424, 454.
57 Tierney, *FDR*, 28.
58 Lipstadt, *Beyond Belief*, 28, 42, 46.
59 Olson, *Roosevelt, Lindbergh*, 384.
60 Lindbergh cited in Cole, *Isolationists*, 435, and O'Neill, *A Democracy at War*, 48; Chadwin, *Warhawks*, 21, 223, 243.
61 Carroll, *Lincoln Brigade*, 234–241; O'Neill, *Democracy at War*, 203.
62 Office of Production Management, 7 June 1941, C. L. Martindale Collection, Box 34, Benson Ford Research Center, Dearborn, MI [hereafter, BFRC]; Herman, *American Business*, 82, 206, 220, 291.
63 Medawar, *Hitler's Gift*, 83. In his 20 August 1940 speech, Churchill declared that British science surpassed its German competitor since "the Germans drove the Jews out." Benjamin Ginsberg, *How the Jews Defeated Hitler: Exploding the Myth of Jewish Passivity in the Face of Nazism* (Lanham, MD, 2016), 71–75.

64 Diggins, *Mussolini*, 350, 359; Joan Keating, "Looking to Europe: Roman Catholics and Christian Democracy in 1930s Britain," *European History Quarterly*, vol. 26 (1996), 66; Olson, *Roosevelt, Lindbergh*, 124; Bernstein, *German-American Bund*, 18, 26–27; Leland V. Bell, "The Failure of Nazism in America: The German American Bund, 1936–1941," *Political Science Quarterly*, vol. 85, no. 4 (December, 1970), 587.
65 William Green, "The Attack on Organized Labor," *Nazism: An Assault on Civilization*, 282; Ludwig Lore, "The Fate of the Worker," *Nazism: An Assault on Civilization*, 113; Eby, *Comrades*, 15.
66 Larry Ceplair, *Under the Shadow of War: Fascism, Anti-fascism, and Marxists, 1918–1939* (New York, 1987), 169.
67 Whiting, *Antifascism*, 81.
68 Ibid., 93–97; Thompson, "Record of Persecution," 3, [italics in original]. Brian Foss, *War Paint: Art, War, State and Identity in Britain 1939–1945* (New Haven, CT, 2007), 162, 169.
69 Cited in Whiting, *Antifascism*, 189.

7 ANTIFASCISMS UNITED: 1941–1944

1 Robert Dallek, *Franklin D. Roosevelt and American Foreign Policy, 1932–1945* (New York, 1979), 3; Roosevelt cited in Tierney, *FDR*, 28–29.
2 Sebastian Haffner, *Churchill* (London, 2003), 118–119.
3 Offner, *Origins*, 200, 203.
4 Ascher, *Riddle*, 173; Chadwin, *Warhawks*, 71. Cf. Robert O. Paxton, "The Five Stages of Fascism," in Brian Jenkins, ed. *France in the Era of Fascism: Essays on the French Authoritarian Right* (New York, 2005), 115.
5 Zietsma, "Sin," 560; Foss, *Art*, 54.
6 Memo by US and British chiefs of staff, cited in Reynolds, "1940," 344.
7 Mark Mazower, *Hitler's Empire: How the Nazis Ruled Europe* (New York, 2008), 135.
8 Hastings, *Inferno*, 279, 287; Cole, *Isolationists*, 433; Chadwin, *Warhawks*, 235.
9 Hastings, *Inferno*, 284; Max Hastings, *Winston's War: Churchill, 1940–1945* (New York, 2010), 144; O'Neill, *Democracy at War*, 214; Pierre Brocheux and Daniel Hémery, *Indochina: An Ambiguous Colonization, 1858–1954*, trans. Ly Lan Dill-Klein (Berkeley, CA, 2009), 351–353.
10 Eduard Mark, "Revolution by Degrees: Stalin's National-Front Strategy for Europe, 1941–1947," Cold War International History Project (February 2001), 6, http://www.wilsoncenter.org/sites/default/files/ACFB11.pdf; Bourdet, *De la Résistance à la Restauration*, 175.
11 Hastings, *Inferno*, 147, 174–175; Karski quoted in Hastings, *Inferno*, 500; Lipstadt, *Beyond Belief*, 170, 217, 277. When Jews became Resistance fighters, for example, in the Warsaw ghetto, the coverage was greater, if still inadequate. Gregor Dallas, *1945: The War That Never Ended* (New Haven, CT, 2005), 310.
12 Hastings, *Inferno*, 638.

13 John Ellis, *The Sharp End: The Fighting Man in World War II* (New York, 1980), 245; Deák, *Europe on Trial*, 157; Alexander N. Yakovlev, *A Century of Violence in Soviet Russia*, trans. Anthony Austin (New Haven, CT, 2002), 174.

14 Richard Wigg, *Churchill and Spain: The Survival of the Franco Regime, 1940–1945* (Brighton, UK, 2008), 54; Joan Maria Thomàs, *Roosevelt y Franco: De la guerra civil española a Pearl Harbor* (Barcelona, 2007), 547.

15 Buchanan, *American Grand Strategy*, 54, 59, 73–74, 220; Casey, *Cautious Crusade*, 118–124; Burrin, *France under the Germans*, 150.

16 Moore, *American Debate on Nazism*, 196; Goebbels cited in Kershaw, *Hitler*, 570.

17 Hastings, *Inferno*, 389; Casey, *Cautious Crusade*, 71; Moore, *American Debate on Nazism*, 135, 234, 265.

18 Moore, *American Debate on Nazism*, 247; Jackson, *France and the Nazi Menace*, 69–71.

19 Ludwig cited in Moore, *American Debate on Nazism*, 250. For similar themes in France, see Michel, *Courants de pensée*, 217.

20 Cited in Calder, *People's War*, 307.

21 David Cannadine, *In Churchill's Shadow: Confronting the Past in Modern Britain* (Oxford, 2003), 72, 84. Cf. Jacques Cantier, "Les horizons de l'après Vichy: De la 'Libération' de l'empire aux enjeux de mémoire," in Jacques Cantier and Éric Jennings, *L'empire colonial sous Vichy* (Paris, 2004), 34, and Levisse-Touzé, *L'Afrique du Nord*, 268, who have labeled US support for Darlan and Giraud as "Vichyism under American control." Yet, unlike Vichy, the United States (and the United Kingdom) allied with counterrevolutionaries only if they were willing to fight the fascist enemy.

22 Charles L. Robertson, *When Roosevelt Planned to Govern France* (Amherst, MA, 2011), 55; Thomas, *The French Empire*, 167; "Saint-Pierre-et-Miquelon," Andrieu, *Dictionnaire de Gaulle*, 1047; Jean-Louis Crémieux Brilhac, *De Gaulle, la République et la France Libre: 1940–1945* (Paris, 2014), 187; Buchanan, *American Grand Strategy*, 87.

23 Michel, *Courants de pensée*, 498; Sadoun, *Socialistes*, 176, 207.

24 Douzou, *La Désobéissance*, 274, 286.

25 Ibid., 296–343; Herbert R. Lottman, *The Purge* (New York, 1986), 28; Wieviorka, *Histoire de la Résistance*, 188.

26 Combes, *La franc-maçonnerie*, 359; Simon Kitson, "L'évolution de la Résistance dans la police marseillaise," in Jean-Marie Guillon and Robert Mencherini, eds. *La Résistance et les Européens du Sud* (Paris, 1999), 263.

27 Chevallier, *Franc-Maçonnerie française*, 3:372; Dominique Rossignol, *Vichy et les Francs-Maçons: La liquidation des sociétés secrètes, 1940–1944* (Paris, 1981), 70; Pétain cited in Combes, *La franc-maçonnerie*, 53.

28 Rossignol, *Vichy et les Francs-Maçons*, 58, 75.

29 Douzou, *La Désobéissance*, 303, 367.

30 Situation à Paris, 28 December 1943; Situation à Paris, 10 January 1944, APP.

31 Situation à Paris, 3 April 1944, APP.

32 Robertson, *To Govern France*, 165.

33 Situation à Paris, 3 April 1944, APP.
34 Roussel, *De Gaulle*, 518; Crémieux-Brilhac, "Leclerc," 137; "Révolution française," Andrieu, *Dictionnaire de Gaulle*, 1021; Sadoun, *Socialistes*, 190.
35 Adams, *Political Ecumenism*, 114; Richard Vinen, *The Unfree French: Life under the Occupation* (New Haven, CT, 2006), 32; Sadoun, *Socialistes*, 184, 191; Muracciole, *France libre*, 78–83; Charles de Gaulle, *The Complete War Memoirs of Charles de Gaulle*, trans. Richard Howard (New York, 1964), 360–361.
36 Steiner, *Triumph of the Dark*, 1061; Crémieux Brilhac, *France Libre*, 11; Jackson, *Fall of France*, 193, 213; Frieser, *Blitzkrieg Legend*; Nord, *France 1940*.
37 Situation à Paris, 7 February 1944, APP.
38 Roussel, *de Gaulle*, 420–421; "Opinion Publique Britannique, 1940–1946," Andrieu, *Dictionnaire de Gaulle*, 841; Muracciole, *France libre*, 89–90.
39 Soviets quoted in Roussel, *de Gaulle*, 414, 461, 466; Julian Jackson, *France: The Dark Years* (Oxford, 2003), 537.
40 Roussel, *de Gaulle*, 285–289, 414; Robertson, *To Govern France*, 127, 131; Hélène Chaubin, "Libération et pouvoirs: un modèle corse," *La Résistance*, 347; "Corse," Andrieu, *Dictionnaire de Gaulle*, 284; Jackson, *Dark Years*, 517; de Gaulle, *Memoirs*, 464–468; Charles-Louis Foulon, "Le Général de Gaulle et la Libération de la France," Comité d'Histoire de la Deuxième Guerre Mondiale, *La Libération de la France* (Paris, 1976), 44.
41 Roussel, *de Gaulle*, 430; Robertson, *To Govern France*, 168; Stein, *Spanish Republicans*, 150, 179; Vinen, *Unfree French*, 337, 340.
42 Roussel, *de Gaulle*, 419, 449, 451, 457; Buchanan, *American Grand Strategy*, 3; Robertson, *To Govern France*, 168; Stein, *Spanish Republicans*, 150, 179; Vinen, *Unfree French*, 337, 340; Jacques Vernet, "Mise sur pied de la 2ᵉ DB: De la diversité à l'unité," *Du capitaine de Hauteclocque au général Leclerc*, 198; de Gaulle cited in John Keegan, *Six Armies in Normandy: From D-Day to the Liberation of Paris* (New York, 1982), 306; Maurice Agulhon, "Les communistes et la Libération de la France," *La Libération*, 72–85; Bourdet, *De la Résistance à la Restauration*, 255, 285.
43 Edward Mortimer, "France," in Martin McCauley, ed. *Communist Power in Europe, 1944–1949* (London, 1977), 154; Wieviorka, *Histoire de la Résistance*, 268, 338, 345, 397; de Gaulle, *Memoirs*, 631–632, 692.
44 Crémieux Brilhac, *France Libre*, 370; Dallas, *1945*, 329, 332.
45 Olivier Wieviorka, "¿Guerra civil a la francesa? El caso de los años sombríos," Julio Aróstegui and François Godicheau, eds. *Guerra Civil: Mito y memoria* (Madrid, 2006), 344; Crémieux Brilhac, *Georges Boris*, 286, offers a higher number.
46 Robertson, *To Govern France*, 177; Buchanan, *American Grand Strategy*, 166.
47 Georges-Henri Soutou, "France," in David Reynolds, ed. *The Origins of the Cold War in Europe: International Perspectives* (New Haven, CT, 1994), 98–100; Georges Bernanos, "Notes on Fascism I," *Commonweal*, XXXVII (19 March 1943), 534–536; Burrin, *France under the Germans*, 224; M. R. D. Foot, *Resistance: European Resistance to Nazism, 1940–1945* (New York, 1977), 40; Roussel, *de Gaulle*, 462; Gildea, *Fighters*, 94; Daniel Lindenberg, *Les années souterraines (1937–1947)* (Paris, 1990), 141; Shannon L.

Fogg, *The Politics of Everyday Life in Vichy France: Foreigners, Undesirables, and Strangers* (New York, 2009), 96.

48 Roussel, *de Gaulle*, 433; Robertson, *To Govern France*, 175–176.

49 Olivier Wieviorka and Jacek Tebinka, "From Everyday Life to Counter-State," in Robert Gildea, Olivier Wieviorka, and Anette Warring, eds. *Surviving Hitler and Mussolini: Daily Life in Occupied Europe* (Oxford, 2006), 168.

50 François Bédarida, "World War II and Social Change in France," in Arthur Marwick, ed. *Total War and Social Change* (New York, 1988), 85; Vinen, *Unfree French*, 344; Lottman, *Purge*, 157.

51 Robertson, *To Govern France*, 184.

8 BEYOND FASCISM AND ANTIFASCISM: WORKING AND NOT WORKING

1 Cited in Jackson, *Dark Years*, 227.

2 Vinen, *Unfree French*, 118. Burrin, *France under the Germans*, 284, puts the figure at 200,000.

3 Situation à Paris, 24 August 1942, APP.

4 Situation à Paris, 13 July 1942, 8 March 1943, APP.

5 Patrice Arnaud, *Les STO: Histoire des Français requis en Allemagne nazie 1942–1945* (Paris, 2010), 1–6; Situation à Paris, 19 and 26 August 1940, 9 February 1942, 22 June 1942, 13 and 27 July 1942, Situation à Paris depuis le 14 juin 1940, 16 July 1940, APP; Burrin, *France under the Germans*, 236; *La Vie Ouvrière*, November 1941, in Allyn, *Le mouvement syndical*, 53.

6 Situation à Paris, 22 June 1942, 13 and 27 July 1942, 16 November 1942, 26 July 1943, APP.

7 Situation à Paris, 21 September 1942, 5 and 19 October 1942, 2 November 1942, APP; Jean-Pierre Le Crom, *Syndicats nous voilà: Vichy et le corporatisme* (Paris, 1995), 339; Frederick Cooper, *Decolonization and African Society: The Labor Question in French and British Africa* (Cambridge, UK, 1996), 110–159; Robert Gildea, Dirk Luyten and Juliane Fürst, "To Work or Not to Work," *Surviving Hitler*, 67–68.

8 Situation à Paris, 9 September 1940, 21 October 1940, APP; *La Vie Ouvrière*, 17 and 24 October 1942, in Allyn, *Le mouvement syndical*, 96, 106.

9 Situation à Paris, 10 August 1942, 2 November 1942, 17 May 1943, 17 April 1944, APP; William I. Hitchcock, *The Bitter Road to Freedom: The Human Cost of Allied Victory in World War II Europe* (New York, 2008), 25; Robert Gildea, *Marianne in Chains: Daily Life in the Heart of France during the German Occupation* (New York, 2002), 280.

10 Situation à Paris, 11–25 January 1943, APP.

11 Situation à Paris, 30 November 1942, 23 August 1943, APP; Vinen, *Unfree French*, 85; Arnaud, *Les STO*, 352, 359.

12 Situation à Paris, 25 January 1943, 8 and 22 February 1943, 22 March 1943, 28 June 1943, APP; Claude Bellanger, *Presse Clandestine, 1940–1944* (Paris, 1961), 145, 149; Jacqueline Sainclivier, "La Résistance

et le STO," in Bernard Garnier and Jean Quellien, eds. *La main d'œuvre française exploitée par le IIIe Reich: Actes du colloque international, Caen, 13–15 décembre 2001* (Caen, 2003), 520; Roderick Kedward, "The Maquis and the Culture of the Outlaw," in Roderick Kedward and Roger Austin, eds. *Vichy France and the Resistance: Culture and Ideology* (London, 1985), 234.

13 Situation à Paris, 19 October 1942, 8 and 22 March 1943, 15, 22, and 28 June 1943, APP. On the French-German bargaining of labor policy, see Allan Mitchell, *Nazi Paris: The History of an Occupation, 1940–1944* (New York, 2008), 66–67, 112.

14 Situation à Paris, 22 June 1942, 19 October 1942, 2 November 1942, 21 February 1944, 3 April 1944, APP.

15 Situation à Paris, 15 and 28 June 1943, 23 August 1943, 20 September 1943, 7 and 21 February 1944, APP; Arnaud, *Les STO*, 22, 368.

16 Kedward, "The Maquis and the Culture of the Outlaw," *Vichy France and the Resistance*, 246; John F. Sweets, *Choices in Vichy France: The French under Occupation* (New York, 1994), 212; Vinen, *Unfree French*, 88.

17 Michel Boivin, "Les réfractaires au travail obligatoire: essai d'approche globale et statistique," *La main d'œuvre française*, 497–498; Gildea, *Marianne in Chains*, 286; Fogg, *Everyday Life*, 131, 146; Arnaud, *Les STO*, 17; Raphaël Spina, "Impacts du STO sur le travail en entreprises: activité productive et vie sociale interne entre crises, bouleversements et adaptations (1942–1944)," in Christian Chevandier and Jean-Claude Daumas, eds. *Travailler dans les entreprises sous l'occupation* (Besançon, 2007), 105.

18 Vinen, *Unfree French*, 184, 300; Wieviorka, "From Everyday Life to Counter-State," *Surviving Hitler and Mussolini*, 153.

19 Vinen, *Unfree French*, 359; Arnaud, *Les STO*, x, 63; Broch, *Ordinary Workers*, 91.

20 Jackson, *Dark Years*, 298; Situation à Paris, 16 February 1942, 13 July 1942, 12 June 1944, APP; Dominique Veillon, *Vivre et survivre en France 1939–1947* (Paris, 1995), 211.

21 Crémieux Brilhac, *Les français*, 2:321; Vigna, *Histoire des ouvriers*, 155.

22 Crémieux Brilhac, *Les français*, 2:334; Philippe Buton, "Les communistes dans les entreprises," 121–128; Courtois, "Action," 91.

23 Etienne Dejonghe and Yves Le Maner, "Les Communistes du Nord et du Pas-de-Calais de la fin du Front Populaire à mai 1941," *Les communistes français*, 238–241; Taylor, *Northern France*, 20, 51; Crémieux Brilhac, *Les français*, 2:323.

24 Le Crom, *Syndicats*, 327; Dejonghe, "Les Communistes du Nord," 250–251; Taylor, *Northern France*, 74.

25 Tollet, *La classe ouvrière*, 81; Taylor, *Northern France*, 92.

26 Field, *British Working Class*, 119, 134; Arthur Marwick, *Britain in the Century of Total War: War, Peace and Social Change* (Boston, 1968), 288; Vigna, *Histoire des ouvriers*, 149; Patrick Fridenson and Jean-Louis Robert, "Les ouvriers dans la France de la Seconde Guerre mondiale: Un bilan," *Le mouvement social*, no. 158 (January–March 1992), 134; Veillon, *Vivre et survivre*, 213, 320; Chapman, *French Aircraft Industry*, 247; Jackson, *Dark Years*, 296;

Fogg, *Everyday Life*, xiv–40; Situation à Paris, 9 February 1942, APP; Fabrice Grenard, "Les implications politiques du ravitaillement en France sous l'Occupation," *Vingtième Siècle*, 94 (April–June 2007), 199–204.

27 Situation à Paris, 21 June 1941, 8 February and 5 April 1943, 7 February 1944; L'état d'esprit de la population et la propagande communiste, Mai 1941, APP.

28 Situation à Paris, 8 December 1941, APP.

29 *La Vie Ouvrière*, 1 November 1941 and 5 May 1944, in Allyn, *Le mouvement syndical*, 38, 42, 117, 212; Situation à Paris depuis le 14 juin 1940, 16 July 1940; Situation à Paris, 21 October 1940, 9 February 1942, 2 March 1942, 7 April 1942, 16 November 1942, 22 March 1943, 17 April 1944, APP.

30 *La Vie Ouvrière*, Novembre 1941, in Allyn, *Le mouvement syndical*, 34, 38; Situation à Paris, 2 and 29 November 1943, APP; Semelin, *Civilian Resistance*, 81; Thomas Fontaine, *Les oubliés de Romainville: Un camp allemand en France (1940–1944)* (Paris, 2005), 39, 63.

31 *La Vie Ouvrière*, 6 March 1944, in Allyn, *Le mouvement syndical*, 178; Tollet, *La classe ouvrière*, 117; Situation à Paris, 17 April 1944, 10 and 24 July 1944, 7 August 1944, APP.

32 Le Crom, *Syndicats*, 319–328; Dominique Veillon, "Les ouvrières parisiennes de la couture," *Les ouvriers*, 177.

33 Situation à Paris, 23 February 1942, 9 March 1942, 20 April 1942, 22 June 1942, 13 July 1942, 22 February 1943, 10 July 1943, 29 November 1943, 20 March 1944, 2 and 30 May 1944; Principaux faits, 1 November 1944, APP; Fridenson, "Les ouvriers," 141; François Bloch-Lainé and Jean Bouvier, *La France Restaurée 1944–1954: Dialogue sur les choix d'une modernisation* (Paris, 1986), 65.

34 Situation à Paris, 19 January 1942, 16 and 23 February 1942, 20 April 1942, 13 July 1942, 28 December 1943, 21 February 1944, 20 March 1944, APP.

35 Situation à Paris, 7 and 20 April 1942, 13 and 27 July 1942, 25 January 1943, 2 May 1944, 7 August 1944, APP; Tollet, *La classe ouvrière*, 72, 212.

36 Situation à Paris, 2 March 1942, 13 and 27 July 1942, 28 December 1943, 17 April 1944, 2 May 1944, APP; Michel Cointepas, "La mise en oeuvre de la Charte du travail par les inspecteurs du travail," *Les ouvriers*, 189.

37 Irina Bilitza, "Les débrayages pendant l'occupation allemande dans l'ancien département de la Seine," in Michel Margairaz and Danielle Tartakowsky, *Le syndicalisme dans la France occupée* (Rennes, 2008), 403; Jackson, *Dark Years*, 162; Situation à Paris, 22 March 1943, 5 April 1943, 18 October 1943, 10 July 1944, APP.

38 Situation à Paris, 6 and 20 March 1944, 3 April 1944, 15 and 30 May 1944, 10 July 1944, APP.

39 *La Vie Ouvrière*, November 1941, 6 March 1944, in Allyn, *Le mouvement syndical*, 50; Situation à Paris, 28 December 1943, 10 January 1944, 21 February 1944, 20 March 1944, APP.

40 Situation à Paris, 19 October 1942, 16 November 1942, 3 April 1944, 24 July 1944, APP.

41 Situation à Paris, 20 September 1943, 18 October 1943, APP.

42 Situation à Paris, 18 October 1943, 17 April 1944, APP.

43 Tollet, *La classe ouvrière*, 117; Gildea, *Marianne in Chains*, 65; Burrin, *France under the Germans* 3, 28; Deák, *Europe on Trial*, 4.

44 Tollet, *La classe ouvrière*, 79, 149–150; Allyn, *Le mouvement syndical*, 16, 50–53, 143; Wieviorka, *Ils étaient juifs*, 120; Situation à Paris, 29 November 1943, APP.

45 Situation à Paris, 2 November 1943, APP.

46 Mitchell, *Nazi Paris*, 115; Burrin, *France under the Germans*, 247–248; Talbot Imlay and Martin Horn, *The Politics of Industrial Collaboration during World War II: Ford, France, Vichy and Nazi Germany* (New York, 2014), 143; Jean-Louis Loubet, "Le travail dans quelques entreprises automobiles françaises sous l'Occupation," Chevandier, *Travailler*, 184; Broch, *Ordinary Workers*, 18, 101–119.

47 Tollet, *La classe ouvrière*, 125–126; *La Vie Ouvrière*, 7 November 1941, in Allyn, *Le mouvement syndical*, 54–55; Situation à Paris, 2 November 1943, APP.

48 Situation à Paris, 25 January 1943, APP; Allyn, *Le mouvement syndical*, 53; Sadoun, *Socialistes*, 159; Fridenson, "Les ouvriers," 144; *La Vie Ouvrière*, November 1941, 1 April 1943, 7 December 1943, in Allyn, *Le mouvement syndical*, 96–160; Courtois, "Action," 80–81. See also Sébastien Albertelli, *Histoire du Sabotage: De la CGT à la Résistance* (Paris, 2016), 341.

49 Situation à Paris, 28 December 1943, APP. On Communist *meneurs* deported to Germany and to Auschwitz, see Annie Lacroix-Riz, "Les relations sociales dans les entreprises," *Les ouvriers*, 225–226.

50 Situation à Paris, 21 February 1944, 2 May 1944, APP.

51 Situation à Paris, 3 April 1944, 15 and 30 May 1944, 12 June 1944, 10 July 1944, APP; *La Vie Ouvrière*, 5 May 1944, in Allyn, *Le mouvement syndical*, 212.

52 Situation à Paris, 15 and 30 May 1944, APP.

53 Situation à Paris, 21 February 1944, 12 June 1944, 10 July 1944, APP; Les rapports mensuels des Inspecteurs divisionnaires du Travail, 1 August 1944, APP.

54 Jackson, *Dark Years*, 561; Situation à Paris, 24 July 1944, 7 August 1944, APP.

55 Mitchell, *Nazi Paris*, 104; Broch, *Ordinary Workers*, 8, 155; *La Vie Ouvrière*, 6 March 1944, 5 May 1944, 5 August 1944, in Allyn, *Le mouvement syndical*, 178, 212, 225; Tollet, *La classe ouvrière*, 174, 202; Vigna, *Histoire des ouvriers*, 55; Situation à Paris, 3 and 17 April 1944, APP.

56 Philip Morgan, "Popular Attitudes and Resistance to Fascism," *Opposing Fascism*, 173.

57 Tollet, *La classe ouvrière*, 98–99, 187; Mitchell, *Nazi Paris*, 114; Albertelli, *Histoire du Sabotage*, 193, 283, 367–382, 424; Emmanuel Chadeau, *L'industrie aéronautique en France, 1900–1950: De Blériot à Dassault* (Paris, 1987), 362; Gildea, *Marianne in Chains*, 111; For a discussion of the meaning of the Resistance, see Laurent Douzou, *La Résistance française: une histoire périlleuse* (Paris, 2005), 20, and Pierre Laborie, *Les Français des années*

troubles: De la guerre d'Espagne à la Libération (Paris, 2003), 65–80; Wieviorka, *Histoire de la Résistance*, 213.

58 Situation à Paris, 9, 16, 23, and 30 March 1942, 7 April 1942, 4, 11, and 26 May 1942, 13 July 1942, 25 January 1943, APP; *La Vie Ouvrière*, 14 March 1942, 17 July 1943, in Allyn, *Le mouvement syndical*, 64, 127; Matt Perry, "Bombing Billancourt: Labour Agency and the Limitations of the Public Opinion Model of Wartime France," *Labour History Review*, vol. 77, no. 1 (2012), 61; Lindsay Dodd and Andrew Knapp, "'How Many Frenchmen did you Kill?' British Bombing Policy towards France (1940–1945)," *French History*, vol. 22, no. 4 (2008), 470–478; Andrew Knapp, *Les français sous les bombes alliées, 1940–1945* (Paris, 2014), 91.

59 Situation à Paris, 19 April 1943, 3 May 1943, 15 June 1943, 20 September 1943, 4 October 1943, 2 November 1943, 10 and 24 January 1944, 7 February 1944, 2 and 15 May 1944, APP; Chapman, *French Aircraft Industry*, 247.

60 Situation à Paris, 15 and 30 May 1944, 12 June 1944, 10 July 1944, 7 August 1944, APP; Gates, *Collapse of the Anglo-French Alliance*,157; Veillon, *Vivre et survivre*, 264; Fridenson, "Les ouvriers," 118.

61 Situation à Paris, 9, 16, and 22 March 1942, 4 May 1942, 1 June 1942, 19 April 1943, 6 and 20 September 1943, APP; Gildea, *Marianne in Chains*, 292; Perry, "Bombing Billancourt," 66–70; Tartakowsky, *Les manifestations*, 456; Knapp, *Les français*, 30, 112, 392–419.

62 Situation à Paris, 9 March 1942, APP.

63 Situation à Paris, 7 August 1944, APP.

64 Hastings, *Inferno*, 514; Dodd, "'How Many Frenchmen,'" 470; Knapp, *Les français*, 22; Principaux faits, 31 October 1944, 1 November 1944; Compte Rendu, 2 November 1944; Opinion publique, 12 January 1945; Situation générale, nd [February ?] 1945, APP.

65 Morgan, *British Communist politics, 1935–41*, 172–189.

66 Field, *British Working Class*, 316; Croucher, *Engineers*, 145, 152.

67 Ministry of Labour, Industrial Relations Department, 22 August 1942, LAB 10/363, National Archives, Kew [hereafter NA].

68 Ministry of Labour, Industrial Relations Department, 2 May 1942, 7 November 1942, LAB 10/363, NA.

69 Calder, *People's War*, 439.

70 Addison, *Road to 1945*, 134; Calder, *People's War*, 348.

71 Ministry of Labour, Industrial Relations Department, 16, 24, and 31 January 1942, 13 and 14 February 1942, 28 March 1942, 9 and 30 May 1942, 20 June 1942, LAB 10/363; Confidential, Weekly Report, 17 October 1942, LAB 10/146, NA.

72 Mr. Hodges, 29 October 1941, LAB 10/153, NA.

73 Confidential, 16 January 1942, LAB 10/153; Industrial Relations, 25 November 1941, LAB 10/153; Solicitor, nd, LAB 10/153; Weekly Report, 8 August 1942, LAB 10/352; Weekly Report, 29 May 1943, LAB 10/394; Confidential, Weekly Report, 10 March 1944, LAB 10/146, Confidential, 20 October 1944, LAB 10/146, NA.

74 Alan Bullock, *Ernest Bevin: A Biography* (London, 2002), 316.

75 Confidential, Weekly Report, 21 November 1942, LAB 10/146, NA.

76 Croucher, *Engineers*, 117–121; Weekly Report, 29 August 1942, LAB 10/352; Weekly Report, 20 March 1943, LAB 10/394; Confidential, Weekly Report, 18 February 1944, 10 March 1944, 27 October 1944, LAB 10/146, NA.

77 Minutes, 29 October 1941, Trade Disputes, 29 October 1941, LAB 10/146; Mr. Hodges, 29 October 1941, LAB 10/153; Weekly Report, 1 August 1942, LAB 10/352; Confidential, Weekly Report, 4 February 1944, LAB 10/146, NA; Calder, *People's War*, 357; Field, *British Working Class*, 101; Henry Pelling, "The Impact of the War on the Labour Party," in Harold L. Smith, ed. *War and Social Change* (Manchester, 1986), 143.

78 Weekly Report, 7 March 1942, 13 June 1942, LAB 10/352; Weekly Report, 30 July 1943, 10 December 1943, LAB 10/394; Stoppages, 14 December 1943, LAB 10/394, NA; Ministry of Labour, Industrial Relations Department, 3 January 1942, LAB 10/363, NA; Croucher, *Engineers*, 204; Bullock, *Bevin*, 353.

79 Croucher, *Engineers*, 255–268; Weekly Report, 18 April 1942, LAB 10/352; Confidential, Weekly Report, 7 January 1944, 5 May 1944, 3 November 1944, 10 November 1944, LAB 10/146; Ministry of Labour, Industrial Relations Department, 28 February 1942, LAB 10/363, NA; Calder, *People's War*, 388; Penny Summerfield, "Women, War and Social Change: Women in Britain in World War II," *Total War*, 106; Harold L. Smith, "The Effect of the War on the Status of Women," *War and Social Change*, 217–221.

80 Weekly Report, 13 June 1942, LAB 10/352; Weekly Report, 10 and 17 July 1943, LAB 10/394, NA.

81 Edgerton, *Britain's War Machine*, 205; Dorothy Kosinski, *Henry Moore: Sculpting the Twentieth Century* (New Haven, CT, 2001), 49, 146; Foss, *Art*, 3; Peter Stansky and William Abrahams, *London's Burning: Life, Death and Art in the Second World War* (Stanford, CA, 1994), 49, 67.

82 Douglas, 9 September 1941, LAB 10/146; Summary, 16 October 1941, LAB 10/146; Message, 18 October 1941, LAB 10/146, Minutes, 29 October 1941, LAB 10/146; Ministry of Labour, Industrial Relations Department, 23 May 1942, 5 and 12 September 1942, LAB 10/363; Weekly Report, 12 September 1942, LAB 10/352, NA; Croucher, *Engineers*, 132, 367.

83 Weekly Report, 29 May 1943, 17 July 1943, 19 November 1943, LAB 10/394, NA; Calder, *People's War*, 433, 441; Croucher, *Engineers*, 231; Bullock, *Bevin*, 262, 356, 365; Hastings, *Winston's War*, 228.

84 Ministry of Labour, Industrial Relations Department, 21 February 1942, 12 September 1942, 17 October 1942, LAB 10/363; Dear Ernest [Bevin], 29 October 1941, LAB 10/146: For a similar plea by Alexander to Bevin, see Dear Ernest, 26 September 1941, LAB 10/146. Dear Macintosh, 14 October 1941, LAB 10/146; Reference, Hodges, 22 October 1941, LAB 10/146; Summary, 18 October 1941, LAB 10/146; Ministry of Labor, 16 January 1942, LAB 10/153, NA.

85 Mr. Emmerson, 30 October 1941, LAB 10/153; Ministry of Labour, Industrial Relations Department, 19 December 1942, LAB 10/363; Weekly Report, 3 October 1942, LAB 10/352, NA; Croucher, *Engineers*, 119–201.
86 Strikes in progress, 10 October 1942, LAB 10/352; Confidential, Weekly Report, 10 and 24 October 1942, LAB 10/146; Ministry of Labour, Industrial Relations Department, 21 and 28 November 1942, LAB 10/363, NA.
87 Field, *British Working Class*, 102, 151, 154; Ministry of Labour, Industrial Relations Department, 18 April 1942, LAB 10/363, NA; Croucher, *Engineers*, 279; Appendix Stoppages, LAB 10/146; Weekly Report, 20 and 27 August 1943, 1 October 1943, 19 and 26 November 1943, LAB 10/394, NA.
88 Confidential, Weekly Report, 16 and 23 June 1944, LAB 10/146, NA; Calder, *People's War*, 117–118.
89 Croucher, *Engineers*, 111–118; Confidential, Weekly Report, 14 July 1944, LAB 10/146; Weekly Report, 8 August 1942, LAB 10/352; Confidential, Weekly Report, 24 March 1944, 30 June 1944, LAB 10/146, NA.
90 Weekly Report, 7 February 1942, LAB 10/352, NA; Calder, *People's War*, 176–405; Penny Summerfield, "The 'levelling of class'," *War and Social Change*, 189–196; Lizzie Collingham, *The Taste of War: World War II and the Battle for Food* (New York, 2012), 363–382.
91 Ministry of Labour, Industrial Relations Department, 25 April 1942, 20 June 1942, 11 and 18 July 1942, LAB 10/363, NA; see also Bullock, *Bevin*, 278–279. Calder, *People's War*, 449. Cf. Edgerton, *Britain's War Machine*, 207, who denies that the United States was ahead in shipbuilding. Weekly Report, 3 and 31 January 1942, 18 April 1942, 20 June 1942, LAB 10/352; Weekly Report, 27 March 1943, LAB 10/394, NA.
92 Bullock, *Bevin*, 353; Calder, *People's War*, 331–404; cf. Edgerton, *Britain's War Machine*, 278. Ministry of Labour, Industrial Relations Department, 10 January 1942, LAB 10/363; Confidential, Weekly Report, 19 December 1942, LAB 10/146; Weekly Report, 11 April 1942, LAB 10/352, NA.
93 Weekly Report, 22 May 1943, 19 June 1943, 31 December 1943, LAB 10/394; Ministry of Labour, Industrial Relations Department, 31 January 1942, 28 April 1942, 2 May 1942, 4 July 1942, LAB 10/363, NA; Jose Harris, "War and Social History: Britain and the Home Front during the Second World War," *Contemporary European History*, vol. 1, no. 1 (March 1992), 25
94 Calder, *People's War*, 351; Confidential, Weekly Report, 3 March 1944, LAB 10/146; Weekly Report, 23 May 1942, LAB 10/352; Ministry of Labour, Industrial Relations Department, 14 and 28 February 1942, LAB 10/363, NA.
95 Ministry of Labour, Industrial Relations Department, 21 March 1942, 16 May 1942, 25 July 1942, 26 September 1942, LAB 10/363; Confidential, Weekly Report, 10 March 1944, 14, 21 and 28 April 1944, 5 and 19 May 1944, 20 October 1944, LAB 10/146; Report of Strikes, 28 February 1942, LAB 10/363, NA; Calder, *People's War*, 329.

96 Weekly Report, 4 April 1942, LAB 10/352; Ministry of Labour, Industrial Relations Department, 18 and 25 July 1942, 1 and 8 August 1942, LAB 10/363; Stoppages of Work, 25 April 1944, 7 November 1944, LAB 10/146; Confidential, Weekly Report, 11 February 1944, 21 April 1944, LAB 10/146; Weekly Report, 23 January 1943, 27 March 1943, 3 April 1943, LAB 10/394, NA.

97 Weekly Report, 3 and 10 January 1942, 29 August 1942, 19 September 1942, LAB 10/352; Confidential, Weekly Report, 25 February 1944, LAB 10/146, NA; Weekly Report, 29 August 1942, LAB 10/352, NA.

98 Weekly Report, 10 January 1942, 25 April 1942, LAB 10/352; Confidential, Weekly Report, 31 January 1944, LAB 10/146, NA. On French employers' Resistance or lack thereof, see Imlay, *Industrial Collaboration*, 7, 244–245.

99 Confidential, Weekly Report, 17 March 1944, 7 April 1944, 19 May 1944, 1 September 1944, LAB 10/146; Ministry of Labour, Industrial Relations Department, 4 July 1942, LAB 10/363, NA.

100 Herman, *American Business*, ix–8, 118, 210–249; Adam Hochschild, *Spain in our Hearts: Americans in the Spanish Civil War, 1936–1939* (New York, 2016), 167–173; Dunn, *FDR*, 60; William H. Chafe, *The Unfinished Journey: America since World War II* (New York, 2003), 8; Edgerton, *Britain's War Machine*, 242.

101 Melvyn Dubofsky and Foster Rhea Dulles, *Labor in America: A History* (Wheeling, IL, 2010), 305; O'Neill, *Democracy at War*, 207; Lichtenstein, *Labor's War*, 81.

102 Herman, *American Business*, 151–248; On unions, Harry Shulman and Neil Chamberlain, *Cases on Labor Relations* (Brooklyn, 1949), 54.

103 Herman, *American Business*, 25–26, 141, 281; Max M. Kampelman, *The Communist Party vs. the C.I.O.* (New York, 1971), 26; O'Neill, *Democracy at War*, 202–204; Lichtenstein, *Labor's War*, 62–65; War Department Air Corps, 10 April 1941, Sorenson Collection, Box 95, BFRC; Irving Bernstein, *Turbulent Years: A History of the American Worker, 1933–1941* (Boston, 1971), 765.

104 North American Aviation, nd, UAW Local 887, Box 1, RL; Nelson Lichtenstein, "Auto Worker Militancy and the Structure of Factory Life, 1937–1955," *Journal of American History*, vol. 67, no. 2 (September 1980), 337–348; Nelson Lichtenstein, "Life at the Rouge: A Cycle of Workers' Control," in Charles Stephenson and Robert Asher, eds. *Life and Labor: The Dimensions of American Working-Class History* (Albany, NY, 1986), 243; James B. Atleson, *Labor and the Wartime State: Labor Relations and Law during World War II* (Urbana, IL, 1998), 132–138; Glaberman, *Wartime Strikes*, 17, 40–49, 99; Departmental Communication, 9 May 1942, Sorenson Collection, Box 95, BFRC.

105 Herman, *American Business*, 246–259; Joel Seidman, *American Labor from Defense to Reconversion* (Chicago, 1953), 150; Atleson, *Labor and the Wartime State*, 20; Sparrow, *Warfare State*, 115, 166; Clive, *Michigan*, 29; Chafe, *America since World War II*, 8; Shulman, *Cases on Labor Relations*, 513–672; Chairman, 14 September 1942, UAW-NWLB, Box 3,

RL; Oral History, Robert Hiser Interview, 6 October 1989, Box 89324, BFRC.

106 Report of Conditions Affecting Production at Willow Run, Local 50, UAW-CIO, 26 February 1943, UAW War Policy Division, Box 16, RL; GMC Chevrolet-Flint, UAW-NWLB, Box 3; Snyder Tool, January [?] 1945, UAW-NWLB, Box 3, RL; Oral History, Robert Hiser Interview, 6 October 1989, Box 89324, BFRC; Jarecki, August [?] 1944, UAW-NWLB, Box 1, RL; Hayes Manufacturing, UAW-NWLB, Box 1, RL; David Brody, *Workers in Industrial America: Essays on the Twentieth Century Struggle* (New York, 1980), 198.

107 Herman, *American Business*, 184, 241, 247; Glaberman, *Wartime Strikes*, 13, 119; Lichtenstein, "Auto Worker Militancy," 344; Lichtenstein, *Labor's War*, 178; Continental Motors, UAW Local 887, Box 1, RL; Confidential, Jarvis Company, 15 January 1944, UAW-NWLB, Box 3, RL; "Incentive Pay," 2 October [1943?], *Detroit News* [press clipping], War Policy Division, Women's Bureau, Box 1, RL.

108 Lichtenstein, "Life at the Rouge," 243–245; Telegram, 6 January 1943, Sorenson Collection, Box 95, BFRC; O'Neill, *Democracy at War*, 211–212; Jarecki, nd, UAW-NWLB, Box 1, RL; Sanders, *Thompson*, 308; Chafe, *America since World War II*, 27.

109 Shulman, *Cases on Labor Relations*, 44–49; Lichtenstein, "Life at the Rouge," 249–250; Atleson, *Labor and the Wartime State*, 67; Seidman, *American Labor*, 189.

110 Shulman, *Cases on Labor Relations*, 47–49.

111 Auto Specialties, 1944, UAW-NWLB, Box 3, RL; Bower Roller Bearing, February 1945, UAW-NWLB, Box 3, RL.

112 Shulman, *Cases on Labor Relations*, 48–50; 432–433; Glaberman, *Wartime Strikes*, 33–34; Lichtenstein, *Labor's War*, 193.

113 Lichtenstein, "Life at the Rouge," 246; Glaberman, *Wartime Strikes*, 70; Lichtenstein, "Auto Worker Militancy," 344; George Lipsitz, *Rainbow at Midnight: Labor and Culture in the 1940s* (Urbana, IL, 1994), 51, 79, 87; Bower Roller Bearing, 5 February 1945, UAW-NWLB, Box 3, RL; Paragon Products, May 1944, UAW-NWLB, Box 1, RL; NWLB, 2 November 1944, UAW-NWLB, Box 1, RL; Memorandum, 15 November 1944, UAW-NWLB, Box 1, RL; North American Aviation, 1 June 1944, 21 August 1944, UAW Local 887, Box 1, RL; GMC Chevrolet-Flint, UAW-NWLB, Box 3, RL; Glaberman, *Wartime Strikes*, 23.

114 Shulman, *Cases on Labor Relations*, 39, 187, 408; Habitual Absentees, 27 July 1942, UAW-NWLB, Box 3, RL; North American Aviation, 13 June 1944, UAW Local 887, Box 1, RL; Lichtenstein, "Auto Worker Militancy," 343; O'Neill, *Democracy at War*, 219; Victor Reuther, 22 March 1944, War Policy Division, Women's Bureau, Box 1, RL; Plants deny Nelson Claim, 16 February 1943, UAW-NWLB, Box 5, RL; Testimony of Wendell Lund, House Labor Committee on Absenteeism, 25 March 1943, War Policy Division, Victor Reuther, Box 1, RL; Lowell J. Carr and James E. Stermer, *Willow Run: A Study of Industrialization and Cultural Inadequacy* (New York,

1952), 209; Testimony of Wendell Lund, 19 June 1942, UAW War Policy Division, Box 16, RL; War Manpower Committee, 29 March 1943, War Policy Division, Victor Reuther, Box 13, RL; Report of Conditions affecting Production at Willow Run, Local 50, UAW-CIO, 26 February 1943, UAW War Policy Division, Box 16, RL; Clive, *Michigan*, 37; Address, Wendell Lund, Director, War Production Board, 9 November 1942, War Policy Division, Box 14, RL.

115 GMC Chevrolet-Flint, UAW-NWLB, Box 3, RL; "Absenteeism Cure" [press clipping], *Detroit News*, 9 March 1943, UAW-NWLB, Box 5, RL; Guide for Plant Labor-Management Committees, February 1943, War Policy Division, Victor Reuther, Box 1, RL; Regional War Labor Board, 28 June 1943, UAW Local 887, Box 1, RL; Snyder Tool, January [?] 1945, UAW-NWLB, Box 3, RL; Arbitration, nd, UAW Local 887, Box 1, RL.

116 General Motors Corporation, nd, UAW Local 887, Box 1, RL; Arbitration Decision, nd, UAW Local 887, Box 1, RL; "Absenteeism Rate" [press clipping], *New York Times*, 26 August 1943, War Policy Division, Women's Bureau, Box 1, RL; Clive, *Michigan*, 190; "OWI Reports" [press clipping], *Detroit News*, 17 May 1943, UAW-NWLB, Box 5, RL; "NAM Exonerates Plant Absentees" [press clipping], nd, UAW-NWLB, Box 5, RL; Statement, 12 April 1943, War Policy Division, Victor Reuther, Box 6, RL; War Manpower Commission, 13 January 1943, War Policy Division, Box 14, RL; Sparrow, *Warfare State*, 193.

117 Cited in Manpower prospects to December 1943, Confidential, War Policy Division, Victor Reuther, Box 8, RL; Federal Security Agency, 12 September 1942, War Policy Division, Victor Reuther, Box 8, RL; Atleson, *Labor and the Wartime State*, 141; Detroit District, 19 January 1943, War Policy Division, Victor Reuther, Box 13, RL; War Manpower Commission, 13 January 1943, War Policy Division, Box 14, RL; Lichtenstein, *Labor's War*, 111.

118 OWI, 7 March 1944, War Policy Division, Women's Bureau, Box 1, RL; Wilson Foundry and Machine Co., nd, UAW-NWLB, Box 5, RL.

119 Problems of Women Workers in Detroit, War Production Board, 20 August 1943, War Policy Division, Women's Bureau, Box 1, RL; *New York Times*, 29 April, 3 May, and 14 September 1943 [press clippings], Sorenson Collection, Box 95, BFRC; OWI, 7 March 1944, War Policy Division, Women's Bureau, Box 1, RL; Hoover Ball, UAW-NWLB, Box 1, RL, 124409; Arbitration Decision, nd, UAW Local 887, Box 1, RL.

120 Shulman, *Cases on Labor Relations*, 188, 571, 574, 668, 670; O'Neill, *Democracy at War*, 9; Ruth Milkman, *Gender at Work: The Dynamics of Job Segregation by Sex during World War II* (Urbana, IL, 1987), 75–77, 87; Bower Roller Bearing, 5 February 1945, UAW-NWLB, Box 3, RL; Stephen Tuck, "You Can Sing and Punch . . . but You Can't Be a Soldier or Man," *Fog of War*, 109; Clive, *Michigan*, 158–160; Atleson, *Labor and the Wartime State*, 172; Sparrow, *Warfare State*, 165.

121 Shulman, *Cases on Labor Relations*, 71, 1167–1239.

122 Ibid., 1222–1224; Lichtenstein, "Auto Worker Militancy," 344.

9 ANTIFASCISMS DIVIDED, 1945

1 Stalin cited in Norman Naimark, "The Sovietization of Eastern Europe, 1944–1953," in Melvyn P. Leffler and Odd Arne Westad, eds. *The Cambridge History of the Cold War* (3 vols.) (New York, 2010), 1:175; Mark Kramer, "Stalin, Soviet Policy, and the Consolidation of a Communist Bloc in Eastern Europe, 1944–53," in Vladimir Tismaneanu, ed. *Stalinism Revisited: The Establishment of Communist Regimes in East-Central Europe* (Budapest, 2009), 61; Vladislav Zubok and Constantine Pleshakov, *Inside the Kremlin's Cold War: From Stalin to Khrushchev* (Cambridge, MA, 1996), 13; John Lewis Gaddis, *We Now Know: Rethinking Cold War History* (New York, 1997), 29; http://www.nationalchurchillmuseum.org/sinews-of-peace-iron-curtain-speech.html [my italics].

2 Antonia Grunenberg, *Antifaschismus – ein deutscher Mythos* (Hamburg, 1993), 12, 52, 114; Anson Rabinbach, "Introduction: The Legacies of Antifascism," *New German Critique*, no. 67 (Winter, 1996), 16.

3 Anne Applebaum, *Iron Curtain: The Crushing of Eastern Europe, 1944–1956* (New York, 2012), xxix, 8, 256, 442; Hugh Seton-Watson, *The East European Revolution* (New York, 1951), 301–303; John Lukacs, *1945: Year Zero* (New York, 1978), 266, 304–306; Deák, *Europe on Trial*, 188; Bradley F. Abrams, "The Second World War and the East European Revolution," *East European Politics and Societies*, vol. 16, no. 3 (2002), 633–652; Jan T. Gross, "Themes for a Social History of War Experience and Collaboration," in István Deák, Jan T. Gross, and Tony Judt, eds. *The Politics of Retribution in Europe: World War II and its Aftermath* (Princeton, NJ, 2000), 20–21; Norman M. Naimark, "Revolution and Counterrevolution in Eastern Europe," in Christiane Lemke and Gary Marks, *The Crisis of Socialism in Europe* (Durham, NC, 1992), 68; Alfred J. Rieber, "Popular Democracy: An Illusion," *Stalinism Revisited*, 108; John Connelly, "The Paradox of East German Communism: From Non-Stalinism to Neo-Stalinism?" *Stalinism Revisited*, 172; Ekaterina Nikova, "Bulgarian Stalinism Revisited," *Stalinism Revisited*, 300; Mark, "Revolution by Degrees," 6; Antoni Z. Kaminski and Bartlomiej Kaminski, "Road to 'People's Poland': Stalin's Conquest Revisited," *Stalinism Revisited*, 221; Cold War International History Project (February 2001), 6, http://www.wilsoncenter.org/sites/default/files/ACFB11.pdf

4 Nikova, "Bulgarian Stalinism Revisited," *Stalinism Revisited*, 297; Ken Jowitt, "Stalinist Revolutionary Breakthroughs in Eastern Europe," *Stalinism Revisited*, 19.

5 Buchanan, "Anti-fascism and Democracy," 47–54; Kaiser, *Christian Democracy*, 175; Robert Mencherini, "Résistance, socialistes, communistes et pouvoirs vus de Marseille," *La Résistance*, 323; Marwick, *Britain*, 302; Jose Harris, "War and Social History," 18–19.

6 William A. Pelz, "The Significance of the Mass Strike during the German Revolution of 1918–1919," *Workers of the World: International Journal on Strikes and Social Conflicts*, vol. 1, no. 1 (June 2012), 56–65.

7 Mayer, *Counterrevolution*, 101; Kenneth O. Morgan, *Labour in Power, 1945–1951* (Oxford, 1984), 190–194, 239–246; Foot, *Resistance*, 70, 181; Field, *British Working Class*, 288, 348; Rieber, "Popular Democracy,"

Stalinism Revisited, 120; Ian Buruma, *Year Zero: A History of 1945* (New York, 2013), 324; Michel, *Courants de pensée*, 705.

8 Principaux faits, 29 October 1944, APP; Adams, *Political Ecumenism*, 304; Andrew Shennan, *Rethinking France: Plans for Renewal 1940–1946* (Oxford, 1989), 39.

9 Fabrice Grenard, "La question du ravitaillement dans les entreprises françaises sous l'Occupation: insuffisances et parades," Chevandier, *Travailler*, 397. See Rancière, *Proletarian*, 154. Lacroix-Riz, "Les relations sociales," *Les ouvriers*, 222; Cooper, *Decolonization*, 161.

10 Étienne Fouilloux, "Les chrétiens pendant la Seconde Guerre mondiale," *Études sur la France*, 159; Jean-Marie Guillon, "Les déchirures du 'Var rouge'," *La Résistance*, 391; Lottman, *Purge*, 95; Gildea, *Marianne in Chains*, 334–335.

11 Pieter Lagrou, "Return to a Vanished World: European Societies and the Remnants of Their Jewish Communities, 1945–1947," Patrick Weil, "The Return of Jews in the Nationality or in the Territory of France," and Poznanski, "French Apprehensions," all in David Bankier, ed. *The Jews Are Coming Back* (Jerusalem, 2005), 16, 69, 47–56; Combes, *La franc-maçonnerie*, 317; http://www.cndp.fr/crdp-reims/memoire/enseigner/memoire_vichy/11spoliation.htm

12 Adler, *Jews*, 39, 178; Gildea, *Marianne in Chains*, 341.

13 Jackson, *Dark Years*, 573; Gildea, *Marianne in Chains*, 18–19, 181, 339; Wieviorka, *Histoire de la Résistance*, 469–476; Robertson, *To Govern France*, 131–132; Adams, *Political Ecumenism*, 182; Kedward, *Occupied France*, 78.

14 Principaux faits, 29 October-2 November 1944, APP; Mencherini, "Résistance, socialistes, communistes," *La Résistance*, 323; Chapman, *French Aircraft Industry*, 254; Reid, *Politics of Memories*, 130–132; Michel Goubet, "Les conditions de la Libération de Toulouse 'la ville rouge'," *La Résistance*, 377; Charles-Louis Foulon, "Prise et exercice du pouvoir en province à la Libération," *La Libération*, 518; Bloch-Lainé, *La France Restaurée*, 60–65.

15 Henry Rousso, "L'Épuration en France: une histoire inachevée," *Vingtième Siècle*, no. 33 (January–March 1992), 82–86; Stanley Hoffmann, "The Effects of World War II on French Society and Politics," *French Historical Studies*, vol. 2, No. 1 (Spring 1961), 45; Le Crom, *Syndicats*, 360; Gross, "Social History of War," *Politics of Retribution in Europe*, 29; Deák, *Europe on Trial*, 208; Peter Novick, *The Resistance versus Vichy: The Purge of Collaborators in Liberated France* (New York, 1968), 54–157; Jean-Pierre Rioux, "L'épuration en France," *Études sur la France*, 164; Grégoire Madjarian, *Conflits, pouvoirs et société à la Libération* (Paris, 1980), 214 [italics in original].

16 Mauriac cited in Lottman, *Purge*, 91; Novick, *Purge*, 187; Rousso, "L'Épuration," 103; Situation à Paris, 17 April 1944, APP; Sweets, *Choices*, 229–233; Deák, "Introduction," *Politics of Retribution*, 11; Moore, *American Debate on Nazism*, 281–283.

17 Stein, *Spanish Republicans*, 192–213; Gildea, *Fighters*, 428; Eden cited in Wigg, *Churchill and Spain*, 113–184.

18 Joan Maria Thomàs, *La Batalla del Wolframio: Estados Unidos y España del Pearl Harbor a la Guerra Fría (1941–1947)* (Madrid, 2010), 243–276.

19 Field, *British Working Class*, 214–339; Jose Harris, "Political Ideas and the Debate on State Welfare," *War and Social Change*, 249; Calder, *People's War*, 223, 528–529; Addison, *Road to 1945*, 33, 217, 264.

20 Marwick, *Britain*, 328; Harris, "War and Social History," 25; Addison, *Road to 1945*, 118, 251; Calder, *People's War*, 97; Field, *British Working Class*, 357; Morgan, *Labour*, 151.

21 Herrick Chapman, "French Democracy and the Welfare State," in George Reid Andrews and Herrick Chapman, eds. *The Social Construction of Democracy, 1870–1990* (New York, 1995), 295–298, 310; Philip Nord, *France's New Deal: From the Thirties to the Postwar Era* (Princeton, NJ, 2010), 118–120; Vigna, *Histoire des ouvriers*, 167.

22 Bullock, *Bevin*, 355; Addison, *Road to 1945*, 276–277; Morgan, *Labour*, 97–132; Marwick, *Britain*, 322; Harris, "War and Social History," 31.

23 Shennan, *Rethinking France*, 214; Novick, *Purge*, 113; Lottman, *Purge*, 226; Jean-Charles Asselain, "Les nationalisations 1944–45," *Études sur la France*, 197–198; Chapman, *French Aircraft Industry*, 264; Duclos cited in Jean-Jacques Becker, "Le PCF" in Claire Andrieu, Lucette Le Van, and Antoine Prost, eds. *Les Nationalisations de la Libération: De l'utopie au compromis* (Paris, 1987), 160; Bloch-Lainé, *La France Restaurée*, 143; Compte-Rendu, 28 September 1944, APP; Tollet, *La classe ouvrière*, 170; Gil Emprin, "Résistance et enjeux de pouvoir en Isère (1943–1945)," *La Résistance*, 370; Margairaz, *L'État*, 778; Novick, *Purge*, 36; François Marcot, "Les ouvriers de Peugeot, le patronat et l'État," *Les ouvriers*, 252–254; Albert Camus, *Camus à Combat: Éditoriaux et articles d'Albert Camus, 1944–1947* (Paris, 2002), 213.

24 Paulhan cited in Lottman, *Purge*, 242; Margairaz, *L'État*, 778; Rioux, "L'épuration," 170; Adler, *Jews*, 134; Bédarida, "World War II and Social Change in France," 85; Teitgen cited in Rioux, "L'épuration en France," 172; Rousso, "L'Épuration," 101.

25 Reid, *Politics of Memories*, 134; Michel, *Les courants de pensée*, 697–703; Margairaz, *L'État*, 791; Gildea, *Marianne in Chains*, 330–347; Nord, *France's New Deal*, 143; Andrieu, *Les Nationalisations*, 189–320; Sadoun, *Socialistes*, 189–215; Mayer cited in Michel, *Les courants de pensée*, 740; Sadoun, *Socialistes*, 270; Bloch-Lainé, *La France Restaurée*, 71.

26 Madjarian, *Conflits*, 424.

27 Antoine Prost, "Une pièce en trois actes," *Les Nationalisations*, 238; Madjarian, *Conflits*, 250; Shennan, *Rethinking France*, 287; Jean Bouvier, "Sur la politique économique en 1944–1946," *La Libération*, 854.

28 Shennan, *Rethinking France*, 100; PP, 26 February 1945, APP.

29 Principaux faits, 29 October 1944, APP.

30 Vigna, *Histoire des ouvriers*, 162–167; Rancière, *Proletarian*, 170–174; Fridenson, "Les ouvriers," 133.

31 Penny Von Eschen, "Civil Rights and World War II in a Global Frame," *Fog of War*, 219; Plummer, *Black Americans*, 127–145; O'Neill, *A Democracy at War*, 138; Lizabeth Cohen, *A Consumer's Republic: The Politics of Mass Consumption in Postwar America* (New York, 2003), 73, 114, 403; Ira Katznelson,

When Affirmative Action Was White: An Untold History of Racial Inequality in Twentieth-Century America (New York, 2005), xv.

10 CONCLUSION AND EPILOGUE

1 James Mark, Nigel Townson, and Polymeris Voglis, "Inspirations," in Robert Gildea, James Mark, and Anette Warring, eds. *Europe's 1968: Voices of Revolt* (Oxford, 2013), 73.

2 Kevin Passmore, *Fascism: A Very Short Introduction* (Oxford, 2002), 88–107; Paul E. Gottfried, *Fascism: The Career of a Concept* (DeKalb, IL, 2016), 72–80.

3 In 2014, by accusing Ukrainian leaders of "neo-Nazis[m]," the national-populist Russian leader, Vladimir Putin, revived the antifascism of the inter-war period to justify his annexation of Crimea. See José María Faraldo, "An Antifascist Political Identity? On the Cult of Antifascism in the Soviet Union and post-Socialist Russia," in Hugo García, Mercedes Yusta, Xavier Tabet, and Cristina Clímaco, eds. *Rethinking Antifascism: History, Memory and Politics, 1922 to the Present* (New York, 2016), 203.

Select Bibliography

ARCHIVES

Archives de la Préfecture de Police (APP), Paris, France
Archivo General de la Administración (AGA), Madrid, Spain
Archivo Histórico Nacional-Sección Guerra Civil (AHN-SGC), Salamanca, Spain
Benson Ford Research Center (BFRC), Dearborn, Michigan, USA
National Archives (NA), Kew, UK
Reuther Library (RL), Detroit, Michigan, USA

PERIODICALS

Catholic World
Commonweal
La Journée industrielle
L'Économie nouvelle
L'Europe Nouvelle
Le Populaire

BOOKS AND ARTICLES

Abrams, Bradley F., "The Second World War and the East European Revolution," *East European Politics and Societies*, vol. 16, no. 3 (2002), 623–664.
Adams, Geoffrey, *Political Ecumenism: Catholics, Jews, and Protestants in de Gaulle's Free France, 1940–1945* (Montreal, 2006).
Adamthwaite, Anthony, *France and the Coming of the Second World War 1936–1939* (London, 1977).
  Grandeur and Misery: France's Bid for Power in Europe 1914–1940 (London, 1995).
Addison, Paul, *The Road to 1945: British Politics and the Second World War* (London, 1975).
Adler, K. H., *Jews and Gender in Liberation France* (New York, 2003).
Agulhon, Maurice, "Les communistes et la Libération de la France," Comité d'Histoire de la Deuxième Guerre Mondiale, *La Libération de la France* (Paris, 1976), 67–90.
Albertelli, Sébastien, *Histoire du Sabotage: De la CGT à la Résistance* (Paris, 2016).

Alía Miranda, Francisco, *La agonía de la República: El final de la guerra civil española (1938–1939)* (Barcelona, 2015).

Allyn, Gustave, *Le mouvement syndical dans la résistance* (Paris, 1975).

Alpers, Benjamin L. *Dictators, Democracy, and American Public Culture: Envisioning the Totalitarian Enemy, 1920s–1950s* (Chapel Hill, NC, 2003).

Álvarez Tardío, Manuel, and Roberto Villa García, "El impacto de la violencia anticlerical en la primavera de 1936 y la respuesta de las autoridades," *Hispania Sacra*, LXV, 132 (July–December 2013), 683–764.

and Roberto Villa García, *El precio de la exclusión: La política durante la Segunda República* (Madrid, 2010).

Amouroux, Henri, *La vie des français sous l'Occupation*, 2 vols. (Paris, 1961).

Andrieu, Claire, Lucette Le Van, and Antoine Prost, eds. *Les Nationalisations de la Libération: De l'utopie au compromis* (Paris, 1987).

Philippe Braud, and Guillaume Piketty, eds. *Dictionnaire de Gaulle* (Paris, 2006).

Applebaum, Anne, *Iron Curtain: The Crushing of Eastern Europe, 1944–1956* (New York, 2012).

Arnaud, Patrice, *Les STO: Histoire des Français requis en Allemagne nazie 1942–1945* (Paris, 2010).

Aron, Raymond, *The Committed Observer: Interviews with Jean-Louis Missika and Dominique Wolton*, trans. James and Marie McIntosh (Chicago, 1983).

"Réflexions sur les problèmes économiques français," *Revue de Métaphysique et de Morale*, vol. 44, no. 4 (October 1937), 793–822.

Ascher, Abraham, *Was Hitler a Riddle?: Western Democracies and National Socialism* (Stanford, CA, 2012).

Asselain, Jean-Charles, "Les nationalisations 1944–45," in *Études sur la France de 1939 à nos jours* (Paris, 1985), 180–207.

Aster, Sidney, "Guilty Men: The Case of Neville Chamberlain," in Robert Boyce and Esmonde M. Robertson, eds. *Paths to War: New Essays on the Origins of the Second World War* (New York, 1989), 233–268.

Atholl, [Duchess of], *Searchlight on Spain* (Harmondsworth, 1938).

Atleson, James B., *Labor and the Wartime State: Labor Relations and Law during World War II* (Urbana, IL, 1998).

Barrett, Neil, "The anti-fascist movement in south-east Lancashire, 1933–1940: The divergent experiences of Manchester and Nelson," in Tim Kirk and Anthony McElligot, eds. *Opposing Fascism: Community, Authority, and Resistance in Europe* (Cambridge, UK, 1999), 48–62.

Becker, Jean-Jacques, "Le PCF," in Claire Andrieu, Lucette Le Van, and Antoine Prost, eds. *Les Nationalisations de la Libération: De l'utopie au compromis* (Paris, 1987), 157–167.

Bédarida, François, "World War II and Social Change in France," in Arthur Marwick, ed. *Total War and Social Change* (New York, 1988), 79–94.

Bell, Leland V. "The Failure of Nazism in America: The German American Bund, 1936–1941," *Political Science Quarterly*, vol. 85, no. 4 (December, 1970), 585–599.

Bellanger, Claude, *Presse Clandestine, 1940–1944* (Paris, 1961).

Berinsky, Adam J. "Assuming the Costs of War: Events, Elites, and American Public Support for Military Conduct," *The Journal of Politics*, vol. 69, no. 4 (November 2007), 975–997.

Bernstein, Arnie, *Swastika Nation: Fritz Kuhn and the Rise and Fall of the German-American Bund* (New York, 2013).

Bernstein, Irving, *Turbulent Years: A History of the American Worker, 1933–1941* (Boston, 1971).

Berstein, Serge, *Léon Blum* (Paris, 2006).

Bilitza, Irina, "Les débrayages pendant l'occupation allemande dans l'ancien département de la Seine," in Michel Margairaz and Danielle Tartakowsky, eds. *Le syndicalisme dans la France occupée* (Rennes, 2008), 401–410.

Birnbaum, Pierre, *Léon Blum: Prime Minister, Socialist, Zionist*, trans. Arthur Goldhammer (New Haven, CT, 2015).

Bjerström, Carl-Henrik, *Josep Renau and the Politics of Culture in Republican Spain, 1931–1939: Re-imagining the Nation* (Brighton, UK, 2016).

Bloch-Lainé, François, and Jean Bouvier, *La France Restaurée 1944–1954: Dialogue sur les choix d'une modernisation* (Paris, 1986).

Bloch, Marc, *Strange Defeat: A Statement of Evidence Written in 1940*, trans. Gerard Hopkins (New York, 1968).

Blower, Brooke L., "From Isolationism to Neutrality: A New Framework for Understanding American Political Culture, 1919–1941," *Diplomatic History*, vol. 38, no. 2 (April 2014), 345–376.

Boivin, Michel, "Les réfractaires au travail obligatoire: essai d'approche globale et statistique," in Bernard Garnier and Jean Quellien, eds. *La main d'œuvre française exploitée par le IIIe Reich: Actes du colloque international, Caen, 13–15 décembre 2001* (Caen, 2003), 493–515.

Bosch, Aurora, *Miedo a la democracia: Estados Unidos ante la Segunda República y la Guerra civil española* (Barcelona, 2012).

Bougeard, Christian, "Éléments d'une approche de l'histoire de la France Libre," in Patrick Harismendy and Erwan Le Gall, eds. *Pour une histoire de la France Libre* (Rennes, 2012), 15–28.

Bourdet, Claude, *L'Aventure incertaine: De la Résistance à la Restauration* (Paris, 1975).

Bouvier, Jean, "Sur la politique économique en 1944–1946," Comité d'Histoire de la Deuxième Guerre Mondiale, *La Libération de la France* (Paris, 1976), 835–862.

Boyce, Robert, "René Massigli and Germany, 1919–1938," in Robert Boyce, ed. *French Foreign and Defence Policy, 1918–1940: The Decline and Fall of a Great Power* (London, 1998), 132–148.

"World Depression, World War: Some Economic Origins of the Second World War," in Robert Boyce and Esmonde M. Robertson, eds. *Paths to War: New Essays on the Origins of the Second World War* (New York, 1989), 55–95.

Brendon, Piers, *The Dark Valley: A Panorama of the 1930s* (New York, 2000).

Brocheux, Pierre, and Daniel Hémery, *Indochina: An Ambiguous Colonization, 1858–1954*, trans. Ly Lan Dill-Klein (Berkeley, 2009).

Broch, Ludovine, *Ordinary Workers, Vichy and the Holocaust: French Railwaymen and the Second World War* (Cambridge, UK, 2016).

Brody, David, *Workers in Industrial America: Essays on the Twentieth Century Struggle* (New York, 1980).

Brookshire, Jerry H., "Speak for England, Act for England: Labour's Leadership and the Threat of War in the Late 1930s," *European History Quarterly*, vol. 29, no. 2 (1999), 251–287.

Buchanan, Andrew, *American Grand Strategy in the Mediterranean during World War II* (New York, 2014).

Buchanan, Tom, "Anti-fascism and Democracy in the 1930s," *European History Quarterly*, vol. 32, no. 1 (2002), 39–57.

"'Beyond Cable Street': New Approaches to the Historiography of Antifascism in Britain in the 1930s," in Hugo García, Mercedes Yusta, Xavier Tabet, and Cristina Clímaco, eds. *Rethinking Antifascism: History, Memory and Politics, 1922 to the Present* (New York, 2016), 61–75.

Britain and the Spanish Civil War (New York, 1997).

The Impact of the Spanish Civil War on Britain: War, Loss and Memory (Portland, OR, 2007).

The Spanish Civil War and the British Labour Movement (Cambridge, UK, 1991).

Bullock, Alan, *Ernest Bevin: A Biography* (London, 2002).

Burrin, Philippe, *France under the Germans: Collaboration and Compromise*, trans. Janet Lloyd (New York, 1996).

Buruma, Ian, *Year Zero: A History of 1945* (New York, 2013).

Buton, Philippe, "Les communistes dans les entreprises travaillant pour la défense nationale en 1939–1940," in Jean-Pierre Rioux, Antoine Prost, and Jean-Pierre Azéma, eds. *Les communistes français de Munich à Châteaubriant, 1938–1941* (Paris, 1987), 119–144.

Calder, Angus, *The People's War: Britain 1939–1945* (New York, 1969).

Campoamor, Clara, *La revolución española vista por una republicana* (Barcelona, 2002).

Camus, Albert, *Camus à Combat: Éditoriaux et articles d'Albert Camus, 1944–1947* (Paris, 2002).

Cándano, Xuan, *El Pacto de Santoña (1937): La rendición del nacionalismo vasco al fascismo* (Madrid, 2006).

Cannadine, David, *In Churchill's Shadow: Confronting the Past in Modern Britain* (Oxford, 2003).

Cantier, Jacques, "Les horizons de l'après Vichy: De la 'Libération' de l'empire aux enjeux de mémoire," in Jacques Cantier and Éric Jennings, *L'empire colonial sous Vichy* (Paris, 2004).

Carrascal, José María, *Autobiografía apócrifa de José Ortega y Gasset* (Madrid, 2010).

Carr, Lowell J. and James E. Stermer, *Willow Run: A Study of Industrialization and Cultural Inadequacy* (New York, 1952).

Carroll, Peter N., *The Odyssey of the Abraham Lincoln Brigade: Americans in the Spanish Civil War* (Stanford, CA, 1994).

Casey, Steven, *Cautious Crusade: Franklin D. Roosevelt, American Public Opinion, and the War against Nazi Germany* (New York, 2001).

Ceplair, Larry, *Under the Shadow of War: Fascism, Anti-fascism, and Marxists, 1918–1939* (New York, 1987).

Chadeau, Emmanuel, *L'industrie aéronautique en France, 1900–1950: De Blériot à Dassault* (Paris, 1987).

Chafe, William H., *The Unfinished Journey: America since World War II* (New York, 2003).

Chalmers, David M., *Hooded Americanism: The History of the Ku Klux Klan* (New York, 1965).

Chapman, Herrick, "French Democracy and the Welfare State," in George Reid Andrews and Herrick Chapman, eds. *The Social Construction of Democracy, 1870–1990* (New York, 1995), 291–314.

    State Capitalism and Working-Class Radicalism in the French Aircraft Industry (Berkeley, 1991).

Chapman, Michael E. *Franco Lobbyists, Roosevelt's Foreign Policy, and the Spanish Civil War* (Kent, OH, 2011).

Chaubin, Hélène, "Libération et pouvoirs: un modèle corse," in Jean-Marie Guillon et Robert Mencherini, eds. *La Résistance et les Européens du Sud* (Paris, 1999), 339–347.

Chaumont, Jean-Michel, *La concurrence des victimes: Génocide, identité, reconnaissance* (Paris, 1997).

Chevallier, Pierre, *Histoire de la Franc-Maçonnerie française*, 3 vols. (Paris, 1975).

Christophe, Paul, *1936: Les Catholiques et le Front Populaire* (Paris, 1986).

Churchill, Winston S. *Step by Step, 1936–1939* (New York, 1939).

    The Gathering Storm (New York, 1948).

    Winston S. Churchill: His Complete Speeches, 1897–1963 (New York, 1974).

Clive, Alan, *State of War: Michigan in World War II* (Ann Arbor, MI, 1979).

Cockett, Richard, *Twilight of Truth: Chamberlain, Appeasement and the Manipulation of the Press* (New York, 1989).

    "Ball, Chamberlain and *Truth*," *The Historical Journal*, vol. 33, no. 1 (March 1990), 131–142.

Code, Joseph B., *The Spanish War and Lying Propaganda* (New York, 1938).

Cohen, Lizabeth, *A Consumer's Republic: The Politics of Mass Consumption in Postwar America* (New York, 2003).

Cointepas, Michel, "La mise en œuvre de la Charte du travail par les inspecteurs du travail," in Denis Peschanski and Jean-Louis Robert, eds. *Les ouvriers en France pendant la seconde guerre mondiale* (Paris, 1992), 181–191.

Coleman, Bruce, "The Conservative Party and the Frustration of the Extreme Right," in Andrew Thorpe, ed. *The Failure of Political Extremism in Inter-War Britain* (Exeter, 1989), 49–66.

Cole, Wayne S., *Roosevelt and the Isolationists, 1932–1945* (Lincoln, NE, 1983).

Collingham, Lizzie, *The Taste of War: World War II and the Battle for Food* (New York, 2012).

Colton, Joel, *Léon Blum: Humanist in Politics* (Cambridge, MA, 1974).

Combes, André, *La franc-maçonnerie sous l'Occupation: Persécution et résistance (1939–1945)* (Monaco, 2001).

Connelly, John, "The Paradox of East German Communism: From Non-Stalinism to Neo-Stalinism?" in Vladimir Tismaneanu, ed. *Stalinism Revisited: The Establishment of Communist Regimes in East-Central Europe* (Budapest, 2009), 161–194.

Cooper, Frederick, *Decolonization and African Society: The Labor Question in French and British Africa* (Cambridge, UK, 1996).

Copsey, Nigel, *Anti-Fascism in Britain* (Basingstoke, 2000).

"'Every time they made a Communist, they made a Fascist': The Labour Party and Popular Anti-Fascism in the 1930s," in Nigel Copsey and Andrzej Olechnowicz, eds. *Varieties of Anti-Fascism: Britain in the Inter-War Period* (Basingstoke, 2010), 52–72.

"Towards a New Anti-Fascist 'Minimum'," in Nigel Copsey and Andrzej Olechnowicz, eds. *Varieties of Anti-Fascism: Britain in the Inter-War Period* (Basingstoke, 2010), xiv–xxi.

Courtois, Stéphane, "Les Communistes et l'action syndicale," in Jean-Pierre Rioux, Antoine Prost, and Jean-Pierre Azéma, eds. *Les communistes français de Munich à Châteaubriant, 1938–1941* (Paris, 1987), 85–98.

Cowling, Maurice, *The Impact of Hitler: British Politics and British Policy, 1933–1940* (Chicago, 1977).

Crémieux-Brilhac, Jean-Louis, *De Gaulle, la République et la France Libre: 1940–1945* (Paris, 2014).

Georges Boris: Trente Ans d'Influence: Blum, de Gaulle, Mendès France (Paris, 2010).

"Leclerc et la France Libre," in Christine Levisse-Touzé, ed. *Du capitaine de Hauteclocque au général Leclerc* (Brussels, 2000), 127–146.

Les français de l'an 40, 2 vols. (Paris, 1990).

"Les Communistes et l'armée pendant la drôle de guerre," in Jean-Pierre Rioux, Antoine Prost, and Jean-Pierre Azéma, eds. *Les communistes français de Munich à Châteaubriant, 1938–1941* (Paris, 1987), 98–118.

Croucher, Richard, *Engineers at War* (London, 1982).

Crouter, Richard, *Reinhold Niebuhr: On Politics, Religion, and Christian Faith* (New York, 2010).

Crowson, N. J., *Facing Fascism: The Conservative Party and the European Dictators, 1935–1940* (London, 1997).

Cruz, Rafael, *En el nombre del pueblo: República, rebelión y guerra en la España de 1936* (Madrid, 2006).

Cueva, Julio de la, "Religious Persecution, Anticlerical Tradition, and Revolution," *Journal of Contemporary History*, vol. 33, no. 3 (1998), 355–369.

Dack, Janet, "It certainly isn't cricket!: Media Responses to Mosley and the BUF," in Nigel Copsey and Andrzej Olechnowicz, eds. *Varieties of Anti-Fascism: Britain in the Inter-War Period* (Basingstoke, 2010), 140–161.

Dallas, Gregor, *1945: The War That Never Ended* (New Haven, CT, 2005).

Dallek, Robert, *Franklin D. Roosevelt and American Foreign Policy, 1932–1945* (New York, 1979).

Deák, István, *Europe on Trial: The Story of Collaboration, Resistance and Retribution during World War II* (Boulder, CO, 2015).

de Gaulle, Charles, *The Complete War Memoirs of Charles de Gaulle*, trans. Richard Howard (New York, 1964).

Dejonghe, Etienne and Yves Le Maner, "Les Communistes du Nord et du Pas-de-Calais de la fin du Front Populaire à mai 1941," in Jean-Pierre Rioux, Antoine Prost, and Jean-Pierre Azéma, eds. *Les communistes français de Munich à Châteaubriant, 1938–1941* (Paris, 1987), 201–265.

Denéchère, Yves, *Jean Herbette (1878–1960): Journaliste et ambassadeur* (Paris, 2003).

Deutsch, Bernard S., "The Disfranchisement of the Jew," in Pierre van Paassen and James Waterman Wise, eds. *Nazism: An Assault on Civilization* (New York, 1934), 39–58.

Diggins, John P., *Mussolini and Fascism: The View from America* (Princeton, NJ, 1972).

Dodd, Lindsay, and Andrew Knapp, "'How Many Frenchmen did you Kill?' British Bombing Policy towards France (1940–1945)," *French History*, vol. 22, no. 4 (2008), 469–492.

Douzou, Laurent, *La Désobéissance: Histoire d'un mouvement et d'un journal clandestins: Libération-Sud (1940–1944)* (Paris, 1995).

La Résistance française: une histoire périlleuse (Paris, 2005).

Lucie Aubrac (Paris, 2012).

Dreyfus-Armand, Geneviève, and Émile Temime, *Les camps sur la plage, un exil espagnol* (Paris, 1995).

Dreyfus, Michel, "Les socialistes européens et les Front populaires: un internationalisme déclinant," in Serge Wolikow and Annie Bleton-Ruget, eds. *Antifascisme et nation: les gauches européennes au temps du Front populaire* (Dijon, 1998), 21–30.

Droz, Jacques, *Histoire de l'antifascisme en Europe, 1923–1939* (Paris, 1985).

Dubofsky, Melvyn, and Foster Rhea Dulles, *Labor in America: A History* (Wheeling, IL, 2010).

Dunbabin, John, "The British Military Establishment and the Policy of Appeasement," in Wolfgang J. Mommsen and Lothar Kettenacker, eds. *The Fascist Challenge and the Policy of Appeasement* (London, 1983), 174–196.

Dunn, Susan, *FDR, Willkie, Lindbergh, Hitler – the Election amid the Storm* (New Haven, CT, 2013).

Dutton, David, *Anthony Eden: A Life and Reputation* (London, 1997).

Ealham, Chris, *Anarchism and the City: Revolution and Counter-Revolution in Barcelona, 1898–1937* (Oakland, 2010).

Eby, Cecil D., *Comrades and Commissars: The Lincoln Battalion in the Spanish Civil War* (University Park, PA, 2007).

Edgerton, David, *Britain's War Machine: Weapons, Resources, and Experts in the Second World War* (New York, 2011).

Edwards, Jill, *The British Government and the Spanish Civil War, 1936–1939* (London, 1979).

Edwards, Mark Thomas, *The Right of the Protestant Left: God's Totalitarianism* (New York, 2012).

Eley, Geoff, "The Legacies of Antifascism: Constructing Democracy in Postwar Europe," *New German Critique*, no. 67 (Winter 1996), 73–100.

Ellis, John, *The Sharp End: The Fighting Man in World War II* (New York, 1980).

Elorza, Antonio, "La nation éclatée: Front populaire et question nationale en Espagne," in Serge Wolikow and Annie Bleton-Ruget, eds. *Antifascisme et nation: les gauches européennes au temps du Front populaire* (Dijon, 1998), 113–128.

Emprin, Gil, "Résistance et enjeux de pouvoir en Isère (1943–1945)," in Jean-Marie Guillon and Robert Mencherini, eds. *La Résistance et les Européens du Sud* (Paris, 1999), 361–371.

Faraldo, José María, "An Antifascist Political Identity? On the Cult of Antifascism in the Soviet Union and post-Socialist Russia," in Hugo García, Mercedes Yusta, Xavier Tabet, and Cristina Clímaco, eds. *Rethinking Antifascism: History, Memory and Politics, 1922 to the Present* (New York, 2016), 202–227.

Field, Geoffrey G., *Blood, Sweat, and Toil: Remaking the British Working Class, 1939–1945* (New York, 2011).

Fogg, Shannon L., *The Politics of Everyday Life in Vichy France: Foreigners, Undesirables, and Strangers* (New York, 2009).

Fontaine, Thomas, *Les oubliés de Romainville: Un camp allemand en France (1940–1944)* (Paris, 2005).

Foot, M. R. D., *Resistance: European Resistance to Nazism, 1940–1945* (New York, 1977).

Foss, Brian, *War Paint: Art, War, State and Identity in Britain 1939–1945* (New Haven, CT, 2007).

Fouilloux, Étienne, "Les chrétiens pendant la Seconde Guerre mondiale," in Jean-Charles Asselain, *Études sur la France de 1939 à nos jours* (Paris, 1985), 156–161.

Foulon, Charles-Louis, "Le Général de Gaulle et la Libération de la France," Comité d'Histoire de la Deuxième Guerre Mondiale, *La Libération de la France* (Paris, 1976), 31–54.

"Prise et exercice du pouvoir en province à la Libération," Comité d'Histoire de la Deuxième Guerre Mondiale, *La Libération de la France* (Paris, 1976), 501–529.

Fox, Richard Wightman, *Reinhold Niebuhr: A Biography* (New York, 1985).

Frankenstein, Robert, *Le prix du réarmement français, 1935–39* (Paris, 1982).

Frank, Robert, "La gauche sait-elle gérer la France? (1936–1937/1981–1984)," *Vingtième siècle*, no. 6 (April–June 1985), 3–21.

Fridenson, Patrick, and Jean-Louis Robert, "Les ouvriers dans la France de la Seconde Guerre mondiale: Un bilan," *Le mouvement social*, no. 158 (January–March 1992), 117–147.

Frieser, Karl-Heinz, with John T. Greenwood, *The Blitzkrieg Legend: The 1940 Campaign in the West* (Annapolis, MD, 2005).

Fronczak, Joseph, "Local People's Global Politics: A Transnational History of the Hands Off Ethiopia Movement of 1935," *Diplomatic History*, vol. 39, no. 2 (2015), 245–274.

Fry, Joseph A., *Dixie Looks Abroad: The South and U.S. Foreign Relations, 1789–1973* (Baton Rouge, LA, 2002).

Fyrth, Jim, "Introduction: In the Thirties," in Jim Fyrth, ed. *Britain, Fascism and the Popular Front* (London, 1985), 9–29.

Gaddis, John Lewis, *We Now Know: Rethinking Cold War History* (New York, 1997).

Gannon, Franklin Reid, *The British Press and Germany 1936–1939* (Oxford, 1971).

García, Hugo, *Mentiras necesarias: La batalla por la opinión británica durante la Guerra Civil* (Madrid, 2008).

Garraud, Philippe, "La politique française de réarmement de 1936 à 1940: priorités et contraintes," *Guerres mondiales et conflits contemporains*, no. 219 (July 2005), 87–102.

Gates, Eleanor M., *The End of the Affair: The Collapse of the Anglo-French Alliance, 1939–40* (Berkeley, CA, 1981).

Gentile, Emilio, *Politics as Religion*, trans. George Staunton (Princeton, NJ, 2006).

Gibson, Ian, *The Death of Lorca* (Chicago, 1973).

Gildea, Robert, and Dirk Luyten and Juliane Fürst, "To Work or Not to Work," in Robert Gildea, Olivier Wieviorka, and Anette Warring, eds. *Surviving Hitler and Mussolini: Daily Life in Occupied Europe* (Oxford, 2006), 42–87.

Gildea, Robert, *Fighters in the Shadows: A New History of the French Resistance* (Cambridge, MA, 2015).

  Marianne in Chains: Daily Life in the Heart of France during the German Occupation (New York, 2002).

Ginsberg, Benjamin, *How the Jews Defeated Hitler: Exploding the Myth of Jewish Passivity in the Face of Nazism* (Lanham, MD, 2016).

Glaberman, Martin, *Wartime Strikes: The Struggle against the No-Strike Pledge in the UAW during World War II* (Detroit, 1980).

Goda, Norman J. W., *Tomorrow the World: Hitler, Northwest Africa, and the Path toward America* (College Station, TX, 1998).

Golan, Romy, *Modernity and Nostalgia: Art and Politics in France between the Wars* (New Haven, CT, 1995).

Gombin, Richard, *Les socialistes et la guerre: La S.F.I.O. et la politique étrangère française entre les deux guerres mondiales* (Paris, 1970).

Gottfried, Paul E., *Fascism: The Career of a Concept* (DeKalb, IL, 2016).

Gottlieb, Julie, "Varieties of Feminist Responses to Fascism in Inter-War Britain," in Nigel Copsey and Andrzej Olechnowicz, eds. *Varieties of Anti-Fascism: Britain in the Inter-War Period* (Basingstoke, 2010), 101–118.

Goubet, Michel, "Les conditions de la Libération de Toulouse 'la ville rouge,'" in Jean-Marie Guillon and Robert Mencherini, eds. *La Résistance et les Européens du Sud* (Paris, 1999), 373–380.

Graves, Robert, and Alan Hodge, *The Long Week-End: A Social History of Great Britain 1918–1939* (New York, 1940).

Green, William, "The Attack on Organized Labor," in Pierre van Paassen and James Waterman Wise, eds. *Nazism: An Assault on Civilization* (New York, 1934), 280–283.

Grenard, Fabrice, "La question du ravitaillement dans les entreprises françaises sous l'Occupation: insuffisances et parades," in Christian Chevandier and Jean-Claude Daumas, eds. *Travailler dans les entreprises sous l'occupation* (Besançon, 2007), 395–410.

"Les implications politiques du ravitaillement en France sous l'Occupation," *Vingtième Siècle*, 94 (April–June 2007), 199–215.

Griffiths, Richard, *Fellow Travellers of the Right: British Enthusiasts for Nazi Germany 1933–9* (London, 1980).

Grill, Johnpeter Horst, "The American South and Nazi Racism," in Alan E. Steinweis and Daniel F. Rogers, eds. *The Impact of Nazism: New Perspectives on the Third Reich and its Legacy* (Lincoln, NE, 2003), 19–38.

Gross, Jan T., "Themes for a Social History of War Experience and Collaboration," in István Deák, Jan T. Gross, and Tony Judt, eds. *The Politics of Retribution in Europe: World War II and its Aftermath* (Princeton, NJ, 2000), 15–35.

Grunenberg, Antonia, *Antifaschismus – ein deutscher Mythos* (Hamburg, 1993).

Guillon, Jean-Marie, "Les déchirures du 'Var rouge'," in Jean-Marie Guillon and Robert Mencherini, eds. *La Résistance et les Européens du Sud* (Paris, 1999), 381–392.

Guttmann, Allen, *The Wound in the Heart: America and the Spanish Civil War* (New York, 1962).

Haffner, Sebastian, *Churchill* (London, 2003).

Hamilton, Alice, "The Enslavement of Women," in Pierre van Paassen and James Waterman Wise, eds. *Nazism: An Assault on Civilization* (New York, 1934), 76–87.

Harris, Jose, "Political Ideas and the Debate on State Welfare," in Harold L. Smith, ed. *War and Social Change* (Manchester, 1986), 233–266.

"War and Social History: Britain and the Home Front during the Second World War," *Contemporary European History*, vol. 1, no. 1 (March 1992), 17–35.

Harris, Joseph E., *African-American Reactions to War in Ethiopia, 1936–1941* (Baton Rouge, LA, 1994).

Hastings, Max, *Inferno: The World at War, 1939–1945* (New York, 2011).

Winston's War: Churchill, 1940–1945 (New York, 2010).

Herman, Arthur, *Freedom's Forge: How American Business Produced Victory in World War II* (New York, 2012).

Hernández Sánchez, Fernando, *Guerra o Revolución: El Partido Comunista de España en la guerra civil* (Barcelona, 2010).

Herndon, James S., "British Perceptions of Soviet Military Capability," in Wolfgang J. Mommsen and Lothar Kettenacker, eds. *The Fascist Challenge and the Policy of Appeasement* (London, 1983), 297–319.

High, Stanley, "The War on Religious Freedom," in Pierre van Paassen and James Waterman Wise, eds. *Nazism: An Assault on Civilization* (New York, 1934), 25–38.

Hinojosa Durán, José, *Tropas en un Frente olvidado: El ejército republicano en Extremadura durante la Guerra Civil* (Mérida, 2009).

Hitchcock, William I., *The Bitter Road to Freedom: The Human Cost of Allied Victory in World War II Europe* (New York, 2008).

Hochschild, Adam, *Spain in our Hearts: Americans in the Spanish Civil War, 1936–1939* (New York, 2016).

Hodgson, Keith, *Fighting Fascism: The British Left and the Rise of Fascism, 1919–39* (Manchester, 2010).

Hoffmann, Stanley, "The Effects of World War II on French Society and Politics," *French Historical Studies*, vol. 2, no. 1 (Spring 1961), 28–63.

Holmes, John Haynes, "The Threat to Freedom," in Pierre van Paassen and James Waterman Wise, eds. *Nazism: An Assault on Civilization* (New York, 1934), 127–142.

Hucker, Daniel, *Public Opinion and the End of Appeasement in Britain and France* (Surrey, 2011).

Imlay, Talbot, "Democracy and War: Political Regime, Industrial Relations, and Economic Preparations for War in France and Britain up to 1940," *Journal of Modern History*, vol. 79, no. 1 (March 2007), 1–47.

   Facing the Second World War: Strategy, Politics, and Economics in Britain and France 1938–1940 (Oxford, 2003).

   and Martin Horn, *The Politics of Industrial Collaboration during World War II: Ford, France, Vichy and Nazi Germany* (New York, 2014).

   "Mind the Gap: The Perception and Reality of Communist Sabotage of French War Production during the Phoney War 1939–1940," *Past and Present*, no. 189 (November 2005), 179–224.

Inboden, William C., "The Prophetic Conflict: Reinhold Niebuhr, Christian Realism, and World War II," *Diplomatic History*, vol. 38, no. 1 (January 2014), 49–82.

Ingram, Norman, *The Politics of Dissent: Pacifism in France, 1919–1939* (Oxford, 1991).

Inquimbert, Anne-Aurore, "Monsieur Blum ... un roi de France ferait la guerre," *Guerres mondiales et conflits contemporains*, no. 215 (2004), 35–45.

Jackson, Julian, *The Fall of France: The Nazi Invasion of 1940* (Oxford, 2003).

   France: The Dark Years (Oxford, 2001).

   The Politics of Depression in France, 1932–1936 (Cambridge, UK, 1982).

   The Popular Front in France: Defending Democracy, 1934–38 (Cambridge, UK, 1988).

Jackson, Peter, *France and the Nazi Menace: Intelligence and Policy Making, 1933–1939* (Oxford, 2000).

   "Intelligence and the End of Appeasement," in Robert Boyce, ed. *French Foreign and Defence Policy, 1918–1940: The decline and fall of a great power* (London, 1998), 234–260.

Jacobs, Joe, *Out of the Ghetto: My Youth in the East End Communism and Fascism, 1913–1939* (London, 1978).

Jenkins, Roy, *Churchill: A Biography* (New York, 2001).

Jennings, Eric T., "La dissidence aux Antilles (1940–1943)," *Vingtième Siècle*, 68 (October–November 2000), 55–71.

Johns, Richard Seelye, *A History of the American Legion* (Indianapolis, 1946).

Johnstone, Andrew, "Isolationism and Internationalism in American Foreign Relations," *Journal of Transatlantic Studies*, vol. 9, no. 1 (March 2011), 7–20.

Jordan, Nicole, "The Cut Price War on the Peripheries: The French General Staff, the Rhineland, and Czechoslovakia," in Robert Boyce and Esmonde M. Robertson, eds. *Paths to War: New Essays on the Origins of the Second World War* (New York, 1989), 128–166.

Jowitt, Ken, "Stalinist Revolutionary Breakthroughs in Eastern Europe," in Vladimir Tismaneanu, ed. *Stalinism Revisited: The Establishment of Communist Regimes in East-Central Europe* (Budapest, 2009), 17–24.

Kaiser, Wolfram, *Christian Democracy and the Origins of European Union* (Cambridge, UK, 2007).

Kaminski, Antoni Z. and Bartlomiej Kaminski, "Road to 'People's Poland': Stalin's Conquest Revisited," in Vladimir Tismaneanu, ed. *Stalinism Revisited: The Establishment of Communist Regimes in East-Central Europe* (Budapest, 2009), 195–228.

Kampelman, Max M., *The Communist Party vs. the C.I.O.* (New York, 1971).

Kanawada, Leo V., *Franklin D. Roosevelt's Diplomacy and American Catholics, Italians, and Jews* (Ann Arbor, MI, 1982).

Katznelson, Ira, *When Affirmative Action was White: An Untold History of Racial Inequality in Twentieth-Century America* (New York, 2005).

Keating, Joan, "Looking to Europe: Roman Catholics and Christian Democracy in 1930s Britain," *European History Quarterly*, vol. 26 (1996), 57–79.

Kedward, Roderick, "The maquis and the culture of the outlaw," in Roderick Kedward and Roger Austin, eds. *Vichy France and the Resistance: Culture and Ideology* (London, 1985), 232–251.

Occupied France: Collaboration and Resistance 1940–1944 (Oxford, 1985).

Keegan, John, *Six Armies in Normandy: From D-Day to the Liberation of Paris* (New York, 1982).

Kersaudy, François, *De Gaulle et Churchill: La mésentente cordiale* (Paris, 2003).

Kershaw, Ian, *Hitler, 1936–1945: Nemesis* (New York, 2000).

Khan, Yasmin, *India at War: The Subcontinent and the Second World War* (New York, 2015).

Kiesling, Eugenia C., *Arming against Hitler: France and the Limits of Military Planning* (Lawrence, KS, 1996).

Kirk, Tim and Anthony McElligot, "Introduction," in Tim Kirk and Anthony McElligot, eds. *Opposing Fascism: Community, Authority, and Resistance in Europe* (Cambridge, UK, 1999), 1–11.

Kirschenbaum, Lisa A., *International Communism and the Spanish Civil War: Solidarity and Suspicion* (New York, 2015).

Kitson, Simon, "L'évolution de la Résistance dans la police marseillaise," in Jean-Marie Guillon and Robert Mencherini, eds. *La Résistance et les Européens du Sud* (Paris, 1999), 257–270.

Knapp, Andrew, *Les français sous les bombes alliées, 1940–1945* (Paris, 2014).

Koestler, Arthur, *Scum of the Earth* (London, 1941).

Kosinski, Dorothy, *Henry Moore: Sculpting the Twentieth Century* (New Haven, CT, 2001).

Kramer, Mark, "Stalin, Soviet Policy, and the Consolidation of a Communist Bloc in Eastern Europe, 1944–53," in Vladimir Tismaneanu, ed. *Stalinism Revisited: The Establishment of Communist Regimes in East-Central Europe* (Budapest, 2009), 51–101.

Laborie, Pierre, *Les Français des années troubles: De la guerre d'Espagne à la Libération* (Paris, 2003).

Lacaze, Yvon, *L'opinion publique française et la crise de Munich* (Berne, 1991).

Lacouture, Jean, *De Gaulle: The Rebel 1890–1944*, trans. Patrick O'Brian (New York, 1990).

Lacroix-Riz, Annie, *De Munich à Vichy: L'assassinat de la Troisième République* (Paris, 2008).

Le choix de la défaite: Les élites françaises dans les années 1930 (Paris, 2010).

"Les relations sociales dans les entreprises," in Denis Peschanski and Jean-Louis Robert, eds. *Les ouvriers en France pendant la seconde guerre mondiale* (Paris, 1992), 221–232.

Lagrou, Pieter, "Return to a Vanished World: European Societies and the Remnants of Their Jewish Communities, 1945–1947," in David Bankier, ed. *The Jews are Coming Back* (Jerusalem, 2005), 1–24.

Lawson, Tom, "'I was following the lead of Jesus Christ,' Christian Anti-Fascism in 1930s Britain," in Nigel Copsey and Andrzej Olechnowicz, eds. *Varieties of Anti-Fascism: Britain in the Inter-War Period* (Basingstoke, 2010), 119–139.

Le Crom, Jean-Pierre, *Syndicats nous voilà: Vichy and le corporatisme* (Paris, 1995).

Le Gall, Erwan, "L'engagement des France Libre: une mise en perspective," in Patrick Harismendy and Erwan Le Gall, eds. *Pour une histoire de la France Libre* (Rennes, 2012), 29–47.

Levisse-Touzé, Christine, *L'Afrique du Nord dans la guerre, 1939–1945* (Paris, 1998).

Levy, James P., *Appeasement and Rearmament: Britain, 1936–1939* (Lanham, MD, 2006).

Lewisohn, Ludwig, "The Revolt against Civilization," in Pierre van Paassen and James Waterman Wise, eds. *Nazism: An Assault on Civilization* (New York, 1934), 143–160.

Lichtenstein, Nelson, "Auto Worker Militancy and the Structure of Factory Life, 1937–1955," *Journal of American History*, vol. 67, no. 2 (September 1980), 335–353.

Labor's War at Home: The CIO in World War II (New York, 1982).

"Life at the Rouge: A Cycle of Workers' Control," in Charles Stephenson and Robert Asher, eds. *Life and Labor: The Dimensions of American Working-Class History* (Albany, NY, 1986), 237–259.

Liebich, Andre, "The anti-Semitism of Henry Wickham Steed," *Patterns of Prejudice*, vol. 46, no. 2 (2012), 180–208.

Lincoln, Mark, *American Interventionists before Pearl Harbor* (New York, 1970).

Lindenberg, Daniel, *Les années souterraines (1937–1947)* (Paris, 1990).

Lipsitz, George, *Rainbow at Midnight: Labor and Culture in the 1940s* (Urbana, IL, 1994).

Lipstadt, Deborah E., *Beyond Belief: The American Press and the Coming of the Holocaust 1933–1945* (New York, 1986).

Llordés Badía, José, *Al dejar el fusil: Memorias de un soldado raso en la Guerra de España* (Barcelona, 1968).

Lore, Ludwig, "The Fate of the Worker," in Pierre van Paassen and James Waterman Wise, eds. *Nazism: An Assault on Civilization* (New York, 1934), 108–126.

Lottman, Herbert R., *The Purge* (New York, 1986).

Loubet, Jean-Louis, "Le travail dans quelques entreprises automobiles françaises sous l'Occupation," in Christian Chevandier and Jean-Claude Daumas, eds. *Travailler dans les entreprises sous l'occupation* (Besançon, 2007), 177–186.

Lukacs, John, *1945: Year Zero* (New York, 1978).

MacDonald, Callum, "Deterrent Diplomacy: Roosevelt and the Containment of Germany, 1938–1940," in Robert Boyce and Esmonde M. Robertson, eds. *Paths to War: New Essays on the Origins of the Second World War* (New York, 1989), 297–329.

"The United States, Appeasement and the Open Door," in Wolfgang J. Mommsen and Lothar Kettenacker, eds. *The Fascist Challenge and the Policy of Appeasement* (London, 1983), 400–412.

MacLean, Nancy, *Behind the Mask of Chivalry: The Making of the Second Ku Klux Klan* (New York, 1995).

Madariaga, Salvador de, *Spain: A Modern History* (New York, 1963).

Madjarian, Grégoire, *Conflits, pouvoirs et société à la Libération* (Paris, 1980).

Marcot, François, ed. *Dictionnaire Historique de la Résistance: Résistance intérieure et France Libre* (Paris, 2006).

"Les ouvriers de Peugeot, le patronat et l'État," in Denis Peschanski and Jean-Louis Robert, eds. *Les ouvriers en France pendant la seconde guerre mondiale* (Paris, 1992), 247–256.

Margairaz, Michel, *L'État, les finances et l'économie: Histoire d'une conversion 1932–1952* (Paris, 1991).

Maritain, Jacques, *France My Country: Through the Disaster* (New York, 1941).

The Social and Political Philosophy of Jacques Maritain: Selected Readings, Joseph W. Evans and Leo R. Ward, eds. (Notre Dame, IN, 1976).

Mark, Eduard, "Revolution by Degrees: Stalin's National-Front Strategy for Europe, 1941–1947," Cold War International History Project (February 2001), http://www.wilsoncenter.org/sites/default/files/ACFB11.pdf

Mark, James, Nigel Townson, and Polymeris Voglis, "Inspirations" in Robert Gildea, James Mark, and Anette Warring, eds. *Europe's 1968: Voices of Revolt* (Oxford, 2013), 72–103.

Martel, André, "Philippe Leclerc de Hauteclocque: Maréchal de France, 1902–1947," in Christine Levisse-Touzé, ed. *Du capitaine de Hauteclocque au général Leclerc* (Brussels, 2000), 23–32.

Martin, Russell, *Picasso's War: The Destruction of Guernica and the Masterpiece That Changed the World* (New York, 2003).

Marwick, Arthur, *Britain in the Century of Total War: War, Peace and Social Change* (Boston, 1968).

Mayer, Arno J., *Dynamics of Counterrevolution in Europe, 1870–1956: An Analytic Framework* (New York, 1971).

Mazower, Mark, *Hitler's Empire: How the Nazis Ruled Europe* (New York, 2008).

Medawar, Jean and David Pyke, *Hitler's Gift: The True Story of the Scientists Expelled by the Nazi Regime* (New York, 2001).

Meisel, James H., *Counter-Revolution: How Revolutions Die* (New York, 1966).

Mencherini, Robert, "Résistance, socialistes, communistes et pouvoirs vus de Marseille," in Jean-Marie Guillon and Robert Mencherini, eds. *La Résistance et les Européens du Sud* (Paris, 1999), 315–326.

Mendès France, Pierre "La portée de ce témoignage," *Les Cahiers de la République* (September–October 1960), 11–16.

Michel, Henri, *Les courants de pensée de la Résistance* (Paris, 1962).

Milkman, Ruth, *Gender at Work: The Dynamics of Job Segregation by Sex during World War II* (Urbana, IL, 1987).

Mitchell, Allan, *Nazi Paris: The History of an Occupation, 1940–1944* (New York, 2008).

Moore, Michaela Hoenicke, *Know Your Enemy: The American Debate on Nazism, 1933–1945* (New York, 2010).

Moorhouse, Roger, *The Devils' Alliance: Hitler's Pact with Stalin, 1939–1941* (New York, 2014).

Moral Roncal, Antonio Manuel, *Diplomacia, humanitarismo y espionaje en la Guerra Civil española* (Madrid, 2008).

Morgan, Kenneth O., *Labour in Power, 1945–1951* (Oxford, 1984).

Morgan, Kevin, *Against Fascism and War: Ruptures and Continuities in British Communist Politics, 1935–41* (Manchester, 1989).

"Une toute petite différence entre La Marseillaise et God Save the King: La gauche britannique et le problème de la nation dans les années trente," in Serge Wolikow and Annie Bleton-Ruget, eds. *Antifascisme et nation: les gauches européennes au temps du Front populaire* (Dijon, 1998), 203–212.

Morgan, Philip, "Popular Attitudes and Resistance to Fascism," in Tim Kirk and Anthony McElligot, eds. *Opposing Fascism: Community, Authority, and Resistance in Europe* (Cambridge, UK, 1999), 163–179.

Mortimer, Edward, "France," in Martin McCauley, ed. *Communist Power in Europe, 1944–1949* (London, 1977), 151–167.

Muracciole, Jean-François, *Les Français libres: L'autre Résistance* (Paris, 2009). *Histoire de la France libre* (Paris, 1996).

Naimark, Norman M., "Revolution and Counterrevolution in Eastern Europe," in Christiane Lemke and Gary Marks, eds. *The Crisis of Socialism in Europe* (Durham NC, 1992), 61–83.

"The Sovietization of Eastern Europe, 1944–1953," in Melvyn P. Leffler and Odd Arne Westad, eds. *The Cambridge History of the Cold War* (3 vols.) (New York, 2010), 1:175–197.

Narinski, Mikhail, "Le Komintern et le Parti Communiste français," *Communisme*, vol. 32–4 (1992–1993), 11–40.

Nikova, Ekaterina, "Bulgarian Stalinism Revisited," in Vladimir Tismaneanu, ed. *Stalinism Revisited: The Establishment of Communist Regimes in East-Central Europe* (Budapest, 2009), 283–304.

Nord, Philip, *France 1940: Defending the Republic* (New Haven, CT, 2015).
France's New Deal: From the Thirties to the Postwar Era (Princeton, NJ, 2010).
Novick, Peter, *The Resistance versus Vichy: The Purge of Collaborators in Liberated France* (New York, 1968).
Offner, Arnold A., *The Origins of the Second World War* (New York, 1975).
Olechnowicz, Andrzej, "Historians and the Study of Anti-Fascism in Britain," in Nigel Copsey and Andrzej Olechnowicz, eds. *Varieties of Anti-Fascism: Britain in the Inter-War Period* (Basingstoke, 2010), 1–27.
Olson, Lynne, *Citizens of London: The Americans Who Stood with Britain in Its Darkest, Finest Hour* (New York, 2010).
Those Angry Days: Roosevelt, Lindbergh, and America's Fight over World War II, 1939–1941 (New York, 2013).
O'Neill, William L., *A Democracy at War: America's Fight at Home and Abroad in World War II* (New York, 1993).
Ortiz Villalba, Juan, *Sevilla 1936: del golpe militar a la guerra civil* (Seville, 1998).
Orwell, George, *Homage to Catalonia* (New York, 1980).
Ovendale, Ritchie, "Why the British Dominions Declared War," in Robert Boyce and Esmonde M. Robertson, eds. *Paths to War: New Essays on the Origins of the Second World War* (New York, 1989), 269–296.
Overy, Richard, *The Twilight Years: The Paradox of Britain between the Wars* (New York, 2009).
Parello, Joseph, "Los republicanos españoles en la Francia Libre," *Memòria antifranquista del Baix Llobregat*, no. 16 (2016), 6–10.
Parker, R. A. C., "British Rearmament 1936–9: Treasury, Trade Unions and Skilled Labour," *The English Historical Review*, vol. 96, no. 379 (April 1981), 306–343.
Passmore, Kevin, *Fascism: A Very Short Introduction* (Oxford, 2002).
Paxton, Robert O., *The Anatomy of Fascism* (New York, 2004).
"The Five Stages of Fascism," in Brian Jenkins, ed. *France in the Era of Fascism: Essays on the French Authoritarian Right* (New York, 2005), 105–128.
Payne, Stanley G., *Civil War in Europe, 1905–1949* (New York, 2011).
"Soviet Anti-Fascism: Theory and Practice, 1921–45," *Totalitarian Movements and Political Religions*, vol. 4, no. 2 (Autumn 2003), 1–62.
Spain's First Democracy: The Second Republic, 1931–1936 (Madison, WI, 1993).
The Spanish Civil War, the Soviet Union, and Communism (New Haven, CT, 2004).
Peden, G. C., "Keynes, the Economics of Rearmament and Appeasement," in Wolfgang J. Mommsen and Lothar Kettenacker, eds. *The Fascist Challenge and the Policy of Appeasement* (London, 1983), 142–156.
Pelling, Henry, "The Impact of the War on the Labour Party," in Harold L. Smith, ed. *War and Social Change* (Manchester, 1986), 129–148.
Pelz, William A., "The Significance of the Mass Strike during the German Revolution of 1918–1919," *Workers of the World: International Journal on Strikes and Social Conflicts*, vol. 1, no. 1 (June 2012), 56–65.
Perry, Matt, "Bombing Billancourt: Labour Agency and the Limitations of the Public Opinion Model of Wartime France," *Labour History Review*, vol. 77, no. 1 (2012), 49–74.

Pigenet, Michel, "Jeunes, ouvriers et combattants: Les volontaires parisiens de la colonne Fabien (septembre-décembre 1944)," in Denis Peschanski and Jean-Louis Robert, eds. *Les ouvriers en France pendant la seconde guerre mondiale* (Paris, 1992), 483–493.

Pike, David Wingeate, *Les Français et la guerre d'Espagne* (Paris, 1975).

Plummer, Brenda Gayle, *Rising Wind: Black Americans and U.S. Foreign Affairs, 1935–1960* (Chapel Hill, NC, 1996).

Plumyène, Jean and Raymond Lasierra, *Les fascismes français, 1923–63* (Paris, 1963).

Pons, Silvio, "La diplomatie soviétique, l'antifascisme et la guerre civile espagnole," in Serge Wolikow and Annie Bleton-Ruget, eds. *Antifascisme et nation: les gauches européennes au temps du Front populaire* (Dijon, 1998), 59–66.

Poznanski, Renée, "French Apprehensions, Jewish Expectations: From a Social Imaginary to a Political Practice," in David Bankier, ed. *The Jews are Coming Back* (Jerusalem, 2005), 25–57.

Prost, Antoine, *Les Anciens Combattants* (Paris, 2014).

"Une pièce en trois actes," in Claire Andrieu, Lucette Le Van, and Antoine Prost, eds. *Les Nationalisations de la Libération: De l'utopie au compromis* (Paris, 1987), 236–246.

Pugh, Martin, *Hurrah for the Blackshirts: Fascists and Fascism in Britain between the Wars* (London, 2006).

Rabinbach, Anson, "Introduction: The Legacies of Antifascism," *New German Critique*, no. 67 (Winter, 1996), 3–17.

Racine, Nicole, "Les Unions internationales d'écrivains pendant l'entre-deux-guerres," in Serge Wolikow and Annie Bleton-Ruget, eds. *Antifascisme et nation: les gauches européennes au temps du Front populaire* (Dijon, 1998), 31–48.

"Université libre," in Jean-Pierre Rioux, Antoine Prost, and Jean-Pierre Azéma, eds. *Les communistes français de Munich à Châteaubriant, 1938–1941* (Paris, 1987), 133–144.

Raghavan, Srinath, *India's War: World War II and the Making of Modern South Asia* (New York, 2016).

Ragsdale, Hugh, *The Soviets, the Munich Crisis, and the Coming of World War II* (New York, 2004).

Rancière, Jacques, *Staging the People: The Proletarian and His Double*, trans. David Fernbach (London, 2011).

Ranzato, Gabriele, *El Eclipse de la democracia: La guerra civil española y sus orígenes, 1931–1939*, trans. Fernando Borrajo (Madrid, 2006).

La grande paura del 1936: Come la Spagna precipitò nella Guerra civile (Rome-Bari, 2011).

Reid, Betty, "The Left Book Club in the Thirties," in Jon Clark, Margot Heinemann, David Margolies, and Carole Snee, eds. *Culture and Crisis in Britain in the Thirties* (London, 1979), 193–208.

Reid, Donald, *Germaine Tillion, Lucie Aubrac, and the Politics of Memories of the French Resistance* (Newcastle, 2008).

Rémond, René, *Les crises du catholicisme en France dans les années trente* (Paris, 1996).

Renton, Dave, *Fascism, Anti-Fascism and Britain in the 1940s* (Basingstoke, 2000).

Rey, Fernando del, *Paisanos en lucha: Exclusión política y violencia en la Segunda República española* (Madrid, 2009).

Rey García, Marta, *Stars for Spain: La Guerra Civil Española en los Estados Unidos* (La Coruña, 1997).

Reynolds, David, "1940: Fulcrum of the Twentieth Century?" *International Affairs*, 66:2 (April 1990), 325–350.

Ribuffo, Leo P., *The Old Christian Right: The Protestant Far Right from the Great Depression to the Cold War* (Philadelphia, 1983).

Riddell, Neil, "Walter Citrine and the British Labour Movement, 1925–1935," *History*, vol. 85, no. 278 (April 2000), 285–306.

Rieber, Alfred J., "Popular Democracy: An Illusion," in Vladimir Tismaneanu, ed. *Stalinism Revisited: The Establishment of Communist Regimes in East-Central Europe* (Budapest, 2009), 103–128.

Rioux, Jean-Pierre, "L'épuration en France," in Jean-Charles Asselain, *Études sur la France de 1939 à nos jours* (Paris, 1985), 162–179.

"Présentation," in Jean-Pierre Rioux, Antoine Prost, and Jean-Pierre Azéma, eds. *Les communistes français de Munich à Châteaubriant, 1938–1941* (Paris, 1987), 11–16.

Roberts, Geoffrey, "Soviet Foreign Policy and the Spanish Civil War," in Christian Leitz and David J. Dunthorn, eds. *Spain in an International Context, 1936–1939* (New York, 1999), 81–104.

Robertson, Charles L., *When Roosevelt Planned to Govern France* (Amherst, MA, 2011).

Robertson, Esmonde M., "German Mobilisation Preparations and the Treaties between Germany and the Soviet Union of August and September 1939," in Robert Boyce and Esmonde M. Robertson, eds. *Paths to War: New Essays on the Origins of the Second World War* (New York, 1989), 330–366.

Rosique Navarro, Francisca, *La Reforma agraria en Badajoz durante la IIa República* (Badajoz, 1988).

Rossignol, Dominique, *Vichy et les Francs-Maçons: La liquidation des sociétés secrètes, 1940–1944* (Paris, 1981).

Roussel, Éric, *Charles de Gaulle* (Paris, 2002).

Rousso, Henry, "L'Épuration en France: une histoire inachevée," *Vingtième Siècle*, no. 33 (January–March 1992), 78–105.

"Où en est l'histoire de la Résistance," in Jean-Charles Asselain, *Études sur la France de 1939 à nos jours* (Paris, 1985), 113–136.

Rubio, Javier, *Asilos y canjes durante la guerra civil española* (Barcelona, 1979).

Ruiz, Julius, *El Terror rojo: Madrid 1936* (Barcelona, 2012).

Sadoun, Marc, *Les socialistes sous l'Occupation: Résistance et collaboration* (Paris, 1982).

Sainclivier, Jacqueline, "La Résistance et le STO," in Bernard Garnier and Jean Quellien, eds. *La main d'œuvre française exploitée par le IIIe Reich: Actes du colloque international, Caen, 13–15 décembre 2001* (Caen, 2003), 517–534.

Sanders, Marion K., *Dorothy Thompson: A Legend in Her Time* (Boston, 1973).

Schirmann, Sylvain, *Les relations économiques et financières franco-allemandes, 24 décembre 1932–1 septembre 1939* (Paris, 1995).

Schivelbusch, Wolfgang, *Three New Deals: Reflections on Roosevelt's America, Mussolini's Italy, and Hitler's Germany, 1933–1939* (New York, 2006).

Schmidt, Gustav, "The Domestic Background to British Appeasement Policy," in Wolfgang J. Mommsen and Lothar Kettenacker, eds. *The Fascist Challenge and the Policy of Appeasement* (London, 1983), 101–124.

Schuker, Stephen A., "France and the Remilitarization of the Rhineland, 1936," *French Historical Studies*, vol. 14, no. 3 (Spring 1986), 299–338.

Schwartz, Paula, "Redefining Resistance: Women's Activism in Wartime France," in Margaret Randolph Higonnet, ed. *Behind the Lines: Gender and the Two World Wars* (New Haven, CT, 1987), 141–153.

Seidman, Joel, *American Labor from Defense to Reconversion* (Chicago, 1953).

Semelin, Jacques, *Unarmed against Hitler: Civilian Resistance in Europe, 1939–1943*, trans. Suzan Husserl-Kapit (Westport, CT, 1993).

Seton-Watson, Christopher, "The Anglo-Italian Gentleman's Agreement of January 1937 and its Aftermath," in Wolfgang J. Mommsen and Lothar Kettenacker, eds. *The Fascist Challenge and the Policy of Appeasement* (London, 1983), 267–282.

Seton-Watson, Hugh, *The East European Revolution* (New York, 1951).

Shay, Robert Paul, *British Rearmament in the Thirties: Politics and Profits* (Princeton, NJ, 1977).

Shennan, Andrew, *Rethinking France: Plans for Renewal 1940–1946* (Oxford, 1989).

Shulman, Harry and Neil Chamberlain, *Cases on Labor Relations* (Brooklyn, 1949).

Siegel, Mona L., *The Moral Disarmament of France: Education, Pacifism, and Patriotism, 1914–1940* (New York, 2004).

Skoutelsky, Rémi, "Les volontaires français des Brigades internationales: patriotisme et/ou internationalisme," in Serge Wolikow and Annie Bleton-Ruget, eds. *Antifascisme et nation: les gauches européennes au temps du Front populaire* (Dijon, 1998), 87–98.

Smith, Denis Mack, "Appeasement as a Factor in Mussolini's Foreign Policy," in Wolfgang J. Mommsen and Lothar Kettenacker, eds. *The Fascist Challenge and the Policy of Appeasement* (London, 1983), 258–266.

Smith, Harold L., "The Effect of the War on the Status of Women," in Harold L. Smith, ed. *War and Social Change* (Manchester, 1986), 208–229.

Soo, Scott, *The routes to exile: France and the Spanish Civil War refugees, 1939–2009* (Manchester, 2013).

Soutou, Georges-Henri, "France," in David Reynolds, ed. *The Origins of the Cold War in Europe: International Perspectives* (New Haven, CT, 1994), 96–120.

Sparrow, James T., *Warfare State: World War II, Americans, and the Age of Big Government* (New York, 2011).

Spier, Eugen, *Focus: A Footnote to the History of the Thirties* (London, 1963).

Spina, Raphaël, "Impacts du STO sur le travail en entreprises: activité productive et vie sociale interne entre crises, bouleversements et adaptations (1942–1944)," in Christian Chevandier and Jean-Claude Daumas, eds. *Travailler dans les entreprises sous l'occupation* (Besançon, 2007), 87–108.

Stansky, Peter and William Abrahams, *London's Burning: Life, Death and Art in the Second World War* (Stanford, CA, 1994).

Steiner, Zara, *The Triumph of the Dark: European International History 1933–1939* (Oxford, 2011).

Stein, Louis, *Beyond Death and Exile: The Spanish Republicans in France, 1939–1955* (Cambridge, MA, 1979).

Stein, Sygmunt, *Ma Guerre d'Espagne: Brigades internationales la fin d'un mythe*, trans. Marina Alexeeva-Antipov (Paris, 2012).

Stone, Dan, "Anti-Fascist Europe Comes to Britain: Theorising Fascism as a Contribution to Defeating It," in Nigel Copsey and Andrzej Olechnowicz, eds. *Varieties of Anti-Fascism: Britain in the Inter-War Period* (Basingstoke, 2010), 183–201.

Stone, Glyn, "The European Great Powers and the Spanish Civil War," in Robert Boyce and Esmonde M. Robertson, eds. *Paths to War: New Essays on the Origins of the Second World War* (New York, 1989), 199–232.

Strachan, Hew, "The Soldier's Experience in Two World Wars: Some Historiographic Comparisons," in Paul Addison and Angus Calder, eds. *Time to Kill: The Soldier's Experience of War in the West, 1939–1945* (London, 1997), 369–378.

Sugrue, Thomas, "Hillburn, Hattiesburg, and Hitler," in Kevin M. Kruse and Stephen Tuck, eds. *Fog of War: The Second World War and the Civil Rights Movement* (New York, 2012), 87–102.

Summerfield, Penny, "The 'Levelling of Class'," in Harold L. Smith, ed. *War and Social Change* (Manchester, 1986), 179–207.

"Women, War and Social Change: Women in Britain in World War II," in Arthur Marwick, ed. *Total War and Social Change* (New York, 1988), 95–118.

Sweets, John F., *Choices in Vichy France: The French under Occupation* (New York, 1994).

Tartakowsky, Danielle, *Les manifestations de rue en France, 1918–1968* (Paris, 1997).

Taylor, Lynne, *Between Resistance and Collaboration: Popular Protest in Northern France, 1940–45* (New York, 2000).

Thomas, Hugh, *Spanish Civil War* (New York, 1961).

Thomàs, Joan Maria, *La Batalla del Wolframio: Estados Unidos y España del Pearl Harbor a la Guerra Fría (1941–1947)* (Madrid, 2010).

Roosevelt y Franco: De la guerra civil española a Pearl Harbor (Barcelona, 2007).

Thomas, Martin, *Britain, France and Appeasement: Anglo-French Relations in the Popular Front Era* (Oxford, 1996).

The French Empire at War, 1940–45 (Manchester, 1998).

Thompson, Dorothy, "The Record of Persecution," in Pierre van Paassen and James Waterman Wise, eds. *Nazism: An Assault on Civilization* (New York, 1934), 1–24.

Thompson, Neville, *The Anti-Appeasers: Conservative Opposition to Appeasement in the 1930s* (Oxford, 1971).

Thurlow, Richard, "The Failure of British Fascism 1932–40," in Andrew Thorpe, ed. *The Failure of Political Extremism in Inter-War Britain* (Exeter, 1989), 67–84.

"Passive and Active Anti-Fascism: The State and National Security, 1923–45," in Nigel Copsey and Andrzej Olechnowicz, eds. *Varieties of Anti-Fascism: Britain in the Inter-War Period* (Basingstoke, 2010), 162–180.

Tierney, Dominic, *FDR and the Spanish Civil War: Neutrality and Commitment in the Struggle that divided America* (Durham, NC, 2007).

Todorov, Tzvetan, *Une tragédie française: Été 44: scènes de guerre civile* (Paris, 2004).

Tollet, André, *La classe ouvrière dans la résistance* (Paris, 1984).

Tooze, Adam, *The Wages of Destruction: The Making and Breaking of the Nazi Economy* (New York, 2006).

Trapiello, Andrés, *Las armas y las letras: Literatura y guerra civil (1936–1939)* (Barcelona, 1994).

Traverso, Enzo, *À feu et à sang: De la guerre civile européenne 1914–1945* (Paris, 2007).

Tuck, Stephen, "You Can Sing and Punch ... but You Can't Be a Soldier or Man," in Kevin M. Kruse and Stephen Tuck, eds. *Fog of War: The Second World War and the Civil Rights Movement* (New York, 2012), 103–125.

Tusell, Javier and Genoveva García Queipo de Llano, *El catolicismo mundial y la guerra de España* (Madrid, 1993).

Tuttle, Charles H., "The American Reaction," in Pierre van Paassen and James Waterman Wise, eds. *Nazism: An Assault on Civilization* (New York, 1934), 250–256.

Ulrich-Pier, Raphäelle, *René Massigli (1888–1988): Une vie de diplomate*, 2 vols. (Paris, 2006).

Varsori, Antonio, "Reflections on the Origins of the Cold War," in Odd Arne Westad, ed. *Reviewing the Cold War: Approaches, Interpretations, Theory* (London, 2000), 281–302.

Veillon, Dominique, "Les ouvrières parisiennes de la couture" in Denis Peschanski and Jean-Louis Robert, eds. *Les ouvriers en France pendant la seconde guerre mondiale* (Paris, 1992), 169–178.

Vivre et survivre en France 1939–1947 (Paris, 1995).

Veil, Simone, *Une Vie* (Paris, 2007).

Vergnon, Gilles, *L'antifascisme en France de Mussolini à Le Pen* (Rennes, 2009).

Vernet, Jacques, "Mise sur pied de la 2e DB: De la diversité à l'unité," in Christine Levisse-Touzé, ed. *Du capitaine de Hauteclocque au général Leclerc* (Brussels, 2000), 191–204.

Vials, Christopher, *Haunted by Hitler: Liberals, the Left, and the Fight against Fascism in the United States* (Amherst, MA, 2014).

Vigna, Xavier, *Histoire des ouvriers en France au XXe siècle* (Paris, 2012).

Vigreux, Jean, *Le front populaire, 1934–1938* (Paris, 2011).

Histoire du Front populaire: L'échappée belle (Paris, 2016).

Vila Izquierdo, Justo, *Extremadura: La Guerra Civil* (Badajoz, 1984).

Vilanova, Mercedes, *Les majories invisibles* (Barcelona, 1995).

Vincent, Mary, *Catholicism in the Second Spanish Republic: Religion and Politics in Salamanca, 1930–1936* (Oxford, 1996).

"The Spanish Civil War as a War of Religion," in Martin Baumeister and Stefanie Schüler-Springorum, eds. *"If You Tolerate This . . . ": The Spanish Civil War in the Age of Total War* (New York, 2008), 74–89.

Vinen, Richard, *The Unfree French: Life under the Occupation* (New Haven, CT, 2006).

Vitoux, Frédéric, *Céline: A Biography*, trans. Jesse Browner (New York, 1992).

Von Eschen, Penny, "Civil Rights and World War II in a Global Frame," in Kevin M. Kruse and Stephen Tuck, eds. *Fog of War: The Second World War and the Civil Rights Movement* (New York, 2012), 171–187.

Wallace, Henry A., *Christian Bases of World Order* (Freeport, NY, 1971).

Ward, Jason Morgan, "A War for States' Rights," in Kevin M. Kruse and Stephen Tuck, eds. *Fog of War: The Second World War and the Civil Rights Movement* (New York, 2012), 126–144.

Watkins, K. W., *Britain Divided: The Effect of the Spanish Civil War on British Political Opinion* (London, 1963).

Watt, Donald C., "The European Civil War," in Wolfgang J. Mommsen and Lothar Kettenacker, eds. *The Fascist Challenge and the Policy of Appeasement* (London, 1983), 3–21.

Weil, Patrick, "The Return of Jews in the Nationality or in the Territory of France," in David Bankier, ed. *The Jews are Coming Back* (Jerusalem, 2005), 58–71.

Weinberg, Gerhard L., *A World at Arms: A Global History of World War II* (New York, 1994).

Weintraub, Stanley, *The Last Great Cause: The Intellectuals and the Spanish Civil War* (New York, 1968).

Wendt, Bernd-Jürgen, "Economic Appeasement – A Crisis Strategy," in Wolfgang J. Mommsen and Lothar Kettenacker, eds. *The Fascist Challenge and the Policy of Appeasement* (London, 1983), 157–172.

Whiting, Cécile, *Antifascism in American Art* (New Haven, CT, 1989).

Wichert, Sabine, "The British Left and Appeasement: Political Tactics or Alternative Policies," in Wolfgang J. Mommsen and Lothar Kettenacker, eds. *The Fascist Challenge and the Policy of Appeasement* (London, 1983), 125–141.

Wieviorka, Annette, *Ils étaient juifs, résistants, communistes* (Paris, 1986).

Wieviorka, Olivier and Jacek Tebinka, "From Everyday Life to Counter-State," in Robert Gildea, Olivier Wieviorka, and Anette Warring, eds. *Surviving Hitler and Mussolini: Daily Life in Occupied Europe* (Oxford, 2006), 153–176.

Wieviorka, Olivier, "¿Guerra civil a la francesa? El caso de los años sombríos," in Julio Aróstegui and François Godicheau, eds. *Guerra Civil: Mito y memoria* (Madrid, 2006), 337–360.

Histoire de la Résistance, 1940–1945 (Paris, 2013).

Wigg, Richard, *Churchill and Spain: The Survival of the Franco Regime, 1940–1945* (Brighton, UK, 2008).

Williamson, Philip, "The Conservative Party, Fascism and Anti-Fascism, 1918–1939," in Nigel Copsey and Andrzej Olechnowicz, eds. *Varieties of Anti-Fascism: Britain in the Inter-War Period* (Basingstoke, 2010), 73–97.

Williams, William Carlos, "Federico García Lorca," *The Kenyon Review*, vol. 1, no. 2 (Spring 1939), 148–158.

Winock, Michel, *Histoire politique de la revue «Esprit», 1930–1950* (Paris, 1975).

and Nora Benkorich, *La trahison de Munich: Emmanuel Mounier et la grande débâcle des intellectuels* (Paris, 2008).

Wise, James Waterman, "Introduction," in Pierre van Paassen and James Waterman Wise, eds. *Nazism: An Assault on Civilization* (New York, 1934), ix–xii.

Wise, Stephen S., "The War upon World Jewry," in Pierre van Paassen and James Waterman Wise, eds. *Nazism: An Assault on Civilization* (New York, 1934), 202–211.

Wiskemann, Elizabeth, *The Europe I Saw* (New York, 1968).

Wolikow, Serge, "Table Ronde: Front populaire et antifascisme en débat," in Serge Wolikow and Annie Bleton-Ruget, eds. *Antifascisme et nation: les gauches européennes au temps du Front populaire* (Dijon, 1998), 251–260.

Yakovlev, Alexander N., *A Century of Violence in Soviet Russia*, trans. Anthony Austin (New Haven, CT, 2002).

Yonnet, Paul, *Voyage au centre du malaise français: L'Antiracisme et le roman national* (Paris, 1993).

Young, Robert J., *France and the Origins of the Second World War* (New York, 1996).

Zagorin, Perez, *How the Idea of Religious Toleration Came to the West* (Princeton, NJ, 2003).

Zamora Bonilla, Javier, *Ortega y Gasset* (Barcelona, 2002).

Zelizer, Julian E., "Confronting the Roadblock: Congress, Civil Rights, and World War II," in Kevin M. Kruse and Stephen Tuck, eds. *Fog of War: The Second World War and the Civil Rights Movement* (New York, 2012), 32–50.

Zielenski, Bernd, "Le chômage et la politique de la main-d'oeuvre de Vichy (1940–1942)," in Denis Peschanski and Jean-Louis Robert, eds. *Les ouvriers en France pendant la seconde guerre mondiale* (Paris, 1992), 295–304.

Zietsma, David, "Sin Has No History: Religion, National Identity, and U.S. Intervention, 1937–1941," *Diplomatic History*, vol. 31, no. 3 (June 2007), 531–565.

Zubok, Vladislav and Constantine Pleshakov, *Inside the Kremlin's Cold War: From Stalin to Khrushchev* (Cambridge, MA, 1996).

Index

Abbott Laboratories, 145
Abraham Lincoln Brigade, 27
absenteeism, 23, 56, 152
  and Bevin, 209
  and collective bargaining, 227
  and drinking, 228
  and Dunkirk spirit, 210
  and Friday pay, 210, 227
  and hunting season, 227
  and lack of alarm clocks, 211
  and physicians, 228
  and UK miners, 211
  and UK shop stewards, 210
  and US opinion, 228
  and weekend labor, 218
  and weekends, 228
  and women, 211, 228
  at US Ford factories, 226
  during German occupation of France,
    200
  during Phoney War, 190
  in postwar France, 249
  in UK shipbuilding, 210
  in United Kingdom, 210
  in United States, 223
  of French miners, 191, 248
  reasons for, 210
absolutism, 9
Abyssinia. *See* Ethiopia
Academic Assistance Council, 88
Action Française, 31, 40, 98, 123
  and Leclerc, 123
  as anti-Catholic, 100
AEU (Amalgamated Engineering Union),
  217, 219
affirmative action, 28
Africa, 26
African-Americans, 7, 230
  and "double victory", 221
  and anti-Semitism, 141
  and competition for victimhood, 142
  and Ethiopia, 130, 131

  and German prisoners of war, 143
  and interventionism, 136
  and Ku Klux Klan, 141
  and Southern racism, 142
  and World War II, 143
  as victims, 135
  discrimination against, 155, 230
  newspapers of, 141
  pastors of, 131
Again, 145
Agir, 99
Aid Spain committees, 35
airlift, 26
Alain (Émile-August Chartier), 75
Albania, 107
Alcalá Zamora, Niceto, 13
alcohol abuse, 24
Alexander, A. V., 213
Alfonso XIII, 17
Algeria, 253
  and de Gaulle, 174
Algerian War, 253
Algiers, 174
Alliance démocratique, 80
Alliance of Antifascist Intellectuals, 44
Alphonsines, 17
Alsace, 146
Alsthom
  and Allied bombing of France,
    204
America First, 41, 148
  as anti-Soviet, 154
American Artists' Congress, 42
American Communists. *See* CPUSA
American Federation of Labor (AFL),
  157
American Legion, 152
  opposes anti-Semitism, 135
American Revolution, 140
Americanophilia, 186
Americans. *See* United States
Amery, Leo, 66